THE GREAT SALMON HOAX

**An Eyewitness Account of the Collapse of Science and Law
and the Triumph of Politics in Salmon Recovery**

by James L. Buchal

To my wife, Cathy, and my children, who suffered patiently through the writing, editing, and publication of this book, and the experiences that engendered it . . .

Visit http://www.buchal.com/hoax.html
for Supplemental Material and
Online Searches

Published by Iconoclast Publishing Company, P.O. Box 677, Aurora, Oregon 97002-0677

Library of Congress Catalog Card Number 97-94732

ISBN Number 0-966195-10-8

First Printing, January 1998
Second Printing, November 1998

The cover drawing is © Anne Buchal 1998

The author's T-shirt in the photo on the back cover is © Ray Troll 1990
(You can buy one at http://www.dbcity.com/troll/trolline.htm)

Table of Contents

Table of Figures

Preface

"I will continue to root for heresy preached by the nonprofessional . . . th[e] hardest of all games to win."
Stephen Jay Gould, *Ever Since Darwin*

I moved to the Pacific Northwest in 1991 from New York City. I wasn't expecting Ecotopia, but I looked for a cleaner better world for me and my family. I didn't think much about salmon; in the back of my mind I expected to be able to take my children salmon fishing. I didn't know much about salmon and their power as a symbol in the Pacific Northwest.

As soon as I arrived, I found myself involved in a lawsuit brought by the Sierra Club Legal Defense Fund to change operations at the dams and reservoirs comprising the Federal Columbia River Power System. I represented a group of industries taking the position that the Sierra Club, allied with commercial salmon harvest interests, was making unreasonable demands that had almost nothing to do with improving the lot of salmon, and more to do with other agendas.

The facts concerning dams and salmon are complex and controversial. Nearly forty years ago, the writer of *Salmon of the Pacific Northwest: Fish vs. Dams* wrote that "[o]n this issue many emotional conflicts have been waged, political campaigns fought, and much blood, sweat and tears expended".[1] That has been true for me. This book documents my sometimes bitter personal experience spending six years collecting the facts on dams and salmon, and seeing them consistently disregarded by every agency with authority for improving the lot of salmon.

People may be skeptical about the views in this book because I acquired some of them while representing corporations with an economic interest in continued hydropower operations. But no one paid me to write this book. It represents my personal beliefs. I brought no prejudice to the salmon problem, other than a prejudice in favor of the scientific method, and a prejudice in favor of the rule of law. I think that real science is based on data you can measure, and real law is specific and clear rules, not vague and general statements that let bureaucrats do whatever they want.

After reviewing the facts, the book provides a case study in how the law of salmon recovery has failed because of a wholesale refusal to enforce it. Citizens attempting to get the federal government to obey any sort of environmental law have little chance of success. Many judges will not apply the plain language of the law to overturn a government decision that is endorsed by politically-potent elements of society. Doctrines invented by the courts have disenfranchised those who would seek to impose scientific rationality and economic sense into environmental decisionmaking, contrary to the plain language and intent of the statutes the courts are supposed to be enforcing. The courts seem to justify all this in the belief that they are serving larger social goals of protecting the environment. Only by fighting battles over and over in the courts, just as environmentalists did, can citizens hope to reshape the body of law back to a more rational, fact-based approach to review of government decisions concerning the environment.

I think I care about the environment more than most people I know. A true environmentalist takes a global perspective to environmental problems, and looks at the environmental costs and benefits of all alternatives. From that perspective, hydropower has enormous advantages over most other forms of energy generation. Once one can see that dam removal is not necessary or sufficient to achieve healthy runs of salmon in the Pacific Northwest, it becomes clear that the best choice is to continue to generate electricity with dams and bring large salmon runs back to the rivers.

We can do it, because technology has given us the tools needed to improve salmon populations. As Gregg Easterbrook has emphasized, "[t]echnology has always created as many problems as it has solved; surely it will continue to create many problems in the future. It's just that the environment is one area where technology has finished a phase of creating problems and now enters a phase of solving them".[2] But the only way we are going to move to that phase is if the ideas in this book become more widely accepted, because those in charge of salmon recovery are pursuing an anti-technological approach that cannot succeed.

There are many parties to thank for assisting in the production of this work. Many people provided helpful comments, particularly Bill Rudolph, the only reporter in the entire Pacific Northwest who seems to perceive the Great Salmon Hoax. A former commercial fisherman, he supplied me with many of the more interesting facts in this book. Other reviewers, principally present or former federal employees, wished to remain anonymous, a sad commentary on the ground yet to be covered in this struggle. Any mistakes are, of course, entirely my own.

NOTES TO PREFACE

[1] A. Netboy, *Salmon of the Pacific Northwest: Fish vs. Dams* vi (Binfords & Mort Portland 1958)

[2] G. Easterbrook, *A Moment on the Earth* 266-67 (Viking 1995).

10

INTRODUCTION: THE NATURE OF THE GREAT SALMON HOAX

On November 20, 1991, the National Marine Fisheries Service listed the Snake River sockeye salmon as an "endangered species" under the Endangered Species Act of 1973.[1] On April 22, 1992, the National Marine Fisheries Service listed two groups of Snake River chinook salmon, a combined spring and summer unit, and a fall unit, as "threatened species".[2] The Snake River chinook were later designated "endangered" as well.

Several years later, in the fall of 1997, these Snake River salmon struggled up the Columbia River. In theory, they were fish of incalculable value, representing the few remaining members of a population that had survived enormous mortality at every stage of its life cycle and would now spawn the next generation of salmon.

Once above Bonneville Dam, the first of the eight dams in their path, the salmon entered the Zone 6 tribal fishery, and ran a gauntlet of gillnets. Hundreds were captured, and sold off the back of pickup trucks in Cascade Locks and other towns along the Columbia for two dollars a pound. The tribes even had an 800 number for potential customers to call. No other endangered species are caught, killed and sold for human consumption.

Federal, state and tribal fishery agencies did not merely fail to stop these harvests; they promoted them. Fishery management could require selective harvest methods that would spare the endangered salmon. But fishery managers refuse even to consider any reform of their own rules and practices.

Instead, their reform efforts are focused on blaming hydropower generation for the decline of salmon. Their attention centers on the Federal Columbia River Power System, a collection of dams along the Columbia and Snake Rivers and their tributaries that the fishery interests have opposed for decades. Without a single vote of Congress, the fishery managers have created, by administrative fiat, the single most ambitious and expensive endangered species recovery program ever devised, all funded by surcharges on electric ratepayers.

So far, the program has expended more than $3 billion with no measurable benefits to salmon. At the same time, power production at the dams has been radically reduced, and navigation, recreation, and irrigation, are threatened (and in some cases already destroyed) by proposals to "draw down" the reservoirs.

11

Outsiders who might be expected to serve as watchdogs are instead lapdogs. Environmentalists, funded by and allied with commercial salmon harvest interests, generally support the efforts of the fishery managers—they file lawsuits against harvesting trees, but not salmon. An uncritical media regards the fishery managers, environmentalists, and fishermen as the protectors of the salmon. Indeed, as of 1997, both environmentalists and the media invoke the utter failure of the program to justify ever-more-extravagant plans.

The past public policy blunders, and the even larger ones now threatened, arise from what I call the Great Salmon Hoax: a collection of mutually-reinforcing and commonly-held beliefs about salmon recovery, all of which lack any basis in sound science. Some of these beliefs are the product of ignorance or reliance on outdated research. Others are the product of deliberate misrepresentations, apparently made in the service of a larger ideological vision: the Northwest without dams.

This book is written to begin debunking these myths and provide a comprehensive summary of the best available scientific evidence on the prospects for salmon recovery. It also tells the many stories of how these myths arose, who is promoting them, and how the promoters have overcome both science and law.

Myth #1: Columbia Basin Salmon Are in Danger of Extinction.

In truth, none of the several biological species of salmon in the Columbia River Basin are in any imminent danger of extinction. A "species" is defined by biologists in the common sense way: if you lose the last two members of it, the species will disappear from the face of the earth forever. The Endangered Species Act was intended to provide a Noah's Ark for species in such dire straits, and enjoys widespread support because that is what ordinary citizens think the Act is doing.

In fact, law and biology have diverged. The Endangered Species Act protects not merely species, but also "distinct population segments" of salmon, a concept that can mean a salmon run in a single stream or lake. So defined, there are thousands of "distinct population segments" of just one biological species: chinook salmon.

There is no scientific evidence that losing any particular distinct population segment of salmon will threaten the survival of any salmon species. To the contrary, in nature such smaller subpopulations ebb and flow, while the larger species continues. Quests for greater diversity in salmon populations are political quests, pushed by a new, politically-active group known as "conservation biologists". We can have plenty of salmon without having hundreds of viable subpopulations, just as we can have plenty of cattle without hundreds of breeds of cows. No one worries that the cow population will collapse if farmers discontinue some breeds.

Myth #2: Salmon Hatcheries Cannot Maintain Abundant Salmon Runs.

Salmon hatcheries maintained salmon populations for decades in the face of ever-increasing harvest pressures. Most people would be surprised to know that the highest total count of salmon and steelhead ever recorded at Bonneville Dam came nearly 50 years after that Dam was constructed:

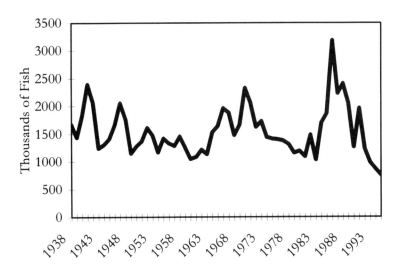

Figure 1: Salmon and Steelhead Returns to the Columbia River[3]

Only recently—many salmon generations after the last dam was completed—have there been sharp drops in salmon abundance.

Many factors have conspired to produce these drops, including poor ocean conditions, harvest pressures, reduced hatchery releases, and truly extraordinary mismanagement of hatchery operations. Hatchery operators do not even issue reports from which their success at returning adults for harvest can be assessed; it is unclear if the data is collected at all. While hatcheries are supposed to mitigate for dam-related losses, no competent estimates exist to determine whether more smolts are now delivered alive to the bottom of the river than before the dams were built.

Myth #3: Overfishing Is No Longer a Significant Factor in Columbia Basin Salmon Decline.

Since fishery agencies have not even attempted to estimate the total number of Columbia River salmon killed in salmon harvest, lacking competent estimates of how many Columbia River fish are caught in the ocean, it is hard to credit claims that harvest is not a problem. They have not even estimated the total legal harvest, much less the very substantial illegal harvest, and other harvest-related losses.

The effects of overfishing, including a net-induced downsizing of fish to half their historic size, continue today. Salmon runs are declining up and down the West Coast even in Canadian rivers with little human development—declines that everywhere else are attributed to overfishing. There is incredible waste and abuse in current salmon harvest management, with millions of pounds of dead salmon tossed overboard as "bycatch".

But people want to believe that we can "save our salmon and eat them too". Attempts to have the federal courts impose limitations on salmon harvest have repeatedly failed, as fishery agencies flout federal law without consequence. Even though the Endangered Species Act flatly forbids all trade and commerce in endangered species, the National Marine Fisheries Service routinely issues permits (called "incidental take statements") for the commercial harvest of endangered salmon. Environmentalists, hypersensitive to clear-cutting on land, ignore it in the sea.

Myth #4: The Eight Mainstem Columbia and Snake River Dams Are a Critical Obstacle to Salmon Recovery

Federal, state and tribal fish managers repeatedly claim that these dams kill 95% of juvenile salmon migrating downstream. Many of them, particularly in the state agencies, know that this is false, yet continue to repeat the lie to uncritical media representatives.

It is true that many juvenile salmon die while migrating downstream, but natural mortality in rivers is always high, whether the rivers have dams or not. That is why each female salmon has thousands of eggs, only two of which need to hatch and survive to adulthood to maintain salmon populations.

While salmon losses were larger twenty years ago while the dams were under construction, and before substantial fish passage improvements, salmon now survive at a higher rate per mile in the dammed part of the Columbia and Snake Rivers than the undammed parts. Comparisons of survival between the Columbia River and the undammed Fraser River in Canada fail to show any effect whatsoever of the dams. The most recent tests show less than 5%

14

mortality for juvenile salmon that go through turbines, and the vast majority of the salmon are routed around the turbines.

Nevertheless, the fishery managers, backed by the Clinton/Gore Administration, have pushed the dam operators to adopt enormously-expensive efforts to reduce mortality at dams by increasing the river's flow and spilling the water over the top of dams, despite evidence that higher flow and spill levels are counterproductive. Backed by credulous politicians, they have also pushed the dam operators to decrease the percentage of salmon transported around the dams, an action that one federal official suggested probably meant ten to fifteen thousand fewer salmon returned in 1995.

The fishery agency hoaxes about the effects of transportation (Chapter 5), flow (Chapter 7) and spill (Chapter 12) have severely damaged the scientific process as applied to salmon recovery. Discredited studies and bogus computer models are repeatedly invoked to justify flow and spill increases, and to reduce the percentage of salmon transported downstream.

The best scientific evidence is ignored and even suppressed. In one particularly egregious case, when observers using ninety-power microscopes found symptoms of gas bubble trauma in tiny juvenile salmon from the agencies' spill increases, the agencies took the microscopes away and gave the scientists magnifying glasses instead.

The legal process was damaged as well, as federal courts swallowed the Great Salmon Hoax hook, line and sinker. They never even permitted opponents of the agencies to present testimony on the effects of dams, repeatedly invoking procedural barriers to reaching the true facts that one judge characterized as akin to the barriers barring the salmon's attempt to return to the spawning grounds.[4]

Myth #5: Dam Removal Will Cause Wild Salmon Populations To Rebound To Historic Levels

It is widely-reported that Columbia Basin salmon runs peaked in the late 1800s at 16 million fish; competent scientific analysis puts the number at half that. Unless we genetically engineer or breed superior salmon, we are unlikely to ever have that many salmon in the Columbia River Basin again, because the ecosystem of the 1800s can never be restored.

The introduction of exotic and competing species, such as shad and walleye, forever limits salmon abundance. The walleye eat salmon; skyrocketing shad populations compete with salmon for food. Soaring bird and marine mammal populations threaten the salmon as well.

More importantly, the effects of natural cycles in ocean conditions dwarf fresh water effects under human control. In the last two decades, ocean conditions have been the worst in 500 years; the fate of salmon hangs largely on changes in those conditions. Both the ocean and river are warmer now, and salmon are cold water fish.

To the conservation biologists who now have the ear of Northwest policymakers, there is but one true path to salmon recovery, as salmon recovery is subordinate to a larger political imperative: the return to a state of nature. They have coined the phrase a "normative river" to describe a river as close to natural as policymakers will go. They and other promoters of the Great Salmon Hoax would simply remove four to six dams along the Columbia and Snake Rivers, and let Nature take its course.

Immense public resources are now devoted to considering the question of dam removal, despite the absence of the most elementary data needed to make a rational decision, or even the means to collect it. Indeed, the U.S. Army Corps of Engineers and the National Marine Fisheries Service have formally committed themselves to making a decision in 1999 on dam removal, taking the legally-unsupportable position that such a decision is required by the Endangered Species Act.

An Alternative

The data we do have suggests that deciding to take out the dams would be a tragic mistake. It would not bring back the salmon in historic numbers, and would waste billions of dollars that could be put to better use. It would have profound and negative effects on the environment. Dam removal would require the thermal generation of unfathomable amounts of electricity, with accompanying pollution. The Northwest would lose not merely electricity, but also valuable flood control, inland navigation, irrigation, and reservoir recreation.

Everyone knows that the fishery agencies charged to recover salmon have failed utterly. Those who read this book can understand how the myths and misrepresentations in the Great Salmon Hoax fuel continuing failure. Increased salmon runs in the Pacific Northwest can only come when we look beyond harvest managers for solutions, and base recovery measures on hard scientific data, not the opinions of agency ideologues.

Most of what we need to do is known. Perhaps the most important step is to adopt selective harvest methods and management regimes that allow us to enforce specific harvest levels for every stock we decide is worth saving. Setting harvest levels based on larger, total abundance inevitably weeds out less-productive stocks, and cannot continue if we are really trying to protect those stocks. Only if and when fishermen are required to fish where they catch only the abundant stocks, or release the less-abundant ones alive, will we make any progress in protecting wild stocks.

Instituting the most elementary measures of management performance for hatcheries can improve hatchery operations immensely. A concerted effort will be required to undo decades of bad salmon breeding, and offset effects of overfishing.

Competent measurements, yet to be undertaken, can direct us to focus on structural improvements at the dams where they will be cost-effective. New surface collector technology will result in even fewer salmon passing through turbines, and new turbine techology will result in less harm to those that do.

We have the technology to run dams and hatcheries while maintaining sufficient genetic diversity for the overall health of salmon in the Columbia River Basin. All that is lacking is political leadership willing to settle the present funding battles and empower a single, accountable entity to mandate competent, science-based salmon management. Knowledgeable and concerned citizens should demand nothing less.

NOTES TO INTRODUCTION

[1] 56 Fed. Reg. 58,619 (Nov. 20, 1991).

[2] 57 Fed. Reg. 14,658 (April 22, 1992).

[3] From Table 1, "Status Report: Columbia River Fish Runs and Fisheries, 1938-95", at 2-3 (WDFW/ODFW Aug. 1996).

[4] *PNGC v. Brown*, 822 F. Supp. 1479, 1483 (D. Or. 1993), *aff'd in part and rev'd in part*, 38 F.3d 1058 (9th. Cir. 1994).

CHAPTER 1: BACKGROUND FACTS ABOUT COLUMBIA BASIN SALMON

We know much more about about salmon than most species of fish. The scientific facts we know about what makes salmon thrive are the facts that ought to be guiding our decisions about salmon recovery programs. At least since the Enlightenment, people have applied science to solve problems. This book proceeds from the premise, increasingly unfashionable, that the salmon problem is a problem that can be solved by applying basic scientific knowledge.

From a scientific perspective, growing salmon is not a problem different in kind than farming any other species. Given ocean conditions, the production of the salmon crop will always be highly variable. But we can measure when farming techniques are working, and when they are not.

Basic Life History of Salmon

Salmon are found throughout the higher, cooler latitudes around the world. In vast forested regions around the world, small gravel-bottomed streams have the potential to support juvenile fish, but do not offer sufficient food to sustain adult fish. Anyone who has ever hiked in the mountains east of the Cascades knows that the mountain streams are clear and cold. The crystal clarity of the water means that the water itself is deficient in the micro-organisms that form the bottom of the food chain to support large numbers of big fish.

Salmon take advantage of this underinhabited habitat by using the stream gravel to deposit their eggs. They dig nests in the gravel which are called "redds". Over the course of several days, a chinook salmon will typically dig a long groove in the gravel, depositing four or five egg pockets in a line running upstream, and covering them as she goes.[1] Salmon have literally thousands of eggs, meaning that but for enormous mortality throughout the life cycle, the world would be quickly awash in salmon. Zoologist Ernest Mayr has pointed out that on average only two of any pair of animal's offspring successfully reproduce.[2]

The type of spawning habitat needed by salmon has been the subject of long and serious scientific inquiry. It has also been the subject of much popular and political attention, as various salmon recovery plans attempt to remake salmon habitat to the specifications of the authors of those plans. Chinook salmon can accept a wide range of spawning habitat, in terms of the depth of the water and its velocity, and the size of the gravel.[3]

The most important factor for chinook salmon appears to be good subsurface flow of water through the gravel, which allows the eggs to "breathe". Because chinook salmon have the largest eggs (and thus the lowest ratio of surface area to volume), good subsurface flow is critical for them. Biologists theorize that spawning salmon sense where gravel has good subsurface flows, and concentrate their redds there, avoiding other areas where the gravel looks fine to human observers.

Once the eggs are deposited in the redds, they are relatively safe from predators. However, one of the largest sources of mortality in the redds is flooding. The flooding can scour out the redds entirely, or bury them in silt that restricts the ability of water to percolate through the gravel.[4] Very high flows can cause survival rates for eggs to fall by a factor of ten or more.[5] Alternatively, redds can dry out if river levels drop, whether the cause is natural or the product of river regulation by dams. Some juvenile salmon have a tendency to burrow in and hide under gravel in the river beds, and sometimes, juvenile salmon trapped by falling water levels can dig deep to keep wet.[6]

There is some evidence that salmon limit themselves to spawning in river reaches with a gradient of 3% or less.[7] Ironically, most of the streams in the Pacific Northwest currently under federal protection as salmon habitat, particularly upland streams at higher elevations, have larger gradients, and are at best sub-optimal salmon habitat.[8]

"Stream-Type" Salmon, Including Endangered Snake River Spring/Summer Chinook Salmon

Salmon begin to diverge in behavior after emerging from the redds into two general groups of salmon. The first, "stream-type", stay in the vicinity of spawning beds over the winter after emerging from the redds. They also return to fresh water months before spawning, typically from February through July. Spring and summer chinook salmon in the Columbia and Snake Rivers typically are regarded as "stream-type" salmon.

In the first year of life in the streams, perhaps 70% of the population is lost to starvation and predators. Birds eat many of them. Dr. Don Chapman is probably the world's greatest expert on the biology of Idaho salmon. Three times, most recently in 1988, he has received an award from the American Fisheries Society for publishing the most significant paper in the Transactions of the American Fisheries Society for the year.[9] Dr. Chapman suggests that by killing colonies of mergansers in Idaho that can consume hundreds of juvenile salmon in a single day, one could cause an appreciable increase in the number of smolts emerging from any particular stream.

Perhaps in order to avoid this predation, juvenile chinook salmon tend to avoid still and clear water, avoiding beaver ponds and off-channel sloughs. Some have theorized that pools of water from beaver ponds, log blockages, etc., are essential to provide "overwintering habitat" for juvenile salmon. However, there does not appear to be much published scientific evidence to suggest that lack of pools is a limiting factor in chinook production, except where habitat is so degraded that water temperatures rise to undesirable levels.

Because stream-type salmon spend much more time in fresh water, they are more vulnerable to the loss of freshwater habitat and, as adults, to land-based harvest pressure. The stream-type of salmon that survive the birds, bull trout, and other problems begin to head downstream as the ice and snow melts. They move quickly, and do not linger in the mainstem rivers.

Once they reach the ocean, another important behavioral difference appears: the stream-type chinook are great ocean explorers. Indeed, samples of chinook salmon captured in the Western Pacific in Japanese fisheries are almost exclusively stream-type chinook. No one is really sure where populations of stream-type chinook salmon from Idaho go in the ocean. Although some tags have been recovered in Canadian and Alaskan fisheries, too few tags have been recovered to draw firm conclusions.

The upriver spring/summer chinook in the Snake River Basin have been in decline for some time, from 1.5 million in the late 1800s, to an average of 125,000 in the 1950s. Over the 1960s and 1970s and 1980s, wild fish in the Snake River seem to have been gradually replaced by hatchery fish. From 1980 to 1988, however, the population of wild fish rose from 3,343 to 21,870 fish,[10] before crashing in the 1990s. According to the Idaho Department of Fish and Game, only about 60,000 wild spring chinook are expected to migrate out of Idaho streams in 1996, along with about 350,000 hatchery smolts.[11]

There are some encouraging signs, however. The population of "jacks" sampled in 1996 was the highest in years. "Jacks" are sexually precocious 2-year old males. Increases in their number typically signal larger returns of the more abundant classes three, four or more years old. And the number of returning adults has increased for three years in a row. The 1997 return of upriver adults is the best in many years.

"Ocean-Type" Salmon, Including Endangered Snake River Fall Chinook Salmon

The second group of salmon, "ocean-type", begin heading for the sea very soon after they emerge from the gravel. They feed along the way, and move more slowly downstream. Sometimes traveling in schools, they will stop

21

for days in spots along the river. Columbia and Snake River fall chinook salmon typically fall into this group of salmon.

This categorization between "stream-type" and "ocean-type" salmon is, like many biological concepts, only rough in nature. Many important salmon populations share some characteristics of both populations. For example, the Warm Springs run of spring chinook salmon is closer to fall chinook salmon in many ways than other groups of Columbia River spring chinook salmon.

Abundance estimates of fall chinook are sketchier than many other stocks. A fish wheel operator near The Dalles, Oregon wrote that that the fall chinook race, entirely absent in the 1920s, seemed to appear out of nowhere in 1933—"Why they came then, or from where, no one knows. Everyone was taken completely by surprise."[12] The fall chinook seemed to displace the fall run of steelhead and coho; "there were a few steelhead left, but the silversides just completely disappeared".[13]

The National Marine Fisheries Service reports that the historical high of the race now considered endangered, Snake River fall chinook, was 72,000. By the 1950s, when only Bonneville Dam had been completed, the run had already fallen to about 29,000.[14] As of 1996, about 600 were counted at Lower Granite Dam.

The National Marine Fisheries Service has proposed that endangered Snake River fall chinook salmon might be removed from the list of endangered species when 2,500 of them are observed to make it past Lower Granite Dam. But that many fall chinook salmon have never been counted at the Dam. In 1975, when the Dam was completed, only 1,000 were counted.[15]

Sockeye Salmon, and the Endangered Snake River Sockeye Salmon

In the early 1900s, sockeye runs in the Columbia River basin exceeded one million fish annually. Sockeye are the third most abundant species of Pacific salmon. There are more sockeye salmon than chinook salmon, but less than pink (*O. gorbuscha*) and chum salmon (*O. keta*). The distinctive feature of sockeye salmon is that they make more use of lake rearing habitat when juveniles. Indeed, there are even subgroups of sockeye that remain in lakes throughout their life—they are called kokanee, and are common in Western lakes, often the product of transplants by fishery agencies.

Sockeye have been successfully introduced into many lakes, including Frazer Lake on Kodiak Island and Lake Washington in Seattle. The Frazer

Lake population rose to 142,000 within twenty years after introduction. The Lake Washington stock was apparently transplanted from Baker Lake in the 1940s.

In the Columbia Basin, however, the story of sockeye is one of blocking lake habitat. At the turn of the century, twenty-seven lakes produced sockeye in the Columbia River Basin. Today, only three are left: Lake Wenatchee, Washington; Lake Osoyoos, Washington and British Columbia; and Redfish Lake, Idaho. About 96% of available habitat has been lost.[16] One commercial salmon harvester wrote that "[d]ams and irrigation had pretty much destroyed the bluebacks on the Columbia River by the middle 1930s",[17] before construction of any mainstem dam.

People who are interested in restoring sockeye populations to historic numbers need to look lake by lake for habitat that can be restored. The sockeye were an important component of the historic Columbia Basin runs, but a lot of lakes would have to be brought back on line for sockeye to resume significant strength.

It is seems clear that it is the loss of lake habitat, not the mainstem Columbia River dams, that limits sockeye salmon production in the Columbia River Basin. The remaining healthy lake systems of Lake Wenatchee and Lake Osoyoos in Washington, are upstream of *nine* dams. The runs continue notwithstanding the dams.

Sockeye used to inhabit several lakes in the Stanley Basin in Idaho. Early development efforts, including small dams and irrigation diversions, blocked anadromous fish migration into several of these lakes. By the 1940s, the sockeye were almost all gone, with only 200 sockeye reported spawning in Redfish Lake; the run was described as "small" and "greatly depleted".[18] By the 1990s, the sockeye had been reduced to a single lake: Redfish Lake.

One reason this happened is that Idaho Department of Fish and Game poisoned most of the other lakes in the Stanley Basin in "deliberate efforts to substitute trout fisheries for kokanee/sockeye".[19] Idaho also constructed small dams at the outlets of some lakes specifically to prevent anadromous and other undesired fish from migrating into the lakes and competing with trout.[20]

In 1990, the Shoshone-Bannock Tribes of Idaho petitioned the National Marine Fisheries Service to protect the Redfish Lake sockeye under the Endangered Species Act. In 1992, the National Marine Fisheries Service granted the petition, and exercised its authority under the Endangered Species

Act to protect the very first endangered "species" of salmon. The listing was limited to the Redfish Lake sockeye population.

The Service ignored scientists who had advised that in all probability the Redfish Lake sockeye were not an endangered species at all, in the sense that the original, native Redfish Lake sockeye were extinct. A dam constructed in 1909-10 by the Golden Sunbeam Mining Company, thirty feet high, blocked all sockeye migration into Redfish Lake from 1910-34, when the south abutment was blown up.[21] That would mean that any sockeye now in Redfish Lake are the progeny of strays, resident kokanee or fishery agency transplants from other locations.

Perhaps anxious for the flood of federal funds an Endangered Species Act listing would provoke, the Idaho Department of Fish and Game mobilized researchers to go and interview elderly residents of the Stanley Basin. Some of them claimed to have seen "red fish" in the Lake when they were children, and on this basis, the National Marine Fisheries Service determined that some native sockeye had somehow swum through the dam, and thus the "species" was not extinct.

Recently, in attempting to explain why Redfish Lake sockeye were in such poor condition relative to Upper Columbia sockeye stocks, the National Research Council has again suggested that the Redfish Lake sockeye "might have originated as residual sockeye . . . after the removal of Sunbeam Dam in the 1920s, whereas Columbia River sockeye have had continuous access to the sea and to their natal areas. Residual sockeye might be less fit for the rigors of anadromy."[22] Most probably, the endangered Snake River sockeye salmon, to the extent they ever constituted a distinct species, have long been extinct; what we now protect as endangered species are probably just part of the kokanee population.

Even today, as millions of dollars are spent annually to "recover" these Redfish Lake sockeye, the Idaho Department of Fish and Game continues to fight against restoring the Stanley Basin sockeye to all the lakes where they used to live in the Stanley Basin. The National Marine Fisheries Services acts as if the Idaho Department of Fish and Game has veto power of the decision to reintroduce the sockeye.

By 1996, NMFS' program to produce fertilized eggs from the few remaining sockeye was such a success that NMFS had over 300,000 such eggs. When NMFS sought to put some of the eggs in Alturas Lake, Keith Johnson, representing IDFG, said that "the Department would certainly oppose such a release, unless IDFG was allowed to conduct a normal rainbow trout stocking and kokanee fisheries . . .".[23] Idaho continues to insist on stocking potential sockeye habitat with both endangered sockeye and their trout predators, and allowing fishermen to catch and kill them both.

The Ability of Salmon to Change and Survive

Jonathan Weiner's Pulitzer-Prize winning book *The Beak of the Finch* articulates the remarkable strides that have been made in the science of evolution in recent decades. While the most exacting studies have been done on the Galapagos Islands, researchers throughout the world have documented how the physical characteristics of species, carried in their genes, rapidly change to optimize the species for survival as their environments change. Mr. Weiner concludes that Darwin "vastly underestimated the power of natural selection. Its action is neither rare nor slow. It leads to evolution daily and hourly, all around us, and we can watch."[24]

Biologists have not yet determined just when the seven races of Pacific salmon evolved. Some argue that because Pacific salmon (the genus *Onchorhychus*) are restricted to the Pacific, and the Pacific was connected to the Atlantic during the late Pliocene era, the salmon race must have originated as recently as 500,000 to 1,000,000 years ago. Others, using DNA testing techniques, argue that the species may be two to three million years old.

But the salmon that we now protect as endangered evolved much more recently. As recently as 12,000 years ago, a tiny moment in geological time, there were no Columbia Basin salmon. Glaciers blocked the Columbia River as North America's last Ice Age was ending. When the ice melted, the salmon began to colonize the Columbia River Basin, and were highly successful at doing so. Other species, like the sticklebacks common in Canadian lakes, were also isolated and formed different "species" within the last 12,000 years.[25]

About 800 years ago, a three-mile chunk of Table Mountain fell into the Columbia River, blocking it entirely.[26] This event probably cut off the upriver tribes from salmon entirely until the river broke through and the salmon came back.[27] No one knows whether the blockage lasted for one, two, three or more salmon generations. There is some chance that the salmon recolonized the upper Columbia and Snake Rivers within the last 800 years. In 1913, the Fraser River was temporarily blocked when blasting unleashed a rock slide that reportedly killed millions of sockeye salmon.[28] Yet Fraser River sockeye recovered and remained abundant for decades.

It may be that salmon runs in the Snake River have always been subject to occasional disappearances. A 1938 researcher reported that "[w]hen running, the [salmon in the upper Snake River] were sufficiently abundant to

25

supply all who could take them. The main limitation on them was their occasional failure to run and the restricted number of convenient fishing places."[29]

Where conditions are favorable, salmon can colonize available habitat at an amazing rate. Chinook salmon from California were introduced into New Zealand at the turn of the century. Without heavy commercial fishing pressure, the salmon spread to run in five New Zealand rivers. And, more significantly, there are demonstrable differences in appearance between the different salmon runs. The authors of one study of the New Zealand salmon concluded that

> ". . . skeptics of the application of the species concept (including the U.S. Endangered Species Act) to salmon populations might argue that the rapid diversification of salmon populations indicates they they are more plastic than has been assumed, and that only a diverse gene pool need be preserved, not every spatially and genetically discrete population."[30]

This "plasticity" is not a phenomenon unique to New Zealand. Recently, a race of spring-spawning chinook salmon has developed in the Great Lakes, which developed from a fall-spawning race.[31] In the language of genetic biologists, the genus *Onchorhychus* has extraordinarily plastic genes.

Although salmon are famous for returning to their natal streams, they also stray and return to the wrong stream or even the wrong river. Biologists retrieving coded wire tags in Alaskan rivers have been known to recover Columbia River salmon.

Straying is useful for the preservation of the species, in that the stray salmon form the nucleus for new colonies of salmon in previously unused habitat. When people have introduced salmon to new places, straying allows salmon to spread rapidly to colonize available habitat. The eruption of Mt. St. Helens provided yet another example of the value of straying: when returning adults from the Toutle River found the the river completely blocked by ash and debris, they were able to change course, go to the Cowlitz River, and spawn there.[32]

That salmon are adaptable does not mean that we should make things worse for them. But as Gregg Easterbrook emphasized in his call for "ecorealism", *A Moment on the Earth*, "understanding the strength and resiliance of life helps us put the environmental issues of the day into a perspective larger than our own. Without such perspective, humankind will not be able to make rational choices regarding which environmental alarms are genuine and which merely this year's fad."[33]

There is some evidence that it is difficult to replace a population of salmon once extinguished, but the evidence is generally limited and anecdotal. Between 1949 and 1975, for example, Canadian fishery managers tried and failed to replace sockeye in the Adams River, a tributary of the Fraser River that had been blocked by a dam from 1908 to 1921.[34]

Some biologists believe that populations of salmon have highly specific adaptations to particular habitat that interfere with efforts to "transplant" salmon, but the evidence is sketchy.[35] This belief, however, is a cornerstone of the prevailing salmon orthodoxy. Bruce Brown's influential *Mountain in the Clouds: A Search for the Wild Salmon*, went so far as to claim that juvenile salmon genes were, in essence, unique to the particular stream in which they are born.[36] Journalists and politicians commonly repeat claims that once salmon are lost from a single river, particular salmon traits are "never to be recovered".[37] This perspective exaggerates the differences in genetic materials and ignores the rapidity of evolution in salmon populations.

The Concept of a Salmon "Species"

Why would NMFS list the sockeye population in a single lake as endangered, when sockeye are plentiful? Few people realize that the Endangered Species Act does not protect just "species", but also subspecies, and even sub-subspecies, or "distinct population segments".

A "species" is something you can look up; a Latin name describing a specific taxonomic group of animals. As Harvard Professor Stephen Jay Gould has explained, the "category of species has a special status in the taxonomic hierarchy" because "each species represents a 'real' unit in nature".[38] A species is simply a population of actually or potentially interbreeding organisms sharing a common gene pool.

Professor Gould notes that both above the species level (taxon, genus, etc.) and below it (subspecies, distinct population segments, etc.), the designations are inherently arbitrary. The boundaries of a subspecies can never be fixed and definite, because by definition the members of a subspecies can interbreed with different subspecies, potentially forming other subspecies. According to him, "[m]any biologists are now arguing that it is not only inconvenient, but downright misleading, to impose a formal nomenclature on the dynamic patterns of variability that we observe in nature".[39]

The endangered Snake River spring/summer and fall chinook salmon are identified as "distinct population segments" of the species *Oncorhynchus tshawytscha*—chinook salmon. In the case of endangered Snake River sockeye salmon, the species is *Onchorhynchus nerka*—sockeye salmon. The world is swimming in chinook and sockeye salmon. There are probably more than a thousand populations of chinook salmon scattered in a ring around the Northern Pacific from California, Oregon, Washington, British Columbia, Alaska and Siberia, and transplanted populations in New Zealand and (perhaps) Chile. Any pair of these salmon can successfully interbreed, even if they are from populations thousands of miles apart.

The endangered and non-endangered Snake River chinook salmon are identical to the naked eye. In fact, it is difficult to tell the stocks apart even with expensive, high-tech genetic testing. NMFS relies on "gel electrophoresis" to identify variations in the frequency of particular salmon genes at particular gene locations.

There are some subtle visual differences in appearance between upriver and downriver chinook salmon stocks in the Columbia River Basin. So while you can't really tell the Snake River salmon apart from the other upriver stocks (like the abundant mid-Columbia stocks), you can tell them apart from lower river stocks. But the visual differences are far less than, for example, differences among different breeds of roses, rabbits or cows. The only way to be relatively sure of what population a salmon comes from is by watching where it returns to spawn; since salmon stray, we can never be sure.

Yet catching a wild chinook salmon in some parts of the Snake River Basin can constitute a federal crime. Catching one in a gillnet in the lower Columbia River is authorized and supported by the National Marine Fisheries Service. Why is this legal? Because when the gillnet is pulled into the boat, with the drowned salmon hanging from it, there is no way to distinguish the "endangered" salmon from the common ones.

In the case of Snake River spring chinook, state and tribal fishery agencies have urged protection of each and every one of 38 subpopulations of this tiny "distinct population segment" of the chinook salmon population. There is no unique genetic material in any of these populations; only the frequency of genes common to all 38 populations varies.[40] And there is no evidence that different frequencies of genes have any measurable effect on the salmon's ability to survive.

The Endangered Species Act allows the bureaucrats to try to protect, as "endangered species", populations of animals identical but for differing gene frequencies. Yet, as the National Research Council has explained, "individual local breeding populations of salmon are expected to have a limited time of persistence on an evolutionary time scale" because the salmon consist of a "metapopulation" in constant "balance between extinction and recolonization of local breeding populations".[41] Trying to freeze one particular pattern of local breeding populations in place is like trying to stop the tide.

When the fact that Snake River salmon are separated into a number of populations that can re-establish each other is taken into account in assessing the likelihood of extinction, the results are striking. Dr. John Emlen of the Northwest Biological Science Center has prepared the only analysis I know of. His conclusion: "the model projections *indicate a virtually certain persistence of Snake River spring chinook over the next 100 years*".[42] While Dr. Emlen warns that models can be misleading, his analysis flies in the face of all conventional wisdom on salmon. The fishery agencies have responded by ignoring his work entirely.

This is not to say that evolution, or metapopulation dynamics, is an excuse for not protecting salmon. Some biologists believe that mankind has produced a great "acceleration" of evolution. This in turn is "an indication of what must have happened again and again in geological history whenever any species or group of species became so ecologically dominant as greatly to upset the habitats of their own times".[43] Short of depopulating the Pacific Northwest, that ecological dominance is not going to disappear.

Moreover, those who claim that the rate of extinctions is at an all time high suffer from what Gregg Easterbrook has called the "Fly Corpse Factor. If species were dropping like flies, the corpses should be piling up by now. Instead species corpses turn out to be exceedingly difficult to locate."[44] He points out that because of the Spotted Owl Hoax, the Northwest forests are among the best-studied ecologies. Yet researchers have not uncovered "a single actual extinction, which seems revealing given that every graduate student involved in a Northwest forest field study is acutely aware that documenting a species loss would make his or her academic career".[45]

While protecting genetic diversity is important, it is worth remembering that

> "[s]cientists now believe Earth's ecosphere has become progressively more diverse, playing host to a greater range of species and gene lines as the ages have passed. Edward O. Wilson of Harvard University, a leading contemporary biologist, thinks that at present global genetic diversity is the highest ever, with perhaps as many as 100 million species walking the earth."[46]

And if each species had a thousand "distinct population units", like chinook salmon, then there would be 100 *billion* distinct population units on the earth.

Mankind is gifted with the choice of how to influence the environment, and the opportunity to choose how its dominance will affect other species. As the biologists who studied Darwin's finches concluded: "Species don't stand still. You can't 'preserve' a species."[47] The historic hundred pound salmon of the Columbia River are gone forever unless we use technology to bring them back. By making the right choices in salmon recovery, we may be able to exercise our dominance in a way that helps to bring back many salmon, even if they are not pristine wild salmon.

NOTES TO CHAPTER 1

[1] M. C. Healey, "Life History of Chinook Salmon", *reprinted in* Pacific Salmon Life Histories 321 (UBC Press 1991).

[2] Cited in G. Easterbrook, *A Moment on the Earth* 144.

[3] *Id.*

[4] *Id.* at 328.

[5] "High water tied to salmon egg decline", *The Spokesman-Review*, May 14, 1997 (Reporting on WDFW research: "On the Cedar and Skagit, the survival rate is about 20% when flows are modest. During the biggest floods, it drops to 2% or less. In seasons with moderately high flows, survival hovers between 5% and 12%).

[6] B. Brown, Mountain in the Clouds 93.

[7] J. Palmisano, Informal Comments to the NWPPC on the ISG's Report, April 15, 1997, at 3.

[8] *Id.*

[9] Dr. Chapman's qualifications are summarized in his affidavit filed Dec. 14, 1993, in *Northwest Resource Information Center v. National Marine Fisheries Service*, No. 93-870-MA (D. Or.).

[10] *PNGC v. Brown*, 822 F. Supp. at 1483

[11] B. Rudolph, "Huge PIT-Tag Study Planned by Long-Term Critics; NMFS Has Doubts", *Clearing Up*, Dec. 23, 1996, at 5.

[12] F. Seufert, *Wheels of Fortune* 7 (Oregon Historical Society 1980).

[13] *Id.*

[14] B. Rudolph, "Fall Harvest Cuts Pay Small Dividend to Northwest Fishers", *Clearing Up*, Dec. 16, 1996, at 7.

[15] *Id.*

[16] The facts in this paragraph can be found in ISG, *Return to the River* 98.

[17] F. Seufert, *Wheels of Fortune* at 6.

[18] "Compilation of Information on Salmon and Steelhead Losses in the Columbia River Basin", Appendix D of the 1987 Columbia River Basin Fish and Wildlife Program, at D-86 (NWPPC Mar. 1986).

[19] D. Chapman, W. Platts, D. Park & M. Hill, "Status of Snake River Sockeye Salmon", Final Report to PNUCC, June 26, 1990, at 49.

[20] *Id.*

[21] *Id.* at 26-36 (recounting history of Sunbeam Dam).

[22] NRC, *Upstream* at 86 (Prepub. ed.). Sunbeam Dam may not have been removed until the 1930s (W. Ebel, pers. comm, May 5, 1997).

[23] Meeting Summary, Stanley Basin Technical Oversight Committee, Sept. 19 1996, at 5 (NMFS Laboratory, Manchester, Washington).

[24] J. Weiner, *The Beak of the Finch* 9 (Vintage 1994).

[25] *Id.* at 185.

[26] R. White, *The Organic Machine: The Remaking of the Columbia River* 10 (Hill & Wang 1995).

[27] *Id.* at 18.

[28] R. Steelquist, *A Field Guide to the Pacific Salmon* 31.

[29] J. Steward, "Basin-Plateau Aboriginal Sociopolitical Groups Bulletin 120 (Smithsonian Inst. 1938), quoted in "Compilation of Information on Salmon and Steelhead Losses in the Columbia River Basin", Appendix D of the 1987 Columbia River Basin Fish and Wildlife Program, at 64 (NWPPC Mar. 1986).

[30] T. Quinn *et al.*, "Origin and Genetic Structure of Chinook Salmon (*Oncorhynchus tshawytscha*) Transplanted from California to New Zealand: Allozyme and mtDNA Evidence" 18 (research conducted under contract to Puget Power, in press as of 1996).

[31] M. C. Healey, *in* Pacific Salmon Life Histories, at 382.

[32] R. Taylor, "Conservation Biology", *Wana Chinook Tymoo*, Issue One, 1996, at 30 (CRITFC); *cf.* R. Steelquist, *Field Guide to the Pacific Salmon* 42 ("When the Toutle River salmon returned to the river, they found it choked with ash and silt, abandoned it, and spawned instead in the Kalama River.")

[33] G. Easterbrook, *A Moment on the Earth* 45.

[34] NRC, *Upstream* at 135 (Prepub. ed.).

[35] Uncharacteristically, the NRC's *Upstream* report cites no studies at all in support of its assertion that there is "strong evidence" that genetics explains "complicated homing behavior, temperature adjustments, unique local mating behavior, and adjustments of smolts to local feeding conditions". *Upstream* at 134 (Prepub. ed.).

[36] B. Brown, *Mountain in the Clouds: A Search for the Wild Salmon* 62.

[37] J. Cone, *A Common Fate* 124.

[38] S. Gould, *Ever Since Darwin: Reflections in Natural History* 232 (W.W. Norton 1992).

[39] *Id.*. at 233.

[40] R. Turner, "Conservation Biology", *Wana Chinook Tymoo*, Issue One, 1996, at 33 (CRITFC).

[41] NRC, *Upstream* at 135 (Prepub. ed.).

[42] J. Emlen, "Population Viability of the Snake River Chinook Salmon (*Onchorynchus tshawytscha*), at 14.

[43] E. Anderson & G. Stebbins, "Hybridization as an Evolutionary Stimulus", quoted in J. Weiner, *The Beak of the Finch* 244.

[44] G. Easterbrook, *A Moment on the Earth* 558.

31

[45] *Id.* at 559.

[46] G. Easterbrook, *A Moment on the Earth* 36.

[47] R. Grant & P. Grant, *Evolutionary Dynamics of a Natural Population,* quoted in J. Weiner, *The Beak of the Finch* 250.

CHAPTER 2: OVERFISHING AND SALMON POPULATIONS

> "We regulate our fisheries. But we concentrate them on the best races and one by one these shrink or vanish and we do not even follow their fate because we have not learned to recognize their independent component groups or to separate them one from the other. We continue our unequal demands, knowing only that our total catches diminish, as one by one small populations disappear unnoticed from the greater mixtures from which we fish." W. F. Thompson (1965).[1]

The decline of Columbia River salmon is mostly another tragedy of the commons; a story of overfishing. Fishery biologists have been warning about the problem for a long time, as populations of salmon disappeared one by one from the Pacific Northwest, in rivers with and without dams. Even after the listing of some Northwest salmon as endangered, we "continue our unequal demands" on them, as endangered Northwest salmon remain subject to commercial harvest and human consumption.

The Rise of Salmon Harvest in the Columbia Basin

The great abundance of salmon in the Columbia River Basin helped shape the development of tribal civilizations throughout the Northwest. When Lewis and Clark toured the Pacific Northwest in 1805-06, they found Native Americans fishing at over 100 sites in the lower Snake and Columbia, and observed them packing 90-100 pound bales of pulverized, dried salmon for commerce with distant tribes.[2] How many salmon were caught? No one will ever really know for sure.

Research continues, however, and there have been recent (but unpublished) reports of archaeological evidence of tribal famines from inadequate salmon runs. In the Native American myths, "there is a recurring motif of a time when sisters imprisoned the salmon—sometimes within a lake or pond, sometimes behind a dam—and how they are freed by Coyote, the lecherous and often foolish culture hero."[3] Perhaps these myths all arise from the collapse of Table Mountain.

We do know that the tribes caught a lot of salmon. They were highly skilled, using spears, dipnets, seines and sometimes even gillnets. Places where the salmon were particularly easy to catch—at the bottom of waterfalls or on spawning grounds—became centers for tribal gatherings. The most famous such location was Celilo Falls, near The Dalles, Oregon, now submerged by the waters impounded behind The Dalles Dam. Before the Dam was built, Celilo Falls was only submerged during spring floods, which halted fishing at the site.[4]

Some historical accounts have claimed that during the heavy fishing season at Celilo Falls, the population swelled from 100 to 3,000.[5] A fishwheel operator in The Dalles, however, reported that "[p]rior to about 1936, Celilo Falls had an Indian population in the fishing season of some 30 or 40 families that lived there permanently or came from the reservations to fish".[6] Most of the fishing spots at the Falls were inaccessible because of swift waters, but once the fishwheel company (which also purchased salmon caught by the tribes) began to string overhead cables for access, "[i]n less than ten years Celilo had developed from a few Indian fishermen to an estimated 1,000 Indians coming to fish there during the fall season".[7] Higher salmon prices at the onset of World War II helped draw Indians from the reservations.[8]

In the 1940s, scientists estimated the peak population of Native Americans in the Columbia River Basin at 50,000, and suggested that if they each consumed a pound of salmon a day, the annual catch was 18 million pounds.[9] These were crude estimates and did not take account of the differences in consumption among the tribes. The tribes centered around Celilo Falls may have derived between 30 and 40 percent of their total caloric intake from salmon; the upriver tribes probably obtained 5 percent or less.[10]

These facts are now of political significance. Anti-dam writers, holding the salmon more important to the tribes, speculate that archeological evidence showing that early Snake River inhabitants ate more meat than fish could be in error because "fish bones don't preserve well".[11] This seems unlikely, since hundreds of thousands of salmon vertebrae have been recovered at 10,000-year-old sites.[12]

As a result of the effects of white settlement, particularly smallpox, the tribal population fell drastically, perhaps by a factor of 6 between 1800 and 1850.[13] By the time Governor Stevens signed several treaties with the tribes in 1855, total tribal harvest may have fallen accordingly, to 3 million pounds.

Early writers theorized that the collapse of tribal populations allowed salmon populations to increase and paved the way for record salmon runs in the late 1800s.[14] More modern writers have questioned whether the tribes' fishing effort was ever sufficient to depress salmon populations.[15]

While we do not know the effects of tribal fishing on salmon, many believe that early Paleo-Indian populations showed no restraint in hunting the wooly mammoth to extinction.[16] Had Northwest tribal civilizations developed into Mayan proportions, including widespread slavery,[17] they might well have produced the same destruction of salmon runs that the white settlers ultimately wrought. One biologist has estimated that "nearly 75 percent of the large mammal and bird genera of the late ice age era were gone from North America by the time Europeans arrived, with some of these extinctions hastened along by Indians in the sort of hyperspeed fashion now presumed an exclusive feature of industrial society".[18]

David Duncan's wonderful book *The River Why* recounts a legend of the Wolf Clan of the Nass River People intended to warn tribal members not to waste the salmon resource.[19] The great Harvard anthropologist Franz Boas came to the Pacific Northwest in the late 1800s and reported on all the taboos that the trickster-god Coyote provided for his people. In the case of chinook salmon, he told the people: "When you have killed many salmon, you must never carry them outside the house. You must roast and eat them at the same place. When part is left you must stay at the same place."[20]

These sorts of rules may be calculated to limit overfishing, and one wonders what Coyote would say about the tribes' modern commercial harvest practices. Perhaps he would tell them that their violation of the taboos has contributed to salmon declines. It seems doubtful that Coyote would approve of stringing up seven gillnets across a 100-foot creek to completely exterminate a wild steelhead run—a practice reported in 1997.[21]

It would not be surprising if the unwritten history of all tribes includes battles between environmentalists and those who would exploit natural resources thoughtlessly, like the contrast in *The River Why* between Thomas Bigeater, the Warm Springs elder, and the young drunken Indians spearing salmon. The holy men of the tribes may have been the environmentalists and custodians of the tribal lore about which we now learn. Thus we now think of the tribes as environmentalists and ignore their frequent slash and burn approach to natural resource management.

We do know, however, that the tribes never adopted high technology fishing methods. Most of the salmon were caught one-by-one, with dip nets and spears. The white settlers quickly invented (or copied from the tribes) mass production techniques. Gillnets, fish wheels, and fish traps littered the river, in a parallel to an orgy of timber harvesting going on at the same time. By the late 1800s, observers warned about the decline in salmon numbers, and urged limits on fishing seasons.

At that time, chinook salmon ran continuously in the Columbia River beginning in February, increasing throughout the summer and gradually decreasing into the fall. They were divided into three races: spring chinook salmon (harvested beginning in February until May), summer (harvested in June, July and August), and fall chinook (harvested after August). Under current management plans, all chinook passing Bonneville Dam from March through May are counted as upriver "spring" chinook. Chinook passing in June and July are summer chinook. Fall chinook can be distinguished visually and generally pass Bonneville in late July through early October.[22]

The most abundant salmon, the summer run, were destroyed first. When settlers first arrived, the "June hogs" were recognized to be the best salmon for eating. This, coupled with the fact that the weather made it easier to fish in the summer, meant that the harvesters focused on summer chinook first. Writer Joseph Cone notes that as early as the 1880s, the June hogs "established the reputation of Columbia salmon throughout the United States".[23]

Today the summer run of chinook salmon in the Columbia River is the smallest of the three runs. And even though large-scale fishing for summer chinook has been outlawed for decades, the summer run has never regained its former size. After the summer chinook were nearly destroyed, the spring and fall races became an important component in commercial salmon harvests.[24] The spring run, however, was regarded as the high quality run, and many canneries only operated in the fall if the spring runs were poor.[25]

The gillnetters became the winners in the battle for control of the salmon resource. The story of how they achieved this is fully told in a number of good books, including Dr. Courtland Smith's *Salmon Fishers of the Columbia*. It was a triumph of trade unionism akin to that prevailing around the country, as the gillnetters formed a union and attacked the owners of fish traps, fish wheels, pound nets, and other harvesters as "moneyed individuals" who "annihilated" salmon and "could take their gold and go elsewhere".[26] Violent controversy and even murder fueled the rise of the gillnetters.

Although concentrated in the lower river, overfishing reached to the farthest hinterlands of the Pacific Northwest. Even in remote Idaho, in streams that provide pristine salmon habitat, large numbers of fishermen, including the tribes, overfished the salmon.

Most Idahoans now lament the fact that the historic Salmon River no longer contains great runs of salmon for which it was named. But the salmon in the Salmon River were largely destroyed decades ago. A 1941 survey of the Salmon river reported that "spearing salmon on the spawning beds at the headwaters formerly resulted in great economic waste and was one of the principal causes of salmon depletion in this region".[27]

Marsh Creek, a tributary of the Middle Fork of the Salmon River, used to support a substantial run of salmon. But a 1950 survey of the Columbia River Basin reported that "in the last 20 years, particularly in the decade preceding 1940, the run had been almost exterminated by the former unrestricted practice of spearing salmon on the spawning beds".[28] The surveyors counted only five redds in the Creek.[29]

One of the goals of the secret "Biological Requirements Work Group" arising from the *Idaho Fish and Game* case (discussed in Chapter 9 below) was to establish very aggressive recovery goals for Snake River tributaries, including Marsh Creek. Perhaps the authors of those goals had no idea that the runs were the remnants of a race exterminated by overfishing, and no idea whether recovery is possible at all in such circumstances—they chose instead to blame the dams for the decline in runs.[30]

There does not seem to be any documentation as to who was doing the spearfishing on the spawning grounds up in Idaho. Circumstantial evidence suggests that it was members of the Shoshone-Bannock Tribe, the same Tribe that led the charge for Endangered Species Act protection for Idaho salmon by petitioning for the listing of Snake River sockeye salmon.

No one really knows what sort of subtle aftershocks influence the salmon populations in the wake of the periods of great overfishing. One government biologist who worked for 30 years in the field concluded:

> "History tells us 80 percent to 90 percent of the run was caught or canned or otherwise gone before Bonneville Dam was constructed. So most of the fish, fishermen, and their profits were long gone before I was born. But the resulting biological and ecological lesions from population decimation would continue, with long-term, pernicious consequences, neither easily nor quickly undone."[31]

Smarter, Faster, More Efficient Fishermen

The rise of downriver gillnetting was defended as giving larger employment. The comparatively few fixed sites for salmon harvest, like Celilo Falls, recognized for generations as the easiest place to catch salmon, were replaced at the front of the salmon harvest line by an entire fleet of gillnetters. At first, those were small (often father and son) sailboats. The gillnetters simply outnumbered their opponents and got the old ways outlawed. In Oregon and Washington, public initiatives outlawed fish traps and fish wheels. In doing so, the States of Oregon and Washington legislated inefficiency and waste in the short-run interest of larger employment.

Technology quickly undermined the premise of that legislative choice. No longer is there a huge fleet of small family-owned boats. Instead, there are large, capital-intensive boats, with large nets pulled in by automatic winches, not hand over fist. The rise of fishing technology was recently summarized in the Scientific American:

> "An explosion of fishing technologies occurred during the 1950s and 1960s. During that time, fishers adapted various military technologies to hunting on the high seas. Radar allowed boats to navigate in solid fog, and sonar made it possible to detected schools of fish deep under the oceans' opaque blanket. Electronic navigation aids such as LORAN (Long-Range Navigation) and satellite positioning systems turned the trackless sea into a grid so that vessels would return to within 50 feet of a chosen location, such as sites where fish gathered and bred. Ships can now receive satellite weather maps of water-temperature fronts, indicating where fish will be traveling. Some vessels work in conjunction with aircraft used to spot fish."[32]

James Bohnsack, a research scientist with the National Marine Fisheries Service, warns that while overfishing was limited for years by deep waters, bad weather and imprecise navigation, "[n]ow we have the technology, the tools, to catch that last fish".[33] Environmentalists ought to view this as the land-based equivalent to clear-cutting ancient forests.

The Environmentalist/Harvester Alliance

Unfortunately, the fishermen have hired the best lawyers the environmentalists have, the Sierra Club Legal Defense Fund (now known as the "Earthjustice" Legal Defense Fund), to focus all attention away from fishing to the dams. As explained below, the litigation offensive mounted by the Sierra Club Legal Defense fund on behalf of its fishery industry and environmentalist clients has been remarkably successful in persuading the public that catching, killing and eating salmon doesn't hurt salmon populations—just dams do.

Given the ecological damage caused by fishing, this unholy alliance of commercial fisherman and environmental organizations ought to receive a lot more attention. Fishing organizations such as the Washington Trollers Association and the Pacific Coast Federation of Fisherman are parties in nearly every lawsuit described in this book. Nearly always, they are capably represented by the Seattle office of the Sierra Club Legal Defense Fund.

38

Because non-profit organizations are not generally required to disclose their sources of funding, we never have found out just what percentage of these suits were bought and paid for by the fishermen.

So powerful is the political alliance between commercial fisherman and environmentalists that Northwest environmental groups have repeatedly opposed legislative initiatives to reform salmon harvest. When the sportsfishermen of Oregon succeeded in getting Measure 8 on the ballot in 1992, which would have required selective harvest techniques in the Lower Columbia River, and thereby outlawed most gillnetting, environmentalists opposed it. Environmentalist Ed Chaney wrote in the Voter's Pamphlet that the measure "will only compound the damage to people and communities already victimized by the real fish killers, the Army Corps of Engineers and the Bonneville Power Administration".[34] The voters rejected the initiative.

The Sierra Club Legal Defense Fund have even assisted the fishermen in their fight against farmed salmon, by providing legal services to challenge the environmental permits for fish farms.[35]

Perhaps people would take a more critical perspective on the claims of environmentalists if people knew where their money was coming from. As liberal environmental reporter Gregg Easterbrook has warned, ". . . money colors the ability of interest groups to see issues clearly. Institutional environmentalism must come to terms with the fact that by the 1990s it had been a long time since greens took any important position that ran counter to their own financial interests."[36]

The Rise of Northwest Ocean Harvest

Ocean trolling for salmon began between 1905 and 1915 as fishermen tried to get around limited fishing seasons introduced on the river in order to allow more salmon upriver to spawn.[37] Trolling was particularly successful with chinook salmon because, as writer Bruce Brown has explained, "[u]nlike sockeye, chinook salmon will strike at a baited line in the ocean. This phenomenon, which is due to their preference for feeding on fish rather than plankton, has made them one of the principal targets of the growing commercial and sport troll fleets."[38]

> "By the 1960s the trollers were the dominant factor in the coastal fishery, often accounting for over half the total catch of chinook and coho in Washington. Between 1940 and 1970, Washington trollers increased their catch of chinook nearly 100,000 to 958,408 fish. The key to the trollers' success was simple: first shot at the fish. The history of commercial

39

fishing on the Pacific is essentially a tale of one group after another finding a way to fish in front of the others".[39]

Since 1970, the trollers' catch continued to rise to an all-time high around 1990, and then dropped as salmon populations fell off up and down the West Coast. It is clear that Canadian and American troll catches of chinook salmon rose in parallel with declines in the Columbia River harvest.[40]

Because the salmon swim through so many jurisdictions, it is extraordinarily difficult to figure out the total impact of harvest on salmon. Reviewing the data, the National Research Council concluded that "data limitations have had a serious influence on our ability to assess and manage salmon appropriately".[41]

Decades ago, many observers recognized that harvesting salmon in the ocean made no sense. This was (and is) true for several reasons. Most fundamentally, it is harder to catch the salmon. Unlike a pool below a waterfall (or dam) where salmon are concentrated, out in the ocean salmon are few and far between. More investment in capital is required to catch them—a boat capable of going out on the open ocean. And much time and energy is expended searching for the salmon. Fleets of gas or diesel powered boats must comb the oceans at enormous expense. No one has ever attempted to analyze the environmental impacts of all these fishing efforts.

A more subtle problem with the ocean harvest is that many of the fish that are caught are immature. Ocean harvest is like a farmer harvesting carrots in mid-summer, when they are not fully grown. If the farmer would wait until fall, he or she would get more crops (and value) per acre. And if the fishermen would wait until the salmon were mature and returning to the river, our enormous investment in hatcheries would give a better return. The only estimate I have ever seen of losses from this factor, made in 1979, is that the total poundage of salmon landed would be more than 50% higher if the fishermen waited until salmon returned to the river.[42] When I looked at the question myself, by dividing pounds of catch per fish landed for ocean and in-river fisheries, the result looked like this:

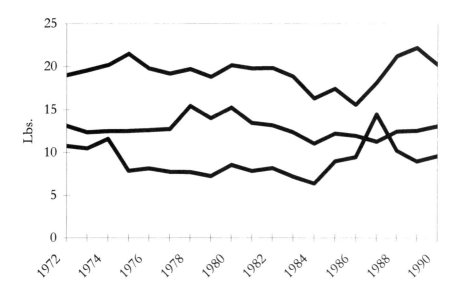

Figure 2: Pounds per fish: Inriver, Washington Non-Tribal Troll, and Tribal Troll[43]

The top line shows the largest, in-river fish; the middle line, the middle-sized fish caught by commercial fishermen trolling off the coast of Washington; and the bottom line, the smallest fish caught in the tribal fishery off the coast of Washington. The tribal ocean fisheries are the most inefficient, essentially wasting half the value of chinook salmon by catching them too soon.

Not every salmon caught in the river will be at the peak of its value. The farther salmon go upriver, the more energy they expend, and the fewer calories are left in their bodies for human consumption. A salmon caught at the mouth of the Columbia River has the maximum caloric value; a salmon caught near The Dalles about 88% of that value; and a salmon caught in the middle Snake River perhaps only 50% or less.[44] In some Canadian rivers, the salmon at the mouths of the rivers are actually too oily to be marketable; on the Columbia the upriver fish with less oil were better for drying as a winter food reserve.

Harvest in the ocean is inherently a "mixed-stock" fishery. Runs of salmon from every river and stream up and down the West Coast and Alaska mix together in one large pool of salmon. There is no practical way to regulate harvest of weak stocks; one can only attempt to regulate the total take of salmon in the pool. This is perhaps the worst vice of ocean harvest, and has long been recognized as a principal cause in the decline of upriver salmon runs in the Columbia River Basin.

Back in 1986, the Northwest Power Planning Council staff warned that in a "mixed-stock fishery, upriver and wild runs already weakened by habitat and passage losses, are fished at the same rate as lower river runs (heavily hatchery-supplemented)."[45] They prepared a chart showing the ratio of ocean harvest to remaining in-river runs for various stocks of salmon in the Columbia River Basin. Total ocean harvest of lower river fall hatchery chinook was 1.4 times the in-river run. Total ocean harvest of upper river fall natural chinook was 3.4 times the in-river run.[46] Upper river and wild stocks simply could not maintain the high harvest rates prevailing in the late 1980s, which set the stage for endangered species listings of upriver stocks.

The Worldwide Problem of Overfishing

The problem of overfishing is not, of course, limited to the Columbia River. The worldwide growth in ocean harvest was explosive after 1970. Between 1970 and 1990, the world's industrial fishing fleet grew twice as fast as harvests. One fisheries biologist estimated that "[t]his armada finally achieved twice the capacity needed to extract what the oceans could sustainably produce."[47]

Study after study has found that overfishing can permanently destroy populations of fish (or at least "permanently" as far as several generations of human beings are concerned). As one fisheries biologist noted, "some of the world's greatest fishing grounds, including the Grand Banks and Georges Bank of eastern North America, are now essentially closed following their collapse—the formerly dominant fauna have been reduced to a tiny fraction of their previous abundance and are considered commercially extinct."[48] The huge cod that fueled trade as America was settled are all gone.

The phenomenon of low vitality following overfishing-induced population collapse remains "puzzling" to state and tribal salmon managers in the Pacific Northwest. Having reduced coastal coho harvests after disastrous miscalculations of coho abundance in the 1980s, and seen no rebound in salmon populations, the Oregon Department of Fish and Wildlife is beginning to recognize that "once a population is reduced to low levels, its resilience is reduced, keeping it from breaking through some threshold to higher levels of productivity".[49] In the Columbia River Basin, however, the fishery agencies refuse to acknowledge this phenomenon. It is assumed that dam passage must be the problem.

Daniel Pauly of the Fisheries Center at the University of British Columbia and Villy Christensen of the International Center for Living Aquatic Resources Management in Manila have pointed out that the vast majority of shallow continental shelves have been scarred by fishing, whereas large untouched tracts of rain forest still exist.[50] The President of the American Association for the Advancement of Science and a panel of other marine scientists recently proposed that nations set aside 20% of the oceans as a reserve from overfishing.[51] As *Ferngully* demonstrates, even children are educated to believe that protecting the rain forests is of vital importance. But the effects of "clear cut" fishing are invisible—except for the absence of fish, which can always be blamed on something else, like dams.

The Failure of Government Regulation of Salmon Harvest

Ocean harvest was unregulated and unlimited from around 1905, when ocean-going boats began going after the salmon, until November 1, 1949, when the Pacific Marine Fisheries Commission closed the season from November 1st to March 14th.[52] Today the Pacific Fishery Management Council, established by Congress in 1976 through the Magnuson Act,[53] regulates the ocean salmon harvest outside the three-mile limit. Inside that limit, the states continue to regulate it.

The United States and Canada Pacific Salmon Treaty was ratified in 1985, and was supposed to limit ocean overfishing on West Coast salmon stocks on an international scale. It did produce some immediate limits in chinook harvests after 1985, which may have been responsible for better returns in the late 1980s. But instead of allowing those increased runs to return to spawning grounds and replenish salmon stocks, they were very heavily harvested in near-shore waters and rivers under state jurisdiction.

Federal and state regulation of harvest has not done much good, since harvest restrictions are generally too little, too late. Ocean harvest regulations have also produced gross waste. Government licenses, permits and quotas mean that tons of the "wrong" fish are caught, killed, and simply tossed overboard. Fishermen allowed to catch only one boatful of fish go out and cast their nets repeatedly, throwing away the less valuable species or smaller fish until the boat is full of the fish that will bring the most money. This is akin to the late 1800s practice of shooting buffalo, cutting their valuable tongues off, and letting the rest of the corpse rot. Now we throw the whole corpses away, salvaging nothing.

43

The harvest managers know what is going on. In the case of salmon, their regulations expressly promote it. For example, as the Pacific Fishery Management Council recently acknowledged, "federal regulations require that salmon caught in the groundfish fishery must be immediately discarded. Fishers are not required to record the number of salmon taken, and there is no comprehensive observer program to monitor bycatch in the shorebased fisheries."[54] This leaves the total damage to salmon populations largely a matter of guesswork, but newspaper accounts suggest that in 1993, for example, more salmon were *thrown away* off the coasts of Oregon, Washington and California than could be legally caught.[55] Scientists warn that bycatch impact is "presently not being addressed by assessment programs.[56]

Huge trawl fisheries operate in the Bering Sea, Gulf of Alaska, and off Oregon, Washington and California and catch largely unknown numbers of salmon, the vast majority of which are chinook salmon.[57] One analysis of the 1995 whiting fishery showed that just 25 tows (out of 2,222 total), captured 60% of the 14,557 chinook bycatch.[58] For all we know, a single sweep of the giant nets can wipe out an entire year class of salmon from an Idaho stream.

When Bern Shanks, director of the Washington Department of Fish and Wildlife, finally put observers on commercial purse seiners in 1997, he characterized the chinook bycatch as "unconscionable" and "obscene". The answer, he said, was to "require the (non-Indian) commercials to release any chinook caught, even though we know there is an estimated 30 percent mortality. We wanted to remove the profit incentive from taking the chinook."[59]

In many of the troll fisheries monitored by the Pacific Salmon Commission, size limits require fishermen to throw back smaller salmon. This process is called "shaking" and can literally involve shaking the salmon off the hook. Obviously, this is not good for the salmon, and there are sharp disputes as to how many of the salmon survive. The fishermen report the total number of fish "caught"; they also report the total number "landed". The difference is those thrown back, dead or alive.

In 1979, for example, the Pacific Fishery Management Council reported 302,000 "adult equivalent mortalities" in fish caught, but not landed.[60] The phrase "adult equivalent" means that the real number of dead fish was probably higher, perhaps 500,000, and that the number of fish shaken off hooks could be in the range of 1.5 million or even higher. These losses continued at very high levels until harvest quota reductions were finally implemented in 1995.[61]

Before the United States asserted jurisdiction over fisheries out to 200 miles (the "Exclusive Economic Zone"), foreign fishermen fished under regulations that required observers to monitor bycatch. When the foreign fishermen were ejected in favor of domestic ones, the requirement of observers was dropped. Regulators apparently assumed that foreign fishermen might not tell the truth about bycatch, but domestic fishermen would scrupulously report it.

As of 1995, there was no monitoring whatsoever in the bottom trawl, shrimp trawl, or long-line fisheries.[62] The National Marine Fisheries Service does have a salmon monitoring program in the North Pacific groundfish fisheries, but only for boats sixty or more feet long. Boats less than 125 feet long need only have 30% coverage in the program.[63] The program has identified enough harvest of endangered salmon to trigger consultations under the Endangered Species Act, but the proportion of salmon caught is small, so the fisheries are not restricted.

Generally speaking, monitoring programs are not audited in any useful way. My colleague and former boss, Jeff Ring, was once flying back from Seattle with a lawyer for the fishermen, who bragged that even where there were observers on the boats, it was in many cases a meaningless exercise. The observers were often retired or disabled fishermen, frequently friends of the boat owners. If they bothered to emerge from their cabins (often, a bottle of scotch is provided to them when they arrived), they would simply peer down into the hold and make an extremely casual judgment as to what was going on.

And no one really knows what is going on in the high seas, where endangered Snake River spring chinook salmon may wander into the illegal drift nets of Taiwanese, Japanese and Korean fishermen. The National Marine Fisheries Service takes the position that this problem was solved by an international moratorium on high seas drift netting. Alaskan fishermen, however, say that foreign boats still put out drift nets on the high seas; when spotted by observers, they simply cut the nets loose, which then continue to kill fish for years. One scientist has suggested that as many as 5.5 million salmon were harvested illegally on the high seas in a recent year.[64] Visitors to Taiwanese markets have seen American steelhead in the markets.[65]

There is a huge, legal drift net fishery for flying squid conducted in the central north Pacific, albeit generally south of the main high seas concentrations of salmonids.[66] Nevertheless, the nets are the same size used for salmon fisheries, and, according to Dr. William McNeil, put Columbia Basin salmon "at risk".[67] No one has even attempted to assess the incidental take of salmon in the squid fishery.

Much more attention is paid to high seas whaling, also the subject of an international moratorium. When travelers reported finding whale meat in Asian markets, researchers used DNA sequencing techniques to confirm the illegal harvest.[68] If anyone bothered to look, we could probably find endangered American salmon for sale in Asian markets too.

The bottom line is that no one knows how many Columbia River salmon are caught in the ocean, and no one seems to care. The Atlantic Salmon Federation took action to protect Atlantic salmon by paying Faroe Islands fishermen $685,600 per year in compensation not to net the salmon in the North Atlantic. Three years later, twice as many salmon returned to native rivers in Iceland and elsewhere in Europe.[69] There may well be one or more classes of ocean harvesters who could be paid off to double salmon runs in the Columbia River.

Surprisingly, government regulation of land-based Columbia River fisheries is only a little more effective that regulation of ocean fisheries. The river fisheries are now managed under a federal court decree supervised by United States District Court Judge Malcolm Marsh in the case of *United States v. Oregon.* As the Idaho Department of Fish and Game recently explained,

> "Basic harvest management decisions under the *United States v. Oregon* process are made in secret by the Policy Committee. The public is excluded from Policy Committee meetings, and the parties are prohibited from revealing what is discussed. To make matters worse, mainstem harvest managers have made little or no attempt to explain these decisions to the public."[70]

The resulting process has continued to sanction heavy harvests on endangered fish. So focused are the parties on allocating the fish among themselves that they have failed to produce any cumulative accounting of the harvest impacts from the lower river commercial and recreational fisheries, tribal commercial and "ceremonial and subsistence" fisheries, and tributary recreational fisheries.[71] In other words, the fishery managers haven't even bothered to assess the impacts of the harvests they authorize.

Nor, more understandably, do the fishery managers know the impact of illegal harvest. Occasional arrests of dealers in illegal salmon have shown uncounted losses from the river of tens of thousands of salmon.[72] From 1992-96, over 500 illegal gillnets were removed from Zone 6 of the Columbia River, which is reserved for tribal harvest.[73] No one has attempted to adjust harvest statistics to account for such losses; instead, they are blamed on the dams.

46

The few studies that focus on the subject are subject to harsh attack. In 1997, the tribes attacked as "racist" BPA's efforts to evaluate a law enforcement assistance program it funded after the evaluators found that the program appeared to be making a dent in illegal harvest by the tribes. When University of Idaho biologists tried to radio-tag fall chinook to find out why they were disappearing, "the program was stopped in its tracks after 50 fish were tagged" by Robert Lohn, head of BPA's fish and wildlife division, because of objections by state and tribal fishery agencies.[74]

When the government is in charge of a business, only that business has the incentive to focus on the details of government decisionmaking. In a phenomenon that is well-recognized by policy analysts, businesses often "capture" the agency. The agency officials begin to think like the business owners. You would expect the government to try and figure out how many salmon from the Columbia River Basin are actually being killed in salmon harvests; you wouldn't expect fishermen to do it. That no one has figured it out speaks volumes.

In a passage that was edited out of its Final Recommendations to the National Marine Fisheries Service, the Snake River Salmon Recovery Team commented:

> "Persons unfamiliar with historic Northwest salmon fisheries might wonder why fisheries management agencies have not actively tried to develop more efficient gear for the [conservation] purposes named here. Avoiding confrontation with user groups, which the agencies have consistently viewed as their clientele as opposed to the general public, is one of the reasons."[75]

After decades of government intervention, the ranks of those "user groups" have been swelled by subsidies. There are so many boats that some fishing seasons in Alaska must be limited to just hours. The shorter the season, the greater the drive to catch anything and everything during the limited time allowed, and the greater the business risk for salmon harvesters.

The current harvest management regime comes under nearly universal attack by fisheries scholars. In another passage stricken from its Final Recommendations to NMFS, the Snake River Salmon Recovery Team noted that

> "A Recovery Plan for Snake River salmon, intended also to prevent further ESA listings, will impose large costs on many people and activities. The cost of maintaining irrational

fisheries should be evaluated in this context. *We use the term irrational to highlight the biological, economical, and managerial inefficiency of the harvesting and management methods now applied to Columbia River salmon.* The overall cost of harvest is far greater than it could be. Excess fishery capacity and resulting intense fishing pressure makes it impossible to gather, process, and apply real time information to manage the fisheries effectively. The inability to adjust mixed stock fisheries results in unbalanced harvesting and makes hatchery production successes an additional threat to natural stocks."

Professor Ray Hilborn of the University of Washington is more succinct: "The commercial fisheries on chinook make little economic sense".[76]

The Recovery Team believed that terminal area fishing and selective fishing offer the best way out of the dilemma posed by non-selective mortality inflicted by traditional gear and harvest patterns.[77] This is not a new thought. In 1976, a representative of the Idaho Department of Fish and Game told his colleagues in the American Fisheries Society:

"As a commercial enterprise, it seems less than intelligent to chase fish all around the ocean when they are ultimately coming back to a home river by themselves and at a greater weight. . . it's rather foolish to chase these fish around the river when they're going to enter fish ladders at some point in their migrations. The mainstem Columbia River fisheries, both sport and commercial, are seldom focused in terms of selective harvest. Tributary or terminal fisheries would be much more sensible."[78]

Only a few in the media perceive the irrationality of salmon harvest. Ross Anderson of *The Seattle Times* once observed that "[s]almon fishing is wonderfully picturesque and romantic, but it never made much sense to employ thousands of people and burn huge quantities of fuel to chase homeward-migrating fish on the open sea."[79]

The economic irrationality of the Northwest salmon fisheries is a reflection of a global problem. Carl Safina, who directs the National Audubon Society's Living Oceans Program, says that

"to catch $70-billion worth of fish, the fishing industry recently incurred costs totalling $124 billion annually. Subsidies fill much of the $54 billion in deficits. These artificial supports include fuel-tax exemptions, price controls, low-interest loans and outright grants for gear or infrastructure. Such massive subsidies arise from the efforts of many governments to preserve employment despite the destruction of so many fisheries."[80]

Many observers, including Mr. Safina, speculate that all those fishermen are not really losing all that money year after year. Rather, they have powerful incentives to underreport harvest, with a huge collective impact on total catches.

The irony of all this regulation is that the push toward capital-intensive techniques for catching fish *limits* employment. Live catch methods are probably more labor intensive. Ocean harvest requires heavier gear, limiting self-employment opportunities. When fish are caught with floating factories out in the Pacific, only a few will be able to own those factories. When they are caught with small boats in rivers and tributaries, many can find the means to buy these boats without subsidies.

Nations like Iceland and Spain have even concluded that commercial harvest of salmon makes no sense, because the finite supply of salmon will deliver the most economic benefits when caught by recreational fishermen.[81] Oscar Thomsen, President of the Oregon Division of the Izaak Walton League of America, has fought gillnetting in the Lower Columbia River, pointing out that

> "The Columbia spring chinook is the most biteable fishery, and provides more recreation to the citizens of Oregon than any other segment of the salmon fishery. The close location of this fishery to the major population centers provides easy access for the fishing public. Recreation is vital to the area, and provides heavy economic income to moorages, motels, hotels, boat builders, motor sales, restaurants and numerous other businesses . . . The gillnet fishery is a wasteful fishery and should be stopped."[82]

While gillnetters come in for almost as much attack as dam interests, there is reason to believe that some of the excesses of the gillnetters were themselves the product of mismanagement by fishery agencies. As Irene Martin has explained in a lucid and succinct history of the Columbia River gillnetters, the gillnetters created, through custom and practice, a process of limiting access to the fishing grounds. The system, known as "drift rights", established specific territories on the Columbia River where fishermen could operate, limiting access to "members". But the courts refused to recognize the system, declaring that the fishery agencies had the responsibility for regulation.[83]   Like any monopoly with a tendency to restrict output, the gillnetters might well have eventually protected the salmon resource—had they not lost all incentive to do so by bad regulation and the sense that the ocean harvesters were taking the fish anyway.

The Subtle Vices of Overfishing

Obviously, overfishing can kill too many adult fish to keep populations healthy.   But overfishing has more subtle effects that conspire to cripple salmon recovery. The most important of these may be the gradual downsizing of salmon.

This results from well-intentioned regulation intended to avoid the waste associated with harvesting immature fish in the ocean. Fishery managers regulate the mesh size of nets used to catch salmon so as to allow smaller, immature salmon to escape. For fish caught in the troll fisheries, they have also established minimum size requirements. This promotes greater biological efficiency, but has a powerful side effect: size, an advantage in the natural system, becomes a disadvantage in the harvest system.

As a result, the size of salmon has been dropping rapidly. As recently as the 1940s, most of the salmon returning were the larger salmon that stayed out in the ocean as long as four or five years.[84] Now they are much smaller. And they don't stay out as long, because each year at sea exposes them to another fishing season. Harvest pressure has selectively eliminated the oldest, largest salmon. A 1980 study by renowned Canadian fish biologist W. E. Ricker concluded that the average size of chinook salmon "has been declining since at least 1920, and continues to decline. Present average weights are half or less than half of those obtained 50 years ago."[85]   Another researcher reported a marked decrease in the average age of fall chinook caught in the ocean from 1919-30 to 1949-63, which he characterized as typical of an overexploited population.[86]   The same phenomenon has been observed in Norwegian cod, Atlantic salmon, red snapper, and red porgy.[87]

Size reductions may have a lot to do with the mysterious loss of "resilience" in overfished salmon populations. Fishery mismanagement can quickly select out the genes for large fish that took centuries (or longer) to develop, and no effort is made to put them back. Large fish got large for a reason. They avoid predators better, and each one of them has a lot more eggs per spawner. Yet it seems to take a very long time for animals to get larger naturally, so that when fishing restrictions are lifted, populations do not rebound. Fisheries scientist John Palmisano suggests that "[t]he failure of many of the Basin's stocks to recover could be a result of the loss of genetic material that occurred during the periods of overharvest . . .".[88]

Size could also explain disproportionately large reductions in upriver salmon runs. Fishermen have long recognized that salmon "destined for upriver areas are larger, as they need more stored fat to enable them to make the journey to their spawning grounds".[89] Size was also an advantage in surmounting obstacles to upstream migration, particularly forceful rapids and waterfalls. Before dams replaced a difficult rapids known as "Goblin's Gate" on the Elwha River, had a reputation for enormous chinook salmon. Only the big ones could get up the rapids.[90] On the Columbia and Snake, fish ladders have replaced the falls, but size may still be important in that larger fish may have greater stores of energy needed for the longer journey.

Many upriver salmon stocks, including Idaho's salmon, have suffered rapid declines that are often blamed on dams. The endangered Snake River spring chinook and sockeye, because they go so far up into the headwaters of the Snake River Basin, have harder migration journeys than most other Columbia River Basin fish.

Smaller salmon are going to have a significant handicap, and the hardest part of their journey may be above the dams. That could be another reason why we have a good deal of high quality salmon habitat in Idaho, far up the tributaries of the Snake River, where salmon are no longer found.

Upriver stocks in the Columbia Basin must pass over many dams, but upriver stocks are declining faster on undammed rivers too. For all we know, the single most important reason for the comparatively greater declines in upriver stocks is the fact that the fish are no longer big enough to get back up there. When I offered this theory to Donna Darm of the National Marine Fisheries Service, who used to assist the Regional Director, Will Stelle, in resolving tough policy issues, she said "keep your day job". Fishery scientists could explore and resolve this question, but the harvest interests and their fishery agencies are not interested in the answer. They would rather blame the dams. The Columbia River Alliance has asked NMFS to study these effects in the Environmental Impact statement it has been preparing pursuant to court order after a legal victory in *Ramsey v. Kantor* (see Chapter 10). NMFS refuses to do so.

The net-based harvest has a second effect, whose long-range implications are entirely unknown: decreasing the age at which salmon are sexually mature. For many years, fishery agencies have kept count of "jacks", which are sexually precocious two-year old males. The proportion of jacks has been rising. This phenomenon was reproduced in a laboratory experiment with two tanks of water fleas. Researchers sieved the tanks every four days, killing all the big water fleas in one tank, and all the little ones in the other tank. After several generations, the fleas in the tanks where big fleas were removed grew more slowly, and began reproducing when they were smaller. In the other tank, the fleas grew faster and did not reproduce until they were larger. In guppies, this change takes about fifty guppy generations.[91] Fishery managers don't seem to be very interested in finding out what the rising proportion of jacks is doing for spawning success.

Another subtle effect comes from the fact that when salmon runs were huge, large numbers of salmon would die after spawning and their bodies would fertilize the streams, providing a reservoir of organic material much richer than rocks or wood. Tiny plankton-like organisms would feed on the dead salmon, and would in turn be eaten by the juvenile salmon overwintering the streams. Insect larvae would colonize the carcasses, then be eaten by fish or escape to the land, spreading the organic materials from the salmon's body to the land itself. One river on the Olympic Peninsula was called the Hamma Hamma or "Stinky-Stinky" because of the magnitude of the rotting salmon bodies. Now that salmon runs have declined, the clarity of these streams may be a barrier to salmon recovery.

Fishery managers have ignored the fertilization phenomenon entirely in setting salmon fishing seasons. To them, any salmon that escapes the gauntlet of nets and hooks is wasted. Fishery managers do set "escapement goals" to allow some salmon to return to the spawning grounds, but the escapement goals are never high enough. Rather than simply manage to allow adequate escapement, the Oregon Department of Fish and Wildlife recently commenced a complicated process to obtain permission from water quality regulators to dump 300 dead fish in Still Creek, a tributary of the Sandy River, as well as several other Oregon rivers.[92]

Ironically, less than two months after the Oregon Department of Fish and Wildlife announced its plan to dump dead fish in the Sandy River, it was trying to keep dead fish out of another Oregon River. The problem arose when the state shut down Klaskanine Hatchery for lack of funding. Instead of letting the returning adult coho salmon spawn in the river, perhaps establishing a naturally-spawning run, the state killed all the salmon and fed them to the inmates at the Yamhill County Correction Center. According to the Hatchery manager, Bob Bivans, salmon carcasses rotting in the river posed a risk of spreading diseases to native cutthroat trout.[93]

Because the parasites are now plentiful in the Columbia River Basin, the best we can probably hope is that resistant strains of fish survive. The benefits of allowing the fish to return upstream to spawn seem pretty obvious; even throwing dead fish in the river probably won't do much harm. But it seems unlikely that hiring biologists to lard Northwest streams with dead fish is a particularly cost-effective means of recovering salmon. Especially if we have to sterilize the carcasses.

The Media's Love of Fishermen

> "Surely environmentalists enjoyed having their claims embraced uncritically by the opinion-making apparatus of society. But this luxury has become counterproductive, allowing the movement to avoid facing the flaws of its arguments. If you love environmentalists, as you should, today the greatest favor you can do them is to toss cold water on their heads." Gregg Easterbrook, *A Moment on the Earth.*[94]

Portland and Seattle newspapers—perhaps the primary information source for the majority of Oregon and Washington citizens—are virtually useless when it comes to covering the pernicious effects of harvest. Indeed, one of the largest newspaper features ever devoted to coverage of the plight of Northwest salmon, an entire pull-out section of the Sunday *Oregonian* called "River of Ghosts", listed the main causes for the decline of salmon populations in large graphics, but omitted overfishing entirely.

The media's image of salmon fishing is a romantic vision of a fisherman on his small boat, pulling in nets filled with Nature's bounty—never a factory trawler. Tribal fishing is especially romanticized.

Yet the growth in tribal gillnetting has a lot to do with the decline of upriver fish. Historically, upriver tribes mostly fished with spears and dipnets, not gill nets. No one has ever analyzed the overall impact of tribal gillnetting. Jake Tanzer, a former Oregon Supreme Court Justice who represented the State of Oregon during the epic court battles over tribal fishing rights, recalls that the named plaintiff in a lead case, Mr. Sohappy, used to leave his nets in the water so long without checking them that whatever was finally hauled out of the water was only good for cat food, if that. Barge operators on the Columbia report that this phenomenon continues today.[95]

Every once in a while, the media will print a letter to the editor that points out the pro-harvest bias. David Kaupanger wrote to the *Idaho Statesman* arguing that Idaho salmon runs thrived for decades while dams were in place, and logging, grazing and mining were in full development, and then declined coincident with the rise of tribal gill netting. The editorial department responded that most people disagreed with him. Nobody bothered to investigate the facts.

Mr. Kaupanger had the right idea, though. Upriver commercial fisheries (harvests above Bonneville Dam) have been reserved for the tribes since 1957. And as more and more dams were going in, they were harvesting more and more chinook salmon. Here is the data:

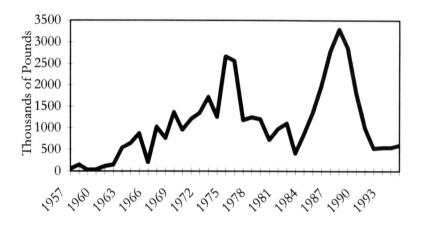

Figure 3: Upriver Tribal Commercial Harvest: 1957-1995[96]

In fact, the real effect of salmon harvest above Bonneville Dam is probably worse than the graph makes it seem, because the graph is based on legal, reported harvest. The number of salmon unaccounted for between Bonneville and McNary Dams seem to vary directly with harvest levels; the fish unaccounted for may have been lost either through illegal harvest (unreported catch) or from the aftereffects of fishing effort (net or hook injuries, etc.).[97]

Other members of the public notice the double-standard for media coverage of salmon fishing, as compared to logging. David Niessner wrote to the Eugene *Register-Guard* to point out:

> "I can pierce the mouth and lips of an endangered species with a metal hook, drag him through the water to the point of exhaustion, handle his delicate skin while determining if he's wild, discard him at the water's edge, and everything is OK. Yet for merely driving a log truck within a half mile of a

spotted owl nest, I can be prosecuted for 'harassing' an endangered species. . . . Why do the media ignore this double standard? Have they become the promoters of a political cause?".[98]

Nobody answered his question, but it's a question I've thought about a lot.

For a long time, I failed to understand why the fishermen—including ocean-based industrialists of a sort—had such an enormous public relations advantage over my clients and other land-based industries. One important reason is that almost no one *sees* what is going on, because most fishing goes on out in the ocean where no one sees it. No news crews venture there. They lack initiative, and the fishermen are smart enough not to encourage them.

On a few occasions, observers have obtained clandestine footage of what goes on out in fishing boats. The waste and destruction caused by some fishing methods, particularly gill and drift-netting, does not show well on film. Observers witness the retrieval of giant gill nets, built to drown fish, hauling up all sorts of "incidental take"—including dead birds and dead marine mammals.

Such footage was used in California television ads supporting a successful initiative to shut down gill netting. When the proponents of a Washington state initiative which would have shut down gillnetting tried to put similar ads on TV in Seattle, the fishermen got two Seattle TV stations to refuse to run them. No one has yet produced any sort of decent documentary that would actually show people the harvest process. Of course, chicken farms aren't pretty either.

In the salmon context, to borrow a sentence from Paul Weaver, the "media are less a window on reality than a stage on which officials and journalists perform self-scripted, self-serving fictions".[99] Fishery officials and environmentalists proclaim that a "crisis" is upon us, as they have been doing for decades. They blame everyone but fishermen. And journalists dutifully reprint their press releases. Contrary press releases, like those issued by Bruce Lovelin of the Columbia River Alliance, are usually ignored or dismissed out of hand as biased.

Despite the constant blast of pro-fishermen, anti-dam propaganda, however, the public is not easily fooled. A 1996 survey conducted by the Washington Department of Fish and Wildlife showed that more than twice as many people blame overfishing, particularly commercial fishing, for the decline in fish populations in Washington as blame hydroelectric production.[100]

The Long-Term Future of Commercial Salmon Harvest

The history of human cultural evolution has seen the replacement of roving bands of hunter-gatherers with agricultural economies, then with industrial-based economies, and now, in developed countries with high agricultural and industrial productivity, the rise of the information-based economy. Fishing for salmon is a throwback to the earliest form of human economic endeavor, which is perhaps why an undeniable romance attaches to it.

But this freedom has always had a cost. Just as the cattle ranchers fenced the west, and put an end to the roving sheepherders, it is time to fence in the fisherman. Their business no longer makes economic sense, at least under the present regulatory scheme. We allow too many fishermen to take too few fish in too inefficient a manner. Many public officials, Oregon's Roy Hemmingway among them, recognize that the fish farmers are going to drive the commercial salmon harvesters out of business. Since 1994, the dollar value of farmed salmon in Washington state has exceeded the dollar value of harvested salmon.[101] The commercial harvesters are fighting back, however, by enlisting environmentalist lawyers to shut down the fish farms as sources of "pollution".

NOTES TO CHAPTER 2

[1] Quoted in ISG, *Return to the River* 76.

[2] A. Netboy, *Salmon of the Pacific Northwest: Fish vs. Dams* 10 (1958).

[3] R. White, *The Organic Machine* 18-19.

[4] F. Seufert, *Wheels of Fortune* at 38.

[5] A. Netboy, *Salmon of the Pacific Northwest: Fish vs. Dams* 13

[6] F. Seufert, *Wheels of Fortune* at 40.

[7] *Id.*

[8] *Id.* at 59 (". . . the profits were good, and the Indians, like the white men, recognized a good thing when they saw it").

[9] J. Craig & R. Hacker, *The history and development of the fisheries of the Columbia River.* U.S. Bureau of Fisheries Bulletin 49(32):133-215.

[10] R. White, *The Organic Machine* 18; *but cf.* B. Harden, *A River Lost* 106 ("Before the [Grand Coulee] dam, each member of the Colville tribe ate, on average, about one and a quarter pounds of salmon a day, according to Verne Ray, an anthropologist who lived among the Colvilles in the 1920s").

[11] K. Petersen, *River of Life, Channel of Death* 48.

[12] *See* "Compilation of Information on Salmon and Steelhead Losses in the Columbia River Basin", Appendix D of the 1987 Columbia River Basin Fish and Wildlife Program, at 31.

[13] D. Chapman, *Salmon and Steelhead Abundance*, at 669. Other estimates put the loss at two-thirds between 1800 and 1875. *See* R. White, *The Organic Machine* 27 (describing outbreaks of smallpox and malaria). Environmentalist writers go so far as to sugges that "perhaps 90% of the Indians of the region had died from outbreaks of malaria", but do not cite any sources for this information. J. Cone, *A Common Fate* 105; *see also* B. Harden, *A River Lost* 61.

[14] *E.g,* Craig, J. A. and R. L. Hacker, "The history and development of the fisheries of the Columbia River, U.S. Bureau of Fisheries Bulletin 49(32):133-215 (1940); Hewes, G. W., "Aboriginal use of fishery resources in northwestern North America", Doctorial dissertation. University of California, Berkeley (1947).

[15] D. W. Chapman, "Salmon and Steelhead Abundance in the Columbia River in the Nineteenth Century", *Transactions of the American Fisheries Society* 115:662-70, at 669 (1986); *see also* B. Harden, *A River Lost* 63 (citing no source for the claim).

[16] G. Easterbrook, *A Moment on the Earth* 316, *cf. id.*. at 87-88

[17] Mr. White tells us that on the lower Columbia, a flattened head denoted freedom, a round head slavery. *The Organic Machine* at 24.

[18] Edward Wilson, in *The Diversity of Life*, cited in G. Easterbrook, *A Moment on the Earth* 97.

[19] D. Duncan, *The River Why* 138 (Bantam 1983).

[20] F. Boas, *Chinook Texts*, Bureau of American Ethnology Bulletin No. 20 (1894), *quoted in* C. Smith, *Salmon Fishers of the Columbia* 13.

[21] Memo, L. Bleakney to File, Aug. 28, 1997 (recording conversation with Milton Fischer concerning Tribal harvest on Herman Creek above Bonneville Dam).

[22] *PNGC v. Brown*, 822 F. Supp. at 1483 n.1.

[23] J. Cone, *A Common Fate* 8.

[24] Van Hyning, J. "Stock-recruitment relationships for Columbia River chinook salmon". Doctoral dissertation. Oregon State University, Corvallis (1968).

[25] C. Smith, *Salmon Fishers of the Columbia* 45.

[26] R. White, *The Organic Machine* 45.

[27] Reported in "Compilation of Information on Salmon and Steelhead Losses in the Columbia River Basin", Appendix D of the 1987 Columbia River Basin Fish and Wildlife Program, at D-81 (NWPPC Mar. 1986). This Appendix goes creek by creek through the salmon-bearing tributaries of the Columbia River and documents enormous destruction of salmon runs entirely unrelated to dams.

[28] F. Bryant & Z. Parkhurst, *Survey of the Columbia River and its Tributaries* 22 (U.S. Fish & Wildlife Service Spec. Sci. Rep. Fish. 1950).

[29] *Id*

[30] *See* Progress Report of the Biological Requirements Work Group § I(D), at 3-4 (Oct. 13, 1994). The list of literature cited in this report evidences no review of the historical circumstances of the "index streams" NMFS identifies as the standard by which salmon recovery should be measured.

[31] G. Bouck, "Thirty years taught that money won't save salmon", The Oregonian, October 20, 1995, at D7.

[32] C. Safina, "The World's Imperiled Fish", Scientific American, Nov. 1995, at 48-49.

[33] Quoted in R. Hill, "Scientists call for protecting oceans", *The Oregonian*, Feb. 17, 1997.

[34] *Excerpted in* J. Cone & S. Ridlington, *The Northwest Salmon Crisis* 330.

[35] S. Doughton, "Farm Salmon: an industry in straits", *The News Tribune*, Dec. 22, 1996.

[36] G. Easterbrook, *A Moment on the Earth* 224.

[37] NRC, *Upstream* 217 (Prepub. ed.); C. Smith, *Salmon Fishers of the Columbia* 85.

[38] B. Brown, *Mountain in the Clouds: A Search for the Wild Salmon* 51 (Simon & Schuster 1982).

[39] B. Brown, *Mountain in the Clouds* 52.

[40] *See, e.g.*, NRC, *Upstream* 229 (Prepub. ed.) (Figure 10-6a showing troll-fishery catch of chinook from 1905 to 1990).

[41] NRC, *Upstream* 222 (Prepub. ed.).

[42] *See* C. Smith, *Salmon Fishers of the Columbia* 90.

[43] Adapted from *Historical Ocean Fishery Data for Washington, Oregon and California* (PFMC Sept. 1993).

[44] R. White, *The Organic Machine* 17

[45] "Compilation of Salmon and Steelhead Losses in the Columbia River Basin", Appendix D of the 1987 Columbia River Basin Fish and Wildlife Program, at 5 (NWPPC Mar. 1986).

[46] *Id.* at 16.

[47] C. Safina, "The World's Imperiled Fish", Scientific American, Nov. 1995, at 50.

[48] C. Safina, "The World's Imperiled Fish", Scientific American, Nov. 1995, at 48.

[49] B. Bakke, "Four wild coho make it back to the Clack", *NW Fishletter*, Mar. 5, 1997, at 6.

[50] C. Safina, "The World's Imperiled Fish", Scientific American, Nov. 1995, at 48.

[51] R. Hill, "Scientists call for protecting oceans", *The Oregonian*, Feb. 17, 1997.

[52] *Historical Ocean Fishery Data for Washington, Oregon and California*, at W-8 (PFMC Sept. 1993) .

[53] 16 U.S.C. § 1801 *et seq.*

[54] Council News, March 1996, at 5.

[55] This showed up in the Oregonian in the first half of 1995.

[56] ISG, *Return to the River*, at 365.

[57] NRC, *Upstream* 222 (Prepub. ed.).

[58] NMFS, "Fishing Conducted under the Pacific Coast Groundfish Fishery Management Plan for the California, Oregon, and Washington Groundfish Fishery", May 14, 1996, at 1, 5 (reinitiation of § 7 consultation).

[59] "Commercial fishermen take too many chinook, state says", *The Oregonian*, Oct. 29, 1997.

[60] ISG, *Return to the River* 364 & Table 8.3 (Pre-pub. ed. 1996).

[61] ISG, *Return to the River* 63.

[62] BPA, "Interim Research, Monitoring, and Evaluation Program to Support the FCPRS Biological Opinion and Recovery Plan", at 53 (Nov. 15, 1995 Draft).

[63] *Id.*

[64] *See* NRC, *Upstream* 226 (Prepub. ed.) ("With the absence of a drift-net fishery on the high seas, illegal harvest should be reduced greatly, but the issue merits monitoring.").

[65] This is based on a report by Seattle lawyer Eric Redman.

[66] Letter, W. McNeil to J. Etchart, April 12, 1997, at 8.

[67] *See id.*

[68] *See* Harvard Magazine, January-February 1997, at 59 (reporting on the activities of Professor Stephen Palumbi).

[69] T. Anderson & D. Leal, "The Rise of the Enviro-Capitalists", *Wall Street Journal*, Aug. 26, 1997, at A16.

[70] Letter, S. Huffaker (Chief, Bureau of Fisheries) to J. Blum (NMFS), Feb. 27, 1997, at 4.

[71] *Id.* at 3.

[72] NMFS, Biological Opinion on FCRPS Operations, Mar. 2, 1995, at 65.

[73] Memo, D. Olsen & J. Pizzimenti to J. Brogoitti (NWPPC), Sept. 24, 1997, at 3.

[74] B. Rudolph, "Fish Cops Worth Cost, But Salmon May Still Be Missing", *NW Fishletter*, Sept. 30, 1997.

[75] Snake River Salmon Recovery Team, *Draft Snake River Salmon Recovery Plan Recommendations*, at IX-16 to IX-17 (October 1993).

[76] R. Hilborn, "Some Reflections on Hatcheries or 'You Don't Have to be a Rocket Scientist to See Some of the Problems'," at 5 (April 3, 1992).

[77] Snake River Salmon Recovery Team, *Draft Snake River Salmon Recovery Plan Recommendations*, at IX-16 to IX-17 (October 1993).

[78] J. Greenley, "The View from the Headwaters in Idaho", in E. Schwiebert (ed.), *Columbia Basin Salmon and Steelhead* 104, Spec. Pub. No. 10 (Am. Fish. Soc. 1977).

[79] R. Anderson, "Settle the salmon wars or go back to square one", *The Seattle Times*, Sept. 29, 1996.

[80] C. Safina, "The World's Imperiled Fish", Scientific American, Nov. 1995, at 50.

[81] D. H. Mills, "Atlantic Salmon Management", in *Developments in fisheries research in Scotland* at 215(Farnham, Surrey, England Fishing News Books Ltd.).

[82] From the 1992 Oregon Voter's Pamphlet, Argument in Favor of Measure 8, *excerpted in* J. Cone & S. Ridlington, *The Northwest Salmon Crisis* 329.

[83] I. Martin, *Legacy and Testament: The Story of the Columbia River Gillnetters* 102-104.

[84] *See* R. Reuberger, "The Great Salmon Mystery", Saturday Evening Post, Sept. 13, 1941.

[85] W.E. Ricker, "Causes of the Decrease in Age and Size of Chinook Salmon (*Onchorhychus tshawytscha*)", Can. Tech. Rep. of Fish. & Aquat. Sci. No. 944 (May 1980).

[86] J. Van Hyning, "Factors affecting the abundance of fall chinook salmon in the Columbia River" (Or. Fish Comm'n 1973), cited in "Complation of Information on Salmon and Steelhead Losses in the Columbia River Basin", at 103

[87] J. Weiner, *The Beak of the Finch* 264.

[88] J. Palmisano, Informal Comments to the NWPPC on the ISG's Report, April 15, 1997, at 13.

[89] I. Martin, *Legacy and Testament: The Story of the Columbia River Gillnetters* 51.

[90] M. Goodman, 20 Envt'l Law at 120.

[91] These experiments are summarized in J. Weiner, *The Beak of the Finch* 263-64.

[92] "Officials want permission to put dead fish in streams", *The Oregonian*, Sept. 27, 1996.

[93] C. Hollander, "End of the line—Hatchery's closure means returning salmon have nowhere to go", *The Daily Astorian*, Nov. 1996.

[94] G. Easterbrook, *A Moment on the Earth* 369.

[95] B. Harden, *A River Lost: The Life and Death of the Columbia* 54 (W.W. Norton 1996); *see generally* R. Crittenden, *Salmon at Risk* 52-53 (Self-published June 1997)(citing examples of "Indian Wastage" of salmon).

[96] Source: "Status Report: Columbia River Fish Runs and Fisheries, 1938-95", at 34-35 (Table 18) (WDFW/ODFW Aug. 1996).

[97] Some data are available from S. Cramer & S. Vigg's 1996 paper on the subject.

[98] *The Register-Guard*, Aug. 6, 1996.

[99] P. Weaver, "Selling the Story", *New York Times*, July 29, 1994, at A13.

[100] *See* Washington Department of Fish and Wildlife Opinion Survey 1996, Summary of Responses, at 6 (Table 29) (24% blame "hydroelectric, 39% "commercial fishing", 8% "recreational fishing", and 12% "fishing by Native Americans").

[101] S. Doughton, "Farm salmon: an industry in straits", *The News Tribune*, Dec. 22, 1996.

CHAPTER 3: NATURAL FACTORS KILLING SALMON

"We will now discuss in a little more detail the struggle for existence." Charles Darwin, *On the Origin of Species*

Most of the popular beliefs about salmon and the problems in their lives are the product of anthropomorphism and ignorance. Like every other species on earth, salmon are locked in a constant struggle for existence against other species, and *homo sapiens* is but one of many competitors.

Much salmon research since 1980 has focused on allocating blame for salmon declines. Nearly all of that research has been conducted by fishery agencies, which have a powerful vested interest in pointing the finger at causes of salmon decline that do not implicate their harvest management, and instead call for them to manage more and more salmon recovery programs. Blaming dams produces greater funding from dam revenues. After overfishing, however, natural salmon cycles are probably the most important factor in recent salmon declines. Nature, however, does not write checks to fishery managers. There is no money in blaming Nature.

A Warmer Climate Depresses Salmon Populations

While many scientific facts about salmon are subject to enormous dispute and obfuscation, practically everyone agrees that salmon are cold water fish, which will die if the water gets too warm. And practically everyone agrees that it is getting warmer in the Pacific Northwest.

I live in a rural community about 30 miles outside of Portland, and the old-timers in the vicinity will talk about how the Pudding River used to freeze in the winter, and there would be skating parties and sleigh rides. The Pudding River never freezes now. The mainstem Columbia River froze over in 1868. It hasn't frozen over since then.

We have been measuring the temperature of the Columbia River since Bonneville Dam was built, and it has been rising steadily ever since we began measuring it. Here is a graph of the date every year when water temperature rises above 15.5 degrees Centigrade—about 60 degrees Fahrenheit.

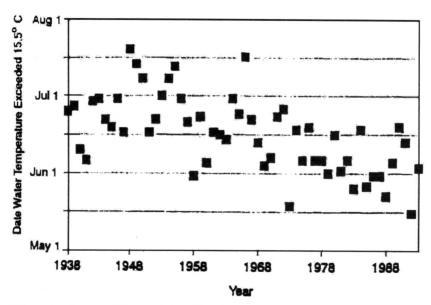

Figure 4: Onset of Warm Columbia River Water Since 1938[1]

Water temperatures have been rising above 60 degrees earlier and earlier in the year, to the point when there is now one full month less of cool water in the summer. Obviously, this is not going to work to the advantage of salmon that are in the river in the summertime.

Some blame dams for the warming trend, but the trend seems to have continued since 1975, even though no new dams have been constructed. The Northwest Power Planning Council staff concluded in 1986 that the "existing reservoir system has caused no significant change in the average annual temperature of the mainstem Columbia River".[2] In fact, the reservoirs have probably acted to dampen extreme swings in temperature. As the Council's Independent Science Group observed in 1996, "[m]aximum temperatures in the mainstem Snake River, where salmon survival is most tenuous, are generally lower in summer than before the series of storage and mainstem reservoirs was installed. This is also true in the mainstem Columbia River."[3] No one has ever attempted to assess what positive effects on salmon, if any, would arise from flattening high temperature peaks.

Notwithstanding the scientific facts, most Northwest fishery agencies continue to assume that dams have raised river temperatures to the detriment of salmon. The official and contra-factual position of the National Marine Fisheries Service is that increased water temperatures, "a result of the impoundment of the river, have been shown to increase predation rates" on salmon.[4] The Clinton/Gore Administration has even enlisted the United States Environmental Protection Agency to opine that dam alteration "may be the only alternative that meets the Clean Water Act" standards for water temperature.[5] An EPA staffer, apparently thrilled to join the dam-bashing, gushed: "This is our coming-out party. We feel like debutantes."[6]

As scientific support for the idea that releasing water from upstream reservoirs will help salmon by making the river run faster has dwindled (the subject of Chapter 7), state and tribal fishery agencies have begun to agitate for reservoir releases to reduce temperatures, even raising the issue in court. But as the Independent Science Group recently pointed out, "[r]elease of deep, cold water from headwater storage reservoirs will not ameliorate high temperatures because the reservoirs are too far upstream".[7]

Another piece of evidence that temperature may be critical results from comparing Upper Columbia stock declines to Snake River stock declines. The state and tribal-dominated "Plan for Analyzing and Testing Hypotheses" (PATH), an ongoing process that was supposed to instill "good science" into salmon decisionmaking, recently released preliminary conclusions. The state and tribal scientists are "reasonably confident" that upriver stocks have declined faster, which they blame on dam development. Yet they have "low confidence" that declines in upper Columbia stocks have correlated with increases in the number of dams.[8] Water in the upper Columbia tends to be colder than water from the Snake, an effect apparently not considered as a root cause in salmon decline by the PATH researchers.

The warmer climate seems to have been loosely associated with lower rainfall in the Columbia River Basin. In recent years, salmon have been adversely affected by drought conditions. Such conditions have persisted in the Snake River Basin, in particular, during much of the 1980s and early 1990s.[9] Low water conditions occurring during droughts destroy important spawning and rearing habitats for salmon. When salmon nests in shallow streams ("redds") become de-watered, eggs and pre-emergent fry perish.[10] Droughts also can reduce overwintering survival of juvenile salmonids, and are usually associated with higher water temperatures in the summer.[11] In addition, agricultural diversions often reduce flow to zero in drought years in streams that would otherwise constitute good habitat for juvenile salmon.

Scientists have considerable evidence about the long-term history of temperatures in the Pacific Northwest. James Chatters of the Pacific Northwest Laboratory and his colleagues have found that fossil remains tend to corroborate climate models suggesting that 6,000 to 7,000 years ago, the temperature in the Pacific Northwest was 2 degrees Celsius higher than at present. Analysis of archeological evidence suggests that salmon populations were anywhere from 30-60% below present populations.[12] Thereafter, the climate became cooler, and salmon populations increased.

Dr. Chatters believes that the "little Ice Age" from 500 to 100 years ago may have represented the best conditions for salmon in the Pacific Northwest in thousands of years, and that efforts to restore salmon to that historic peak of abundance are unrealistic in the face of the warming trend since then. He thinks the late 1800s are "unrepresentative of the region's long term productivity".[13]

From a scientific perspective, it is entirely possible that the effect of rising water temperatures is larger than all the salmon mitigation measures that could be devised. No one has tried to figure out whether and to what extent all the efforts we undertake to recover salmon will make any difference in the face of rising temperatures. Generating electricity by burning fossil fuels instead of running hydropower plants—a major consequence of current salmon recovery efforts—is not likely to have a positive effect on the temperature problem.

In an era where most rivers in the Pacific Northwest never freeze over, longing for a return to 1850s salmon populations makes about as much sense as longing for a return of the Gold Rush. Trying to restore wild salmon populations to such historic levels makes no sense, unless we can somehow engineer salmon to survive in warmer climates.

Changes in Ocean Conditions

Warm fresh water is not the only problem the salmon have. Warm ocean water is also a problem. It brings predators from the South. In the early 1960s, during the last major El Niño episode, fishermen complained about the large populations of mackerel that had migrated north from California. In the 1990s, the mackerel came back, venturing as far north as Southeastern Alaska.

At a conference on ocean conditions in Newport, Oregon in March 1996, a Canadian researcher reported on the effects of mackerel predation off the west coast of Vancouver Island. As the researcher put it, if he had taken a long weekend, he would have missed the story. A release of eight million smolts from a hatchery on the Island hit the ocean, and a huge school of mackerel showed up to feast on them. One mackerel was found to have 13 salmon smolts in its stomach.

But aside from anecdotal evidence like this, fishery agencies have made no effort to estimate the amount of damage done to salmon runs in the 1990s from the influx of mackerel. Nor have they made any effort to promote a mackerel fishery. Truly optimal and adaptive fishery management would single out fish populations that are rapidly growing, particularly at the expense of other valued populations, and promote fishing for such fish.

Localized effects, like the mackerel attacks, are symptoms of large scale cycles in the ocean that tend to have a very significant effect on overall salmon populations. During the 1960s and 1970s, ocean conditions were good for salmon populations south of Vancouver Island. But in the winter of 1975/1976, there was a major shift in regional climate that "produced unfavorable marine conditions for salmonid production in the area south of Vancouver Island, and highly favorable conditions farther north in the Gulf of Alaska".[14] This commenced a climate-driven "downward spiral in ocean conditions and onshore weather patterns salmon need to survive" off the coasts of Washington, Oregon and California.[15]

While harvest agencies craft salmon recovery plans based on river flow as the most important variable in salmon survival, as Drs. Chapman and Giorgi have pointed out, "[o]cean conditions overrode any effect that may have been caused by flows during the outmigrations of 1992 and 1993".[16] "The 1993 smolts left the river during outstandingly good flow conditions with high spill and high discharge, yet will return a run in 1995 about half as large as the smolt run of 1992, or about 10% of the ten-year average. Both runs likely were decimated as smolts when they reached the continental shelf rearing areas."[17]

Many scientists believe that good ocean conditions are correlated with cooler, wetter weather in the Pacific Northwest. On the positive side, 1996 had the highest rainfall measured at the Portland, Oregon airport since 1950: about 60 inches. But during the historic peaks of salmon runs, rainfall in downtown Portland was 67 inches.[18] And in the summer of 1894, the greatest recorded flow in the history of the Columbia actually drowned the famed Cascade Rapids. A steamboat attempted to race upriver, but could not combat the current.[19]

Unfortunately, as of 1997, a new, and very strong, El Niño event seems to be occurring.[20] And temperatures remain above average. There is still room for optimism, however. According to a recent paper by three Northwest scientists, the cycle of poor ocean conditions prevailing since the late 1970s "appears to be one of the longest in the past five centuries".[21] They think more patience is required in salmon recovery programs. "[W]ith costly decisions with regard to altering operations of, or removing Columbia River dams being imminent, we urge decision makers to consider newly-acquired information on the potential for a climate shift."[22]

The Rise of Competing Fish

The popular vision of the Columbia River is one devoid of fish, for the media does not focus on fish besides salmon. The author of one of the many books on the Columbia River wrote, with apparent surprise, that "standing by the fish ladder at Ice Harbor, the first dam on the Snake River, I see fish everywhere. There are large carp and schools of shad, neither native to the river, but only a few chinook, no sockeye, and only a scattering of steelhead."[23]

I had the same experience when I first visited Bonneville Dam. The first thing I noticed in the charts in the fish counting room was that populations of shad had gone up ten-fold as the salmon populations dwindled.

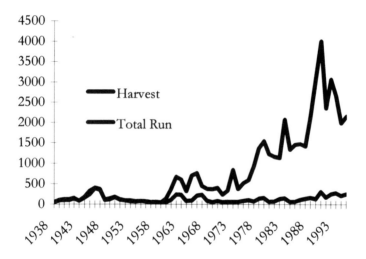

Figure 5: Rising Shad Populations in the Columbia River Basin (in thousands)[24]

The real number of shad in the Columbia River is even higher than the numbers in this chart, according to biologist John Paul Mazzano, because these population estimates are "minimum numbers" made with dam counts, and large numbers of shad spawn before they get to the first dam.

At the turn of the century, shad roe was a delicacy favored by eastern gourmets. It still sells for several dollars a pound. Fishery managers thought it would be a good idea to transplant shad to the West Coast, never stopping to consider whether the rivers were big enough for both shad and salmon. Looking at the chart of shad abundance, it appears that shad were heavily overfished for many years, with harvests approaching the total run sizes. Later, fishermen (and/or the fish-consuming public) lost interest in shad and populations began to skyrocket.

One scientist has compared the increase in shad populations and decrease in salmon populations from a "biomass" perspective.

> "If the average American shad adult weighed four pounds in 1990, the Columbia River production was about 16 million pounds. Together with 1990 salmonid production, the Columbia River production was about 36 million pounds. This compares to a historical high production estimate of 50 million pounds of salmonids before gross habitat losses. There is strong inference for food competition between shad and juvenile salmonids in the Columbia River and estuary today."[25]

From an ecological perspective, the Columbia River Basin has only finite energy resources to support fish and other aquatic life. Like a giant fish bowl, it can only hold so many fish. "When you add up the biomass from the shad population," says oceanographer Curt Ebbesmeyer, "the Columbia is producing as much fish as it did when it was full of salmon".[26]

Many people have a hard time understanding how shad could compete with salmon, envisioning competition as two creatures actually fighting with each other. When resources are limited, competition takes more subtle forms. On the Galapagos Islands, the finches are "locked in the most deadly competition even when they feed together in flocks", for "their lives depend on how efficiently they can forage for food—how little energy they can expend in getting how much energy in return".[27]

And one species can easily displace another. Some of the islands in the Galapagos have no bees, and are populated by smaller, nectar-drinking finches. But the islands that have bees, the bees have apparently displaced these smaller finches. "We never see them fight over a flower, but there is no peace between the birds and the bees."[28] No fishery manager has ever even attempted to estimate the extent to which shad have displaced salmon.

Charles Darwin regarded it as "deeply-seated error" to consider "the physical conditions of a country as the most important for its inhabitants; whereas it cannot, I think, be disputed that the nature of the other inhabitants, with which each has to compete, is at least as important, and generally a far more important element of success".[29] *This "deeply-seated error" is precisely the prevailing orthodoxy among fishery managers.* They focus on the physical conditions in the river, and ignore the nature of the other inhabitants. For all we know, the introduction of shad permanently capped salmon production in the Columbia River Basin.

The negative influence of the shad population is not limited simply to competition for food. There are so many shad in the river that

> "Shad also are interfering with juvenile and adult salmonid passage at Columbia River projects. Basham et al. (1982, 1983) found that juvenile shad created passage problems for subyearling chinook salmon at the McNary Dam juvenile bypass system and caused mortalities. Chapman et al. (1991) reported that adult shad reduce orifice passage efficiency and fish guiding device efficiency at Columbia River projects. USACE (1982) reported that upstream migrating adult shad caused an avoidance and delay for upstream migrating adult salmon at dam fish ladders. Shad numbers have risen dramatically since then. Adult shad migrate upstream from May to August, the same season as adult sockeye and summer chinook salmon."[30]

Of course, if salmon are prevented from ascending the ladders, they cannot get upstream to spawn, putting further downward pressure on salmon populations.

The fact that shad populations have skyrocketed in recent years, notwithstanding the presence of the dams, provides some evidence that dams are not the limiting factor in Columbia Basin salmon production.[31] As Dr. Gerald Bouck points out, "[s]had 'smolts' migrate downstream in the fall when there is little if any spill and ... flows are at their lowest levels. Both salmon and shad smolts pass downstream via repeated passages through turbines, but shad travel under far worse conditions than salmon smolts."[32]

Indeed, "[s]had are considered to be more fragile than salmon, and go into cardiovascular collapse, often dying from 'shock' if handled".[33] There is every reason to believe that the adverse effects of passing through turbines at the dams would be substantially greater on shad. Why shad thrive notwithstanding negative effects of dams is not a subject that fishery agencies choose to investigate.

Other scientists, like Dr. Wes Ebel, point out that shad produce anywhere from 20,000 to 150,000 eggs per adult female, whereas chinook produce at most perhaps 5,000 eggs per adult female. Thus shad could suffer larger losses from dams and still maintain population levels. On the other hand, shad are pelagic spawners and have lower egg survival independent of any dam-related effects. It is also possible that the dams that have created conditions conducive to shad production—although this theory seems inconsistent with shad problems caused by eastern dams.

Slowly but surely, people are beginning again to exploit the shad runs, although the shad are a bony fish chiefly valuable for their roe. Ironically, one of the most significant efforts to control the shad populations may be doing more harm to salmon populations than good. In 1995, the Yakama Tribe obtained permission to string nets across the top of fish ladders at The Dalles Dam to catch shad. Eventually, the Corps of Engineers pointed out that the adult salmon swimming up the fish ladders were spotting the nets and turning around and going back down the ladders. But the fishery managers weighed in and required the Corps to continue the program, although the nets were moved a little farther away.

By 1996, the Yakama were catching upwards of 40,000 pounds of shad a day. Their boats, however, continued to bump against the dam and cause the fish to go back down the fish ladder.[34] The National Marine Fisheries Service continued to allow the harvests. Although the Service acknowledged "[t]he possibility that these effects are large, possibly resulting in degradation of a significant portion of the run (including listed fish)", the Service is unwilling to offend the tribes by limiting the tribal fishery.[35]

Ironically, even other salmon species can compete with Pacific salmon. When 60,000 adult Atlantic salmon being raised in a Puget Sound fish farm escaped in 1996, they began migrating up local rivers, particularly the Elwha River. The media was quick to alarm the public with cries of "biological pollution", reporting that "environmentalists are increasingly asking the government to treat non-native species as pollution".[36] The local Environmental Protection Agency official had advice for Pacific Northwesterners wanting to know what to do with non-native species: "It sounds a little harsh, but the best thing for the environment is to kill them."

No one knows whether the Atlantic salmon will spawn naturally and reproduce (past escapees have failed to do so). If Atlantic salmon begin to thrive in the rivers of the Pacific Northwest, they may pose yet another competitive threat to Pacific salmon. Because they are smaller, they may have a comparative advantage in evading fishermen's nets.

Outside the Pacific Northwest, these competing species are the subject of expensive recovery programs. Pennsylvania utilities are paying to bring back the Eastern Shad. Maine businesses shoulder the cost of trying to bring back the Atlantic salmon. Even carp are venerated, although not usually in this country. To environmentalists, suckers, catfish and carp, which do well in warm and even polluted water are creatures "of disgust" and a badge of "humilation" from environmental degradation.[37]

The Rise of Salmon Predators and Parasites

Fishery managers are also responsible for more direct attacks on salmon populations, through the introduction of species that eat them. There are at least five non-native species of fish that eat juvenile salmon that have been introduced to the Columbia River, and we are now unlikely to be able to get rid of any of them, even if we take out the dams.[38]

For example, in the 1980s, the Washington Department of Fisheries introduced walleye into the Columbia River above Grand Coulee Dam. By the 1990s, the walleye had spread to the Snake River and were supporting trophy-sized walleye fisheries. Unfortunately, walleye are voracious predators, and eat juvenile salmon and sturgeon.[39]

Fishery managers are not promoting programs to exterminate shad and walleye. They are promoting programs to exterminate squawfish, which are, ironically, native fish. In the squawfish management program, because electric ratepayers are picking up the tab, cash bounties are paid for catching squawfish. Unfortunately, unlike mackerel and shad, which can be a gourmet item, most people don't like the taste of squawfish. But they have not gone to waste. They are ground up and fed to the juvenile salmon at the hatcheries.

The recent and headlong rush to "restore the natural ecosystem" has even produced programs to increase salmon predators. The fishery managers placed "Level 1" priority for 1997 BPA funding on a program "directed at learning more about the status of, and options for restoring, populations of Pacific lamprey". Why electric ratepayers should pay for this is unclear, but the motivation is: "Pacific lamprey were an important component of the natural ecosystem, but their numbers have declined dramatically in recent years".[40]

While there is little research on the effect of lamprey populations in the Columbia River, research in Canada suggests that lamprey feed on juvenile salmon and cause significant mortality.[41] If there were more lampreys in the Columbia River, they'd be eating more salmon. If, as some claim, the dams are making life difficult for lamprey, we ought to be happy if our goal is to have larger salmon populations.

In any event, the fishery managers are taxing citizens of the Pacific Northwest $5 million a year to kill one salmon predator (squawfish), and $334,560 to reintroduce another (the lamprey).[42] Right now, squawfish are politically unpopular, while politically-potent tribes cite a historic practice of harvesting lamprey. The impact of restoring lamprey on endangered salmon does not seem to be considered; citizens who pay for the lamprey program have no idea how their money is being spent.

Salmon diseases have also spread rapidly in recent years throughout the Columbia River Basin, sometimes through poor hatchery practices. *Ceratomyxa shasta*, a small worm that preys on salmonids, used to be rare. As recently as twenty years ago, it was only found in the Lower Columbia, below the Deschutes River. Now it can be found as far upstream as the Hell's Canyon complex.[43] Fish tuberculosis and bacterial kidney disease (discussed in greater detail in Chapter 6) also have spread rapidly.

The overall impact on these diseases is presently ignored in salmon recovery programs, in that no one has even attempted to estimate the extent to which overall survival has dropped, and whether and to what extent this drop can be offset by any means. It is possible that until salmon evolve with greater resistance to these diseases, salmon populations may be permanently depressed. Efforts have been made to reduce the spread of disease from hatchery operations, but no one has assessed whether there has been any improvement in overall disease levels.

All salmon have to migrate through the Columbia River estuary, which is rife with predators. Islands at the mouth of the Columbia River, favored by birds, are littered with the identification tags (called "PIT" tags) that scientists have put into salmon. Populations of cormorants, Caspian terns, and other fish-eating birds have increased in recent years, but until very recently, no attempts have been made to quantify the impact on Columbia River salmon.[44]

Radiotagging studies by Oregon State University researcher Carl Schreck have discovered that cormorants and terns eat 30-40% of the smolts that make it to the mouth of the Columbia River.[45] Cormorants take an especially heavy toll. A single cormorant can consume up to twenty pounds of smolts in a single prolonged feeding session. In 1997, Oregon State University researchers focused on the Caspian tern population on Rice Island, which was created by the U.S. Army Corps of Engineers from dredged material. The population has increased 600% in the past 12 years, and it appears that during 1997, *the terns on this one island ate between six and twenty million juvenile salmon.*[46]

No one has prepared any comprehensive review of whether total estuarine bird populations are higher or lower than historical levels and what

71

effect this might have on salmon abundance. It certainly seems as if putting a breeding pair of weasels on Rice Island might produce tens if not hundreds of thousands of additional adult salmon, a singularly cost-effective approach to salmon recovery.

Marine Mammal Populations Decimate Salmon

Marine mammal predation has also increased sharply in recent years. For decades, populations of marine mammals were depressed in the wake of significant human harvest. But populations of marine mammals have increased dramatically on the West Coast since passage of the Marine Mammal Protection Act in 1972.[47] By some accounts, the populations are increasing at 10% a year, and doubling every eight years.

Seals and sea lions are major predators which consume vast numbers of salmon.[48] These animals prey primarily on returning adult salmon but also consume large numbers of juveniles and subadults.[49] Seals and seal lions follow migrating adults well into freshwater environments. A population of 10,000 harbor seals (the near-Columbia River population estimate) would consume 1.8 million pounds of salmon in a year. This is over 60 percent of the 2.8 million pounds landed in the 1990 Oregon troll fishery.

With respect to sea lions, a 10 percent diet of salmon is a conservative estimate. At 25 pounds of fish per day for northern sea lions (2.5 pounds of salmon) and 15 pounds of fish per day for California sea lions (1.5 pounds of salmon), the seasonally migrating California sea lions and the resident northern sea lions could consume 851,000 pounds of salmon per year. This is about 30 percent of the 2.8 million pounds of salmon landed in 1990.[50]

In 1994, forty percent of the adult salmon showing up at Bonneville Dam had marine mammal bites or scars on them. Only twenty percent had the marks at Lower Granite Dam.[51] This suggests, not surprisingly, that the fish bitten by seals are not surviving as well as they migrate upstream—deaths that are attributed by fishery agencies to the effects of dams.

Some scientists believe that marine mammals are not a major factor in the decline of salmon, principally because salmon and marine mammals coexisted for thousands of years before the current declines in salmon. But thousands of years ago, conditions were cooler and much more favorable for salmon. And there were large marine predators on marine mammals. Today, the most significant predators, human beings, cannot lawfully kill marine mammals.

The Overwhelming Dominance of Natural Cycles

As we have seen, many natural factors harming Columbia Basin salmon populations have been on the rise since the 1970s. More generally, looking over periods from 10,000 to 100,000 years, the populations of many marine animals exhibit huge fluctuations. Examples include Dungeness crabs, Maine lobsters, Pacific anchovy, and many other species.[52]

As a general matter, the popular conception of a "balance of nature" is misleading. Modern science is moving toward what Gregg Easterbrook has called "the action-packed balance of nature": at any given time, forces are at work disturbing any particular trend toward equilibrium.[53] From this perspective, efforts to avoid any and all extinctions make no sense.

Nature would laugh at the idea that a salmon population at any moment is perfectly optimized for the natural conditions at that moment, so that its genetic purity must be preserved at all costs. Species that exist now are survivors of all kinds of catastrophic changes in the environment, and may only loosely fit conditions at the moment. They have many, many genes whose purpose only becomes apparent as conditions change.

NOTES TO CHAPTER 3

[1] NRC, *Upstream* at 196 (Prepub. ed.) (Figure 9-3).

[2] "Compilation of Information on Salmon and Steelhead Losses in the Columbia River Basin", at 147.

[3] ISG, *Return to the River* at 166.

[4] NMFS, Biological Opinion, "Reinitiation of the Consultation on 1994-98 Operation of the Federal Columbia River Power System and Juvenile Transportation Program in 1995 and Future Years", Mar. 2, 1995, at 64.

[5] Mary Lou Soscia, quoted in J. Brinckman, "EPA adds new twist to dispute on salmon", *The Oregonian*, Nov. 7, 1997, at B1.

[6] *Id.*

[7] ISG, *Return to the River* at 266.

[8] Report in B. Rudolph, "PATH Researchers Report Preliminary Conclusions", *Clearing Up*, Jan. 13, 1997, at 7.

[9] Proposed Snake River Salmon Recovery Plan at II-25, 26.

[10] *Id.*

[11] *Id.*

[12] J. Chatters, "A paleoscience approach to estimating the effects of global warming on salmonid fisheries of the Columbia River Basin", *reprinted in* National Research Council of Canada, *Symposium on Climate Change and Northern Fish Populations*, at 489 (1992).

[13] Quoted in B. Rudolph, "Archeologist Takes Long Look at Salmon Recovery", *Clearing Up*, Jan. 20, 1997, at 7.

[14] U.S. Army Corps of Engineers, "Interim Status Report", at 2-8 (citing Graham, "Simulation of Recent Global Temperature Trends", 267 Science 666-69 (1995)).

[15] AP, "Global climate changes may affect salmon", *Tri-City Herald*, June 27, 1997.

[16] D. Chapman & A. Giorgi, "Comments on Work of Biological and FCPRS Alternative Work Groups", at 5 (1994).

[17] *Id.*

[18] S. Tomlinson, "Heavy rains make a run on a 46-year record", *The Oregonian*, Dec. 3, 1996, at A1

[19] R. White, *The Organic Machine* 30.

[20] W. Rudolph, "Mackerel Are Back—Another Sign of Impending El Nino", *Clearing Up*, June 30, 1997, at 9.

[21] J. Ingraham, C. Ebbesmeyer & R. Hinrichsen, quoted in W. Rudolph, "Another Possible Sign of Shift to Colder, Wetter Climate Regime", *Clearing Up*, July 14, 1997, at 3.

[22] *Id.*

[23] R. White, *The Organic Machine*, at 90. Mr. White attributes the rise of shad and carp to man-made changes in the River, rather than an inherent consequence of introducing exotic species.

[24] From Tables 72-73, "Status Report: Columbia River Fish Runs and Fisheries, 1938-95", at113-16 (WDFW/ODFW Aug. 1996).

[25] NWPPC, Strategy for Salmon Administrative Record, P3, Vol. 11, AF3-0168 at 23.

[26] Quoted in B. Rudolph, "Shad No Fad on the Columbia", *NW Fishletter*, Mar. 5, 1997, at 9.

[27] J. Weiner, *The Beak of the Finch* 63 (Vintage 1994).

[28] *Id.* at 156.

[29] C. Darwin in *The Origin of Species*, quoted in *id.* at 225-26.

[30] NWPPC, Strategy for Salmon Administrative Record, P3, Vol. 11, AF3-0168 at 23.

[31] G. Bouck, "Thirty years taught that money won't save salmon", The Oregonian, Oct. 20, 1995, at D7 (". . . our shad use the same dams and migration routes as salmon and have grown abundant").

[32] Letter, G. Bouck to R. Baumgartner, Dec. 22, 1994, at 2.

[33] Letter, G. Bouck to R. Baumgartner, Dec. 22, 1994, at 2.

[34] Draft TMT Meeting Minutes, June 12, 1996, at 3.

[35] *See, e.g.*, NMFS, "Biologial Opinion on Impacts of the 1996-98 Management Agreement for upper Columbia River spring chinook, summer chinook and sockeye on listed Snake River salmon", Feb. 16, 1996, at 9.

[36] D. Westneat, "Atlantic salmon in the Elwha River: good for anglers, bad for native fish?", *The Seattle Times*, Nov. 12, 1996.

[37] T. Palmer, *The Snake River* 39.

[38] U.S. Army Corps of Engineers, "Interim Status Report", at 2-4.

[39] J. Lilly, Letter to the Editor, *Northwest Steelheader*, Summer 1996. Mr. Lilly, like many recreational fisherman up and down the rivers of the Columbia Basin, believes that dam turbines have been wrongly blamed for the salmon's decline. "I would like to know", he asks, "who . . . is able to count dead fish coming out of turbines".

[40] CBFWA, Public Review (Draft) FY 1997 Anadromous Fish Recommendations, May 15, 1996, at 9.

[41] R. Beamish & C-E. Neville, "Pacific salmon and Pacific herring mortalities in the Fraser River plume caused by river lamprey (*Lampetra ayresi*)", Can. J. Fish. Aquat. Sci. 52: 644-50 (1995).

[42] BPA, "Fish and Wildlife Budget Tracking Report, Fourth Quarter, Fiscal Year 1996, Dec. 23, 1996, at 13 (1996 funds "in process or obligated).

[43] G. Bouck, pers. comm. (Nov. 20, 1996).

[44] BPA, "Interim Research, Monitoring, and Evaluation Program to Support the FCPRS Biological Opinion and Recovery Plan", at 37 (Nov. 15, 1995 Draft).

[45] C. Schreck, Memo to D. DeHart, W. Weber & B. Schmidt, Oct. 16, 1996.

[46] B. Rudolph, "Birds Getting Fat on Salmon Recovery Dollars", *NW Fishletter*, Oct. 28, 1997.

[47] 16 U.S.C. § 1361 *et seq.*

[48] P2, Vol. 30, 91-25/0997 at 96-97

[49] P3, Vol. 11, AF3-0168 at 18.

[50] *Id.* at 20.

[51] BPA, "Interim Research, Monitoring, and Evaluation Program to Support the FCPRS Biological Opinion and Recovery Plan", at 37 (Nov. 15, 1995 Draft).

[52] *See generally* G. Easterbrook, *A Moment on the Earth* 659.

[53] *Id.*

CHAPTER 4: THE RISE OF DAMS AND THEIR IMPACT ON SALMON

"Now what we need is a great big dam
To throw a lot of water out across that land
People could work and the stuff would grow
And you could wave goodbye to that old Skid Row"
Woody Guthrie, *Washington Talkin' Blues*

Back in the 1930s and 1940s, when Franklin Delano Roosevelt pushed his New Deal across the country, dams were politically correct. People attempting to scratch out a hardscrabble existence in small towns along the tributaries of the Columbia could see the difference that dams would make. It was that vision, coupled with a contract from the Bonneville Power Administration, which moved Woody Guthrie to write his songs promoting the construction of dams.

Many believed that the dams would cause the extinction of salmon, though most were prepared to run the risk for the benefits of dams. In 1937, as Bonneville Dam neared completion, reporter (and later Senator) Richard Neuberger wrote: "Prevalent throughout the principal salmon-producing region of the world today is the almost unshakable opinion that within a few years the fighting fish with the flaky flesh will be one and the same with the dodo bird—extinct."[1] In 1946, the U.S. Fish and Wildlife Service claimed that the construction of McNary Dam would by itself eventually exterminate all upriver salmon.[2] Today we have "scientific" panels presenting the same message. The unshakable opinions were wrong in 1937 and 1946 and they are wrong now.

Most widespread public beliefs about the specific impacts of dams are also wrong. Fishery agencies and environmentalists have successfully promoted the idea that the reservoirs behind the dams are "lethal slackwater pools", full of predators that devour young salmon. But federal fishery scientists have found very little mortality in the Snake River reservoirs, and the highest rates of predation below Bonneville Dam. And while turbines cause some mortality, the vast majority of the salmon do not go through the turbines, so that survival through the dams and reservoirs as a whole is remarkably high.

Incredibly, no one has any empirical evidence to prove whether the mortality of salmon migrating up and down the Columbia River is higher now than before the dams were built. Early evidence from the 1970s did show significant mortality to salmon from the dams. But after many years of refining dam operations, mortality is far lower. There is some evidence that the total mortality rate now may be *lower* than in a natural river—a result achieved by averaging somewhat higher-than-natural mortality in the river with much higher-than-natural survival of transported fish.

The Mainstem Dams on the Columbia and Snake Rivers

Prior to the 1930s, the Columbia and Snake were free-flowing rivers. In their natural state, they created significant flooding problems and rendered transportation of commercial goods virtually unfeasible. It was to solve these problems, and provide for hydropower, irrigated agriculture, and recreational benefits, that Congress authorized the construction of numerous dams to regulate water flow and produce electric power.

Eight mainstem dams on the Columbia and Snake Rivers form the target of most salmon advocates. The first—Bonneville—was constructed in 1938 pursuant to the Bonneville Project Act of 1937 and earlier authority.[3] The Act directed the U.S. Army Corps of Engineers to operate and maintain the project subject to the powers and duties of the Bonneville Power Administration to sell and transmit electric energy.[4] Congress further required the Corps to construct, operate, and maintain such additional hydropower facilities as the BPA Administrator deemed necessary to meet growing demands for federally-generated electricity.

Even after the construction of Bonneville Dam, the City of Portland remained vulnerable to devastating flooding from the Columbia River. In 1948, in a single hour on a sunny May afternoon, the Columbia River destroyed Vanport, which, with 20,000 people, was the second largest city in Oregon.[5] And the flood levels then were well below the record levels of 1894.[6] In February 1996, the river came within inches of flooding downtown Portland.

Few think (or at least publicly admit) that we should remove Bonneville Dam and the other upstream dams that have prevented disastrous floods. But environmentalists have begun to attack flood control efforts in earnest, drawing extensive media publicity by blaming flood control for killing salmon.[7] The state and tribal salmon managers have begun to lobby against flood control as well; the first "system operational request" they made in 1997 was to object to attempts by the U.S. Army Corps of Engineers to control the largest runoff in 60 years.[8]

The state of Idaho urged the Corps in March 1997 to "modify flood control rule curves" and maintain the "highest possible reservoir level by mid-April" at Dworshak Dam[9]—just when reservoir levels should be low to catch and control spring runoff. The year before, flooding caused extensive damage to property along the Clearwater River below the Dam.

Luckily, the U.S. Army Corps of Engineers is continuing flood control efforts (and privately regards the salmon managers' requests as "incredible"), but there is no active lobby in favor of flood control. People take it for granted. I'm glad I don't rely on U.S. Army Corps of Engineers flood control, because unless things change, greater and greater risks will be taken with human lives and property, for unmeasurable and largely imaginary benefits for salmon.

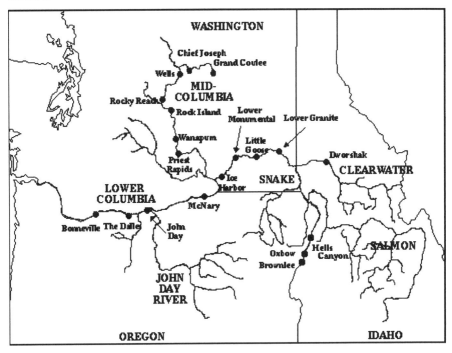

Figure 6: Major Columbia Basin Hydroelectric Dams[10]

Following the completion of Bonneville Dam, the hydrosystem gradually expanded over the next several decades. McNary Dam was constructed in 1953, The Dalles in 1957, Ice Harbor in 1961, Lower Monumental and John Day in 1969, Little Goose in 1970, and Lower Granite in 1975. In the State of Washington, three public utility districts in Grant, Douglas, and Chelan counties spearheaded the development of hydroelectric projects along the Columbia River above its confluence with the Snake: Rock Island, Priest Rapids and Wanapum Dams. Until recently, these three projects have been less controversial because no endangered salmon migrate past them.

The mainstem Columbia and Snake River dams, along with Grand Coulee Dam, are the backbone of the Federal Columbia River Power System, which generates the low-cost power sold by the Bonneville Power Administration. Because the dams are not very high, river commerce and river species are easily passed over, under, or around mainstem dams. Every one of the mainstem dams was built with fish passage facilities.

Storage Dams Impassable to Salmon

Grand Coulee Dam and the Hell's Canyon Complex, built by Idaho Power Company (Brownlee, Oxbow, and Hell's Canyon Dams), are a different species of dam. They are so high that neither boats nor salmon can get through them, the better to store enormous quantities of water.

While the dams are now attacked as violations of nature, the engineers promoting the Grand Coulee project explained that "[t]he dam will accomplish intentionally the result achieved capriciously by the rampant natural forces of the Pleistocene period."[11] At that time, a sheet of ice blocked the Columbia River, which was running through a deep canyon. A huge lake formed, and the overflow from that lake carved a new channel fifty miles long at a 90 degree angle to the former River channel. When the ice dam melted, the River returned to its original course, leaving the new channel—the "Grand Coulee"—high and dry.

The huge natural pools carved during the ice age turned out to be ideal for storing water for irrigation, which could flow downhill to irrigate an area of land twice the size of Rhode Island: the Columbia Basin Project. The chief engineer of the Panama Canal, Major General George Goethals, touted the site in 1922 and proclaimed that development of the dam and Columbia Basin Project would add more to the national wealth of the United States than either the Panama Canal or the Alaskan Railroad.[12] As Richard White wrote, the dam promoters believed that "[w]hat nature had so artfully arranged, it would be criminal for humans to neglect to improve and finish"—"[t]he dam was the final piece necessary to reveal nature's latent harmony".[13]

The Grand Coulee Dam would provide what was at the time the world's largest supply of electricity. Nevertheless, it was regarded at the time largely as an irrigation project. The United States Commissioner of Reclamation declared that the project would irrigate "the largest compact body of undeveloped land remaining in the United States and the most fertile".[14]

At the time, the Pacific Northwest was the destination of choice for tens of thousands of refugees fleeing the Dust Bowl, many of whom hoped to continue to farm, it being the only occupation they had ever known. In his weekly radio speeches, President Roosevelt encouraged these migrants. Others attacked them as "Okies".

Now the descendants of the Okies are attacked as the recipients of federal subsidies. Their long-standing effort to expand the Columbia Basin Project seems doomed politically. But organizations like the Columbia Basin Development League soldier on.

The National Research Council has estimated that of the original salmon and steelhead habitat available in the Columbia River Basin, "55% of the area and 31% of the stream miles have been eliminated by dam construction".[15] The vast majority of these losses occurred from construction of Grand Coulee Dam and the Hell's Canyon Complex.

The Hell's Canyon Complex, constructed by Idaho Power Company, eliminated all remaining anadromous fish production in the upper Snake River Basin, including sockeye, spring/summer, and fall chinook salmon, in 1967.[16] This was especially offensive to fishery interests because Idaho Power Company's federal license to build the dam required passage for salmon.[17] No such promises were made when Grand Coulee was built. It eliminated the famed Kettle Falls fishery and all remnants of many upriver runs.

Environmentalists view the Columbia River and its tributaries as a giant living tree, with dead branches above Grand Coulee and Hell's Canyon. But what few people realize is that those branches were diseased even before the dams were built.[18] And runs "were sustained or even increased over the ensuing 40 years" after construction of Grand Coulee Dam through the use of hatcheries.[19] While the hatcheries could not get salmon past Grand Coulee and the Hell's Canyon Complex, they could keep large runs going in the rivers below the dams.

Despite much talk of dam removal, there is little talk of removing either Grand Coulee or the Hell's Canyon Complex, even though they are the only large dams with indisputedly negative effects on salmon. Idaho environmentalists, who are among the most rabid opponents of the four lower Snake River dams, have long turned a blind eye to water projects in their own state. In 1996, Fred Nampa, president of the Idaho Wildlife Federation, boasted that an average user's annual power bill from Idaho Power Company was $703, and of that amount "only $1.23 came from the socialized power of the four lower Snake River dams. This $1.23 seems to be a small price to pay in order to save our salmon and steelhead populations."[20] He didn't discuss the power that came from the Hell's Canyon Complex.

Effects of Irrigation on Salmon

Long before the Hell's Canyon Complex was constructed, large areas in the Upper Snake were removed from salmon production by early irrigation development. One Corps of Engineers biologist explained that this process was well underway by 1910, and that

> "Large irrigation storage dams completely blocked fish migration and diverted water from river channels leaving them with insufficient flow or altering water temperatures adversely for fish many miles downstream from the dam. . . the major source of damage here was the hundreds of unscreened irrigation canals that diverted millions of juvenile salmon and steelhead to die in the farmers' fields for periods as long as three and four decades."[21]

Along the upper Snake River in Idaho, the U.S. Fish and Wildlife Service estimates that eighty percent of the habitat has been lost.[22]

It does not seem likely that the reduction in flow from river irrigation has itself had any great adverse effect on salmon downriver. In 1990, the total amount of water withdrawn for irrigation in the Pacific Northwest was only about 7% of the average annual flow of the Columbia River.[23] There are localized adverse effects from irrigation withdrawals in the Snake River, where Idaho state policy was and is to reduce the River's flow to zero at Milner Dam. Keith Higginson, the Director of the Idaho Department of Water Resources, said in 1988: "we do not require, expect, need or want any flow to pass Milner."[24]

Counting tributaries, there is almost 13.5 million acre-feet of storage capacity in the Snake River Basin.[25] Irrigators probably remove 7-8 million acre feet of water from the Snake River every year.[26] But since the Hell's Canyon Complex stopped the salmon from going upstream anyway, it is hard to assess the adverse impact of irrigation.

The biggest problem with irrigation is a problem of governance: since state and federal governments have been incapable of providing clear and reliable property rights in water, irrigators are unable to sell or lease excess water for experiments in fishery management.[27] The government has a simple answer: to shut down any future water withdrawals from the Columbia or Snake Rivers. The proposed Snake River Salmon Recovery Plan calls for such a moratorium to extend to "tributaries and those groundwater resources that are part of the Snake and Columbia River System".[28]

In May 1997, the National Marine Fisheries Service even declared that a single Oregon irrigator's application to remove 303 cubic feet of water per second (peak) from the John Day pool would jeopardize the continued existence of Snake River salmon.[29] All the irrigators together in Oregon take less than 1% of Columbia River flow—even in a low flow year.[30] No one really believes that a single irrigation withdrawal will spell the death knell of the salmon, but no single farmer can afford to invest the effort to try and persuade a court that this is not true.

Other Habitat Loss

It is not just dams that cause salmon to be cut off from salmon habitat. Salmon fishing on the South Fork of the Salmon River ended in 1965 after extensive landslides, caused by logging and poorly constructed roads, smothered miles of spawning grounds with mud.[31] Countless other such incidents have, tributary by tributary, reduced available habitat for salmon. Many comprehensive surveys are available showing, on a tributary by tributary basis, how particular examples of human development destroyed salmon habitat. If success in salmon recovery is defined to require naturally-spawning populations, salmon recovery may be a hundred-year war of trying to undo these developments piece by piece.

Rather than try to assess what the piece-by-piece habitat losses mean for attempts to recover salmon runs, fishery agencies tend to blame the dams for the effect of habitat loss. In 1973, the Fish Commission of Oregon reported that the number of redds per "standard spawning ground survey unit" in Idaho per 100 fish counted at the uppermost dam had dropped precipitously from the early 1960s to the early 1970s.[32] The sharpest drop was from 1965 to 1966, which correlated with the mudslides in the Salmon River, not with anything relating to dams.

Yet the Fish Commission blamed the declines on delayed mortality, which they speculated was caused by dams. They did not explain how the effects only appeared after fish had passed all the dams. This was a precursor to the same "delayed mortality" claims fishery managers are now making about smolt transportation (see Chapter 5).

Assessing the Effect of Dams by Comparing Dammed and Undammed Rivers

Dams low enough to have fish ladders are fundamentally similar to a natural obstacle in the river, like a waterfall or rapids. The balance of this Chapter focuses on that sort of dam. All of the eight dams that form the backbone of the Federal Columbia River Power System, situated on the mainstem Columbia and Snake Rivers, do have fish ladders and are entirely passable to fish.

Few people look beyond the Columbia and Snake Rivers and compare the decline of salmon in other, undammed rivers to assess the effect of the dams. The fishery agencies will not do this because if you look outside the Columbia River Basin (and even in it, on tributaries without dams), you will immediately begin to wonder if the dams cause any measurable problem with salmon production.

One run of sockeye, which ascends the Columbia River to Lake Okanogan, has not declined significantly even though that run must pass *nine* dams.[33] (Scientists have suggested that the reason these sockeye have not declined, while the Snake River sockeye have, is because large populations of hatchery fish in the Snake River basin "may interact in negative ways with Snake River sockeye".[34]) The American Fisheries Society recently released a study showing that more than 140 salmon runs in British Columbia are already extinct, almost none of which have any contact with dams.[35]

In the Columbia River, lower river coho salmon populations dropped sharply, to the extent that the National Marine Fisheries Service considered whether to list them as endangered. In 1993, the Service refused to do so, on the ground that they were extinct. The Service made this decision even though an analysis of coho scales suggested that wild populations continued to spawn,[36] and expert geneticists testified that that the coho were not extinct.

As one writer documented, the decision not to list the coho "looked [to environmentalist Bill Bakke] like maybe the agency had dropped the lower river coho so it could keep the public's attention focused on the faults of the hydropower system. The upriver chinook were best for making that case."[37] That was also what my boss, Jeff Ring, my co-worker, Gary Firestone, and I believed. At Jeff Ring's urging, our clients had filed formal comments with the Service urging it to list the lower river coho as endangered. As things turned out, the decision not to list the coho was a spectacular success for the Service, as the public's attention focused almost exclusively on the dams.

Another way to compare survival in undammed and dammed rivers is even more direct: comparing survival per mile in the upriver, undammed reaches, with the lower river, dammed reaches. Dr. McNeil prepared survival rates per mile for stream-type chinook salmon and steelhead using data collected since the 1960s for other purposes. The results: "survival does not differ greatly between dammed and undammed reaches . . ."[38] Dr. McNeil attempted to correlate the survival per mile with the fraction of the reach that was dammed and obtained a result "suggesting that there is little or no correlation between the two variables".[39]

His cautious conclusion: if the findings stood up to additional testing, "man-induced incremental mortality caused by dams would be of a low magnitude".[40] A less cautious conclusion would be that when we try and measure the effect of the dams, *it is so small as to be undetectable.*

Dr. McNeil's study does not account for the fact that the undammed reaches were higher up in the river, where juvenile salmon are younger and may die at a higher rate per day. Generally speaking, in most species there is greater "culling" of the population in the earliest life phases. But no one has tried to figure out the extent to which that could explain Dr. McNeil's result.

Yet another way to look at the total effect of dams is to compare the survival of hatchery salmon from upstream and downstream hatcheries. If river mortality were a major problem, one would expect to see a big difference in the survival of upriver and downriver fish.

Professor Ray Hilborn of the University of Washington studied hatcheries in the Columbia River Basin, and made a remarkable discovery: the effectiveness of a fall chinook hatchery is entirely independent of its distance from the ocean—and the number of dams the fall chinook had to traverse. Here is his data on the percentage of adult fall chinook returns from fall chinook hatcheries in the Columbia River Basin:

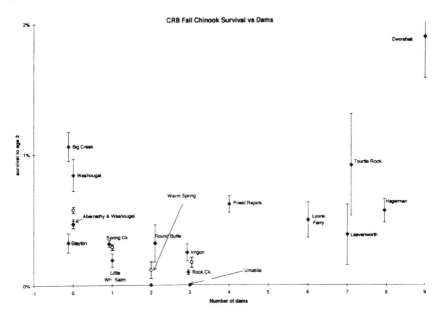

Figure 7: Effectiveness of Fall Chinook Hatcheries vs. Number of Dams

Reviewing these results, Professor Hilborn offered three hypotheses: "(1) there is a trend in hatchery productivity that increases as we move upstream which masks the effect of downstream passage loss, (2) the barge transportation system has been effective at reducing downstream loss so that any remaining loss is masked by the noise in the data, [or] (3) the detailed studies of dam passage loss ... have overestimated the loss."[41] While it is always possible that upriver hatcheries, which may use different stocks of salmon, are more effective, the most reasonable explanation is that dam mortality is small and perhaps reduced to an invisible level by transportation.

It is especially noteworthy that fall chinook survival does not seem to depend on the number of dams because juvenile fall chinook salmon tend to slip through bypass systems and go through turbines more than juvenile spring chinook salmon.

Professor Hilborn did not find the same results for spring chinook salmon hatcheries. The data suggest that the effectiveness of hatcheries raising spring chinook declines as the hatcheries get further upriver.

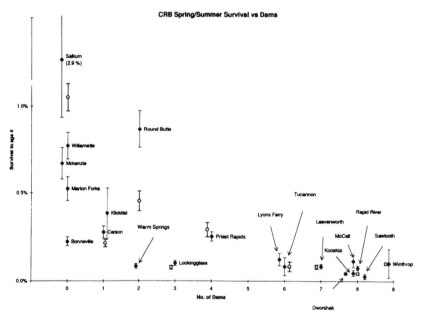

Figure 8: Effectiveness of Spring Chinook Hatcheries vs. Distance Upriver

But just because survival from upriver hatcheries decreases with the number of dams does not mean the effect is related to dams. It could be related to distance, with or without dams. Professor Hilborn decided to see how spring chinook hatcheries performed going up the Fraser River in Canada, which is not dammed. The results:

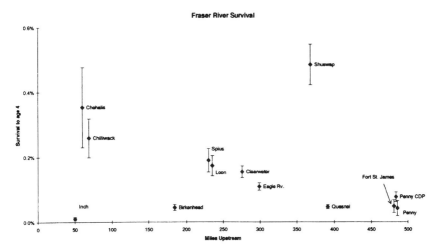

Figure 9: Effectiveness of Fraser River Spring Chinook Hatcheries vs. Distance Upriver

Generally speaking, the spring chinook hatcheries are less effective upriver whether there are dams or not. As Dr. Hilborn noted, "[i]f we accept the Fraser River as a reference 'control' on the dams of the Columbia, then we conclude that the decline in survival seen in hatchery spring/summer stocks as we move upriver may be largely due to the biology of cultured spring/summer [fish] rather than passage".[42]

The National Research Council has noted that the Fraser River "shares many biogeoclimatic features" with the Columbia River, and that salmon catches in the Fraser tend "to show an abundance similar to that observed historically in the Columbia", despite "the absence of dams on the mainstem Fraser River".[43] Here is a comparison:

87

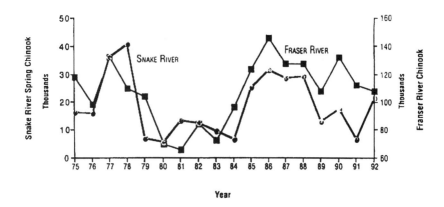

Figure 10: Snake River vs. Fraser River Chinook Salmon Runs[44]

One would think that if the eight dams in the migration path of Snake River salmon had any ascertainable effect on salmon populations, there would be bigger differences in population trends than are evident here.

Dr. McNeil has also investigated ratios of "recruits to escapees" for both Columbia Basin and Canadian salmon stocks. When hatchery and wild fish are lumped together as a group, "[e]stimated ratios of recruits per escapee are similar for chinook and sockeye salmon in the Columbia Basin upstream from Bonneville Dam and in pristine rivers of British Columbia and Alaska".[45] Dr. McNeil thinks that this ratio is associated with carrying capacity and production limits, and that "[s]uccessful actions to increase abundance of wild fish may require concurrent reductions in hatchery fish".[46]

The few scientists familiar with all this data perceive its significance. Dr. Gerald Bouck is a biologist who spent 33 years working for the U.S. Environmental Protection Agency, the U.S. Fish and Wildlife Service and the Fish and Wildlife Division of BPA. At the American Fisheries Society annual meeting in 1997, he received a lifetime achievement award for his work on preservation and protection of salmon. His conclusion: "Frankly, I believe that the Columbia River salmon runs most likely would have declined to their present condition even if no main-stem dams had been built."[47] Dr. Doug Neeley, a biologist specializing in statistics and genetics, thinks that reduced survival through Columbia and Snake River dams "is not the major contributor of decline" for endangered Snake River salmon populations.[48]

No government agency has ever prepared a written explanation of the significance of Professor McNeil's work, Professor Hilborn's work and all the other work that shows that the total effect of dams on salmon is small.

Instead, the government agencies hold fast to data from the 1970s, when dams did injure salmon populations, and pretend that all the improvements since then never happened.

It is one of the principal ambitions of administrative law, having abandoned any effort to judge the wisdom of administrative decisions, to at least ensure that an administrative agency has considered all the relevant issues when making decisions. But for reasons explained in Chapter 9, the courts have so far refused even to rule on whether the government agencies must consider this body of scientific research.

The Historical Coincidences that Support Attacks on the Dams

Certainly the *construction* of some dams has had an enormous adverse effect on salmon, and for this reason it is easy for salmon advocates and the media to assign blame to dams. This blame is a central component of the Great Salmon Hoax. Some who know the truth persist in what one writer has called "framing the guilty"—using misleading information and outright lies to cast the blame unfairly. As liberal environmental reporter Gregg Easterbrook acknowledged, "[f]raming the guilty has become a central operating tactic of environmentalism . . ."[49] He thinks it is "sometimes defensible".[50] I don't think it ever is.

Rob Walton works for the Public Power Council on salmon issues. He recently attended a dinner party where, after learning his occupation, one of the guests blurted out "I just think we ought to take out all those dams. I don't want my children to grow up without salmon". This sort of thinking is common among citizens throughout the Pacific Northwest, at least in the large metropolitan areas far from the dams. Most people have never bothered to think through the details of how dams affect salmon. They have a simple theory for blaming dams: over time, we have built more dams and salmon populations have dropped, so dams must be killing salmon.

One of the favorite graphs used by those who perpetrate the Great Salmon Hoax is the graph of commercial salmon harvest in the Columbia River. James Lichatowich, one of many conservation biologists urging removal of the dams, has even used it four times in a single paper.[51]

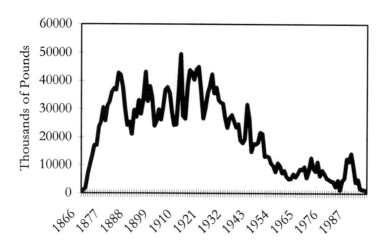

Figure 11: Columbia River Commercial Salmon Harvest

As the National Research Council has pointed out, "casual readers might assume that the depiction of reduced catch reflects the magnitude of the decline of salmon in the Columbia River without recognizing that in-river catch has been largely supplanted by large ocean fisheries".[52] Failing to transcend the status of "casual readers", the Northwest Power Planning Council's Independent Science Group prepared a "Harvest Summary of Chinook Salmon" declaring that from 1958 to the present, harvest has been at "a depressed level of production of about 5 million pounds".[53]

There is some possibility that until quite recently, the decline in in-river harvest masked a *rise* in overall harvest. The Northwest Power Planning Council reported in 1986 that "Columbia River chinook salmon caught in ocean fisheries (including Canada and Alaska) now account for about 73 percent of total harvest".[54] I really would have liked to put in this book a single graph showing the total harvest rate on the three endangered Snake River stocks of fish, showing how, over the years, rising ocean harvests replaced in-river harvests, and fishery managers never came to grips with overfishing until the mid-1990s—if then.

Unfortunately, the only analysis I have ever seen that attempted to figure out whether ocean fisheries had risen to take the place of in-river fisheries was prepared by Dr. Courtland Smith back in 1979. He compared chinook salmon catches from 1969 to 1973 in several fisheries to the 1880 to 1930 average catch of 26.4 million pounds of chinook salmon. By 1969-73, the catch in the gillnet fishery had fallen to 5.2 million pounds. But catch in the troll fisheries had risen to 8.1 million pounds. And Dr. Courtland made a statistical adjustment, usually ignored, to account for the fact that the fish caught by trollers were immature and, had they been caught at maturity, would have been larger. This adjustment alone accounted for 4.2 million pounds of salmon. Dr. Courtland then added in the recreational fishery, taking 5.2 million pounds of fish, and the tribal fishery, taking 1.3 million pounds.

The result: from 1969 to 1973, the total catch of Columbia River chinook salmon was 90% of the historic amounts.[55] Personally, I think it was higher than the historic peaks, because Dr. Courtland left out three critical factors. He left out "the shakers"—fish lost because they were shaken off the hook as too small. At the time, shaker loss was estimated at 7.5% of the total catch, which would have added an additional 0.9 million pounds of loss associated with trolling.[56] More modern estimates suggest that perhaps 25% of chinook salmon die after being caught and released in the troll fisheries, which represents another enormous inefficiency in ocean harvest.[57] Perhaps 30% of chinook salmon die after being caught and released in the Puget Sound commercial purse seine fishery.[58] Dr. Courtland's estimates also ignored all catches by foreigners other than Canadians, which many, especially domestic trollers, believed were substantial at the time.[59] And Dr. Courtland did not attempt to assess the quantity of Columbia River salmon discarded as bycatch in non-salmon fisheries.

If these three factors are taken into account, it is possible that up until the 1990s, chinook salmon from the Columbia River Basin were harvested as heavily as ever. This is a stunning tribute to the success of hatcheries, but the heavy mixed-stock harvest pressure doomed less productive wild runs.

Another problem with the "blame the dams" theory is that upriver salmon populations *increased* for several years in the 1980s after the last dam was in place. The very wild fish now listed as endangered increased in numbers for several years after the dams were all in place. There was better weather in some of those years, but the fact that the population can rebound like that certainly suggests that dams are not going to jeopardize the continued existence of the salmon.

That rebound is even more significant when you consider the degree to which a number of factors of salmon decline have accelerated since 1975. One of the many inadequacies of the fisheries agencies is their inability to present a coherent set of data for salmon management. Because so many agencies are involved, there is no place to look up total salmon harvest information, much less harvest by stocks.

One of my clients hired a consultant to dig up total harvest numbers. The consultant assembled all the different harvest figures from a great number of official sources. The resulting total numbers show a dramatic increase in Pacific Northwest salmon harvest, beginning almost exactly after the last dam was completed in 1975.

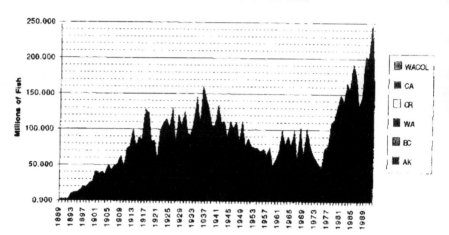

North American Commercial Salmon Catch

Figure 12: West Coast Salmon Harvest

This chart has its limitations. It includes all salmon species, not just chinook salmon, and salmon from all over the West Coast, not just the Columbia River Basin. Most of the increase has been in Alaska. It does not include foreign harvest of U.S.-origin salmon.

If I knew where to look up overall harvest, including Canadian, Alaskan and foreign harvest, on Columbia River stocks, I would present that chart. But as far as I know, the data are not reported anywhere. It is not clear that the harvest managers have even *collected* sufficient data to produce reasonable estimates of the total harvest of Columbia River fish. They have long failed in their most basic role: figuring out who has caught how many fish from where.

Nevertheless, this chart suggests a significant expansion of overall fishing effort after 1975, just as the last mainstem dam was finished. The "coincidence" of a rise in harvest was not limited to ocean harvest.

The number of gillnet licenses issued annually on the lower Columbia River rose from about 600 in 1969 to about 1,500 in 1979.[60] And as we have seen, tribal chinook harvest rose very rapidly after 1975.

There is some evidence that harvest increases after 1975 were a particularly significant factor rendering the Snake River sockeye salmon an endangered species. Although in-river commercial harvest on sockeye was curtailed from 1974 to 1983, it began again in 1984. Dr. Graham Gall, of the University of California at Davis, has prepared a graph showing how rapidly rising harvest levels on sockeye in the 1980s, including substantial tribal harvest, affected endangered Snake River sockeye salmon:

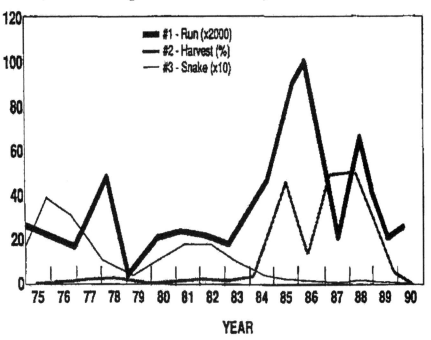

Figure 13: Sockeye Harvest after 1975

The Snake River sockeye were clearly in trouble, but fishery agencies continued to harvest nearly half of them in the river because the total sockeye runs were rising. Most of these sockeye were killed to be sold for commercial gain, not for sport fishing or tribal "ceremonial and subsistence" fishing. An unknown number, not shown on this chart, were also taken in the ocean.

The increased in-river harvest in the late 1980s was one of the many products of the court-dominated regulatory scheme that arose from the case of *United States v. Oregon*. Ironically, some environmentalists and politicians now herald this process as the governance model for future salmon recovery decisions. The States of Oregon and Washington have actually filed formal court papers asking the *United States v. Oregon* Court to take over.

"Across the Concrete Mortality" in Mainstem Dams

> ". . . the fish passage and propagation facilities of the Corps of Engineers are essentially designed, constructed, and operated on the basis of recommendations and criteria received from the fish and wildlife agencies. Therefore, when a facility works well we can all share a sense of pride. Conversely, when facilities do not perform to meet our expectations, we all must share that responsibility as well." E. Mains (1976).[61]

Application of a scientific perspective propelled the federal government to supply nearly all the dams in the Pacific Northwest with fish ladders. The fish ladders were widely recognized as a success. The U.S. Department of Interior observed that salmon climbed the fish ladders with "far less effort than their forebears that fought upstream through the swirling rapids that are now buried beneath fifty feet of water"; the Oregon Fish Commission considered them "entirely successful".[62]

From the perspective of removing obstacles to salmon migration, even the drowning of Celilo Falls by construction of The Dalles Dam was helpful to salmon. As one fishery agency official candidly told reporters at the time, "it would be easier for the fish to go over a ladder in the dam than to fight their way over Celilo Falls".[63] Today such statements are cited as examples of "at least a lack of sensitivity toward Indians among government officials".[64] Truth and sensitivity are often at odds.

Science was not perfect, because providing fish ladders alone is not enough. Forty years ago the question of the downstream migration was rising to prominence, as public figures like reporter (and later Senator) Richard L. Neuberger asked: "But what, in the roaring darkness of the turbines and penstock shafts, what happens to the tiny fingerlings on their turbulent voyage to salt water?"[65]

Environmentalists often proclaim the dams are "rigged with turbines that churn like giant Cuisinarts making salmon and steelhead puree"[66], like the infamous "Bass-o-Matic" demonstrated by Dan Ackroyd on *Saturday Night Live*. The Idaho environmentalists, the most extreme of their breed, went so far as to run a television ad in the spring of 1995 that showed a blender, followed by a red screen leaving the results to the audience's imagination.

94

This is a hoax too. Turbines rarely kill salmon by cutting them up. They have large flat blades that spin about the same speed as bicycle tires—80 rpm. The vast majority of salmon get through untouched.

In the early days, before the engineers learned to run the turbines so as to minimize injuries to salmon, they were run in a way that involved "cavitation", in which bubbles form because of the extreme turbulence and shear forces in the water. Fishery biologists putting marked groups of juvenile salmon through the turbines found mortality anywhere from 4% to 19%. But it is hard to recover marked salmon in a huge river, and the precision of early estimates of losses is highly suspect.

More advanced studies in the 1980s produced a wide range of results at different projects, ranging from 2.3% losses at the second (and newer) powerhouse at the Bonneville Dam to as high as 16.9% at Lower Granite Dam. Behind these figures are enormous experimental problems and difficulties in the interpretation of data.

For example, fishery managers object to running the second powerhouse at Bonneville, even though, because of through advanced design, its direct turbine mortality of 2.3% is low. That is because predator concentrations seem to be particularly high below the second powerhouse, cancelling out the benefits of good turbine design. Conversely, the 16.9% figure at Lower Granite is regarded as suspect by the scientists who conducted the study, because a critical statistical assumption—that control and test groups mixed—did not appear to be true.[67] The devil is always in the details.

By the 1990s, technology had advanced to the point where researchers could attach tiny balloons to salmon that inflate after a delayed chemical reaction.[68] Salmon passed through the turbine pop to the surface quickly after turbine passage. Sometimes a dead and battered salmon comes up. But not very often—about three times out of a hundred. Researchers have observed salmon passing through turbines to compute 120 hour survival estimates, so that immediate and delayed mortality can be computed. The results: 95% survival through the turbines at Lower Granite Dam.[69] Even those results may overstate turbine mortality if "culling" is occurring; it is possible that the weakest members of the population may be weeded out at the first dam, tending to lead to higher estimates of turbine mortality there.[70] Similar results have been obtained at Rocky Reach Dam in the upper Columbia River.

There is also good reason to believe that turbine design can be improved substantially.[71] Since many of the mainstem dams on the Columbia and Snake Rivers will need substantial renovation over the coming decades, there will be many opportunities to reduce turbine mortality even further.

The studies on turbine mortality have had little impact on the turbine component of the Great Salmon Hoax. Newspaper articles continue to report that "[s]almon are being spun around and chewed to bits in the giant turbines of the Columbia-Snake River dam system".[72] Harvest managers and environmentalists continue to assert as a scientific fact that turbines kill 10-15% or even more of the salmon that pass through them.[73] The Northwest Power Planning Council's Independent Science Group essentially ducked its charge to apply science to the question of turbine mortality, instead declaring that "[a] generally accepted figure now is 15%" per dam.[74] In salmon recovery, what is "generally accepted" and what is true are often very different things.

Even if everyone agreed that direct turbine mortality was 5% or less per dam, the cumulative result, over eight dams, is significant. Statistically, if every salmon had to go through the turbines at all eight dams, it would work out to 34% mortality over the course of the migration. That sounds pretty bad. Luckily, that's not the right calculation.

First, the mortality is not entirely additive. Some of the 34% of salmon killed by dams would have been killed by something else, particularly predators. There is a surplus population which is doomed; the cause of death varies but the certainty of loss is invariable. This is a well-recognized phenomenon common to all animal populations called "compensatory mortality" or "competing causes of death". In human populations, for example, curing a disease that kills some fixed percentage of population will not increase the population by that same rate, because other causes of death "compete" to fill the void.

Thus we cannot get a one-for-one increase in salmon populations by reducing any single source of mortality, and we get even less for solving a juvenile mortality problem, because the other causes of death have a long time to compete to fill the void. The fishery agencies, biased to ignore adult mortality, refuse to acknowledge this phenomenon. Indeed, as far as I know, no one has ever even tried to make a quantitative estimate of the extent to which dam-related mortality is compensatory.

It is hard to estimate how much incremental harm that 34% mortality would do to salmon populations. If half the salmon were likely to die anyway, would the dams be killing an additional 10%? 20%? 30%? While both the Northwest Power Act, the Endangered Species Act and other federal law requires agencies to assess the true effects of the dam operations, they have never done so, claiming ignorance.

Instead, all involved simply assume that the turbines could, collectively, kill a third or more of the fish. And to fix the problem, the U.S.

Army Corps of Engineers has put in fish bypass systems so that the vast majority of the salmon never go through the turbines.

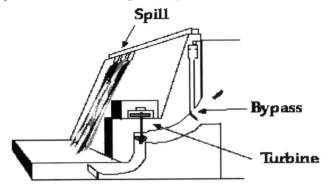

Spill

Bypass

Turbine

Figure 14: Schematic Drawing of Dam Passage Routes

The most expensive devices are huge, submerged traveling screens that guide the fish away from the turbines (identified as "bypass" in the drawing). Current extended screen technology is highly effective at helping fish avoid the turbines. The screens deflect 80% or more of the yearling chinook, including endangered Snake River spring/summer chinook, at Little Goose and McNary Dams. Results on smaller subyearlings, including endangered Snake River fall chinook, range upwards of 50% at many projects. Thus at projects with screens (not including The Dalles),[75] most salmon never go through the turbines, so the turbine losses are far lower.

The screens are not perfect, in that, in theory, fish can be damaged by bouncing against them. However, studies at Lower Granite dams have found that "juvenile fish suffer minimal injury and delay with extended screens".[76] There is another problem associated with all bypass systems: large numbers of juvenile salmon collected in the system are released from pipes below the dam. Critics have theorized that this makes it easier for predators to catch the juvenile salmon, an effect that has been demonstrated at the bypass system of the second Bonneville powerhouse.[77] Evidence suggests much less of an effect at upriver dams, perhaps because predator concentrations are lower upriver. Of course, no one knows how many predators used to concentrate below rapids and waterfalls before the dams were built.

Yet another way salmon can avoid the turbines is when the turbines are turned off and water is spilled over the top of the dams. Survival of fish passing over a spillway can be as high as 98% or more. Spill is the favored passage method of environmentalists, but destroys the economic benefit of dams since spilled water cannot be used to generate electricity. About 20% of the annual planned resources for salmon recovery are presently squandered on spill programs, the subject of Chapter 12. The principal vice of spill, beyond the enormous economic waste, is that at several projects, a decision to spill water siphons fish away from the bypass systems where they could collected for "transportation".

Smolt transportation means collecting juvenile salmon with a bypass system and putting them into barges. They are towed through the locks of the dams, and avoid "across-the-concrete" mortality as well as natural predators. The overwhelming success of this "transportation" program—discussed in Chapter 5—makes it a key target of environmentalists. The transportation program stands as the single most significant obstacle to their ultimate goal: removal of the dams.

As a result of transportation, bypass and spill the vast majority of migrating salmon and steelhead never go near a turbine. Federal fisheries scientists acknowledge that "transportation mitigates for direct losses through the hydropower system under a broad range of flows".[78] Overall survival rates through the Columbia and Snake Rivers, with maximum transportation, can be upwards of 80%. Even without transportation, the most recent analyses by scientists at the National Marine Fisheries Service suggest that in-river survival is at least "66% of historic rates".[79] The true number is probably higher.

The Question of Natural Mortality

With modern methods that can get more than 80% of the juveniles migrating downstream alive, you would think that we would have some idea whether we had mitigated adverse effects of the dams. One of the most amazing facts about salmon management is that federal, state and tribal fisheries managers refuse even to consider whether current rates of survival are above or below survival rates in rivers without any dams.

Before the dams were built, juvenile salmon had to navigate miles of violent rapids that would destroy man-made rafts, including Cascade Rapids, the rapids that stopped Lewis and Clark in their tracks. Early accounts note that fish arriving below these and other rapids were bruised and battered. No one knows whether waterfalls and rapids are more harmful to salmon than modern hydroelectric projects.

Until very recently, none of the fishery agencies would even acknowledge the *concept* of natural mortality. We went so far as to hire a retired professor from Oregon State University, Dr. William McNeil, to investigate it. Dr. McNeil was initially skeptical of our claim that conventional wisdom concerning the dams was wrong, but he had what all government fisheries bureaucrats seemed to lack: an open mind. After conducting a number of scientific studies on the subject for us, he finally became convinced that conventional wisdom attributing significant mortality to the dams was off base.

He wrote Will Stelle on December 15, 1994, advising him that NMFS

"can make meaningful estimates of natural mortality, that being mortality which occurs in the pre-project river. My review of the scientific evidence . . . comparing mortality in dammed and undammed rivers leads me to conclude that *most of the juvenile passage mortality occurring as juvenile salmon migrate through the dams and reservoirs comprising the [Federal Columbia River Power System] is mortality that would have occurred without the projects.*"

A lot of data supports Dr. McNeil's observations. For example, from 1964 to 1967, in-river survival of spring/summer chinook salmon from the Clearwater River confluence with the Snake to below Bonneville Dam, was estimated at 42 to 67 percent.[80] Now, after the construction of four more dams, in-river survival is generally estimated at 40 to 50 percent.[81]

Until 1993, there were no really accurate measurements of in-river survival. PIT-tag technology allowed such measurements, by providing for the first time a way reliably to count individual juvenile salmon as they migrated downstream. The most recent PIT-tag data analysis by the National Marine Fisheries Service measured survival of yearling chinook salmon migrating from the uppermost and eighth dam, Lower Granite, to the third dam, John Day, at 56% during 1996—and that reflected a probable reduction in survival resulting, in part, from ill-conceived spill programs.[82] This translates to about 89% survival per dam and reservoir, including turbine mortality (for fish passing through turbines) and reservoir mortality.

A lot of reservoir mortality from predation would probably happen in a natural river. Yet anti-dam tracts bearing catchy titles like *River of Life, Channel of Death* ignore such natural mortality, complaining that even the spill promoted by harvest managers is "a relatively ineffective measure; thousands of fish are killed or eaten by predators here because there is no safe way through the dam".[83] But no one bothers to think how many thousands of fish would die when passing through any particular undammed section of the river. Or how any equilibrium in salmon populations *requires* that the vast majority of juvenile salmon die.

Late in 1996, nearly four years after we began calling for an assessment of natural mortality, an inter-agency group dominated by the states and tribes has produced an estimate that only 10-20% of the smolts would have been lost during migration before the dams were built.[84] They provided no supporting data; the estimate was essentially pulled out of a hat. If it were true, the pre-dam river would have to have become dramatically safer for smolts once they reached the site of Lower Granite Dam, because the death rate per mile would have to fall drastically from the levels measured in the natural river above Lower Granite Reservoir. The group did not review or address Dr. McNeil's work finding that survival per mile does not differ greatly between dammed and undammed reaches.[85]

Again, it is entirely possible that when the positive effects of transportation are included, passage downriver is now safer for salmon than it was before the dams were built. The Great Salmon Hoax is great indeed, because it pushes us to spend hundreds of millions of dollars to get even smaller increments in survival when from a common sense perspective, "if it ain't broke, don't fix it." There are still a few problem areas, like the Ice Harbor to McNary reach where the Columbia joins the Snake, but maybe natural survival was lower there too. A fisherman's perspective suggests that maybe predators feed more there.

Unraveling the 95% Mortality Hoax

"... by the 1990s fishery biologists had ably demonstrated that federal dams accounted for more than 95% of salmon losses on the Columbia/Snake system. Of course, biologists had known that for years." K. Petersen, *River of Life, Channel of Death* (1995).

Why do we read in newspapers, magazines and books that dams kill 95% of the salmon? This is perhaps the greatest hoax perpetrated by fishery advocates, ranging from environmentalists, to commercial fisherman, and, most regrettably, to the fishery agencies of the States of Oregon, Washington, Idaho, and Alaska. Long after federal fishery officials had recognized that these figures were wrong (although remaining mum about it), fishery officials like Oregon's Doug DeHart continued to repeat the 95% figure to the media. Books and legal opinions echo the figure as well.[86]

Strong willed biologists working for the U.S. Army Corps of Engineers Walla Walla office grew so tired of hearing this lie repeated over and over again that they prepared a special "Information Paper"—"Not True says Corps Review!".[87]

As the Corps explained, the 95% figure traces back to Congressional testimony by the godfather of salmon advocates, a man named Ed Chaney who continues, according to legal papers filed on his behalf, to derive substantial economic benefit from contracts associated with salmon advocacy. When questioned by the Corps about the source of the 95% figure, "Mr. Chaney replied that all the state agencies were using the figure, so it must be true".

After an exhaustive review of fishery research, the Corps did come up with one scientific study by Raymond, estimating that in one year, 1973, 95% of the salmon migrating from the Salmon River perished before they reached The Dalles Dam.[88] As the Corps explained, most of these fish perished before they ever reached the first dam (Lower Granite):

> "In recent years, an average of 50 to 60% of the hatchery chinook have been lost before they reach Lower Granite Dam. More surprising, in PIT tag studies by the federal fishery agencies, 80 to 99% of wild fish marked in the summer did not survive to Lower Granite Reservoir the next spring."[89]

This suggests that a great deal of the mortality Raymond measured had nothing to do with the dams. Moreover, though the Corps did not point this out, because it was not known at the time, Raymond's estimates were compromised to begin with because of very significant flaws in estimation techniques.[90] (These problems are discussed in more detail in Chapter 7.)

The Corps also pointed out that back in 1973, the dams had not yet been modified to protect fish in very significant ways:

> "In 1973, seven dams were in place, with a total of 65 turbines in operation. Only one turbine was screened at Little Goose Dam for experimental purposes. In 1994, eight dams are in place with 94 turbines operational. All of the turbines at Lower Granite, Little Goose, Lower Monumental, Ice Harbor, McNary, John Day, and Bonneville Dams are screened. Two of 22 turbines at The Dalles Dam are screened, with full screening due in 1998."[91]

The Corps also pointed out that "in 1973, turbines were operated at 115% rated capacity with an average of 15% mortality through each turbine. In 1994, turbines will be operated within 1% of peak efficiency which decreases turbine mortality to less than 10%".[92] (Again, the more recent balloon-tag studies show less than half that mortality.)

As Drs. Chapman and Giorgi have explained,

> "It is too easy to forget that in the 1960s and 1970s, there existed no accepted operating criteria for turbine operations to assist fish passage. Bypasses were at rudimentary stages and

hardly fish-friendly. Debris at trashracks and in collection systems was a severe problem."[93]

But the dams have been modified to be much safer for fish since the 1970s.

Finally, as the Corps explained in its paper, not only had in-river survival increased, but also the transportation program had dramatically increased the "system survival"—the total average survival of in-river and transported fish—since the 1970s. As they explained, "in 1973, insignificant numbers of fish were transported, compared to over 80% being transported in the 1990s".[94]

The net effect of all these changes was substantial. Professor Jim Anderson at the University of Washington has used sophisticated computer modeling techniques to plot the gradual increases in survival:

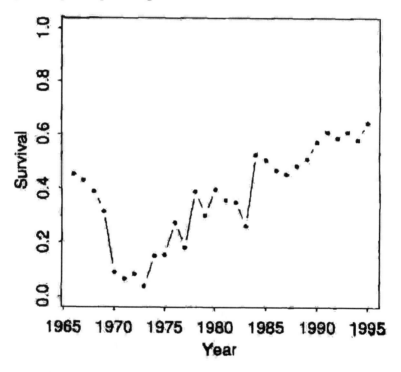

Figure 15: CRiSP Estimates of Survival Improvements[95]

For the most part, critics have completely ignored the improvements. The media does not report them. Leading politicians ignore them. "Vice President Gore has written, in *Earth in the Balance*, that journalists should downplay scientific findings of ecological improvement because good news may dilute the public sense of anxiety."[96]

Even the more perceptive critics lament that "given the gravity of the situation, the changes were modest; they failed to achieve their goal".[97] But given all the other factors working against salmon, fixing the dams could never, by itself, achieve the goal of improving salmon runs. A goal of bringing back salmon by removing or improving dams is a goal that can never be achieved.

Government Efforts to Avoid Disclosure of the True Impacts of Dams on Salmon

> "Dams are good scapegoats. These concrete monoliths serve as tributes to a technocratic age. They cannot talk, and they weather the abuse heaped on them while continuing to slave for those of us who benefit from their power." Courtland L. Smith, *Salmon Fishers of the Columbia*[98]

The Corps' attempt to expose the 95% figure fell upon deaf ears. No news outlet ever picked it up. The Clinton/Gore Administration response? The individuals involved were censured. The Walla Walla office of the Corps was so badly bruised by this and other experiences that friendly sources in the Corps who would reveal information about the Great Salmon Hoax told us they were afraid their phone calls were tapped in the office, and would speak only at home. The Clinton Administration's gag orders extended throughout the federal bureaucracies, constraining all those who dared challenge the conventional "wisdom" about salmon. The U.S. Army Corps of Engineers and the Bonneville Power Administration have become silent scapegoats and monoliths.

The Corps office at Walla Walla has a long history of blurting out the truth about salmon and dams and being slapped down for it. Keith Petersen's anti-dam tract chronicles efforts by the Walla Walla office in 1955 to publicize scientific information about salmon passage that triggered such outrage from the fishery agencies that Brigadier General Louis Foote was forced to reprimand the District to keep the peace.[99] In 1968, a study showing lesser effects than those claimed by fishery interests was the subject of pointed attacks.[100] And again in 1970, the Walla Walla District "published a brochure responding directly to [environmentalists'] accusations" about adverse effects of Lower Granite Dam, triggering another round of adverse publicity.[101]

But by 1994, when Walla Walla had apparently forgotten what happens when it tells the truth about salmon, its efforts didn't even make an impression on the public. The media simply ignored them.

I have frequently talked to scientists employed by the federal agencies, including the National Marine Fisheries Service, who will admit that the official Snake River Salmon recovery plan has no hope of making measurable changes in salmon populations. They acknowledged that the pro-flow and pro-spill biases introduced by political appointees lack any scientific support. They will deride the pseudo-scientific "studies" offered in support of these initiatives as "crap". They lament the increasing role of political appointments in fishery agencies, as "consultants" are engaged to fill policymaking roles formerly held by career civil servants. But when I ask them to take a stand publicly, they all refuse. Some are near retirement, and fear outright termination. Others take a moralistic stance, suggesting that would be lowering themselves by becoming public advocates for any particular issue.

From my perspective, this is an instance when "all that is necessary for evil to triumph is that good men do nothing". But from their perspective, this is not a question of good and evil; all that is at issue is whether a great deal of money is wasted.

The climate of fear extends beyond federal officials to academia. Professor Ray Hilborn of the University of Washington submitted an extraordinarily frank paper to the National Marine Fisheries Service in connection with its listing of Snake River sockeye salmon, but requested that it be kept "confidential" because "enough people hate me already".[102]

The unwillingness to speak the truth about the effects of dams on salmon is only one example of a more general politicization of salmon issues. Almost no one speaks the truth about harvest either. United States fishery experts involved in setting ocean salmon harvests, the subject of international disputes with Canada, admit that harvest rates are too high, but are unwilling to say so publicly. Instead, they tell reporters, off the record, that current harvest levels are so high that if they had been in place earlier, "Washington coastal fall chinook, Snake River chinook and mid-Columbia summer chinook would have gone extinct".[103]

In 1995, I became aware that industrial interests, agricultural interests, and, most importantly, the mid-Columbia Public Utility Districts, were having tentative discussions to form a group that would fund a public relations drive to spread the truth about Northwest salmon recovery. The mid-Columbias, as they are called for short, are the Public Utility Districts of Grant, Douglas and Chelan Counties, Washington. They hold licenses from the United States Federal Energy Regulatory Commission to operate hydroelectric projects on the middle Columbia above the confluence of the Snake.

Their regulation of flow to keep mid-Columbia fall chinook redds covered has produced the largest naturally-spawning salmon run in the Columbia River. The Wells Dam was constructed with a unique design diverting excess flow directly over the powerhouse which turned out to provide excellent fish passage for juvenile salmon.

I was personally hopeful that the group, which had the working name of "Northwesterners for More Fish", would make a real difference in dispelling the Great Salmon Hoax. Reportedly, the mid-Columbias were willing to devote $1 million to the initial public relations campaign. While that is but a fraction of the amount handed out by the government and foundations to promote the Great Salmon Hoax, it was enough to make a difference.

But the group came under immediate scrutiny by the news media, and was attacked over and over before it had ever even done anything. It's not often that the media can destroy a group before it really begins meeting, which is a testament to the power of those promoting the Great Salmon Hoax. At the time, I thought the effort fell apart because of the adverse publicity. Later, I learned that Vice President Gore had personally called one of the board members of the mid-Columbias and told him that they would have regulatory troubles with their NMFS-regulated habitat conservation plans if they went forward.[104] Without the habitat conservation plans in place, the mid-Columbias face their own huge fight over dam removal in relicensing proceedings before the Federal Energy Regulatory Commission.

Dams in the Ecosystem of the Pacific Northwest

One of the main things missing from the debate over the impacts of dams on salmon is a social accounting of the costs and benefits of dams. Fishery managers have no incentive to measure benefits of dams. Their efforts go into attempts to quantify economic benefit from fisheries. The environmentalists focus on accounting for costs of the dams, and release "studies" like *River of Red Ink,* purporting to show the dams are a losing proposition. This seems pretty unlikely, since the Bonneville Power Administration sends a check to the Washington, D.C. Treasury of almost a billion dollars a year.

Though few people think about it, one key advantage of the dams is an environmental one. Hydropower is a substitute for thermal power—burning things. By attacking hydropower, salmon advocates have forced a huge fuel-switching exercise, requiring utilities to burn fossil fuels that are asserted to cause global warming. (Attacking hydropower has had the side effect of encouraging a competitive market in electricity, also anathema to environmentalists, by creating huge bulges in supply during the spring.)

Fish advocates have so successfully demonized hydropower that government promotion of "renewable" energy resources does not extend to hydropower. Government consideration of plans to remove Snake River dams that generate 3,000 megawatts of electricity—enough to supply 300,000 homes—is now serious front page news in the Pacific Northwest.[105] Few people remember that the Northwest Power Planning Council already eliminated 27 percent of potential hydropower production by declaring in 1988 that huge sections of the Columbia River Basin would be "protected areas" where no hydropower dams can be built.[106] The Bonneville Power Administration enforces the Council's decision by refusing to transmit any electric power generated by projects constructed in protected areas.

My personal experience with environmentalists who were utterly blind to the environmental consequences of their attack on dams came in making a speech at the Northwest School of Law at Lewis and Clark College in Portland. In the speech, I explained how warmer temperatures had driven the salmon north to Alaska, and speculated that if global warming theories were correct, they were unlikely to come back at all. Dan Rohlf, a panel member on the faculty of the Law School and frequent litigant in salmon lawsuits, asked me what my clients were doing about the global warming problems. Unable to contain my glee, I told him that we were making an enormous contribution through our struggle to maintain hydropower generation on the Columbia River Basin, much to the amusement of the audience.

Environmentalists often claim that conservation can substitute for power production, but this is a pipe dream. No matter how successful conservation is, the Pacific Northwest is going to require very substantial amounts of electric power. Apart from effects on salmon (but not shad and many other fish), dams offer the cleanest, safest means of generating that power. Decisions to reduce power production at dams are decisions to drill oil and gas wells, dig coal mines, manufacture large quantities of electric generation equipment, and build new power plants.

I can imagine how people might think about taking out dams if such actions would actually bring back salmon in truly historic numbers. But when the best and the brightest fishery scientists frankly acknowledge that the Columbia River hydropower system does not limit the recovery of salmon,[107] it is hard to fathom why we are spending millions of dollars considering dam removal. The best and brightest, however, are ignored; the media simply reports, over and over and over again, that the dams are "considered by most scientists to . . . block salmon recovery efforts".[108]

NOTES TO CHAPTER 4

[1] R. Neuberger, *Saturday Evening Post*, Nov. 1937.

[2] R. White, *The Organic Machine* 96.

[3] 16 U.S.C. §§ 832-832i

[4] 16 U.S.C. § 832.

[55] R. White, The Organic Machine 74.

[6] *Id.*

[7] *See, e.g.,* J. Brinckman, "Flood control actions draw criticism", *The Oregonian*, Feb. 28, 1997.

[8] R. Boyce, System Operational Request #97-1, Feb. 11, 1997, at 2 (Mr. Boyce, an employee of the Oregon Department of Fish and Wildlife, is identified as "Chairperson, Salmon Managers").

[9] "Measures to Enhance Salmon and Steelhead Migration Success During 1997", at 5 (Idaho Governor's Office Mar. 25, 1997).

[10] Picture from http://www.cqs.washington.edu/crisp/hydro/index.html, with additional formatting courtesy Suzanne Iltis. This Website contains comprehensive data on these and other Columbia Basin hydroelectric projects.

[11] Carl Magnusson, quoting in R. White, *The Organic Machine* 37.

[12] Reported in Neuberger, R., Our Promised Land 67 (MacMillan 1938)

[13] R. White, *The Organic Machine* 57.

[14] Quoted in Neuberger, R., Our Promised Land 63 (MacMillan 1938)

[15] NRC, *Upstream* at 53 (Prepub. ed.).

[16] *Snake River Salmon Recovery Team: Final Recommendation to the National Marine Fisheries Service* at II-8 (1994) [hereinafter Recovery Plan]); Northwest Power Planning Council, *Strategy for Salmon*, Vol. I at 28, 33 (1992) [hereinafter Strategy for Salmon].

[17] T. Palmer, *The Snake River* 189.

[18] For example, ODFW fish biologist Kurt Beiningen wrote in the early 1970s that "While erection of Grand Coulee Dam locked out a large portion of habitat in the upper Columbia, it is doubtful that the project alone was the cause of the demise of upriver stocks. Even prior to the construction of Rock Island Dam in 1933, observers reported that substantial depletions of stocks indigenous to tributaries above and below Grand Coulee had already occurred.".

[19] *Id.*

[20] F. Christensen, "Hydropower isn't the cheapest, and it causes a lot of problems", *The Idaho Statesman*, Aug. 1, 1996. Mr. Christensen, woefully ignorant of nearly every fact about which he writes, goes so far as to claim that wind power is cheaper than hydropower.

[21] Ed Mains, quoted in O. Bullard, *Crisis on the Columbia* 111.

[22] T. Palmer, *The Snake River: Window to the West* 13 (Island Press 1991).

[23] NRC, *Upstream* at 61 (Prepub. ed.).

[24] Quoted in T. Palmer, *The Snake River* 142.

[25] T. Palmer, *The Snake River* 54 (citing Northwest Power Planning Council study).

[26] T. Palmer, *The Snake River* 103 (1987 figures from the Idaho Department of Water Resources show 8.2 maf consumption).

[27] T. Palmer, *The Snake River* 131.

[28] NMFS, Draft Snake River Salmon Recovery Plan, at 70. NMFS refuses to release the draft to the public, although it is circulating to State and Tribal fishery agencies and the Northwest Power Planning Council's Independent Science Advisory Board as this book goes to press in October 1997. The citation comes from some pages of the plan that were anonymously faxed to the Columbia River Alliance.

[29] NMFS, Endangered Species Act Section 7 Consultation, Inland Land, Inc., May 16, 1997.

[30] Fred Ziari (pers. comm.)

[31] R. Barker, "Will anglers have a shot at South Fork's salmon?", *The Idaho Statesman*, Jan. 15, 1997.

[32] Appendix to Special Report on the Lower Snake River Dams", at 12 (Fish Comm'n of Oregon March 1973).

[33] G. Bouck, "Thirty years taught that money won't save salmon", The Oregonian, Oct. 20, 1995, at D7.

[34] NRC, *Upstream* at 86 (Prepub. ed.).

[35] Reported in T. Warner, "Expensive talk of dam removal", The Wenatchee World, Oct. 18, 1996.

[36] J. Cone, *A Common Fate* 157.

[37] *Id.*

[38] W. McNeil, "Survival of Marked Juvenile Chinook and Steelhead Migrants in the Columbia Basin", Dec. 10, 1994, at 1.

[39] *Id.* at 6.

[40] *Id.* at 1.

[41] R. Hilborn & C. Coronado, "Survival Trends in Columbia River hatchery chinook salmon", at 4-5 (3/96 Draft Report). Dr. Hilborn offered a fourth hypothesis, that the data were too noisy to see the pattern, but rejected it because of the significant sample sizes involved.

[42] *Id.* at 5.

[43] NRC, *Upstream* at 74.

[44] HARZA Northwest, "Salmon Decision Analysis Lower Snake River Feasilbility Study: Final Report", Oct. 4, 1996, at 3-4 (Figure 3-5).

[45] W. McNeil, "Recruits per Escapee for Columbia Basin Anadromous Salmonids", Dec. 5, 1994, at 1.

[46] *Id.*

[47] G. Bouck, "Thirty years taught that money won't save salmon", The Oregonian, Oct. 20, 1995, at D7.

[48] Declaration of Doug Neeley, Feb.7, 1993, at 2, filed in *IDFG v. NMFS*, No. 93-1603-MA (D. Or.).

[49] G. Easterbrook, *A Moment on the Earth* 117; *see also* I. Suggs, "Defenders of Wild*lies*?", CEI UpDate, Feb. 1997, at 1 (citing G. Hodges, "When Good Guys Lie", *The Washington Monthly*).

[50] *Id.*

[51] J. Lichatowich, "A History of Frameworks Used in the Management of Columbia River Chinook Salmon", at 4, 14, 30, 47 (May 1996).

[52] NRC, *Upstream* at 69 (Prepub. ed.).

[53] ISG, *Return to the River* 93.

[54] "Compilation of Information on Salmon and Steelhead Losses in the Columbia River Basin", Appendix D of the 1987 Columbia River Basin Fish and Wildlife Program, at 5-6 (NWPPC Mar. 1986).

[55] C. Smith, *Salmon Fishers of the Columbia* 100.

[56] *Id.* at 88 (shaker loss excluded because the "calculation is tenuous and subject to considerable controversy").

[57] A. Wertheimer, "Hooking Mortality of chinook released by commercial trollers. North Am. J. Fish. Mgmt. 8:346-55 (1988); A. Wertheimer *et al.*, "Size-related hooking mortality of incidentally caught chinook salmon, *Onchrynchus tshawytscha*", NMFS Fisheries Review 51(2): 28-35 (1989).

[58] "Commercial fishermen take too many chinook, state says", *The Oregonian*, Oct. 29, 1997.

[59] C. Smith, *Salmon Fishers of the Columbia* at 90.

[60] "Compilation of Information on Salmon and Steelhead Losses in the Columbia River Basin", at 125 (Figure 18).

[61] E. Mains, "Corps of Engineers Responsibilities and Actions to Maintain Columbia Basin Anadromous Fish Runs", in E. Schwiebert (ed.), *Columbia River Salmon and Steelhead* 40-41, Spec. Pub. No. 10 (Am. Fish. Soc. 1977).

[62] Quoted in K. Petersen, *River of Life, Channel of Death* 109.

[63] Memo to File, S. Hutchinson (U.S. Fish & Wildlife Service), Jan. 16, 1951 (recounting conversation with reporter Herb Lundy); *excerpted in* J. Cone & S. Ridlington, *The Northwest Salmon Crisis: A Documentary History* 207 (OSU Press 1996).

[64] J. Cone & S. Ridlington, *The Northwest Salmon Crisis: A Documentary History* 213.

[65] Quoted in A. Netboy, *Salmon of the Pacific Northwest: Fish vs. Dams* xi (Binfords & Mort Portland 1958)

[66] B. Matsen, *Ray Troll's Shocking Fish Tales* 91 (Ten Speed Press 1993).

[67] The research results are summarized in ISG, *Return to the River* 273-75.

[68] *See generally*, D. Mathur & P. Heisey, "Debunking the Myths about Fish Mortality at Hydro Plants", *Hydro Review*, April 1992, at 54-60.

[69] J. Skalski *et al.*, "Turbine Passage Survival of Juvenile Spring Chinook Salmon (*Onchorhynchus tshawytscha*) at Lower Granite Dam, Snake River, Washington", U.S. Army Corps of Engineers Contract No. DACW68-95-C-0031 (October 1995), Table 3-6.

[70] *See* C. Steward, "Assessment of the Flow-Survival Relationship Obtained by Sims & Ossiander (1981) for Snake River Spring/Summer Chinook Salmon Smolts", Final Report, BPA Contract No. DE-AM79-93BP99654, at v (April 1994) ("evidence suggest that a disproportionate percentage of chinook smolts died at the first dam encountered on the Snake River, presumably due to the culling of unfit fish").

[71] *See generally* J. Ferguson, "Improving Fish Survival through Turbines", *Hydro Review*, April 1993, at 54-61.

[72] "Our debt is overdue", *The Astorian*, May 13, 1997.

[73] B. Harden, *A River Lost* 71 (10-15% mortality).

[74] ISG, *Return to the River* 273.

[75] Plans are in place to install extended screens at The Dalles. Unfortunately, the States and tribes have begun resisting structural improvements to bypass systems dams they think should simply be removed.

[76] "Fish Research: Filling the Gaps", *Salmon Passage Notes*, at 2 (USACE NPD Feb. 1996).

[77] Ledgerwood *et al.* (1991).

[78] *Id.* at 9.

[79] J. Willliams, G. Matthews & J. Myers, "The Columbia River Hydropower System: Does It Limit Recovery of Spring/Summer Chinook Salmon?", at 4.

[80] U.S. Army Corps of Engineers, "Interim Status Report", at 2-3.

[81] *Id.*

[82] Memo, M. Schiewe to W. Stelle, Jr., July 12, 1996, at 3 (the memo notes that the survival estimates "should be considered minimal estimates that will increase slightly"; I was later told that survival to John Day was 56.4%).

[83] K. Petersen, *River of Life, Channel of Death* 21.

[84] Marmorek *et al.*, *Plan for Analyzing and Testing Hypotheses (PATH): Final Report on Retrospective Analyses for Fiscal Year 1996* (ESSA Technologies 1996).

[85] W. McNeil, "Survival of Marked Juvenile Chinook and Steelhead Migrants in the Columbia Basin", Dec. 10, 1994.

[86] *See, e.g.*, R. White, *The Organic Machine* 102; J. Cone, *A Common Fate* 127; K. Petersen, *River of Life, Channel of Death* 169.

[87] Information Paper, "Subject: Federal Dams cause 95% of the Human-Caused Mortality to Snake River Salmon—Not True says Corps Review", May 1, 1994 (USACE Walla Walla District).

[88] Information Paper at 1.

[89] *Id.* at 2

[90] *See, e.g.*, J. Williams & G. Matthews, "A review of flow/survival relationships for juvenile salmonids in the Columbia River Basin", manuscript submitted to *Fishery Bulletin* (NMFS CZESD March 1994).

[91] *Id.*

[92] *Id.*

[93] D. Chapman & A. Giorgi, "Comments on Work of Biological and FCRPS Alternative Work Groups", at 8 (1994).

[94] Information Paper, at 2.

[95] From Chart presented by Dr. James Anderson at CRA Salmon Symposium, Nov. 19, 1996.

[96] G. Easterbrook, *Earth in the Balance* xviii.

[97] R. White, *The Organic Machine* 103.

[98] C. Smith, *Salmon Fishers of the Columbia* 4.

[99] K. Petersen, *River of Life, Channel of Death* 117-118.

[100] *See, e.g.*, O. Bullard, *Crisis on the Columbia* 114 ("a study that showed that the newer turbines would result in a loss of only five percent at each dam came in for heavy criticism and charges . . ."),

[101] *Id.* at 144-45.

[102] R. Hilborn, "Some Reflections on Hatcheries or "You Don't Have to be a Rocket Scientist to See Some of the Problems" (April 3, 1992).

[103] P. Koberstein, "Shipwreck! Is the Pacific Salmon Treaty Lost at Sea?", *Big River News* (Fall 1996).

[104] Gore was previously noted for telling DuPont personally that it had to go on producing CFCs, which he had previously termed "the greatest crisis humanity has ever faced"—destruction of the ozone layer—because the White House "feared a political rebellion" if citizens could not recharge their automobile air conditioners. G. Easterbrook, *A Moment on the Earth* 545.

[105] J. Brinckman, "Army Corps considers removing dams", *The Oregonian*, Nov. 9, 1996.

[106] T. Palmer, *The Snake River* 195-96.

[107] *See, e.g.,* J. Williams, G. Matthews & J. Myers, "The Columbia River Hydropower System: Does It Limit Recovery of Spring/Summer Chinook Salmon?", at 20 (Their answer: "Most probably not.").

[108] J. Brinckman, "Panel gets Kitzhaber's hard stand on salmon", *The Oregonian*, Aug. 6, 1997, at A1.

111

CHAPTER 5: THE ATTACK ON SALMON SMOLT TRANSPORTATION

> "The Buddha, the Godhead, resides quite as comfortably in the circuits of a digital computer or the gears of a cycle transmission as he does at the top of a mountain or in the petals of a flower." Robert M. Pirsig, *Zen and the Art of Motorcycle Maintenance.*

History is riddled with examples of political misadventures with science. Perhaps the most famous of these occurred during the 1930s in Soviet Russia. Stalin's personal friend Lysenko had his own theories about evolution and genetics, and attempted to implement those theories all over the land. Starvation resulted as agricultural cooperatives were forced to plant to his specifications. Lysenko was executed, but today's fish managers are promoted.

The annals of federal government misadventures in applied science should make anyone a skeptic about the likely success of big government programs. Recent decades have seen government efforts to distill oil from rock ("shale oil"), a promotion of unneeded nuclear reactors (like WPPSS), and a program to clean up toxic wastes by paying lawyers to fight about them (CERCLA) that rivals salmon recovery as the most expensive environmental boondoggle in history.

This history of failure may be what gives the U.S. Army Corps of Engineers smolt transportation program a bad name. But there have been government successes in science, like the space program. And smolt transportation is another.

Measuring the Effects of Transporting Juvenile Fish

The idea is simple. By barging the salmon around the dams, they can avoid turbine mortality, which cumulated over many dams may be significant. Even more importantly, they can also avoid predators in hundreds of miles of river.

The transportation program started as an emergency measure in response to drought conditions in the 1970s, when most of the salmon were dying before they got downriver. Later, after research confirmed the benefits of transportation, the program was expanded. There is some possibility that many salmon runs would be extinct today if they hadn't been saved by the transportation program.

The research itself was simple and convincing. The National Marine Fisheries Service tagged two groups of fish, left one in the river, and put one in a barge. The barge took the transported group downriver and released it below the dams. Then, two, three, four or more years later when the fish returned as adults, NMFS compared the ratio of barged to in-river returns. For years this ratio was generally called the TBR, or Transportation Benefit Ratio. When the TBR is greater than one, transports outnumbered controls. Starting around 1996, the conservation biologists deemed it improper to speak of the Transportation *Benefit* Ratio, and the politically-correct term is now the Transportation In-river Ratio or TIR.

Positive transportation ratios have been observed for all the major races of salmon. So far, roughly 32 experiments have been conducted with spring and summer chinook salmon transported from Snake River Dams to below Bonneville Dam. In 13 of the experiments, enough adults came back to make the resulting TBR statistically significant. Every one of those TBRs was greater than one; their average is 4.89, a figure that is inflated by very high TBRs in 1973 (averaging 16.1).[1]

Sockeye experiments have been conducted with transportation from Priest Rapids Dam in the Mid-Columbia River. In three out of five years, the TBR exceeded one. The data for fall chinook are primarily based on tests at McNary Dam, just downstream of the confluence of the Columbia and Snake Rivers, and again the TBRs have been consistently high. They are even higher for steelhead.

The positive results of transportation are not unique to the Columbia River Basin. As Dr. William McNeil, Professor Emeritus at Oregon State University has pointed out, "European workers have been evaluating transport of Atlantic salmon smolts for nearly two decades".[2] High positive TBR values have been found in Swedish rivers, Norwegian rivers, and also in Japan.[3]

Snake River salmon have continued to decline despite an extensive transportation program, but the best science suggests that the decline would have been a lot worse without transportation. Drs. Chapman and Giorgi compared the number of smolts getting downriver from the Upper Columbia (transported from only one dam, McNary) with smolts getting downriver from the Snake (transported from McNary and two other dams). They found that from 1979 to 1988, the Snake River escapements (returning adults) increased at a greater rate than the Columbia River escapements.[4] This provides evidence of the efficacy of transportation notwithstanding the general downward trends in population abundance.

The success of transportation should not surprise anyone, since it was invented precisely to overcome the objections of fishery advocates. They have a litany of complaints about the condition of the river. It is too hot. There are too many predators. There is not enough water. The dams kill the salmon. By putting salmon in a barge, and having a tugboat push them down the river, all these problems are avoided.

Critiques of Transportation

For a while, it was feared that the barging process would interfere with the homing instinct. But National Marine Fisheries Service researchers paid attention to this question "from the inception of their studies".[5] They found no evidence that transported fish lost the homing instinct, probably because the salmon had already migrated many miles in the river before being collected for transportation. In addition, the transportation barges constantly recirculate water while they are going downstream. If juvenile salmon do imprint on the chemical composition of the mainstem water, they can do so in the barges. By 1997, Idaho officials would privately admit "there is no evidence that fish are somehow losing their homing instinct from the barging process[, because d]am to spawning beds conversion rates are the same as they were before the barging process started".[6]

Because most of the fish marked for transportation research are hatchery fish, there have also been persistent suggestions that wild fish do not benefit as much from transportation as hatchery fish. But if you exclude all the hatchery fish from the calculations, the TBRs are even more positive.

Another well-promoted hypothesis is delayed mortality. No one can really can think of a good reason why transported salmon should die long after leaving the barges. One idea is that piping the salmon into the barges stresses the juveniles. Bert Bowler, an Idaho Department of Fish and Game biologist, has gone so far as to tell reporters that "the stress of the fish from splashing them into the barges is responsible for the decline in returning adults".[7] This notion lacks any basis in fact.

In fact, tests show no difference in survival rates of marked groups of chinook salmon that are subjected to high stress before release and those that are not.[8] Tests show no difference in swimming endurance of yearling chinook tested before and after barging.[9] Other evidence suggests that any stress-caused reduction in ability to evade predators would disappear within an hour.[10] And above all else, we know that transported juvenile salmon stay alive for hundreds of miles after they leave the barge at the same rates as untransported fish.

The Northwest Power Planning Council's Independent Science Group has recently put forth a more sophisticated version of the "delayed mortality" theory. They point out that juvenile salmon "die at rates related to physical conditions existing during the time of emigration in the river" and that there is an "*apparent dependence* of the survivals of both transported and untransported juvenile salmon on conditions in the hydroelectric system".[11] For this reason, they claim (in a widely-quoted passage), that "transportation alone, as presently conceived and implemented, is unlikely to halt or prevent the continued decline and extirpation of listed species of salmon in the Snake River Basin".[12]

The fallacy here is the "apparent dependence". What they are really saying is that in dry years, when conditions are worse in the river, death rates seem to be higher in the ocean too. With blame-the-dams blinders on, conservation biologists assume that the higher death rate in the ocean is somehow related to passage through the river. The obvious countervailing hypothesis, that dry years on land are correlated with poorer conditions in the ocean, is ignored.

The Independent Science Group does acknowledge, in another section of its report, that

> "during periods of warm ocean conditions and reduced flow
> of the California Current, freshwater habitat conditions may
> also decline due to reduced stream flows and increasing river
> temperatures in Western Oregon. These effects suggest a
> kind of 'double jeopardy' for salmon stocks . . ."[13]

It is precisely this "double jeopardy", and other adverse effects on salmon, that has hidden the positive effects of the transportation program. Transportation can't alone offset the effects of bad ocean and freshwater conditions, but nothing can. As National Marine Fisheries Service scientists John Williams and Gene Matthews have explained, "this unproven theory [of transportation failure] has turned to fact in the minds of many because data were incorrectly interpreted . . ."[14]

Because transportation speeds up the migration process, it puts fish into the estuary sooner than they would otherwise get there. This was long thought to offset migration delay from the dams. However, there is evidence that survival of later-transported fish is higher.[15] This could be because it is better for fish to arrive later, or it could be because conditions in the river are less favorable later, killing off more of the control groups compared to transported fish.

Over the next few years, substantial additional data will become available to measure changes in salmon survival within the river at each project, and the survival of transported fish. We may well find a time, early in the year, when transportation does not help the fish. But the good news will be that that is because in-river conditions are so good.

Torturing the Data Until It Confesses: The Anti-Transportation Review Groups

My personal introduction to the attack on transportation came when the environmentalists filed their first lawsuit specifically targeting transportation. The United States Fish and Wildlife Service, apparently led by one of the many instigators of the Great Salmon Hoax, Fred Olney, commissioned a review of the extensive literature on transportation experiments. This itself was peculiar since the Fish and Wildlife Service has no jurisdiction over anadromous fish; they fall under the jurisdiction of the National Marine Fisheries Service. The review was conducted by a number of anti-transportation activists in the state and tribal fishery agencies who called themselves the "Ad Hoc Transportation Review Group".

Their report managed to turn the review of a collection of papers proving transportation worked into an indictment of the transportation system. A consultant in the process, Phil Mundy, put an "Executive Summary" on the document that was harshly, and unjustifiably critical of transportation.

This is an old trick, not unique to those promoting the Great Salmon Hoax. Environmental journalist Gregg Easterbrook, investigating the science behind a number of environmental issues, warned that "the summary is the only portion of a science document any journalist or politician ever actually reads—an important factor to keep in mind when the subject turns to global warming".[16]

In addition to the biased summary, the Report is laced with anti-transportation speculation so extreme that one reviewer told the National Marine Fisheries Service that it was both "laughable and professionally disappointing".[17] For example, the Report speculates that transportation does not return more adults all the way to the spawning grounds, speculation recently echoed by the Northwest Power Planning Council's Independent Science Group.[18] While the studies were only designed to measure returns back to the uppermost dam, there is some data based on spawning ground surveys, and although it is not statistically significant, the transportation ratio is even higher when measured at the spawning grounds.

117

When the Ad Hoc Report came out, the Pacific Northwest Utilities Conference Committee (PNUCC) was still active on salmon issues, and willing to pay independent biologists to review the claims of the states and tribes. (Later, when PNUCC's investor-owned utility members began to see that the Great Salmon Hoax could cripple the Bonneville Power Administration as a competitor, PNUCC lost its funding to continue to combat the Hoax.)

PNUCC asked Dr. Don Chapman to review the report. Dr. Chapman observed that "[g]ood scientific practice would secure outside scientific review. Had the Group done so, it would surely not have released this report, which contains many faulty analyses and erroneous conclusions."[19] With considerable understatement, Dr. Chapman suggested that "the Group seems to need to draw conclusions beyond the limits of the study design and data".[20] Worse still, Dr. Chapman identified instance after instance of what he politely termed "selective data treatment"[21]—what would in law constitute misrepresentation or outright fraud.

His ultimate conclusion: "Each Review Group participant bears responsibility for this misleading and biased document."[22] Don Park, who retired from the National Marine Fisheries Service in 1990, and participated in all of NMFS' transportation studies, noted that the Review Group was attacking "the research and methodology they formerly approved", called the Report "infamous", and concluded that it "lacked scientific credibility".[23] Over and over again, former NMFS researchers have come out of retirement to protest elements of the Great Salmon Hoax, but they are usually ignored by their own agencies.

Phil Mundy later continued his anti-transportation efforts when he was hired by the National Marine Fisheries Service to develop a "rule curve" to describe when to use transportation, based on conditions prevailing in the river. His former professor, and Dean Emeritus of the School of Fisheries, Don Bevan, privately advised the NMFS scientists in Seattle that much of the analysis should be "dismissed as nonsense". Dr. Bevan pointed out that Mundy created his curve using "the wrong data set". "A reasonable approach", commented Dr. Bevan, "would be to use the coefficient fitted to the data". Doing so "would result in always transporting".[24] This, however, was apparently not the "right" answer.

The Legal Attack on Transportation

Armed with the report of the Ad Hoc Transportation Review Group and a raft of affidavits from the anti-transportation activists, the Sierra Club Legal Defense Fund filed suit in the United States District Court in Portland.

Like all the other salmon cases, it was assigned to Judge Malcolm Marsh. On April 22, 1993, Judge Marsh held a hearing on their motion for emergency injunctive relief against the transportation program. We filed a motion to intervene in the case before the hearing, but Judge Marsh would not rule on our motion, entitling us to participate as parties. We could be mere observers until he ruled on our motion.

I was personally disappointed because, guided by Dr. Chapman's critiques of the Review Group, I was prepared to cross-examine the state and tribal experts criticizing transportation and demonstrate that they lacked any scientific credibility. The highlight of my examination was going to be an attack on their claims that transportation didn't work for wild fish. Using the studies they had purported to review, it was possible to simply count the fish and show that transportation was twice as effective for wild fish—if one followed the experts' unscientific practice of drawing conclusions from the limited set of data that was available. I was also prepared to show, by walking the experts through the data charts in the transportation studies, that returns to the spawning grounds were higher for transported fish.

Instead of allowing us to question the witnesses, Judge Marsh ordered them into the jury box as a group and began questioning them himself. Luckily, he knew enough about the issues that his "talk show" method of conducting proceedings elicited some relevant evidence, although not as much as we would have.

It quickly became clear that the NMFS scientists who supported the program were more credible than the state and tribal witnesses who attacked it. Only after the hearings were over did Judge Marsh allow us to intervene in the case, explaining later that he had done so because of the "potential power loss" of 2.2 million megawatt-hours from the changes sought by plaintiffs.[25] Though the environmentalists were allowed to file their own expert affidavits, we were not. On December 13, 1993, Judge Marsh refused to "supplement the record" with an affidavit from Dr. Chapman.

Ultimately, Judge Marsh may have been persuaded that transportation was a good thing for the fish, for he denied plaintiffs' claims that transporting the fish violated the Endangered Species Act. When the environmentalists sought to appeal, the Ninth Circuit dismissed their Endangered Species Act claim as moot.[26]

NEPA: Considering Alternatives in Environmental Decisionmaking

The environmentalists had a second claim: that the transportation program was conducted in violation of the National Environmental Policy Act (NEPA). They claimed that an environmental study done pursuant to the Act, the 1993 Supplemental Environmental Impact statement (SEIS), was inadequate.

The SEIS was a peculiar document which studied different kinds of flow increases as a primary salmon recovery policy for the federal government despite the absence of evidence that flow increases would have any effect on salmon survival (see Chapter 7). Given the politically-driven policy choice to release water from reservoirs, no alternatives to flow augmentation were studied.

We privately agreed with the environmentalists that it would be have been useful to have had a comparison of *all* the alternatives for recovering salmon in a single environmental analysis. Such a document could have quickly educated decisionmakers that transportation worked, flow augmentation didn't, and there were far fewer environmental side effects from transportation.

Judge Marsh decided that transportation of salmon was sufficiently "connected" to the question of changing flows that the two should have been considered in the same SEIS, and thus held that the Corps of Engineers had violated NEPA. On June 1, 1995, the Ninth Circuit reversed Judge Marsh. The three judges refused to agree that transportation and flow augmentation were "connected actions" that had to be considered in the same EIS.

"On this rationale", they explained, "measures involving harvest limits, hatchery releases, and habitat maintenance are also interdependent parts of every action taken to benefit the salmon."[27] The Court could just as easily have decided that these were all "connected actions" because they fit precisely within the definition of the NEPA regulations: they were "interdependent parts of a larger action"—saving salmon—"and depend on the larger action for their justification".[28]

Then the Corps of Engineers would have had to compare the environmental effects of all the different ways of trying to produce salmon. For the first time, there would have been a document that permitted a rational comparison of the environmental costs and benefits of all salmon recovery alternatives. As of 1997, no one has prepared such a document and no one probably ever will.

Some people think that the requirement of analyzing "connected actions" or "alternatives" is pointless. But the law only requires this sort of analysis for major federal actions "significantly affecting the human environment". There is real benefit to pointing out the pros and cons of different ways of meeting the same public policy objectives, rather than letting agencies put blinders on to ignore disfavored alternatives. As the regulations point out, the analysis must provide "a clear basis for choice among options by the decisionmakers and the public".[29]

The whole idea of NEPA is that citizens of the United States can turn to the courts and demand some minimal analysis before major federal action with a significant effect on the human environment. Unfortunately, they can't, at least not unless they are perceived to be on the side of the salmon. The United States Court of Appeals for the Ninth Circuit has repeatedly ruled that the NEPA cannot be used to challenge federal action that the Court deems pro-environmental—ordinary citizens lack "standing" to raise questions about NEPA's application.

And just to shut things down for those people who do have standing, like other government agencies, the Ninth Circuit has decided that the Endangered Species Act "trumps" NEPA, making it unnecessary for the federal agencies to comply with NEPA when purporting to implement the Endangered Species Act. When Douglas County, Oregon, sued the federal government to require NEPA analysis of the federal decision to designate a substantial part of Douglas County as "critical habitat" for the spotted owl, the Ninth Circuit found three reasons that the government did not have to comply with NEPA.

According to Judge Pregerson, (1) the Endangered Species Act's procedural requirements were close enough to NEPA's that NEPA need not apply; (2) NEPA analysis was not required because the critical habitat designation would merely "preserve the physical environment"; and (3) the Endangered Species Act furthered the goals of NEPA without requiring further analysis.[30]

But Douglas County had provided sworn testimony that the critical habitat designation, by forbidding insect, disease and fire control in the forests, might well cause enormous damage to the environment. NEPA was designed precisely to consider *all* environmental impacts, not just impacts on a single "species". By allowing the federal government to ignore the broader consequences of its decisionmaking, the Ninth Circuit could be accused of burning the forest to save the owls in it.

Fourteen years earlier, Judge Pregerson had accurately stated the prevailing rule, which is that if two federal statutes apply to a situation, both should be enforced unless they are "repugnant" to each other.[31]   Now, however, Judge Pregerson was reluctant to allow Douglas County to enforce NEPA's requirements because he perceived doing so as an "obstructionist tactic".[32]   One of the most frustrating aspects of attempting to enforce environmental laws in the Ninth Circuit is that the Court will bend over backwards to allow the federal government to violate the law if the Court thinks that the violation is a good thing.

NMFS Splits the Baby

Despite the best efforts of the state and tribal anti-transportation zealots, NMFS endorsed continued transportation of juvenile salmon in its biological opinion on Federal Columbia River Power System operations for 1995 and future years. NMFS even recommended a few improvements to the transportation system, including buying more barges to permit the direct loading of fish from all four collector dams.[33]

As a sacrifice to the states and tribes, NMFS recommended that spring transportation from McNary Dam be halted. The stated reason? Even though the scientific tests had found about twice as many transported fish returning, as a statistical matter, there was some (small) chance that there would be no benefit from transportation.[34]

As a result, the $15 million facility at McNary Dam has been idle every spring since 1995.   And because spring chinook are no longer being transported from McNary, there is no further research to remove the remaining statistical uncertainty.   The only evidence we have is that transportation at McNary nearly doubles the survival of fish, the evidence is deemed to be not good enough, and no one may collect any further evidence.

In the meantime, less political reviews of dam management continued to endorse transportation.   In late 1995, the National Reseach Council concluded that based on the available information, "transportation appears to be the most biologically effective and cost-effective approach for moving smolts downstream".[35] Indeed, they declared that it "is the mitigation tool of choice until inriver migration shows higher survival rates than does barging fish".[36] The reason: "No investigator to date has provided the Columbia River region with experimental results that demonstrate higher survival of inriver migrants than transported migrants at any discharge level.   Until such experimental data become available, transportation should continue to be used."[37]

An interim review of transportation by the U.S. Army Corps of Engineers in December 1996 concluded that critiques of transportation lack support in sound science, and that

"In light of the research, it appears that transportation is successful and, therefore, Snake River salmon should be recovering. One explanation for the poor recent adult returns, regardless of the treatment group, is the prolonged drought and poor resulting environmental conditions that have plagued the region in the past 12 years. Other survival inhibitors may include massive increases in hatchery releases during a period of low, near-ocean productivity, anomalous concentrations of huge schools of mackerel farther north than normal during the recent and persistent El Niño events (mackerel feed on smolts entering the ocean), recent large increases in pinniped (seals, etc.) populations that feed on adults returning to spawn, and a massive non-native shad population that may be competing with juvenile salmon for scarce resources."[38]

The Latest Attacks on Transportation

Rebuffed in the Courts, state and tribal bureaucracies followed a time-honored approach to dealing with independent science groups like the Snake River Salmon Recovery Team and the National Research Council that didn't give the right answer on transportation. The tactic was simple: the state and tribal forces urged the Northwest Power Planning Council to appoint yet another scientific review group to assess transportation: the Independent Science Group.

The Independent Science Group's conclusions on transportation were a product of its general anti-technological bias. The Group argued that

"Efforts to develop technological solutions to individual human-imposed ecosystem changes have been based on the best of intentions and often on sound, if narrowly focused, science. . . . Yet the fact remains that salmon have continued to decline despite actions based on these assumptions. It is our belief that this is the result of the guiding premise that for each identified source of mortality there is an individual technological solution. This piecemeal approach to ecosystem restoration presumes that we have sufficient knowledge to identify all direct, indirect, synergistic and cumulative impacts of our actions and that we can identify a technological solution for each impact. The recognized complexity and dynamic nature of ecosystems and the lack of success of this paradigm identifies this as an act of hubris."

Packed into this paragraph is the whole basis of the current "back to nature" fad for salmon recovery. The simple goal of putting more salmon in rivers is quietly replaced with the overriding imperative of "ecosystem restoration", so that all measures must be judged inadequate. The fact that salmon have declined—largely due to climate, overfishing, and competition—is cast as a failure of technology and science. *And science itself is replaced with a quasi-religious confession of unworthiness to the task of salmon management.*

The ISG provided a complete list of the Transportation Benefit Ratios based on the studies discussed above. But as usual, the summary was misleading. The ISG asserted: "Transportation appears to have increased the survival of fish to the point of release in about half the experiments conducted during 1968-1990".[39] The unspoken implication is that transportation did not increase survival in half the experiments. The truth is that not enough fish returned in half the experiments to get a statistically-significant result.

With a biased summary of the research results, and an anti-technological bias, the ISG concluded that "[t]ransportation should be considered an experimental, interim measure pending restoration of normative conditions . . .".[40] The ISG's report was good enough for the *Oregonian*, which asserted that transportation, a "traditional salmon recovery strategy", was "supported by pretty flimsy data". The editorial was entitled "Self-evident salmon truths".[41]

When somebody tells you that a truth is self-evident, it is apt to be a sign that we have passed from the realm of science to the realm of politics, as in "we hold these truths to be self-evident . . ." The *Oregonian's* Declaration of Independence from science is echoed throughout the Northwest. Environmental groups are distributing flyers all the time that ask citizens to write to their politicians and tell them that barging doesn't work. Nobody bothers to look at the facts. The bottom line is simple: transportation works. It has not succeeded in recovering the salmon by itself, but should not be expected to.

The state and tribal forces have also continued their attacks on the transportation system through their increased involvement in federal salmon spending. Throughout the fall of 1996, in meeting after meeting, state and tribal representatives (albeit not those from Idaho and Montana) urged NMFS to recommend to the Corps that it not proceed to buy additional barges to improve the transportation system, as specified in the Biological Opinion. The battle did not end until November 22nd, when NMFS finally terminated the debate and directed the Corps to award the contract less than a week later.[42] Doubtless the delays increased costs.

Oregon Representative Elizabeth Furse, a mouthpiece for harvest managers, and Idaho Representative Mike Crapo, the heir to the Cecil Andrus "blame the dams" strategy for saving Southern Idaho irrigators, have joined forces to promote attacks on transportation. They are demanding that federal dam operators uncritically "accept and implement the recommendations of state and tribal fish agencies" to cut transportation.[43]

Idaho's Governor Phil Batt told Idaho citizens in early 1997 that "[m]ost reports recommend a gradually declining use of barging" and that he "accept[ed] that wisdom".[44] He has convinced the entire Idaho Congressional Delegation and other Idaho interests to sign off on a plan to restrict transportation operations so as to leave two-thirds of the juvenile salmon leaving Idaho in the river.[45]

At this point, the only group of fishery agency scientists still willing to stand up for transportation are the elite federal fisheries scientists at the National Marine Fisheries Service Montlake Lab in Seattle. Unfortunately, NMFS' policy branch has all but silenced them. When their chief Michael Schiewe sought during a meeting of the biological opinion Implementation Team in March 1997 to offer scientific criticism of Idaho's plans, policy enforcer Brian Brown told him, in substance, to shut up. Other scientists in the Lab have found outright misrepresentations of scientific papers in Idaho's "analyses" of efforts to assist juvenile salmon. The Montlake Lab is one of the last bastions of science in Northwest fishery agencies, perhaps because of its close proximity to, and close relationship with, the University of Washington.

On March 25, 1997, the Columbia River Alliance delivered a notice of intent to sue the National Marine Fisheries Service and several other federal agencies because, among other things, the Service had caved in to state and tribal pressure in reducing the fraction of salmon transported. Shortly thereafter, on April 4th, the Service held a meeting of the "Executive Committee" of high-ranking federal, state and tribal officials to consider a proposal by the state of Idaho and several of the tribes to barge only one-third of the fish in the river. The U.S. Fish and Wildlife Service broke ranks with the other federal agencies to support the proposal. But the National Marine Fisheries Service turned it down, with NMFS Regional Director Will Stelle pointing out that if they transported less than half the fish, they'd probably get sued, and probably lose. This I counted as one of our litigation successes.

The state and tribal forces continue to inflict the death of a thousand cuts on the transportation system. No attention is paid to further improvements that could increase survival dramatically. For example, research conducted by private salmon ranching companies has demonstrated that the survival of released smolts can be *doubled* by towing a net pen full of smolts several miles out to sea, beyond the range of many of the salmon predators in the estuary (particularly birds).[46] Other research found a 50% survival increase when coho were released downriver at Tongue Point rather than immediately below Bonneville Dam.[47]

But the fishery agencies ignore this research, and no one is modifying the current transportation program to take advantage of this knowledge. It would be inconsistent with efforts to promote the Great Salmon Hoax to make transportation more effective.

Lacking any scientific evidence against transportation, the opponents have become more and more vitriolic. Idaho salmon activist Ed Chaney calls it a "huge scientific hoax", claims that the data are "cooked", and says that claims of benefits from transportation are "fairy tales".[48] Environmentalists call the barges "iron coffins".[49] In a successful (albeit short-lived) attempt to shut down transportation at two dams during the spring of 1997, the Oregon Department of Fish and Wildlife's Ron Boyce declared that BPA's demands for scientific evidence amounted to "a witch hunt", and that the further information was "irrelevant" in deciding to shut down the transportation system.[50]

By the fall of 1997, environmentalists even went so far as to bring television news reporters to watch smolt releases from barges. Some juvenile shad, much more fragile than the salmon, die in the barges. Seagulls gather to eat them when the barges are unloaded. The gullible reporters produced "a deluge of negative press, the gist of the news coverage being 'look at all of the gulls eating our salmon and steelhead'".[51] But the fish being eaten were shad; the juvenile salmon and steelhead swim straight down upon release and avoid the birds.[52] And, after all, the studies show that transported groups still have double the chance of surviving to adulthood, even if birds catch some of them coming out of the barges. This fact was not reported.

As the claims of anti-transportation zealots are echoed in the media, the federal and academic scientists who actually measure and know its benefits remain publicly silent. Over time, transportation has acquired a bad name for no legitimate reason.

Yet the data continue to mount that transportation works, although it is not publicized. In December 1996, the HARZA consulting firm reported that a preliminary study of 1994 outmigrants showed that 7.5 times more wild Snake River salmon that were transported returned to the river, compared to untransported ones.[53] As of the end of May, 1997, the preliminary data including 1995 outmigrants showed that 2.7 times as many transported wild fish were returning as untransported ones.[54] Donna Darm of the National Marine Fisheries Service even acknowledged publicly in June 1997 that according to this preliminary data, if full transportation had been in effect in 1995, there would have been ten to fifteen thousand more adult salmon returning in 1997. In August 1997, NMFS scientists reported that they expect that salmon juveniles transported downriver in 1995 may wind up returning at rate of "about 2.3%, which is consistent with return rates observed prior to full Snake River hydropower development".[55]

Over the next couple of years, there is every reason to believe that the data will continue to show transportation works. Nevertheless, every state and tribal fishery agency in the Pacific Northwest continues to support *decreasing* the percentage of fish transported. In September 1997, Dr. Chapman warned that this position was "at best simply not consistent with the tenets of adaptive management"; "[t]o deliberately send smolts through the system to make a political point in support of dam breaching is, at worst, irresponsible, hypocritical, and criminal . . ."[56] Stephen Mealey, Director of the Idaho Department of Fish and Game, responded by asserting that the pro-transportation "perspective has been relegated to the fringe of scientific thought . . ."[57]

Ironically, as we engineer better and better dam passage for salmon, transportation *should* show less effectiveness—if dam passage is at all a significant source of mortality. Killing fewer fish in the river will make transportation look worse, because more untransported fish will return. The fact that transportation benefit ratios have remained roughly the same despite big changes in river operations seems to suggest, consistent with the evidence in Chapter 4, that expensive changes in dam operations don't even make a measurable difference for salmon survival.

NOTES TO CHAPTER 5

[1] Data from Table 7.2, ISG, *Return to the River* 330-31.

[2] W. McNeil, "Transport of Juvenile Salmonids to Increase Survival" (unpublished July 2, 1991 paper prepared for the Public Utility District of Grant County, Washington).

[3] *Id.*

[4] D. Chapman & A. Giorgi, "Comments on Work of Biological and FCRPS Alternative Work Groups", at 13 (1994).

[5] ISG, *Return to the River* 327.

[6] B. Rudolph, "Latest Survival Research Highlighted at IT Meeting", *NW Fishletter*, Nov. 11, 1997 (information attributed to "NMFS sources").

[7] "Barging of salmon debated", Eugene Register Guard, Nov. 24, 1995, p. 8. To give Mr. Bowler the benefit of the doubt, there is some chance that the reporter misquoted him.

[8] *See* ISG, *Return to the River* 304.

[9] C. Schreck *et al.*, "Evaluation of facilities for collection, bypass and transportation of outmigrating chinook salmon", Draft Annual Report for U.S. Army Corps of Engineers by Oregon Coop. Fish. Res. Unit, OSU (1994).

[10] D. Chapman & A. Giorgi, "Comments on NMFS Draft Biological Opinion on FCRPS Operations", at 12.

[11] ISG, *Return to the River* 328 (emphasis added).

[12] *Id.*

[13] *Id.* at 483 (citation omitted).

[14] J. Williams, G. Matthews & J. Myers, "The Columbia River Hydropower System: Does It Limit Recovery of Spring/Summer Chinook Salmon?", at 7; *see also* Memo, M. Schiewe to W. Stelle, Aug. 1, 1997, at 1 (dismissing several critiques of transportation as "unfounded" based on most recent data).

[15] Hinrichson *et al.* (1996).

[16] G. Easterbrook, *A Moment on the Earth* 165.

[17] Memorandum, Dr. Al Giorgi to NMFS, Feb. 24, 1993, at 3.

[18] ISG, *Return to the River* 328.

[19] Letter, D. Chapman to P. Barrow (PNUCC), Jan. 31, 1993, at 1.

[20] *Id.* at 2.

[21] *See, e.g., id.* at 9.

[22] *Id.* at 28.

[23] D. Park, "Public Testimony for Snake River Transportation Issues", Feb. 25, 1993.

[24] Letter, D. Bevan to U. Varanasi, April 25, 1996 (Draft).

[25] *NRIC v. NMFS*, slip op. at 6, No. 93-870-MA (D. Or. Dec. 22, 1993) (motion granted April 4, 1993)

[26] *NRIC v. NMFS*, 56 F.3d 1060 (9th Cir. 1995).

[27] *NRIC v. NMFS*, 56 F.3d 1060, 1069 (9th Cir. 1995).

[28] 40 C.F.R. 1508.25(a)(1).

[29] 40 C.F.R. 1508.8.

[30] *Douglas County v. Babbitt*, 48 F.3d 1495 (9th Cir. 1995), *cert. denied*, ___ U.S. ___.

[31] *Grindstone Butte Project v. Kleppe*, 638 F.2d 100 (9th Cir. 1981)

[32] *Douglas County*, 48 F.3d at 1508.

[33] NMFS, Biological Opinion on FCRPS Operations, Mar. 2, 1995, at 127 (RPA #25).

[34] NMFS, Biological Opinion on FCRPS Operations, Mar. 2, 1995, at 110.

[35] NRC, *Upstream* at 9 (Prepub. ed.)

[36] *Id.* at 206.

[37] *Id.* at 216.

[38] U.S. Army Corps of Engineers, "Interim Status Report", at 4-11.

[39] ISG, *Return to the River* 326.

[40] *Id.* at 62.

[41] *The Oregonian*, Oct. 1, 1996.

[42] Letter, B. Brown (NMFS) to Lt. Col. D. Curtis (USACE), Nov. 22, 1996, at 1.

[43] Letter, E. Furse & M. Crapo to R. Hardy *et al.*, Dec. 9, 1996, at 2.

[44] P. Batt, "State of the State Address", Jan. 6, 1997.

[45] Press Release, Mar. 27, 1997, and accompanying "Measures to Enhance Salmon and Steelhead Migration Success During 1997", at 3 (Idaho Governor's Office). Governor Batt was willing to allow half the fish to be transported, but only so long as flows in the Snake dropped below 100,000 cubic feet per second, which "Idaho does not anticipate" would happen during the spring migration period.

[46] W. McNeil, R. Gowan & R. Severson, "Offshore Release of Salmon Smolts", *American Fisheries Society Symposium* 10:548-553 (1991).

[47] M. Solazzi, T. Nichelson & S. Johnson, "Survival, contribution and return of hatchery coho salmon (*Onchorhynchus kisutch*) smolts", 37 Can. J. Fish. & Aquat. Sci. 765-69 (1991).

[48] Quoted in K. Petersen, *River of Life, Channel of Death* 186.

[49] Quoted in B. Rudolph, "Stelle Says Half the Fish Will Stay in Barges", *Clearing Up*, April 14, 1997, at 5.

[50] Quoted in B. Rudolph, "TMT Wrestles with Questions of Barging and Spill", *Clearing Up*, May 19, 1997, at 8.

[51] Draft TMT Meeting Minutes, Oct. 1, 1997, at 13 (http://www.npd-wc.usace.army.mil/TMT/1997/minutes/tmt1001.htm (downloaded 10/20/97)).

[52] *Id.*

[53] HARZA Consultants, "Salmon Decision Analysis Lower Snake River Feasibility Study Final Report", at 11-7.

[54] Testimony of Will Stelle, reported in W. Rudolph, "House Subcommittee Hears Testimony on Drawdowns", *Clearing Up*, June 9, 1997, at 6

[55] Memo, M. Schiewe to W. Stelle, Aug. 1, 1997, at 2.

[56] Letter, D. Chapman to Interested Parties, Sept. 4, 1997.

[57] Quoted in B. Rudolph, "Debate Heats Up After Consultant Calls for More Barging", *Clearing Up*, Nov. 14, 1997, at 9.

CHAPTER 6: THE HATCHERY MACHINE AND ITS POTENTIAL

"The vast volume of fresh water coming down the Columbia will make it almost impossible ever to pollute it sufficiently to drive away the salmon, and it is hardly possible that civilization will ever crowd its banks to an extent that will endanger that [salmon] industry, so I suppose it is safe to say that Columbia-river salmon will always continue to be a choice dish in all parts of the world. Of course, the increasing demand for fish and growing scarcity of the same will call for more aid toward artificial propagation in order to keep up the supply." W. A. Wilcox (1896).[1]

". . . the several fishery agencies have made good progress toward the objectives that have been established in the past. Losses have been replaced to a surprising degree, entirely new runs have been started in barren drainages, and vigorous fisheries are still being established. The fishery agencies are gradually developing better methods of producing fish in hatcheries." F. Cleaver (1976).[2]

"If restoring the fishery is the goal, then revamped hatcheries could perform a useful role. But if the goal is saving wild fish, then most of the scientific evidence points toward weaning ourselves out of the hatchery business, not expanding it". Editorial, *The Oregonian*, Jan. 7, 1997.

The current salmon "crisis" is in great measure the result of a rising tension between the goal of putting more fish in the rivers vs. putting wild fish in the rivers. Hatcheries can put more fish in the rivers, but then fishermen catch them along with less productive wild stocks, and inevitably extinguish wild stocks. The Pacific Northwest needs to make a choice between more fish and wild fish, but instead, politicians are promoting yet another component of the Great Salmon Hoax: we can have our salmon, and eat them too.

This is an issue that may someday split the environmentalists from the harvest agencies and their fishermen allies. Right now, environmentalists write law review articles about the vices of hatcheries,[3] and gradually gain ground in fishery agencies as more and more policies are promoted to protect the genetic purity of wild fish from hatchery miscegenation. Ultimately, the fishing interests may wake up and regret their alliance with the environmentalists, because there might be a backlash against enormously expensive wild fish programs that don't put more fish in the rivers.

Given all the factors working against salmon, there is probably no way to get significant numbers of salmon into the Columbia River Basin without extensive hatchery operations. After all, four-fifths of the adult salmon returning to the Columbia River now are hatchery fish.[4] Many people think of this as a recent development, but hatcheries have been supplanting natural production for a very long time. As early as 1898, 26 million salmon fry were being released from hatcheries in the Columbia River Basin each year.[5] The August 1905 issue of *Pacific Fisherman* reported that: "There seems no question but that 75 percent of the salmon entering the river are directly attributable to artificial production."[6] This claim may be inflated, but by the 1920s, annual hatchery releases approached 100 million per year.[7] Throughout the 1980s and 1990s, hatchery production has hovered around 200 million per year.[8]

Most people who think that we can shut down hatcheries and restore "wild" salmon naturally don't understand that much of what they are trying to restore has been gone since the turn of the century. Generally speaking, with the possible exception of strong or recoverable natural runs, it seems more practical to try and get the hatcheries working again. Competent harvest and hatchery management could accomplish this.

The Early Promise of Hatcheries

The architects of the early dams that blocked off access to salmon habitat hoped to maintain the promise of salmon in the river with salmon hatcheries. Biologists carefully captured salmon at the Grand Coulee Dam, and using a fish hatchery at Leavenworth, Washington, the race was transplanted widely below the Dam. Contemporary accounts report the scale of the federal government's efforts: in 1941 the program cost $3,510,000, involving specially-built tank trucks cooled with cracked ice.[9]

In 1938, Congress passed the Mitchell Act, which was, according to the House Committee Report, "to take care of situations in the salmon industry which arise from the construction of certain government works and particularly from the building of the Bonneville Dam across the Columbia River, near Portland . . ."[10] In 1947, water development and fisheries agencies formed the Lower Columbia River Fisheries Development Program to plan and coordinate the use of Mitchell Act funds.

The initial focus was on downriver hatcheries and only the states of Oregon and Washington were involved. Mitchell Act funding built and operated 25 salmon and steelhead hatcheries, 23 of which were located in the

132

Lower Columbia River. The Act also funded the construction of 45 fishways (ladders) throughout the Columbia River Basin and the screening of over 800 irrigation diversions.[11]

In 1956, Congress directed the Interior Department, administering the Program, to develop fishery resources above McNary Dam. The word "Lower" was dropped, so that the effort became known as the Columbia River Fisheries Development Program.[12]

When the Corps of Engineers constructed the four lower Snake Dams, they commissioned a review by University of Washington Professor Ernest Salo, who reported that the dams would ultimately cause the loss of 134,500 salmon and steelhead annually.[13] Consistent with modern practice, Dr. Salo did not make any truly scientific estimate of the losses to be expected from the projects. Instead, he used a 15% loss per project figure which was, he said, "generally accepted" by "agreement among all parties".[14] As we have seen, these losses significantly overstate current losses.

The Lower Snake River Compensation Plan was designed to mitigate for the estimated losses by releasing some 26,701,600 additional hatchery juvenile salmon and steelhead annually.[15] If only 1/2 of one percent of those hatchery fish returned, the adverse effects of the dams would presumably be fully mitigated. Most years, that goal has been (or could, with competent hatchery management, be) achieved. When it couldn't, as in the case of poor ocean conditions, natural runs would not have been that large anyway.

By 1978, National Marine Fisheries Service research biologist Howard Raymond suggested that hatcheries offered the only hope for improved upriver runs of anadromous fish in the Columbia River Basin. He advised that "[e]ven with improved downstream survival, it is doubtful that these [upriver] stocks will ever return to their former levels", but "[w]ith improved rearing techniques, hatcheries should provide an even greater contribution to the total run than is presently indicated . . ."[16]

Areas where salmon no longer can pass upriver can *only* rely on hatcheries to return large numbers of salmon to the immediate vicinity. Elsewhere, many, many factors have combined to degrade salmon habitat, including logging, mining, and irrigation. Many federal and state regulations are now in place to halt further degradation, many of which range far beyond what is actually needed to protect salmon habitat.

But some changes in habitat may take hundreds of years to undo, and regulation cannot turn back the clock. For example, some biologists believe that some salmon, particularly coho, find beaver ponds create useful habitat.[17]

With the decline of beaver in the Pacific Northwest as a result of intensive trapping beginning in the mid-1800s,[18] such habitat cannot be restored simply by banning logging.

As noted above, historical numbers of salmon and steelhead returning to the Columbia River have remained at high levels since 1937, when Bonneville Dam was constructed.

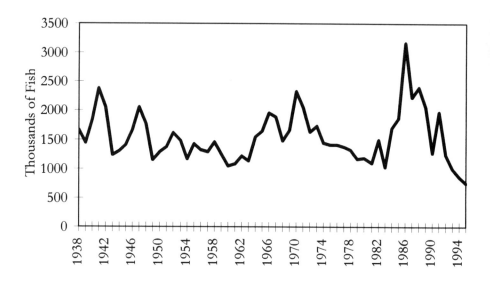

Figure 16: Salmon and Steelhead Returning to the Columbia River[19]

Note that the all time high count was reached fifty years after dam construction began.

The hatcheries did not just produce fish returning to the river. They fueled huge ocean harvests. As we have seen, as late as the 1970s, the hatchery program was a success and the Basin was still producing more than *ninety* percent of the 1880-1930 average catch despite the drastic reduction in available spawning grounds.

For years this represented the great achievement of hatcheries: as eight dams were put in the path of migrating salmon, and available habitat shrank, returns remained roughly constant. So long as natural conditions remained favorable, the hatcheries could offset the loss of freshwater habitat. Even harsh critics of hatcheries, like the Northwest Power Planning Council's Independent Science Group, admit that "[f]rom a cursory examination of the overall numbers, it could be argued that in recent decades the hatchery program has accomplished its objective . . ."[20] To critics, however, the program is a failure because it has not prevented the depletion of natural populations, and has probably hastened their decline.

Most dissatisfaction came, however, because a far higher percentage of the catch was now in the ocean, so that fewer fish were available for commercial harvest in the river. And upriver interests were also dissatisfied, because, as the Northwest Power Planning Council staff concluded in 1986, a "dramatic effect of mitigation activities for hydropower and for multipurpose developments has been to strengthen fish propagation in the lower Columbia River Basin without attempting to rebuild upriver runs."[21]

By the 1990s, as we have seen, many factors had turned against the salmon, including bad weather, the rise of natural predators, and overfishing. Just as transportation was proclaimed a failure for failing to offset these factors, so too have hatcheries—as another technological solution—come under attack.

Conservation biologist Jim Lichatowich, echoing the simplistic attack on smolt transportation, sums up the politically-correct view of hatcheries: "The only way you can look at the situation in the Columbia River right now is to point out that the status quo hasn't worked. Hatcheries have been a major part of the status quo for 120 years."[22] By that standard, water pollution laws, stream restoration efforts, and flow manipulation should all be tossed on the ash heap of failed recovery measures, as parts of a status quo that hasn't worked.

Writer Joseph Cone aptly summarizes another environmentalist view of hatcheries:

> "Faced with abundance, most people didn't recognize a need for moderation. They didn't recognize the inevitability of limits. When the abundance was clearly disappearing, their response was not to change their behavior. Instead, unequipped to struggle within themselves, they fought each other harder and looked outside themselves for a solution. Hatcheries became popular."[23]

But most people don't recognize "the inevitability of limits". The "limits to growth" theorists have been proven wrong again and again, ever since Malthus invented the theory hundreds of years ago.

We can choose to abandon hatcheries, concentrate human populations in urban areas, and de-populate rural areas in the service of Nature and natural river restoration. But the choice won't be made because of "limits". It will be an aesthetic judgment that it is more important to protect remnant wild salmon stocks than to have lots of hatchery salmon.

The "Soft Underbelly" of Hatchery Mismanagement: Bad Breeding Techniques

> "It is far too common a practice for farmers to cross the stock of two herds. . . . All stock breeders should keep pure-bred animals. Each breed has been produced because the animals are best for some particular purpose. The breeder should determine what his purpose is and then choose the proper pure breed for that purpose. The animals of that breed are sure to be more satisfactory than any cross breeds or grades. Pure-bred animals have fixed characteristics and may be expected to come *true to type*. The superior qualities of the parents will be found in the offspring." Dr. Kary Davis, *Productive Farming* (1917).

What ordinary farmers have known since the turn of the century, government fish breeders have been slow to recognize. Bill Bakke, the founder and former leader of Oregon Trout, refers to hatchery operations as the "soft underbelly" of fishery management. The bureaucrats running the hatcheries made a lot of mistakes. Most were mistakes that animal breeders dealing with other species have known not to make for decades.

No attempts were made to keep track of the genetic history—bloodlines—of hatchery releases. Eggs from one hatchery were moved to another hatchery willy-nilly, with no documented regard for preserving existing runs. Anyone who has ever gotten involved with purebred dogs or horses or any animal knows that the first things the breeders worry about are the ancestors, and they keep a careful record of those ancestors.

Not coincidentally, some of the largest-scale and poorest hatchery practices occurred in areas where salmon are now in the worst shape: the Middle Snake River and its tributaries. In the Snake River Basin hatchery releases grew from 1-2 million per year in the 1960s and 1970s to over 20 million in the late 1980s and early 1990s. The Rapid River hatchery,

136

constructed by Idaho Power Co. to mitigate for the effects of the Hell's Canyon Complex, used spring chinook broodstock whose spawning grounds were above the Complex.[24] While those stocks were at least from the same river basin, biologists question whether their life history was compatible with wild stocks in the lower Snake.[25]

In addition, hatchery operators in the Snake River Basin also imported eggs from many other stocks outside the Snake River Basin, including the Carson, Klickitat, Cowlitz, Leavenworth, Marion Forks and South Santiam stocks from west of the Cascade Mountains.[26] Studies have demonstrated that the genetic structure of "native" Snake River stocks in some streams, like Catherine Creek, now resembles the imported stocks more than native stocks.[27] Thus many Snake River spring chinook now protected as endangered on account of their valuable genetic structure are in fact mongrels.

State and tribal hatchery operators would use sperm from one captured male to fertilize eggs from literally dozens of females. In nature, the practice is just the opposite, where more than one male frequently fertilizes the eggs of a single female.[28] Culls from the hatchery tanks, often unfit or diseased, were released to the streams.[29]

Worse still, bacterial kidney disease (BKD) was pandemic among hatchery salmon. Many biologists believe that the disease was transferred from hatchery to wild stocks. Juvenile salmon with BKD may have significantly lower survival rates, dying salmon slowly over a period of one to three months.[30] In a 1988 review of the effects of dams and hatcheries on Columbia Basin salmon and steelhead, Howard Raymond of the National Marine Fisheries Service asked:

> "Why the poor returns of hatchery fish when downriver survival from the Snake River has improved in recent years? I suspect the major problem is mortality of hatchery fish from bacterial kidney disease (BKD) either during migrations through dam complex, or, more likely, shortly after entry into the ocean."[31]

While Raymond speculated that dam passage exacerbated the effects of BKD, no one has any solid documentation of such an effect.

After nearly two decades, fishery managers have finally learned how to control BKD, pasteurizing the ground-up fish they served to juveniles in the tanks. Anecdotal accounts suggest that by the mid-1990s, outbreaks of the disease are less prevalent. However, BKD may now be pandemic among hatchery fish—like the common cold among humans. Unless and until salmon populations evolve resistance to BKD, losses from BKD may continue to bar the achievement of historic return rates.

Nearly all hatcheries tried to cut costs by speeding the growth of the juvenile salmon and releasing them earlier. At least one writer has speculated that this "tends to make the succeeding stages of their life correspondingly brief, and means that they weigh less at maturity than wild salmon", but I have seen no scientific evidence of this phenomenon.[32] There are a number of studies that show that hatchery fish show poorer growth after release, but that is largely because they have been fed for many months and have some trouble learning to hunt for themselves.

Indeed, the longstanding feeding method at many hatcheries was to fling the food by hand into the tanks. The juvenile salmon learned to associate the shadow of the hatchery worker with food, and rise to the surface. Out in the river, when attacked by birds, that is a fatal instinct. There is also evidence that hatchery juveniles don't get the idea that they should wander out to shallow areas to find food while migrating downstream.[33]

The poor biological practices at hatcheries went hand in hand with poor management practices. But as science gradually promoted improvements in biological practices, government gradually promoted decay in management practices.

The Effectiveness and Costs of Hatcheries

The basic management flaw was (and is) in measuring hatchery success in "pounds of product" where product was defined as smolts released alive into the river. But the mission of hatcheries is to produce harvestable adults. Success in that endeavor depends not only upon the pounds of smolts, but also their quality, and how, when and where they are released.

Only rarely did fishery managers attempt to figure out whether hatcheries were succeeding in their basic mission. A series of cost-benefit studies conducted on fall chinook releases from 1961 to 1964 showed cost-benefit ratios ranging from 2:1 to 7.2:1.[34] Another evaluation based on releases from 1978 to 1982 showed a cost-benefit ratio of 5.7:1.[35] Average survival (or percentage of returning adults) had fallen from 0.7 percent to 0.33 percent, but no one paid much attention to that problem.

By the 1980s, assessing the effectiveness of hatcheries was all but taboo among fishery managers. When Reagan's Office of Management and Budget began an effort to remove Mitchell Act hatchery funding through appropriations and substitute Bonneville Power Administration funding through surcharges on electricity (an effort started by the Nixon OMB in 1973), someone mailed our clients an anonymous assessment of the Mitchell Act hatcheries.

It reported that by the late 1980s funding for the Mitchell Act hatcheries was running in the $7-8 million range. The hatcheries were producing over 100 million smolts annually. From 1973 to 1987, the cost per pound of smolts produced ranged from $2.03 to $3.04. The report did not provide the cost per harvestable adult, but if 1% of the smolts had survived to harvest, the cost would have been $7-8 per fish—still a bargain by today's standards.

There has been little oversight of Mitchell Act and most other hatchery spending. In 1996, Bonneville engaged a consultant to audit hatchery operations, producing comprehensive reports on many of the hatcheries in the Columbia River Basin. But the reports are marred by the lack of the most basic data needed to assess effectiveness; what data are available suggests that the cost per fish has risen substantially. By my calculation, we spent $51 per adult for Bonneville Hatchery fall chinook and $273 per fish for Rapid River Hatchery spring chinook for a few years of releases in the late 1980s; no data is available since then.[36]

Some of these hatcheries have had years in which none of their fish were recovered in fisheries at all. The worst upriver spring chinook hatcheries appear to be spending over a thousand dollars per harvested adult salmon. There is no government report, anywhere, which presents the cost hatcheries per returning adult salmon for all hatcheries in the Columbia River Basin.

Professor Ray Hilborn of the University of Washington recently analyzed the effectiveness, in terms of returning adults, of hatcheries in the Columbia River Basin. Since hatcheries often produce more than one salmon stock, he divided his analysis between fall chinook production and spring chinook production.

Professor Ray Hilborn's data, presented in Chapter 4, show the huge variation in the effectiveness of hatcheries. Some hatcheries are consistently more effective. For example, somebody should take a closer look at the Shuswap Hatchery on the Fraser River to see what its managers are doing right. Unfortunately, fishery managers have made no effort to distinguish the hatcheries that work from hatcheries that don't, and the most inefficient Snake River hatcheries remain in operation.

Many Northwest salmon decisionmakers will admit, in private, that running failing hatcheries no longer makes economic sense. But they do nothing in public, because of the political imperative to produce salmon. The fishery managers have no incentive to make these hatcheries work. As hatchery opponent Bruce Brown pointed out in 1982, "[f]or government agencies with resource responsibility, allowing the degradation of wild salmon has been a self-fulfilling prophesy of greater hatchery production, expanding budgetary allocations and increased agency power".[37]

By 1996, hatcheries have come under so much criticism that but for their pork barrel attributes, they probably would have failed to secure funding in Congress. The Clinton/Gore Administration has continued to try on several occasions to eliminate Mitchell Act funding, in favor of sticking the Bonneville Power Administration with the bill.

The biggest push in hatchery management right now is to move more production upriver. Driven by tribal demands and increased pressure from upriver interests on the Northwest Power Planning Council, BPA has been spending more and more money on hatcheries:

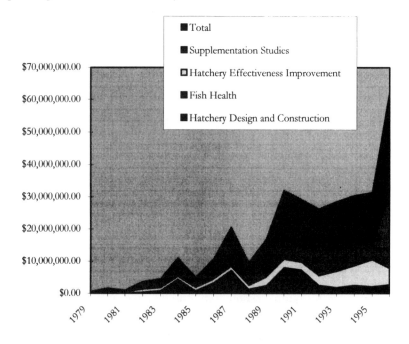

Figure 17: BPA Hatchery and Hatchery-Related Spending[38]

The fish produced at these hatcheries will be some of the most expensive animals ever raised in captivity. With this much money, we could start captive breeding programs for dozens of truly endangered species.

One of the reasons spending is rising so fast is that politicians are pursuing inherently conflicting objectives. In directing expansion of upriver hatcheries, Congress "emphasize[d] that only projects which protect, maintain or enhance biological diversity of existing wild salmon stocks should be pursued".[39] As the U.S. Army Corps of Engineers noted, Congress' direction had an inherent "conflict", in that to "initiate hatchery construction projects" would not "increase the biodiversity of the listed [endangered Snake River salmon] stocks".[40]

The concept of cost benefit analysis has begun to lose all meaning, because no one can measure the benefits of making fish more "wild". Instead, we assume that this is of incalculable value, and spend immense sums of money building hatcheries that are supposed to make "wild" fish. When the U.S. Army Corps of Engineers first proposed the Lower Snake River Compensation Plan, they reported that they expected to pay $46,000,000, with operation and maintenance costs of $3,000,000, for a benefit to cost ratio of two-to-one.[41] Twenty-one years later, they reported having spent $215,696,000, with an estimate of $268,288,000 to complete the project, since the Corps has only completed five of nine hatcheries.[42] Contrary to the Corps' own regulations, its 1996 progress report does not even mention benefits—other than to report on the poundage of smolts produced at the hatcheries. There is no cost-benefit analysis whatsoever.

The Wild v. Hatchery Choice: How Much Diversity Do We Really Need?

Most people think that the Endangered Species Act was written in such absolute terms because it was meant to protect the very last few members of a species. Probably the members of Congress who voted for the Act thought that was what they were doing. If there were just a few sockeye or chinook salmon left in the world, the Act's provisions would make a lot of sense.

The provisions are draconian, as befits an act to save the last few members of a species. For example, once the government designates "critical habitat" for the salmon, no "adverse modification" of that habitat is supposed to be allowed. What is "adverse modification"? Environmentalists argue that *any* change in the habitat that interferes with the salmon should be a prohibited "adverse modification".

Activities that "jeopardize" the salmon are not allowed to go forward either. "Jeopardize" means whatever federal regulators want it to mean. The most significant salmon case yet decided by the courts, described in Chapter 9, affirmed the National Marine Fisheries Services' assertion that a plan that *improved* salmon survival "jeopardized" the salmon. While we persuaded a higher court to vacate that opinion, the federal agencies continue to act as if improving salmon survival through agency action is not enough to comply with § 7 of the Endangered Species Act.

But if salmon hatcheries were evaluated under the same legal standards as logging or running hydroelectric dams, they would probably be closed by application of the Endangered Species Act. There is mounting evidence that hatchery fish compete with wild fish for food and space. Studies have found that when hatchery fish are released in a stream, they tend to displace the wild fish, sometimes even "residualizing" and remaining in the stream without migrating.[43] Hatchery-released juveniles tend to be larger than wild juveniles, and comparatively more vulnerable to predators.

Biologists think that flooding rivers with hatchery juveniles may increase predation on wild stocks, causing an adverse effect on wild juveniles. Large steelhead smolts released from hatcheries even eat smaller chinook smolts. Many writers have observed that hatchery coho "bred and reared to attain larger size by the time of release can swamp a stream system and displace the smaller (and more fit) wild coho".[44] The National Marine Fisheries Service even declared lower Columbia River coho extinct in part because of past hatchery operations.

One question that the citizens of the Pacific Northwest ought to be facing is: do we want all this absolute protection for every single river with salmon in it, or do we want more rivers full of salmon? People who have weaker stocks of salmon (upriver interests) think we need near absolute prohibitions on development. People with big hatchery operations (lower river states and tribes) want to continue running their hatcheries.

Somebody needs to look at the larger picture. When protecting one creek of salmon causes repercussions all the way to Alaska, somebody needs to think about whether this makes sense. Nobody does. We continue to apply absolutist protections that can never recover upriver runs, while maintaining huge hatchery operations that continue to extinguish wild stocks given continued heavy harvests.

At the moment, the world is swimming in salmon. There is a glut of salmon in Alaska, with salmon prices plunging. There are salmon farms in Norway that flood the market with chinook salmon, being the best species to eat. Today, four out of ten salmon sold are raised in farms.[45] By the summer of 1996, prices for pink salmon seined in the coves and inlets of Southeast Alaska were sinking to record lows of 10 to 14¢ per pound.[46] By the fall of 1996, wholesalers in Portland, Oregon were offering 30¢ a pound for Columbia River chinook salmon, 20¢ a pound for steelhead, and 10¢ a pound for "tule" stock (fall chinook salmon).[47]

Only a few public figures have had the courage to point out the irony of this situation, and they have all been vilified for it. During her campaign for office, Idaho Representative Helen Chenoweth held up cans of salmon and had salmon bakes to point out the problem, and now faces students who ridicule her rallies by throwing cans at the podium and bumper stickers that say "can Helen, not salmon". Washington Senator Slade Gorton, who was identified as supporting the idea of getting more salmon in the rivers but abandoning efforts to save particularly weak stocks, continues to be the subject of hostile pieces in the media.

The Indian tribes believe that NMFS has gone overboard in its attempts to preserve each and every salmon population as inviolate. They complain that "NMFS is insisting on the reproductive isolation of Snake River salmon, which can easily lead to inbreeding and the loss of genetic diversity within those populations . . ."[48] Ted Strong, the Executive Director of the Columbia River Inter-Tribal Fish Commission, has even come out against listing additional anadromous fish species under the Endangered Species Act. "The tribes fully expect that NMFS will use this action [a proposed listing of mid-Columbia steelhead] to keep the tribes from putting fish in the river."[49]

Professor Ernest Brannon of the University of Idaho's Aquaculture Research Institute has observed that the Northwest Power Planning Council's Independent Science Group has no expert in aquaculture science and worries that "the valuable role hatcheries can play in the Columbia Basin can easily be under-rated or even ignored".[50] He wrote the Independent Science Group with evidence of the potential for success with hatcheries, warning that "[w]ithout the same intense attention given to aquaculture science that each of you give to your own disciplines, opinions can easily follow the popular view espoused by most biologists familiar primarily with just the failures."[51]

In other words, if you hire ecologists and conservation biologists to tell you how to recover salmon, they'll tell you to take out dams. If you hire aquaculture experts, they'll tell you you can grow the fish. Ordinary people know something is fishy about the sudden attack on hatcheries. As one told me, "I don't understand it. We breed salmon in hatcheries and cows in farms. Nobody worries about endangered cows."

A Breeder's Approach to Hatcheries

Bruce Brown's *Mountain in the Clouds* contains one of the most extensive collections of history relating to hatchery operations. There are no really comprehensive efforts. He recounts the story of Ernie Brannon's work running a hatchery on the Elwha River on the Olympic Penninsula in Washington state. "Brannon thought he was practicing 'selective breeding' to create a large hatchery fish, but in fact he was draining off the last of the *tyee* for no proven gain."[52] But the reason no gain was proven is that Brannon worked in isolation, and the work was never adequately documented. Brannon's viewpoint—that the chinook breed could be improved—was never adopted as official policy by the state of Washington. Indeed, today, under the outspoken leadership of Bernard Shanks, the state purports to be against hatcheries even as it operates them.

But as one fishery biologist observed in 1976, "[g]enetics have played an important role in developing superior strains of plants and animals basically suited to changing environments, and why not use these principles for fish?"[53] He pointed out successful efforts with genetic culling of steelhead at Skamania Hatchery over many years. Nearly twenty years ago, renowned Canadian fish biologist W. E. Ricker recommended that hatcheries should breed selectively from larger and older fish to offset the effects of overfishing.[54]

Another pioneer whose efforts are recounted by Mr. Brown was Lauren Donaldson, a University of Washington professor who wanted to breed fish that could survive in urban environments. According to Mr. Brown,

> "By the mid-1950s, he had established a small run of Chinook
> and steelhead that were larger for their age than anything that
> had ever been observed in the wilds. The result of systematic
> selective breeding, Donaldson's fish were thick bodied and
> extremely fecund (one rainbow produced more than 23,000
> eggs, more than twenty times the number a wild fish could
> carry in one spawning). His fish were shorter lived and
> smaller at maturity than wild fish (which reach forty-five
> pounds and live as long as nine years), but when he laid one of
> his two-year-old fish weighing ten pounds out on the campus
> grass next to a wild fish of the same age weighing a few
> ounces, who could doubt that man had bettered nature?"[55]

Modern biologists, blind to the possibility of breeding salmon, disparage Donaldson's work as merely proving that fish that were fed more would grow faster, but they ignore the solid evolutionary foundation for Donaldson's work.

144

Past selective breeding efforts in hatcheries were narrowly focused on the short-term interests of the hatchery managers. First and foremost, the selective breeding was to enhance survival in the hatcheries rather than throughout the whole life cycle, focusing on fast growth and ease of production. As one writer explained, "[t]he most successful fish in hatcheries are those that are tolerant of crowding, learn to swim toward mechanical or human feeders at the right times, and can outcompete other fish in the pursuit of pelletized food".[56]

But there is no reason that hatchery managers cannot focus on a more advanced measure of "fitness": survival over the entire life cycle, not just to the point of release. The simple device of giving hatchery managers their performance evaluations based on adult returns might accomplish more than any other single means of improving salmon hatcheries.

We can breed salmon just like we breed cows. Even the harshest critics of hatcheries acknowledge that "inbreeding, genetic drift, hybridization and competition can be drastically reduced if proper guidelines are adopted".[57] A letter to the Editor of the Capital Press put it in simpler terms: "Is the Fish and Game [Department] saying that their biologists can't raise anything but genetically inferior fish? If so, then maybe we ought to get some 14-year-old farm child to guide them through a genetics course."[58]

It is probably true that if we don't take care to preserve an adequate genetic diversity among hatchery stocks, we run the risk of losing the whole population to unexpected problems. The classic example is a disease that wipes out every hatchery stock, while certain wild strains, had they not gone extinct, might have survived.

Of course, there are far greater threats to the human race from losses in genetic diversity than arise from salmon breeding. There is less genetic diversity in the plant species like corn, wheat and rice that form our basic food supply than in salmon, yet society is unwilling to make the investment to preserve every distinct population segment of those species.

In the long run, genetic engineering techniques may offer the ability to give salmon greater resistance against parasites, warm water, and other factors limiting salmon production. Scientists in Norway, coping with the problem of water that is too cold, are already attempting to put the cold-resistant genes of winter flounder into Atlantic salmon.[59]

Some sportsfishers say they can tell the difference between hatchery-raised and naturally-spawning salmon (or more often, steelhead) as soon as they are hooked. It may well be true that even after four years out in the ocean, hatchery salmon are not as "wild" as wild salmon. These are subtle differences, however, and all but a tiny minority of purists would find excitement in hooking a forty-pound hatchery chinook salmon in the Columbia River.

The overwhelming "problem" with hatcheries is political, not scientific. As Gregg Easterbrook has explained:

> "Environmental orthodoxy rejects hybridization of species as a horrifying offense against nature, though in nature hybridization has been ongoing since the beginning of life, being essential to the system by which species radiate into new forms. Here is the Stop-in-Place Fallacy at work—a conceit that somehow on the day when the Endangered Species Act was signed a Correct global alignment of habitat and species was in effect, and any change after that must be seen as ghastly . . .

> "It's disquieting to hear some environmentalists go on without a hint of irony about how 'locally distinct populations' must have their 'unique genetic ecotypes' preserved against 'non-native populations' encroaching at the border. How can racial barriers be awful for humankind and vital for animals? To nature this entire line of thought must seem detached from reality. Genes constantly mingle in nature. That's part of the point of the enterprise."[60]

In other words, laws against miscegenation, and in favor of apartheid, anathema to liberals everywhere, are the cornerstone of environmental orthodoxy.

But for the fact that the harvest managers reject this aspect of environmental orthodoxy (and properly so), they would have voluntarily shut down salmon hatcheries. And if the environmentalists weren't taking money from the harvesters, lawsuits under the Endangered Species Act probably would have forced the shut down of hatcheries.

Some among the tribes, more connected to the land, recognize that salmon "farming" with hatcheries makes sense as a relationship between humans, salmon, and the Pacific Northwest. They believe they can operate hatcheries that will bring runs of salmon back to the river for tribal harvesters. They might have trouble competing with fish farmers who raise salmon in pens, but their salmon would probably be a tastier product. As of 1997, the Northwest Power Planning Council, relying on the advice of its Independent

146

Science Group (re-christened the Independent Science Advisory Board) has told the Bonneville Power Administration to defer millions of dollars of funding to the tribes hoping to do this.

The Problem of Carrying Capacity

A potentially serious problem with the hatchery solution is that all the salmon are sent to the same pasture: the North Pacific Ocean. To the extent that the pasture is getting overgrazed, the more new hatcheries we build, the fewer salmon will come back. And it is not just the ocean that may have limits to carrying capacity; some biologists believe that the draining and diking of the Columbia River estuary may have created a "bottle-neck to production" there.[61]

The facts are surprising. It has been estimated that during the historic peaks of salmon production in the 1850s, approximately 264 million salmon smolts were produced in the Columbia River Basin.[62] While this is probably an overestimate, until very recently, we producing even more salmon smolts every year, mostly in Columbia Basin hatcheries. As the Corps of Engineers recently observed:

> "Based on hatchery releases of nearly 203 million fish, and an estimated 145 million naturally-produced fish, a total of nearly 348 million salmonid smolts were present in the Basin in 1990. This is 32 percent above estimated smolt production numbers prior to 1850, yet adult returns remain low."[63]

There was some truth to environmentalist historian Keith Petersen's charge that "Dam-fodder smolts became official government policy."[64] As the Lower Snake River Compensation Program and other efforts got underway in the late 1960s and early 1970s, dams were killing a lot of juvenile salmon, mostly because of gas supersaturation and other construction-related problems that were later solved.

But after survival problems were fixed at the dams, hatchery production and harvest levels remained very high, inevitably wiping out less-productive wild runs. The hatchery smolts survived their migrations and probably reached the ocean in greater-than-historic numbers. As hatcheries raced to "mitigate" overestimated dam losses with higher and higher production, harvest levels set based on hatchery output not only weeded out wild runs, but also less productive upriver hatcheries.

As adult returns to the hatcheries began to drop, hatchery managers responded by pumping out more and more smolts. They are unwilling to do what farmers putting too many sheep on a pasture must do: take some of the sheep off. By the 1990s, it seemed possible that the river, the estuary, and even the North Pacific Ocean might all be overgrazed, but nobody was was willing to do anything about it.

Biologists are beginning to recognize that to understand the effect of changes in dam operations on salmon populations, we need to understand the whole ecosystem used by salmon, including the freshwater and saltwater components. The saltwater component, the ocean, has until recently been a black box. No one really knew what happened in the ocean. Massive hatchery releases in the ocean could actually reduce adult returns.[65] The National Marine Fisheries Service did call for BPA to fund studies of this phenomenon in 1995, but the states and tribes de-prioritized the research.

Thus it is unknown whether it is even possible to increase salmon given such carrying capacity constraints.[66] The Northwest Power Planning Council's Independent Science Group has suggested that it is "speculative" and that there is "little empirical support" for the idea that the salmon bearing ecosystem in the Pacific Northwest and Northeast Pacific Ocean has considerable excess carrying capacity.[67]

Carrying capacity is not just a problem with building hatcheries. *It is a problem with any means used to increase the survival of juvenile salmon.* The possibility that we have already gotten enough smolts downriver alive to exceed carrying capacity means that the idea that we can significantly increase salmon production in the Columbia River Basin above present levels *at all* is inherently speculative. Our only hope for having more salmon in the river may be to limit adult harvest in the ocean.

Improving Hatchery Management

It has long been obvious to all the fisheries managers that more coordination of hatchery operations was necessary. In 1993, they began a comprehensive review, called the Comprehensive Environmental Assessment, which was supposed to look at the global impacts of hatcheries on the Columbia River Basin. The review was also supposed to document compliance with the National Environmental Policy Act.

National Marine Fisheries Service representatives now say (privately) that the Fish and Wildlife Service people "hijacked" the Comprehensive Environmental Assessment. In the Northwest, the Portland, Oregon office of the U.S. Fish and Wildlife Service has traditionally allied with state and tribal agencies against the National Marine Fisheries Service Regional office in Seattle.

In December 1996, the hijacked product was released as a draft programmatic environmental impact statement (DPEIS) called "Impacts of Artificial Salmon and Steelhead Production Strategies in the Columbia River Basin". The authors, anonymous representatives of the Columbia Basin Fish and Wildlife Authority, adopted a clever strategy to downplay the significance of hatcheries: they proclaimed that the study "is limited in scope to the *mainstem migration corridor*".[68] Jim Lichatowich correctly observed that "by limiting their scope to the mainstem, it appears that they define away the problem. Most of the problem is in the tributaries or the ocean fisheries".[69]

Thus the authors proclaimed that their review of the scientific literature found "no explicit evidence of adverse effects caused by hatcheries in the Columbia River migration corridor (with the exception of impacts on weak stocks in mixed-stock harvests)."[70] The conclusion that there was no direct evidence that hatcheries undermined the health of wild fish in the Columbia Basin was sufficiently counter to the mass of evidence that it even triggered adverse media comment.[71]

The authors of the DPEIS know that high hatchery output fueling high harvests inevitably wipes out weaker stocks, including the endangered Snake River salmon. Their "preferred action" to improve hatchery operations does nothing about it, and includes "[l]imiting overall basinwide production to current levels or very small increases".[72] The DPEIS is a remarkable document in that it lacks the most basic supporting data that would be necessary to draw conclusions about the impacts of hatcheries. Nowhere does it contain a complete history of hatchery releases, or an explanation of what was supposed to have been accomplished by those releases, and what success the hatchery program has enjoyed in the past.

That is because the fishery managers have never bothered to collect the data in many cases, and certainly never to summarize it in any useful fashion. No one makes them do it; everyone relies on their assertions that the problems with salmon production lie elsewhere.

NMFS currently advocates releasing hatchery smolts into the river to "supplement" natural populations. The term "supplement" has no precise definition. Apparently, under the "supplementation" approach, hatcheries are to be used to restock natural streams, with hatchery releases to be phased out once the natural production gets going.

But "much hope is being placed in a concept that remains to be tested and proven each time it is applied".[73] There have only been a few attempts to use supplementation, and it was "rarely successful in increasing natural production".[74] A review by the U.S. Fish and Wildlife Service of 300

149

"supplementation" projects found that "only a few were successful at increasing existing natural runs".[75] Other conclusions of the Service included: "successes were primarily for returning adult fish to harvest; supplementation adversely affects wild stocks; chinook salmon are one of the most difficult species to supplement; and supplementation works better for fish stocks having a shorter run to the ocean".[76] In short, supplementation projects seem to have all the characteristics of hatchery projects generally, except the bad name.

By early 1997, the Northwest media was so hostile to hatcheries that *The Oregonian* editorialized that "we wonder why state and federal agencies and Indian tribes are still fooling around with the notion that hatcheries can still rebuild the wild runs".[77]

Supplementation might work if we pay very careful attention to the question of spawning habitat, including artificial improvement to spawning habitat. Hatchery technology coupled with spawning channels has been very successful in building sockeye runs in Canada, for example.[78] But releasing a batch of smolts and hoping that they come back and spawn in the river is like a farmer throwing some seed out in the field and hoping for crops. The farmer will do much better if he or she prepares the ground first.

Hatchery programs are also never going to work unless and until the hatchery operators adopt the attitudes and practices of other breeders of animals. Through careful selection of parents, breeders of pigeons, dogs and even goldfish have been able to shape not only the bodies of these animals but also, in the case of the dogs, their very instincts. Darwin became a pigeon breeder himself in the process of writing the *Origin of Species*, to better understand the processes of natural selection.[79]

Natural selection itself will tend to produce fish of the maximum fitness for a particular environment. Hatchery operators, if they are careful, can accelerate the process, by focusing on selecting successful broodstock. Their success will always be apparent two, three, four and five years later, as measured by the percentage of returning adults. Simply publishing measures of success would help hatchery operators figure out what works and what doesn't. All that is needed is a scientific approach to the problem.

Although a hatchery-based program to restore salmon runs makes the most sense if having more salmon is the goal, right now, having more salmon is not the goal. All other salmon goals in the Columbia River Basin have been displaced in pursuit of a single-minded focus on endangered Snake River salmon. Unless and until the Endangered Species Act is amended or administratively re-interpreted to remove the Snake River salmon from the

150

endangered species list, law, politics and resource constraints will gradually reduce the role of hatcheries from the Columbia River Basin, and the overall numbers of salmon will decline. This process might help a few wild stocks, but will not put salmon in the rivers for people to catch.

NOTES TO CHAPTER 6

[1] Quoted in J. Cone, *A Common Fate* 114 (Mr. Wilcox was an agent of the U.S Fish Commission).

[2] F. Cleaver, "Role of Hatcheries in the Management of Columbia River Salmon", in E. Schwiebert (ed.), *Columbia River Salmon and Steelhead* 91, Spec. Pub. No. 10 (Am. Fish. Soc. 1977).

[3] *See, e.g.*, M. Goodman, "Preserving the Genetic Diversity of Salmonid Stocks: A Call for Federal Regulation of Hatchery Programs", 20 Envt'l Law 111 (1990).

[4] U.S. Army Corps of Engineers, "Interim Status Report", Dec. 1996, at ES-3.

[5] ISG, *Return to the River* 377.

[6] Cited in C. Smith, *Salmon Fishers of the Columbia* 74.

[7] ISG, *Return to the River* 387B (Figure 8.4).

[8] *Id.* at 396A (Figure 8.11).

[9] R. Neuberger, "The Great Salmon Mystery", Saturday Evening Post, Sept. 13, 1941.

[10] House Rep. No. 2235, 75th Cong., 3d Sess. (Merchant Marine and Fisheries Comm.).

[11] Anonymous, "Discussion Paper on Mitchell Act Hatcheries", at 5 (1989).

[12] *Id.*

[13] E. Salo, "Special Report to the U.S. Army Corps of Engineers on Two Reports Concerning Proposed Compensation for Losses of Fish Caused by Ice Harbor, Lower Monumental, Little Goose, and Lower Granite Locks and Dam Projects", at 32 (USACE Walla Walla Dist. June 26, 1974) (20,700 adult fall chinook, 58,700 spring- and summer-run chinook and 55,100 steelhead.

[14] *Id.* at 31.

[15] "Compilation of Information on Salmon and Steelhead Losses in the Columbia River Basin", at 223.

[16] Summary of workshop "The Biological Basis for Listing Species or other Taxa of Salmonids Pursuant to the Endangered Species Act of 1973" (Portland, Oregon Dec. 7-8, 1978), at 70; *excerpted in* J. Cone & S. Ridlington, *The Northwest Salmon Crisis* 211.

[17] *E.g.*, NRC, *Upstream* at 41 (Prepub. ed.).

[18] ISG, *Return to the River* 141.

[19] From Table 1, "Status Report: Columbia River Fish Runs and Fisheries, 1938-95", at 2-3 (WDFW/ODFW Aug. 1996).

[20] ISG, *Return to the River* 396.

[21] "Compilation of Information on Salmon and Steelhead Losses in the Columbia River Basin"

[22] Quoted in *The Oregonian*, editorial page, Jan. 7, 1997.

[23] J. Cone, *A Common Fate* 116.

[24] Declaration of Doug Neeley, Feb. 7, 1993, at 7, filed in *IDFG v. NMFS*, No. 93-1603-MA (D Or).

[25] *Id.*

[26] *Id.*

[27] R. Waples, D. Teel & P. Aebersold, "A genetic monitoring and evaluation program for supplemented populations of salmon and steelhead in the Snake River basin", BPA Project No. 89-096 (1991).

[28] B. Brown, *Mountain in the Clouds* 118-19.

[29] J. Cone, *A Common Fate* 194.

[30] H. Raymond, "Effects of Hydroelectric Development and Fisheries Enhancement on Spring and Summer Chinook Salmon and Steelhead in the Columbia River Basin", N. Am. J. Fish. Mgmt. 8(1):1-24, at 18 (Winter 1988) (reviewing studies).

[31] *Id.*

[32] B. Brown, *Mountain in the Clouds* 102.

[33] ISG, *Return to the River* 206.

[34] *Id.* at 385-86; *see also* J. Richards, "An Economic Evaluation of Columbia River Anadromous Fish Programs", Ph.D. Thesis, Department of Agricultural Economics, Oregon State University, 1968, at 212, cited in C. Smith, *Salmon Fishers of the Columbia* 79 (showing cost-benefit ratio of only 1.6 to 1).

[35] ISG, *Return to the River* 386.

[36] Montgomery Watson, "Hatchery Evaluation Report: Bonneville Hatchery—Tule Fall Chinook ", USDOE Contract No. 95AC49468, May 1996 (using minimum program cost from § 6 divided by total average returns from § 5); Montgomery Watson, "Hatchery Evaluation Report: Rapid River Hatchery—Spring Chinook", USDOE Contract No. 95AC49468, May 1996 (same).

[37] B. Brown, *Mountain in the Clouds* 231-32.

[38] This data comes from BPA's contract management computer database and reflects contract "obligations"; actual spending figures may vary slightly.

[39] Conference Report for H.R. 4506, P.L. 103-316 (Aug. 26, 1994), *quoted in* "Interim Report: Lower Snake River Fish and Wildlife Compensation Plan, Lower Snake River, Washington and Idaho", at 2 (USACE Walla Walla Dist. April 1996).

[40] Interim Report: Lower Snake River Fish and Wildlife Compensation Plan, at 14.

[41] "Special Report, Lower Snake River Fish and Wildlife Compensation Plan, Lower Snake River, Washington and Idaho", Syllabus (USACE Walla Walla Dist. June 1975).

[42] "Interim Report, Supplement to Special Report, Lower Snake River Compensation Plan, Lower Snake River, Washington and Idaho, June 1975", at 26 (USACE Walla Walla Dist. April 1996).

[43] B. Brown, *Mountain in the Clouds* 118-19.

[44] *E.g.*, R Steelquist, *Field Guide to the Pacific Salmon* 15 (Sasquatch Books 1992).

[45] S. Doughton, "Salmon glut puts fishermen in troubled financial waters", The News Tribune, June 17, 1996.

[46] *Id.*; one person told me that prices hit lows of five to eight cents a pound.

[47] C. Thompson, "Tribal fisherman net scores of eager customers", *The Sunday Oregonian*, Sept. 22, 1996. Bypassing the wholesale markets, the Tribal fishermen were selling salmon off their boats for $2 per pound.

[48] R. Turner, "Conservation Biology", *Wana Chinook Tymoo*, Issue One, 1996, at 32 (CRITFC).

[49] Quoted in *Clearing Up*, Aug. 5, 1996, at 6.

[50] E. Brannon to M. Walker, April 8, 1997.

[51] E. Brannon to M. Walker, April 8, 1997.

[52] B. Brown, *Mountain in the Clouds* 102.

[53] J. Ayerst, "The Role of Hatcheries in Rebuilding Steelhead Runs of the Columbia River System", in E. Schwiebert (ed.), *Columbia River Salmon and Steelhead* 84, Special Pub. No. 10 (Am. Fish. Soc. 1977).

[54] W.E. Ricker, "Causes of the Decrease in Age and Size of Chinook Salmon (*Onchorhychus tshawytscha*)", Can. Tech. Rep. of Fish. & Aquat. Sci. No. 944, at 14 (May 1980).

[55] B. Brown, *Mountain in the Clouds* 150. Some people accuse Donaldson of force-feeding the fish, but I have never seen any proof of it.

[56] M. Goodman, 20 Envt'l Law at 128.

[57] M. Goodman, 20 Envt'l Law at 146.

[58] J. Austin, Jr. of Sixes, Oregon, Capital Press, Oct. 3, 1997.

[59] Reported in G. Easterbrook, *A Moment on the Earth* 421.

[60] G. Easterbrook, *A Moment on the Earth* 571.

[61] *See, e.g.*, Declaration of Douglas Neeley, Feb. 7, 1993, at 13, filed in *IDFG v. NMFS*, No. 93-1603-MA (D. Or.).

[62] NWPPC, "Compilation of Information on Salmon and Steelhead Losses in the Columbia River Basin", Appendix D of the 1987 Fish and Wildlife Plan.

[63] U.S. Army Corps of Engineers, "Interim Status Report", at 2-9.

[64] K. Petersen, *River of Life, Channel of Death* 12.

[65] *See* NRC, *Upstream* at 46 (Prepub. ed.)

[66] *See generally* W. Pearcy, *Ocean Ecology of North Pacific Salmonids*, at 26-28, 91-94 (1992) (noting food limitation and competition in estuaries and North Pacific ocean).

[67] ISG, *Return to the River* 48 (The principle is given "level 4" support, described at p. 47 as "speculative, little empirical support")

[68] DPEIS at 2 (CBFWA Dec. 10, 1996) (emphasis in original).

[69] Quoted in B. Rudolph, "Hatchery Study Finds Little Impact on Wild Fish", *Clearing Up*, Jan. 6, 1997, at 6.

[70] DPEIS at 4 (emphasis deleted).

[71] *See, e.g.*, "Hatcheries: a failed fix", *The Oregonian*, Jan. 7, 1997; B. Rudolph, "Hatchery Study Finds Little Impact on Wild Fish", *Clearing Up*, Jan. 6, 1997, at 6.

[72] DPEIS at 5.

[73] ISG, *Return to the River* 398.

[74] *Id.* at 400.

[75] Cited in "Interim Report, Supplement to Special Report, Lower Snake River Fish and Wildlife Compensation Plan, Lower Snake River, Washington and Idaho, June 1975", at 15 (USACE April 1996).

[76] *Id.*

[77] "Hatcheries: a failed fix", *The Oregonian*, Jan. 7, 1997.

[78] "Alaskans Say They're Not Targeting Canadian Sockeye", *NW Fishletter*, July 22, 1997, § 9.

[79] J. Weiner, *The Beak of the Finch* 31.

CHAPTER 7: THE RISE OF THE FLOW THEORISTS AND THE FALL OF SCIENCE

"One day when I was a junior medical school student, a very important Boston surgeon visited the school and delivered a great treatise on the large number of patients who had undergone successful operations for vascular reconstruction. At the end of the lecture, a young student at the back of the room timidly asked, 'Do you have any controls?' Well, the great surgeon drew himself up to his full height, hit the desk, and said: 'Do you mean did I not operate on half of the patients?' The hall grew very quiet then. The voice at the back of the room hesitantly replied, 'Yes, that's what I had in mind.' Then the visitor's fist really came down as he thundered, 'Of course not. That would have doomed half of them to their death.' God it was quiet then, and one could scarcely hear the small voice ask, 'Which half?'" Dr. E. Peacock, Jr.[1]

That small voice is the voice of science. Today's fishery agencies, like the great surgeon, are quite sure that more and more flows are good for salmon because, after all, salmon must have flowing rivers to survive. For six years, I have played the role of the small voice in the back of the room, questioning those who promote higher and higher river flows for salmon.

When questioned, they can present no competent scientific evidence that the millions of acre-feet of water they have released from upstream reservoirs for nearly fifteen years have had any measurable effect on salmon survival. Their theories for why the water should help are contrary to the available data. Yet the flow augmentation program remains the single most expensive component of the Clinton/Gore Administration's salmon recovery program, and as of 1997, negotiations are underway to saddle the Bonneville Power Administration with funding even larger flow augmentation programs for another decade.

Biological Science, Politicized Science, and Government

Science aims for black and white answers, or at least measurable shades of gray. Nearly always, something is either true, or it isn't, or we need to learn more before we know whether it's true or not. If you are talking about something that can't be measured, you are not talking about science. It will always be subjective; no one can prove or disprove it. To be sure, where there is ignorance, there is room for reasonable differences of opinion about what the scientific truth is likely to be. But the genius of the scientific process is that it marches gradually toward removing grounds for disagreement, by disproving hypotheses that are not consistent with reality.

Applying the scientific process is not easy. There is always more than one theory to explain what is going on. In the case of salmon decline, there are many theories. The most important step is to figure out what we would measure if one of the competing theories were correct. After that, experiments must be done to collect the empirical evidence to weed out the theories that don't fit the real world data.

Those who think they perceive the truth without need of experimental confirmation have what philosopher Thomas Sowell calls "the vision of the anointed". As he explains, visions of the anointed have long driven government policy in the social arena, where

> "To a remarkable extent . . . empirical evidence is neither sought beforehand nor consulted after a policy has been instituted. Facts may be marshalled for a decision already taken, but that is very different from systemmatically testing opposing theories by evidence. Momentous questions are dealt with essentially as conflicts of visions".[2]

The scientific process is "[s]eldom . . . used by those who believe in the vision of the anointed. More typically, they look through statistics until they find some numbers that fit their preconceptions, and then cry, 'Aha!'"[3] This behavior characterizes precisely the approach of those anointed to craft salmon recovery programs in the Pacific Northwest. They have vision of the Northwest without dams, and are prepared to act in furtherance of that vision without regard to empirical evidence.

Scientists have always had an uneasy relationship with the government, because real science is uncompromising. It is the province of idealists, like me. It is a province under a growing siege from social theorists, a struggle well-documented in the proceedings of a 1995 conference sponsored by the New York Academy of Sciences called *The Flight from Science and Reason.* As one of the participants in those proceedings pointed out, "the very ideals of science itself are the only real antidote to its misuse".[4] Social theorists claim that scientific conclusions are the product of economic interests or social conventions among scientists, and deny the very concept that there are such things as objective scientific facts. This is delusional thinking, but it passes for scholarship in the minds of many.[5]

In the Pacific Northwest, politics has consistently overruled science in fishery management. As the Director of the University of Washington Fisheries Research Institute has lamented, "[f]isheries scientists who work for various constituency groups may be compelled by their employer to espouse a particular 'party line' with which they may or may not agree".[6]

One reason the problem is so bad is that nearly all the scientific research is funded by federal, state and tribal agencies with overwhelmingly powerful political agendas that stifle useful research. Because the harvest agencies all decided long ago that the primary problem with salmon survival is the dams, nearly all of the research focuses on problems at dams and reservoirs. The little research that looks beyond the dams focuses on other freshwater aspects of salmon survival, and is aimed at proving that cows kill salmon, logging kills salmon, and just about anything except fishing kills salmon.

Congressman Norm Dicks once asked Ross Heath, the Dean of the University of Washington College of Ocean and Fishery Sciences, whether there was any way to improve salmon research in the Northwest. Dean Heath outlined several of the most critical problems.[7] First, he said, no one was allowed to use the fish necessary for useful experiments because "the state agencies and tribes have a stranglehold on this—we couldn't get approval to run 1000 steelhead smolts through a turbine to measure its effect, for example".

We are still using turbine designs from the 1940s and 1950s because fishery managers don't want to fix the turbines; they want the turbines out. It literally took an Act of Congress mandating research on improving turbine designs to overpower the fishery managers; Idaho's Senator Kempthorne deserves the credit. People inside the Corps of Engineers who have been pushing for such research for years are pretty cynical about it. Researchers have to get as far away as the University of Iowa before they can do useful work to make turbines safer. At the current pace of research, it will be years before we get past the conceptual stage and get permission to put some fish through new turbine designs.

When a research project does get funded that generates politically-incorrect results, they disappear into a black hole. According to Dean Heath, "agencies refuse to release 'unfavorable' data gathered with public funds—even to a group as visible and influential as the [Snake River] Salmon Recovery Team". Conversely, the results of projects and studies of the flimsiest scientific merit are invoked whenever they are "favorable".

Lacking scientific evidence, critics attack independent scientists personally. As the Director of the University of Washington Fisheries Research Institute has pointed out, "[u]niversity scientists, who in past years were viewed as being an independent source of information, now find that their scientific opinions are discounted based on the source of their research funding".[8] I once watched Roy Hemmingway, a key policy advisor to Oregon's Governor Kitzhaber, urge a University of Washington professor to be sure to put the source of his funding on the cover page of his research reports, apparently so that he could discount the reports that were funded by interests he opposed, like my clients. He was utterly oblivious to the scientist's disgust with this attitude.

Finally, all the scientific research is processed and prioritized through layers of committees that simply appoint their own agencies to do the research. Dean Heath suggests that "[m]uch, if not most, of the research is being done by individuals with glaring conflicts of interest". By the summer of 1996, this aspect of the problem finally caught the attention of the politicians, who appointed another committee to deal with this problem. While their intentions are good, their "fixes" do not begin to cope with the problem.

Research that survives the gauntlet of federal, state and tribal review seldom produces new information. Each year, enormous sums of money are spent paying scientists to review the work of other scientists. One conspicuous exception is research that finally got underway in 1993 to measure the effects of dams on juvenile salmon survival through several reservoir reaches.

Former Northwest Power Planning Council Member Angus Duncan once told me that he was responsible for pushing this politically-unpopular "reach survival" research. To his credit, he did. But when it came out contrary to his predispositions (the reservoirs were not "lethal slackwater pools"), he continued to vote for policies (like drawdown) that the research predicted would simply not work. He indulged in every conceivable speculative reason why the research might be wrong.

The Political Science of Conservation Biology

"The best lack all conviction, while the worst/Are full of passionate intensity." W. B. Yeats, *The Second Coming*

As the government has exerted more and more influence over scientific research, the role of politics in science has grown larger and larger. And as government-driven environmental spending creates more and more environmental scientists, they then promote attention to environmental causes. As one writer noted,

"The number of 'biological and life scientists' doubled [from 1983 to 1995] to 110,000. The influence of this waxing class of 'hard' scientists, increasingly savvy about public relations and self-promotion, contrasts with the waning clout of social scientists, who have lost prestige in recent decades as their proffered solutions made many problems worse. These days it is the natural scientists who benefit from calamity or the prospect of it . . .".[9]

Over the coming decades, the waxing class of salmon recovery experts now in control of salmon spending may lose prestige, as their programs fail to return more salmon to the rivers of the Pacific Northwest (unless they succeed in claiming credit for improving climatic conditions). Right now, however, their influence continues to rise, premised on the Hoax that we have yet to begin the struggle to save salmon.

It is not just the number of scientists that has changed, but their nature as well. In the field of biology, a new "science", "conservation biology", has been created. Conservation biology mingles old-fashioned biological science with New Age mysticism. In many respects, it is not so much science as religion.

It takes as a postulate—an assumption never to be questioned—the superiority of "natural" conditions, which are usually imagined to be the conditions that prevailed just before some identifiable human development intruded on the environment. Unlike traditional scientists, conservation biologists are all highly political, in the sense that their willingness to embrace new scientific truth is subordinate to the larger political goals of reducing human influence on the environment.

Conservation biologists are also active in legal and political processes, where their recommendations receive great weight because of their status as "scientists". Organizations like the "Society for Conservation Biology" and "The American Institute of Biological Sciences" have actually intervened in lawsuits to challenge forest management.[10] The same "scientists" advise policymakers on "science" and politicians on how to rewrite the Endangered Species Act.[11]

One law review article promoting the new "science" of "conservation biology" explained:

"A distinguishing feature of conservation biology is that it is mission oriented. Underlying any mission is a set of values. Philosophers of science now recognize that no science is value free, despite all we were taught in school about the strict objectivity of the scientific method. Conservation biology is more value-laden than most sciences because it is not concerned with knowledge for its own sake but rather is directed toward particular goals. Maintaining biodiversity is an unquestioned goal of conservation biologists."[12]

Conservation biologists "view species extinction and loss as a crisis of major proportions that requires a drastic shift in our governing policies".[13] This crisis mentality drives conservation biologists to an anti-development political agenda that seems extreme to those who do not share their perception of imminent crisis. From the crisis perspective, the "unquestioned ends" of "biodiversity" justify the means of ignoring scientific evidence. To conservation biologists, objectivity is a vice if it stands in the way of accomplishing the "mission".

Many have an underlying philosophy, exemplified by the Norwegian Arne Naess, that "nature had rights of its own, which were primary. Rivers had a right to be rivers, salmon had a right to be salmon, trees had a right to be trees, just as they were, without human interference".[14] Since no one can communicate with trees or salmon, giving them rights really means giving additional political power to those who purport to speak for the trees or salmon.

Conservation biologists have taken the leading public role as salmon advocates in the Northwest. Joseph Cone chronicled their organization in his 1995 book *A Common Fate*. A small group of individuals, working loosely together, brought Endangered Species Act listings to the Pacific Northwest and popularized the cause of salmon recovery. Gordon Reeves led the politicization of the Oregon chapter of the American Fisheries Society. Jim Lichatowich quit the Oregon Department of Fish and Wildlife because it was not friendly to his world view of an industrial economy at war with a "natural" economy, and has worked tirelessly to popularize his views. Kai Lee, a professor of "environmental studies and political science", who served as Washington's member on the Northwest Power Planning Council, motivated the Council's staff, particularly Willa Nehlsen, to adopt the conservation biology viewpoint.[15]

By 1990, the Oregon Chapter of the American Fisheries Society focused on such questions as "the realistic prospects for sustainable resource use in a consumption-oriented society" and "prospects for natural-resource sustainability as long as local, national and global population growth went unchecked".[16] When fisheries scientists decide to worry about these questions instead of disease vectors for *Ceratomyxa shasta*, evolutionary changes in salmon species, or statistical techniques for counting the number of fish harvested, we all suffer. Everyone wants to be a policymaker, and no one wants to do the hard scientific work that give us the information we need to make intelligent policy choices.

A small and closely-knit group of conservation biologists who are mostly state and tribal bureaucrats in Portland, Oregon[17] have come to exercise enormous influence over government salmon policy. Their unquestioned postulate is that salmon can be recovered to historic levels by manipulating river flows and drawing down reservoir levels. With the assistance of the Clinton/Gore White House Office of Environmental Policy, and a friendly federal court in Portland, they have effectively overruled the federal fish biologists since 1992, and launched a program that quickly expanded to cost more than $500 million a year ($200 million being lost revenues to the Bonneville Power Administration).

These individuals, including the husband-and-wife team of Doug and Michelle DeHart, Howard Schaller, Margret Filardo, and Bob Heineth, deserve credit for a single-minded focus on and dedication to their particular vision of salmon recovery. Unfortunately, they seem to have all lost the capacity to consider objectively the scientific evidence concerning the effects of dams on salmon. Others have a harsher view, calling them "fish terrorists", "blinded by their hatred for the power system", who "believe anything that destroys megawatts has to help salmon".[18]

Real scientists would take a serious interest in considering the data set forth in these pages. The Portland group has taken the opposite approach, attempting to stop the collection of that data, and to harm the careers of those who collect it. They have even reached up to Seattle to try and shut down the thesis projects of fishery students at the University of Washington whose research might undermine their dogma.

Another particularly influential group of conservation biologists, the Northwest Power Planning Council's Independent Scientific Group, issued a widely-heralded report entitled *Return to the River* on September 18, 1996. The Group asserts that the virtue of the report is not to provide new scientific information to policymakers. Rather, the Group proclaims that it has provided a "conceptual foundation", meaning a "set of scientific principles and *assumptions*"—"the filter through which information is viewed and interpreted".[19]

Their "filter" amounts to little more than rose-colored glasses through which they look at "back to nature" solutions for salmon recovery. Because higher spring flows were present before dams, many conservation biologists simply filter out the evidence that increasing spring flows with flow augmentation doesn't help recover salmon. But real scientists don't filter out data. They revise their theories to be consistent with the data. Data are real. Theories may not be.

For the most part, the public and the media cannot tell the difference between real scientists and those who apply the filter of conservation biology; the end result is that science itself is slowly corroded.

Conservation biologists may be well-intentioned, and profess to be trying to use the scientific process, but their objectivity is poisoned by an overwhelming anti-development bias. This bias is held by many who are frankly antiscientific, and opposed to scientific and industrial progress. The rise of such modern-day Luddites recently caused some 2,600 scientists, including 72 Nobel Prize winners, to issue the *Heidelberg Appeal,* expressing concern about

> "the emergence of an irrational ideology opposed to scientific and industrial process. . . . We contend that a Natural State, idealized by movements with a tendency to look toward the past, does not exist and probably has not existed since man's first appearance in the biosphere. . . . The greatest evils that stalk our Earth are ignorance and oppression, not technology and industry."[20]

Ignorance about what has caused salmon decline and what we can do about it stalks the Pacific Northwest. So too does oppression of citizens who try and tell the truth about it.

The Impact of Dams on Natural Flows

Dams have unquestionably altered the natural flow of the Columbia and Snake Rivers. Flow proponents point to changes in the natural "hydrograph"—a graph of average flow over the course of a year. Hydropower production is optimized when the peak on this hydrograph (in the spring) is smoothed, and the water saved in storage reservoirs for release during lower flow times (the fall and winter). Flow proponents argue that the dams, by storing spring runoff for use in generating power in the fall and winter, have an adverse effect on salmon.

Flow theorists have succeeded in destroying a principal benefit of reservoirs: storing spring runoff for fall and winter electric power production. Instead, they require the dam operators to drain the reservoirs in the spring and summer to release water for salmon. In an attempt to "mimic the natural hydrograph", they require smaller reservoir releases in the fall and winter, to save the water until the spring.

This wastes money that the Bonneville Power Administration could otherwise make selling power generated in the fall and winter. Then, in the spring, there is too much water coming down the river for the turbines to handle. As a result, much of the water goes over the spillways instead of generating power, another source of waste. And in some high-flow years, like 1996-97, too much power is generated all at once in the spring for BPA to sell, yet another source of waste.

One obvious problem with the "changes in the hydrograph killed salmon" theory is that the salmon runs in the worst shape are in the Snake River Basin, where there has not been that much alteration of the shape of the natural hydrograph. The Columbia River runs are in far better shape, yet the alteration of the natural river hydrograph is far greater (mostly because of storage reservoirs in Canada). Here are two graphs that the National Research Council used to show natural vs. regulated flows at the Snake River at its mouth (left) and at the Columbia River at The Dalles (right):

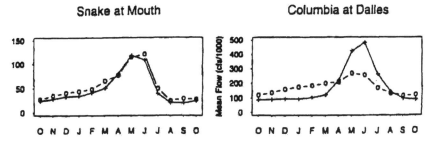

Figure 18: Effects of Reservoir Storage on Hydrographs[21]

As one can see, the natural flows in the Columbia River (denoted with crosses) had a substantially sharper peak than the present regulated flows (denoted with circles)—but natural flows in the Snake didn't.

The National Research Council recently noted that it was a "common misperception" in the Pacific Northwest "that there has been a major shift in the mean discharge hydrograph of the Snake River". "Because there has not been a major shift in the Snake River hydrograph", the Council continued, "it is doubtful a priori [i.e., even before looking at evidence] that the declines in Snake River stocks are due to or reversible by changes in the seasonality of the flow regime of the Snake River alone".[22]

If flow changes were of much importance, we would expect the mid-Columbia stocks to be in much worse shape than the Snake stocks. But upriver salmon runs are in worse shape in the middle Snake River, and healthiest in the mid-Columbia River.

This "misperception" about the significance of flow later came to dominate the thinking of United States District Judge Malcolm Marsh in a series of cases concerning salmon and dams, discussed in Chapter 9. In the first in a series of opinions unwittingly promoting the Great Salmon Hoax, Judge Marsh opined that a "primary" cause of the decline in endangered Snake River salmon is a "failure to meet guidelines, such as water budgets set aside to improve juvenile salmon migration".[23] In a footnote, Judge Marsh lamented that in a recent year, dam operators had only provided 440,000 to 480,000 acre-feet of water despite a fishery agency request for 1,190,000 acre-feet.[24] There was no scientific evidence before him, however, that adding such additional water to the Snake River would accomplish anything for salmon.

The Birth of the Flow/Survival Hypothesis

Flow theorists had another fact on their side that Northwest fishermen have always known: after heavy rains, salmon begin to move upriver. Observers at dams counting returning salmon eventually detected another phenomenon: three or four years after a particularly wet spring, more adult salmon would return. Some salmon biologists began to focus on the relationship between river flow and salmon populations.

In the late 1970s, biologists at the National Marine Fisheries Service began for the first time to estimate the survival of juvenile salmon migrating downstream in the Columbia and Snake Rivers. There were two seminal papers. The first, by Howard Raymond, used mark/recapture techniques to estimate survival for groups of juvenile chinook salmon and steelhead.[25] Later, Carl Sims and Frank Ossiander constructed a flow/survival relationship using that data.[26]

The flow/survival relationship was ultimately based on what NMFS scientist John Williams has somewhat derisively termed the "seven points of light": seven flow/survival years from which the researchers drew a graph of the supposed relationship between river flow and the survival of juvenile salmon.

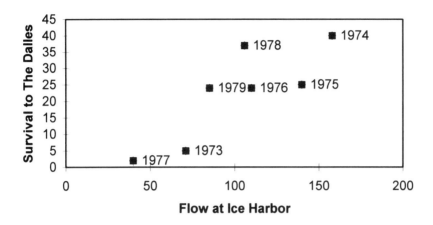

Figure 19: Early Correlations of Flow and Survival[27]

One can see why the original researchers might be tempted to draw a line to fit these points, deriving a rough and ready relationship between flow and survival. The flow theorists, however, went much farther. They declared that if the dam operators would simply release water from upstream reservoirs, the survival of salmon would improve, in amounts to be predicted by using the same mathematical relationship.

When NMFS scientists returned to re-examine the original data used by Raymond, Sims and Ossiander, they found an extraordinary "plasticity in survival estimates based on these techniques", and that if proper techniques were applied, the early estimates of survival were perhaps a factor of two too low.[28] Another researcher who studied the original data even more closely found the studies riddled with questionable assumptions, and pointed out that by comparing the original data on treatment and control group recovery rates, survival "exceeded 100% on 8 out of 22 occasions for fish traveling from the lower Snake River to Ice Harbor Dam"[29] Per project survival estimates were even skewed by a failure to count the number of dams correctly.

These scientists advised that conditions at the dams were far different during the 1970s, something the Corps of Engineers had long tried to point out. In particular, the two low flow/low survival years that provided most of the slope to the flow survival curve—1973 and 1977—were years when poorly designed fish passage facilities (since improved) clogged with trash and descaled and ultimately killed the fish.[30] The NMFS scientists concluded that "the Sims and Ossiander (1981) flow/survival relationship developed from studies in the 1970s does not predict the current survival of spring-migrating juvenile chinook salmon, particularly those migrating under low flow conditions".[31]

The independent reviewer concurred: "Fisheries managers, the public, and the fish themselves would be better served by data collected under present conditions using current technological and analytical techniques".[32] He was certainly right about the public and the fish themselves. Fishery managers eager to extract money from the hydropower system, however, continue to use the older data to this day.

Another major problem with most of the papers cited by flow theorists was the failure to account for spill at hydroelectric projects which, can, at moderate levels, improve salmon survival. For example, flow proponents and harvest agencies often cite a 1993 draft paper by Ray Hilborn in support of their claims that flow affects survival.[33] They fail to disclose that the draft was withdrawn for revision in light of criticism that "it did not examine spill, prevailing water temperature, degree of transportation . . . and may not have used suitable controls".[34] As far as I know, a revised paper was never issued, but they continue to cite the defective draft. The same problems apply to the 1992 work of Idaho Fish and Game biologist Charles Petrosky, whose oft-cited work ignored both spill and increasing numbers of turbines over the period of his study.[35]

The best fisheries scientists, including members of the Snake River Salmon Recovery Team appointed by the National Marine Fisheries Service to recommend a recovery plan for Snake River salmon, acknowledge that "there is no direct evidence that increasing flows in the spring increases reservoir or dam passage survivals for spring chinook".[36]

Testing the Idea that Flow Augmentation Increases Salmon Survival

Harvest agencies have steadfastly refused to conduct any competent experimental testing of whether releases from upstream reservoirs will increase the survival of salmon. Instead, they simply assume that releasing water from a reservoir can mimic the constellation of natural events that correspond with high river flow, including (typically) lower temperatures, greater rainfall, and better ocean conditions. The available data suggests that these other factors are much more important to the survival of salmon than the speed of the water they are swimming in.

Given the state and tribal opposition to such research, until quite recently, no one had conducted much formal analysis of week-by-week changes in survival and flow. No one really knew whether increasing river flows by

166

upstream reservoirs decreases the travel time of fish, much less by how much. All of the major reviews of salmon science conducted in the past couple of years have ignored the importance of within-year measurements of flow and survival.

The first analysis I ever heard of came when my clients induced the Oregon Department of Environmental Quality to require the National Marine Fisheries Service to make a statistical evaluation of the available PIT-tag data to determine week-by-week survival changes (see Chapter 12). The results? High variability in the daily estimates showed no correlation between survival, flow, or several other variables. But when the data were "smoothed", "fairly strong *negative* correlations were found between survival and flow".[37] Biologist Steve Cramer has found the same inverse relationship between flow and survival from PIT-tag data in 1995, 1996 and 1997 in his studies of spill discussed in Chapter 12. The available data are utterly inconsistent with any survival benefits from flow augmentation.

In September 1997, the National Marine Fisheries Service finally released (in draft form), a more comprehensive analysis of the PIT-tag data they had been collecting since 1993. Notwithstanding a general inclination to give every benefit of the doubt to flow theorists, the scientists concluded that "despite a large data base collected over several years using contemporary techniques, relationships between flow and survival . . . were not strong or consistent".[38]

There is some evidence that after spikes in river flow, more juvenile salmon are detected downstream at the dams. Below is a graph of Snake River flow in 1994 versus the number of juvenile salmon detected at Lower Granite Dam.

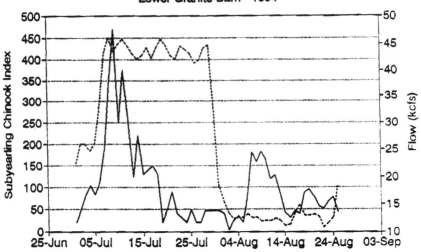

Figure 20: Flow and Juvenile Counts at Lower Granite (1994)[39]

The plateau of flow (dotted line) was caused by releases from Dworshak Reservoir. You can see that when flow rose rapidly, so did the numbers of salmon detected (solid line). But this could be a coincidence; the flow peak could have been timed coincident with a natural peak in migration. After all, when flow dropped sharply in early August, the number of detections also rose. When flow was high and flat, the number of detections dropped. Even assuming that the first pulse of water had any effect on fish, it looks as if most of the water after the first pulse was wasted. Some biologists look at data like this and speculate that *changes* in flow cause fish to move.

But this does not mean that increasing flows will have any measurable effect on the overall population of salmon. A reservoir release may be like blowing air at a tree full of robins: the robins will fly away, but they will not necessarily start flying south for the winter. Natural flows in the summer tend to become warmer, but the flows released from reservoirs are colder. No one knows whether the signal of a blast of cold water is sending the message to juvenile salmon that it is time to migrate. The true signal probably comes from the salmon's own natural development—an internal alarm clock. Nevertheless, leading promoters of the Great Salmon Hoax, like Northwest Power Planning Council member Ken Casavant, continue to promote the idea that "more natural spring flow" will "better trigger the juvenile migration impulse".[40]

There have been many studies that, while not focusing on actual changes in migration speed in a single year, looked to see whether salmon tended to migrate earlier in high flow years. The 1993 Supplemental Environmental Impact Statement (SEIS), which was prepared to rationalize the beginning of the government's foray into large-scale flow augmentation, acknowledged that "only 5 of 117 tests of linear correlation of migration timing to flow quantity had a significant positive relationship".[41] Dr. McNeil's work suggests that "the data tend to favor . . . an alternative hypothesis that migration is advanced by low flow and delayed by high flow. This is the antithesis of the NMFS theory which influences public policies on flow management during juvenile migration".[42]

When my clients and others filed formal comments on the SEIS to point out the lack of any scientific basis for believing that increasing flow would increase salmon survival, the government responded:

> "The comments on this issue demonstrate that opinion within the region on the existence of such a relationship is sharply divided, and that the debate cannot be resolved in the SEIS. . . . no attempt in this SEIS has been made to resolve the issue and render a firm conclusion as to the existence and strength of a flow/survival relationship . . ."[43]

The basic rationale for spending hundreds of millions of dollars? "[T]he cumulative weight of the research does not demonstrate that absolutely no relationship exists."[44] In short, rather than relying on factual support for the flow/survival hypothesis, the government announced that so long as no one could prove beyond doubt that it didn't work, it would go forward with the program. Since 1992, that policy has continued. It is striking testimony to the political power of the flow theorists.

Most recently, the conservation biologists forming the Council's Independent Science Group have come out against efforts to try and measure any sort of flow/survival relationship. "[W]e suggest abandonment of the search for the elusive 'correct' or 'optimum' flow and instead we advise focusing on the restoration of a riverine velocity structure as close as possible to the pre-impoundment hydrograph."[45] In short, we should all just *assume* that higher velocities will advantage salmon. Like conservation biologists generally, the ISG members have abandoned the scientific process in favor of the marketing slogan: just do it!

How Much Do Dams Slow Down Juvenile Salmon?

Most proponents of the importance of flow also argue that the dams have substantially lengthened the time it takes juvenile salmon to migrate to the sea, so that hundreds of thousands of smolts die in the river that would have made it to the sea. (Whether or not they would have died anyway in the sea is not discussed.) One particularly influential paper on this subject, has asserted that juvenile stream-type salmon required 26 days to reach The Dalles from the Salmon River before construction of dams and 65 days after construction.[46]

But this research was later determined to suffer from a critical flaw. The researchers compared marked groups of fish, *but they assumed that time of release had no effect on migration speed.*[47] Dr. William McNeil examined the data and found that "early migrating juveniles move slowly and late migrating juveniles move rapidly. The correlation between migration speed and release date is consistently direct and highly significant . . . . The correlation between migration speed and stream discharge, on the other hand, is equivocal."[48] Dr. McNeil notes that this result "contradicts the theory that migration is a passive behavior".[49]

The newest research by the National Marine Fisheries Service has found that 91.2 percent of the variance in travel time for groups of juvenile salmon released in Lower Granite Reservoir and detected downstream could be explained by a simple model using only date and temperature and a year-specific constant.[50] The same data showed "absolutely no correlation between flow exposure and median travel time".[51]

Dr. McNeil has also determined that the time of passage for juvenile salmon populations migrating down the Columbia River "remained consistent among years for four species of stream-type and one species of ocean-type juvenile salmon *even though stream discharge fluctuated nearly two-fold annually.*"[52] Records of the Seufert Brothers Company in The Dalles, going back to 1885, show that "there may have been more salmon in the earlier days than there are now, but the pattern for the runs, *when they came* and so on, is definitely the same".[53]

The only response to Dr. McNeil's work that I have ever seen, offered by the Northwest Power Planning Council's Independent Science Group, is that "the preponderance of thought clearly supports the links between flow and migration rate" and that "[t]his view is reflected in proposed salmon restoration plans".[54] But scientists are not supposed to uncover scientific truth by looking for the "preponderance of thought" or what the government says the truth is. They are supposed to look at data.

170

There are even claims that increasing the duration of the downstream migration causes fish to become "confused" or lose their urge to migrate. The story is that the transformation of juveniles from fresh to salt water is "delicate and easily disrupted" so that delays experienced while migrating through reservoirs cause fish to "lose their migratory drive".[55] When I couldn't find any scientific evidence at all in support of this notion, I called up a scientist at the National Marine Fisheries Service in Seattle to ask him about it. He laughed and said he had had the same problem. When he checked the references, he found that they said precisely the opposite: that the salmon were flexible.[56]

Despite the absence of competent scientific evidence suggesting that juvenile migration delays have had a measurable adverse effect on salmon populations, death from delay is accepted as acknowledged truth and repeated over and over again in most popular books on salmon recovery.[57]

The Flow/Travel Time/Survival Hypothesis

Until very recently, the cornerstone of flow theory was that lower flows slow down the salmon, and that conversely, if flow in the river is speeded up, the salmon migrate faster. Most people appear to assume that juvenile salmon are like tiny pieces of flotsam, drifting downstream with the current, but this is plainly untrue. As the Northwest Power Planning Council's Independent Science Group recently concluded, "once migration is initiated, downstream migration is more aptly characterized as a discontinuous, spiraling movement rather than as the continual linear progress characteristic of a water particle".[58] The salmon swim actively, and often remain stationary at particular locations to feed or wait until dark when it is safer to move downstream.

Fall chinook salmon in particular do not seem to migrate downstream faster with higher flows.[59] A detailed review of fall chinook migration behavior led the Northwest Power Planning Council's Independent Science Group to conclude that "[r]iver flow and velocity seem to be little involved".[60] There are many examples where fall chinook have experienced longer travel times and higher survival.[61]

Results on juvenile spring/summer chinook salmon seem to show little relationship between travel time and flow. The most recent completed study was conducted by five biologists using tens of thousands of PIT-tag interrogations of individual juvenile salmon between 1992 and 1995. Their work, published in the *North American Journal of Fisheries Management* in 1997, covered spring/summer chinook, fall chinook, and other salmonids. Their conclusions? First, "there is no evidence that subyearling [fall] chinook

171

respond to changes in river discharge, as observed over a broad range of flow levels".[62] "Evidence for flow effects was not apparent [for spring/summer chinook]" either.[63]

Since the best scientific evidence suggests no measurable benefits will accrue from flow augmentation, conservation biologists are beginning to speculate that there are many stocks of salmon with different migration strategies, some of which might be advantaged by efforts to increase flows and some of which might be disadvantaged.[64] No one really knows.

The latest speculation from the flow theorists is that there is some sort of "event horizon", a magic window of time during which flow may assist fish. Unfortunately, it would be almost impossible to measure because the effects would be different for each fish—only when the fish are developmentally ready to move would there be any effect, and no one knows when the fish are ready. Measurements of large groups of fish cannot disprove the theory.[65]

The Northwest Power Planning Council's Independent Science Group has gone even farther, finding it "tempting to suggest" that yearling chinook salmon catch waves from flow surges "much like a surfer catching a wave on a beach".[66] They admit, however, that "[n]o fisheries research could be found on this subject".[67]

Ironically, even if one assumes that the salmon migrate precisely at the same speed as water particles, the effect of flow augmentation on the travel time of water particles is not very large. A multi-year study conducted by the Corps, BPA and the Bureau Reclamation, the System Operation Review, concluded that (again *assuming* that flow augmentation speeded fish) that no matter how one operated the dams and reservoirs, travel time of Snake River fish could be speeded up by only four days, and mid-Columbia fish by three days—a small portion of the overall migration time.[68]

The National Research Council agreed, concluding in 1995 that flow augmentation "is unable to reduce the water-particle travel times through the pools in average flow years by more than a few days—probably biologically insignificant—beyond the levels already achieved by [the Northwest Power Planning Council's] 85-kcfs [thousand feet per second] Lower Granite Dam target".[69] Regrettably, the National Research Council did not examine the question whether additional flows beyond earlier, lower targets than the 85 kcfs made much difference. In all likelihood, flow augmentation has no measurable effect except in the very driest of years, when salmon populations have always suffered.

Avoiding Reservoir Mortality By Reducing Travel Time May Not Help Salmon at All

While the most fundamental dispute among Northwest fishery biologists has been whether and to what extent reservoir releases can speed up salmon, few have bothered to stop and ask whether speeding up salmon does much good. The biologists instead assume the mainstem reservoirs are "lethal slackwater pools" where juvenile salmon are exterminated by hordes of predators and lose their way because there is no swift guiding current, so that speeding salmon through the reservoirs is unquestionably a good thing.

But there are large numbers of predators in undammed reaches too, both above and below the dams. For example, in 1996 the National Biological Service produced data that were "the first to document rapid switching by northern squawfish from a mostly nonfish diet to one of primarily juvenile salmonids in a location away from a hatchery release or hydroelectric dam."[70] After a hatchery release many miles upriver, squawfish in the Clearwater River in Idaho relied on juvenile salmon for 80% of their food. What happens in this undammed reach is downplayed by the harvest agencies: lots of juvenile salmon die, in ways that cannot reasonably be attributed to the effects of dams.

Each and every flow proponent has failed to recognize the simple fact that getting juvenile salmon quickly out of the reservoirs to avoid reservoir predators is only helpful if the net effect is to reduce exposure to predators. If the density of predators is *lower* in the reservoirs than in the lower river and estuary, the survival per day may be *higher* in the reservoirs. Thus, as Dr. James Anderson and Richard Hinrichsen have pointed out, it is conceivable that getting juveniles out of the reservoirs faster could even reduce overall salmon populations, especially if they wind up hitting the estuary at a time of high predation.[71]

I have seen no evidence that predator densities are higher in the reservoirs than in a free-flowing river. I have heard biologists acknowledge that the density of predators appears to be higher below Bonneville Dam than in the reservoirs above it. The National Research Council recently concluded that "[t]here is some evidence that predators, such as northern squawfish, have increased in abundance in the lower Columbia River".[72] The Northwest Power Planning Council's Independent Science Group notes that some data indicates "a 54.5% loss of smolts from the tailrace at Bonneville Dam to Rainier Beach, Oregon".[73] This is consistent with European studies of the survival of Baltic salmon in estuarine conditions, which show mortalities as high as 50% for the last 50 kilometers of salmon migration before the ocean. Survival though the hundreds of miles of Columbia and Snake River reservoirs is far higher everywhere we have measured it.

Biologists have also theorized that as dams raised the water level and slowed river velocities, more silt washed over the rocks at the bottom of the river, leaving the juveniles no space to hide from predators.[74] But no one has ever done experiments to test this theory either, beyond measuring the proportion of juvenile salmon migrating downstream consumed by predators. The Snake River is already so turbid that in 1995, scientists trying to find salmon redds with underwater video cameras could not do so because the water was not clear enough.[75]

The data offer every reason to believe that juvenile salmon are safer from predators in the reservoirs in terms of mortality per mile than they are both above and below the reservoirs. Yet the most fundamental axiom of fishery agency management is to try and rush them through the reservoirs, as if the reservoirs were an especially dangerous place.

Arrival Timing at the Estuary

As the travel time foundations of the flow theorists have failed to appear in experimental testing, flow theorists retreat to their intuition that it is inherently better for salmon to get to the estuary earlier in the year. The primary basis for this belief is that before there were dams, it is believed that juvenile salmon got to the estuary faster—perhaps as much as a month earlier for juvenile spring and summer chinook.[76] That is almost certainly an overestimate, but it seems likely that it takes juvenile salmon longer to get to the sea now.

The question of arrival timing is a difficult one, because estuary and ocean conditions vary from week to week and year to year. Salmon have evolved to adapt to these natural variations. It is probably true that hatchery and barging systems, in addition to the construction of the dams, have altered the timing when juveniles appear in the estuary, but it is also true that scientists have never measured whether the effect is positive, negative, or statistically insignificant.

Transportation gets juvenile salmon downstream faster than natural conditions, but this is never cited as an advantage of transportation. Indeed, studies of salmon which have been transported down below Bonneville Dam produce exactly the opposite result supposed by flow theorists: salmon transported later in the year have substantially higher survivals.

This could be a byproduct of hatchery management that dumps huge quantities of juvenile salmon into the river at the same time earlier in the year, so that there is not enough food for all the salmon and most perish. No one really knows. We do know that one of the most productive stocks of wild chinook salmon in the Columbia River Basin, the Lewis River, Washington stock, happens to migrate through the estuary two months later than all the other salmonid stocks.[77]

There have been huge changes in the estuary since the late 1800s. Scientists believe that the destruction of wetlands has caused a fundamental shift away from macroscopic plants (algae) toward microscopic plants (phytoplankton). This change in the food base is thought to favor shad over salmon. Shad eat the zooplankton that eat the phytoplankton; juvenile salmon prefer larger prey that eat algae.[78] If that is true, that is yet another reason that removing dams won't bring back salmon: we'd have to restore all the wetlands too. And if we took out the dams, we'd reduce the amount of food for the shad, since it appears that algae production in the reservoirs and the resulting "microdetritus input to the estuary is nearly equivalent to the macrodetritus cut off from the estuary by diking the wetlands".[79]

From a long-term perspective, natural processes gradually turn estuarine marshes into swamps, and eventually dry ground, as plants trap sediment and cause the ground to rise.[80] This natural process is much slower than human effects, but it too works against salmon, and could be yet another reason why historic peaks of salmon production can never again be attained— unless and until another ice dam breaks and scours out the Columbia River Gorge again.

Adverse Effects of Flow Augmentation on Adults

The focus on survival of juvenile salmon is a relatively recent phenomenon. Biologists recognized decades ago that the primary problem likely to be caused by the dams was that the adults returning to the spawning grounds could not ascend them. As Bonneville Dam was constructed, controversy raged as to whether its fish ladders would work. As one writer observed, "noted scientists who have studied the situation claim it is extremely important that the salmon find the big stairways with an absolute minimum of delay. Salmon on their way to spawn have only a limited amount of energy. They never eat from the time they enter fresh water from the sea until they die high in the mountains after breeding. If the female salmon, each carrying from twenty-five hundred to five thousand eggs, spend their strength fighting the dam, they will not be able to ascend the long series of pools when they finally discover them. The men building the dam are aware of this."[81] Fortunately, the fish ladders were an enormous success.

At the time, effects on juvenile salmon were neglected. Now the pendulum has swung, and the effects on adults are ignored. The lack of focus on adults seems to be a byproduct of having harvest agencies in charge of protecting endangered salmon: once the salmon reach harvestable size, the agencies' conflict of interest becomes overpowering. Juvenile Snake River salmon are protected as endangered, but adults are caught and sold for food. The fishery agencies consistently refuse to evaluate the effects of their efforts to improve dam passage for juveniles on the returning adults, probably because in most cases they are making things worse for adults.

A picture is worth a thousand words, and the problem that flow augmentation poses for adults is best illustrated by a cartoon that appeared in *The Oregonian*:

Figure 21: *Oregonian* Cartoon[82]

What is wrong with this picture? Put yourself in the salmon's place. The salmon is trying to swim against a raging torrent of water. The last thing in the world the salmon could possibly be thinking is that it needs a stronger current to swim against. This cartoon illustrates the remarkable degree to which worship of flow has displaced rational thought in fisheries management (and the media).

Fishermen have long recognized that "[i]n order to conserve energy in their upstream passage, salmon tend to 'sound' or move to the bottom of the river where the current is not so strong, especially during the ebb tide and during periods of freshet".[83]   Scientific studies confirm that the progress of returning adult salmon up the Columbia River is impeded by higher flows. Delays of up to several days at each dam from higher flows are well documented.

As Dr. William McNeil has explained,

"Summer chinook and sockeye exhibit delayed passage time at high flow along with spring chinook. Sustained upstream movement against river currents and possible delays in locating ladders at dams places demands on finite energy reserves. Adult salmon fast during their spawning migration, and expended energy is not replaced. *Artificially increasing water velocity through flow augmentation and/or reservoir drawdown is likely to delay migration of spring and summer chinook and sockeye spawners.*"[84]

As Dr. McNeil points out, the adverse effects would be strongest on the endangered "Snake River spring chinook salmon which migrate the farthest distance from the ocean to reach spawning grounds".[85]

Dr. McNeil suggests that "it remains to be determined whether prespawning survival is compromised" as a result of the delays".[86]   Fishery agencies have long blamed the dams for delaying adults and causing salmon mortality, going so far as to claim that "[d]elays of three to four days often killed the fish".[87] The U.S. Army Corps of Engineers estimates that some of the "natural river" drawdown plans under consideration would increase adult travel time from 10-30%.[88] Thus if the fishery agencies were consistent, they would have to state that dam removal or reservoir drawdown would decimate adult salmon.

As a matter of elementary population biology, each returning adult is literally thousands of times more important to the perpetuation of the species than one of the thousands of juvenile salmon heading downstream. Adults returning up the Columbia River have survived anywhere from 2 to 6 years of competition in the river, the estuary and the open ocean. They have run a gauntlet of predators, both human and animal. They are returning with thousands of eggs to deposit in the spawning grounds. Without success in returning these adults to the spawning grounds, salmon populations cannot hope to recover.

Flow augmentation has also caused extraordinary adverse effects on the fish and wildlife in the reservoirs drained to provide flows. Chapter 11 discusses the effects in the reservoir behind Dworshak Dam in Northern

Idaho. Similar if not worse effects are found in reservoirs in Montana which have been drained for flow augmentation.[89]

It ought to be shocking that since 1980, the largest single component of the $3 billion or more spent on salmon restoration has gone to increase flows, yet we do not know one of the most basic facts necessary to tell whether or not these flows help: whether benefits to juveniles (if any) outweigh known adverse effects on adults. How this came about is, in part, a product of what passes for "law" in salmon recovery.

Flow Theory and the Northwest Power Planning Council

Shortly after the pioneering but flawed works of Raymond, Sims & Ossiander, power interests went before Congress with a plan to allocate hydropower produced from the dams among themselves. Congressman Dingell, at the urging of environmentalists, declared that the bill would not go forward unless it contained measures to promote fish and wildlife protection in the Columbia River Basin.

Obviously, without some minimal level of flows in the river, no fish are going to survive. Minimum outflows were already in place for each of the projects on the Columbia and its tributaries. This was not enough for the fishery interests, which sought and obtained language creating a Regional Council charged with preparing a fish and wildlife program. And they succeeded in getting Congress to declare that the Council's Fish and Wildlife Program should include measures to "provide flows of sufficient quality and quantity between [the dams] to improve production, migration and survival of [anadromous] fish . . ."[90]

Like proponents of the federal income tax, which began as less than 1% of high incomes, the flow proponents downplayed the significance of the provision. And just like no one ever thought that income tax rates would rise to 50% or higher, no one ever thought that flow augmentation would come to demand so much water. Over the years, the Congressional command to achieve flows of sufficient quantity and quality for salmon became an end in itself, rather than a means to improved salmon survival.

In 1982, the Northwest Power Planning Council recommended a "water budget" for salmon that would supplement spring flows with 1.2 million acre-feet of water, an amount later increased to 3.5 million acre-feet. An agricultural lobbyist once told me that one million acre-feet of water can grow enough wheat to feed the residents of the City of Portland for five years. The 1982 Council program was a significant amount of water to devote to salmon recovery, but it was only the beginning.

178

The Council explained that through "adaptive management", the results of this experiment in providing flows would be monitored carefully. As one early member of the Council, Kai Lee of Washington, explained, the Council's "[m]easures should make an observable difference. Natural populations of fish and wildlife fluctuate for reasons beyond human control or prediction. If an experimental probe is to have a discernible signal, it must have an impact sufficient to overcome the noise of natural variations."[91]

No one ever demonstrated any impact on salmon survival from artificial increases in flows in the Columbia River Basin. By 1992, the Council's program increased the water budget to about 8 million acre feet (a program denounced by the United States Court of Appeals for the Ninth Circuit as inadequate—see Chapter 9). The National Marine Fisheries Service, acting under the White House's extraordinary interpretations of the Endangered Species Act, later increased the amount to 10-11 million acre feet (a program denounced by the United States District Court for the District of Oregon as inadequate—see Chapter 9), and later further increased it to 13-16 million acre-feet.[92]

If one followed the simplistic approach salmon advocates apply to transportation of juvenile salmon (it increased, but the salmon didn't, so the program is a failure), the flow augmentation program has clearly been an enormous failure: these drastic increases in flow have produced no increases in salmon populations whatsoever. Flow theorists, however, adopt the common posture of government program advocates—the program has not yet been funded enough to really make a difference. Demands for still higher flows persist to this day, with lawsuits pending to force even higher flows.

As of 1996, there is such unquestioning allegiance to "flow targets" that the staff of the Northwest Power Planning Council proudly released a computer game (actually a spreadsheet program with gamelike graphics) to allow interested citizens in the Northwest an opportunity to see how manipulating reservoir levels throughout the Columbia River Basin could influence achievement of the flow targets. The program allows users to manipulate reservoir levels and flow targets and (under)estimates the resulting costs. *But the program presents no quantification of benefits at all.* For Council staff, manipulation of dam operations has become a game it itself, a game in which no one cares about whether, and to what extent, biological benefits are being achieved through the manipulation.

The Council's Independent Science Group, discussing the concept of "adaptive management" generally, concluded that

"... adaptive management has since [1987] been used to justify a variety of actions on the premise that they may provide new information. We contend that adaptive management is intended as a much more rigorous scientific approach. The term should only be used in reference to explicit management experiments that include hypotheses, test conditions and a detailed experimental design. The concept of adaptive management should not be used as justification for every action about which the outcome is uncertain."[93]

The ISG went so far as to suggest, correctly, that "[i]t is not clear that the Council or any other regional management entity is politically equipped to effectively utilize adaptive management".[94]

Unfortunately, while the ISG could recognize science in the abstract, when it came to flow augmentation, the Group concluded that it would simply redefine "old" flow augmentation as "purely technological and unsubstantiated", while "new" flow augmentation was obviously desirable as part of the "establishment of normative river conditions".[95] The National Research Council was more straightforward, concluding in 1995 that: "[t]he effectiveness of flow augmentation alternatives has not been demonstrated."[96]

My clients funded a study focusing on how many endangered Snake River salmon you would get for the lost power production from Columbia River flow augmentation, and gave it to the National Marine Fisheries Service, for guidance as to whether flow augmentation constituted a "reasonable and prudent" measure under § 7 of the Endangered Species Act. Put succinctly, NMFS wanted to try to help Idaho fish by moving more water from Canada and Montana through Washington. The cost was in excess of $10,000,000 per returning adult salmon. Nevertheless, NMFS recommended that the Corps and BPA do it, and the White House ordered them to do it.

We later heard that the critical decision was made in a Saturday meeting at the White House. The White House Office of Environmental Policy listened to the delegation from Northwest federal agencies. BPA and the Corps said that more flow would not help the salmon; the fishery agencies said it would. The White House knew that BPA would hide costs in its rates, so it didn't cost the White House anything to give the fishery agencies what they wanted.

The Clinton/Gore Administration has, in substance, forbidden the dam operators from questioning fishery managers about the biological benefits of their schemes. During meetings of the federal, state and tribal Implementation Team in 1996, agency officials from BPA and the Bureau of

Reclamation who asked for an explanation of the biological benefits of flow decisions were repeatedly ruled out of order.

Most of the people I work with now think that flow augmentation demands are really just a tool used by the state and tribal harvest agencies to extract money from the dam operators. As more and more evidence mounts that flow augmentation accomplishes nothing, the harvest managers are now becoming willing to "trade" the costs of flow augmentation for new adventures in salmon mitigation. The Chairman of the Northwest Power Planning Council, John Etchart, has even asked power industry lobbyists whether they wouldn't be willing to take out a dam or two in exchange for eliminating the flow augmentation tax on Bonneville.

The Computer Modeling Wars

"When you can measure what you are speaking about and express it in numbers you know something about it, but when you cannot measure it, when you cannot express it in numbers, your knowledge is of a meagre and unsatisfactory kind; it may be the beginning of knowledge, but you have scarcely, in your thoughts, advanced to the state of *science*, whatever the matter may be." Lord Kelvin (1883).

In the spring of 1994, I came upon a two-page paper by Dr. James Anderson of the University of Washington that suggested that there were two possible views of the salmon world: one in which in-river survival is very low, and ocean survival high, and one in which in-river survival is higher, but ocean survival was lower. The paper suggested that existing data could not exclude either possibility. I thought to myself, here at last is someone with an open mind on these issues.

So I traveled to Seattle, wandered down the halls of the University of Washington's School of Fisheries, and knocked on Professor Anderson's door. He was (and is) eager to explain his salmon work, which consisted of the construction of a huge and complex model of salmon survival called CRiSP (short for Columbia River Salmon Passage).

Most of us recognize that computers are essential to deal with complicated problems facing our society. That is why computers are used in nearly every facet of economic activity. One of the ways computers are useful is in modeling natural phenomena which are too complex for the human mind to assess and predict. Thus, we use computer models to build airplanes. We use computer models to study the weather. And we should use computer models to study salmon.

After all, the greatest challenges faced by salmon managers is attempting to figure out what effect any particular human action will have upon salmon. If you open up a reservoir and increase the flow downstream, without some sort of quantitative model, assessing the relative magnitude of the effects on both juvenile and adult salmon, you have no idea what the net effect on salmon populations will be.

Unfortunately, it is the deliberate policy of Northwest fishery managers to operate in such ignorance. The Bonneville Power Administration, which makes extensive use of computers in its own operation, has long recognized the importance of building computer models that can assess the effects of human actions on natural salmon populations. Beginning in the late 1980s, they began to fund the development of computer models of salmon migration in the Columbia River and its tributaries. Other federal funds have created complicated models of harvest and models to predict adult returns to the river.

State and tribal fishery managers and the Northwest Power Planning Council pressured BPA to provide funding to develop their own models. The leading state and tribal model of juvenile salmon passage is called FLUSH, standing for "Fish Leaving Under Several Hypotheses". A derivative model developed by staff at the Northwest Power Planning Council Model is called PAM for "Passage Analysis Model". Over the years, FLUSH has been invoked to support all kinds of expensive changes to dam operations. Yet, no one knows how the FLUSH model works because there is no manual explaining its operations. Nor is the model code available to anyone.

CRiSP, on the other hand, is available to anyone. You can call up to Dr. Anderson and get a copy of it. You can run the model on the Internet. There is a large and comprehensive manual that explains everything the model does, and the formulas that contain its assumptions. The manual is available on the Internet as well. (Dr. Anderson also runs the website with the single best collection of Columbia Basin salmon data, located at http://www.cqs.washington.edu, and hosted by the University of Washington.)

To construct a computer model, the model builder relies on data gathered about what he is modelling and the relationships among the various factors. In the context of the Columbia River salmon migration, there are very detailed data available going back many years for river flows, temperatures, historic dam operations, harvest levels, and many other factors. The model must account for mortality across the concrete at the dams and for predation in the reservoirs. It must account for the percentage of fish that are transported around the dams.

There is such a wealth of data that the construction of models proceeds in two phases. First, the model is *calibrated* against some of the data. This is, in a sense, the data that goes into building the model. Then, as new data become available or more old data are discovered, the model can be *validated* against this second set of data by using the model to predict what the first set of data says the second set of data will be.

For example, if we have flow and survival data for the 1980s and build a model calibrated against that data, when new data become available in the 1990s, we can run the model with new flows and see whether the predicted survivals with 1990 flows match the actual survivals measured in the 1990s.

In 1993, 1994 and 1995, new data became available based on a new and better method for estimating survival based on PIT-tags. The CRiSP model predicted survival consistent with the new data. The FLUSH model did not.

I asked Dr. Anderson to review the limited information that was available about the operation of the FLUSH model. He concluded that the assumptions that went into it were wildly unrealistic. For example, one of the chief characteristics of the FLUSH model is that it predicts very great survival increases from fairly small increases in river flow, because it is based, in part, on the long-discredited Sims and Ossiander flow/survival relationships.[97] Dr. Anderson discovered that the way this was accomplished was by inserting a relationship under which, as flows increased and travel time decreased, survivals went above 100%—an impossibility.[98] The model is also hard-wired to pretend that smolt transportation does not work.

As the National Marine Fisheries Service prepared its biological opinion on hydropower operations for 1995 and future years, we were able to persuade them that the CRiSP model is more accurate. Nevertheless, as a political matter, NMFS declared that because the FLUSH model represented the judgment and skill of the state and tribal fishery managers, it too should be looked at in making management decisions.

I thought that if a federal agency was going to make a decision based, in part, on the results of a computer model, the model ought to be available to the public. It is hard to understand how a government agency like the National Marine Fisheries Service can make a decision based on a model when it does not have the model, cannot run the model, has no idea what assumptions are built into the model, and can rely only upon the assertions of state and tribal managers as what the model does. Many of the researchers within NMFS have long been frustrated by this state of affairs, but the power of the state and tribal bureaucracy is such that none of them dared challenge it.

After seeing the FLUSH model used to justify actions that we knew made no sense, we asked the state and tribal fish authorities for a copy of it. Specifically, in the *Idaho Fish and Game* case (discussed in Chapter 9), we made a formal request for production of the model pursuant to the Federal Rules of Civil Procedure, which call for disclosure of any document "reasonably calculated to lead to the discovery of admissible evidence".

The state and tribal fishery agencies refused to allow us access to the model, so we filed a motion before Judge Marsh for an order compelling production of the model. After we filed the motion to compel discovery, we also brought to the attention of many Northwest decisionmakers the idea that the FLUSH model was a secret model and that it was improper to make salmon decisions based on a secret model.

The State of Oregon, taking the lead in resolving this issue for the state and tribal fishery agencies, finally agreed to produce the model shortly before Judge Marsh was to rule on our motion, but only if we agreed to a rather stringent set of rules governing it use. In particular, we could make no use of the model without promptly informing the state and tribal fishery managers what we were doing. Anxious to get the model, we signed a stipulated order with the limitations in it.

As initially produced, the model would not run; many of the files were missing. After months of foot dragging, we finally persuaded the state and tribal fishery managers to produce the additional files and ran the model. Our first occasion to use it came in 1996 in the context of attempting to resolve the question whether additional spill was appropriate to benefit salmon. The state and tribal fishery managers argued that survival in 1995 was higher than 1994 because there were higher spills.

I was convinced that the FLUSH model would have predicted much higher survivals in 1995 than actually occurred. Thus if you took the model as accurate, something had to be killing the fish to bring the survivals down. For reasons explained in Chapter 12, we thought that was the spill.

I asked Dr. Anderson to run the FLUSH model and forwarded the results to the State of Oregon for review. The State Attorney General's Office then threatened to file a motion holding us in contempt of court if we showed the results to the state water quality regulators.[99] So we told the water quality regulators that the fishery managers wouldn't let them see what their own model predicted. In proceedings detailed in Chapter 12, the Oregon water quality regulators rubber-stamped the spill requests anyway.

The harvest managers know that the lack of complete and comprehensive computer models prevents criticism of their policies. In its recent decision to allow continued heavy harvest on endangered Snake River fall chinook from 1996 to 1998, the National Marine Fisheries Service claimed:

> "It has not been possible to distinguish natural mortality from human-induced mortality in any life stage (except perhaps in the harvest sector) or allocate proportions of human-induced mortality between life stages. Without such a model, and without first resolving remaining uncertainties, it is not possible to calculate with any confidence tradeoffs in survival improvements that may be necessary as a result of a change in mortality that may be contemplated in any life stage."[100]

This is not true, as computer models can already predict with some confidence the effects of harvest managers' decisions, not only with respect to harvest, but also with respect to operation of the dams. But so long as NMFS claims it is true, and the states and tribes block the funding of even better computer models, harvest managers can and will continue to pretend that dams cause most of the problems with salmon in the Columbia River Basin.

How the Church of Flow Deals with Heretics

> "Our political discourse has become so jejune that the natural habits of a powerful mind—sharp reasoning and imaginative rhetoric—are mistaken for petulant temperament." John McGinniss (1997).[101]

From the moment my clients engaged a fisheries scientist in the Pacific Northwest, that scientist was called a "biostitute". Many independent scientists, sensitive to the political ramifications of taking money from electricity interests, refused to be hired by my clients. (Later, as they grew more and more disgusted at the oppression of science by opponents of positions we were asserting, some changed their minds, and were willing to work for us.)

But mere *ad hominem* attacks are not enough of a weapon to silence critics. Some, like Dr. Anderson, are even spurred to greater efforts. The real way to silence a scientist is to cut off his or her funding. There are few scientists who can afford to work on anything they want to. They must get grants to conduct their research. And the grant money comes from the government. No private entity could or would spend hundreds of millions of dollars on salmon research.

185

Operating through the Columbia Basin Fish and Wildlife Authority (CBFWA), the salmon managers prioritized spending for fiscal year 1997 in a way that ensured that BPA would fund no projects likely to challenge the prevailing orthodoxy. CBFWA's adverse effects on the scientific process are common knowledge in the scentific community. One Bonneville Power Administration employee told fisheries consultant Steve Cramer, "[a]s you know, the CBFWA prioritization has greatly impacted our ability to fund independent analyses/reviews which are necessary for responsible stewardship and management of natural resources".[102] He expressed the hope that independent scientific efforts "will help to swing the pendulum back towards technical science-based rather than politically based water management to benefit Columbia River fisheries resources".[103]

Dr. Anderson is a chief target of the salmon managers, who have never forgiven him for producing CRiSP runs that showed that their salmon measures made no sense, and for proving that their FLUSH model made no sense either. By August of 1996, the Salmon Managers had formally declared that they "do not support the use of CRiSP as a management decisionmaking tool", and that the model had "sufficient unresolved problems including input parameters, their structure, and predictive capabilities, that preclude its use as a basis for management decisions".[104] As Dr. Anderson aptly responded, their opposition to CRiSP was "a political statement, not a scientific one".[105]

By the spring of 1997, the state and tribal fishery managers had prepped Joyce Cohen, one of Oregon's two representatives on the Northwest Power Planning Council, to make an extraordinary public attack on Dr. Anderson during a conference to present scientific research results associated with the Council's Fish and Wildlife Program. She attacked his work as "redundant". When he told her that was a lie, she began shaking a fist in his face and got so angry observers thought she would strike him.

The state and tribal fishery managers have also attacked John Skalski, a professor of biological statistics at the University of Washington, who has produced a model forecasting salmon detections at dams that is far more accurate than the model used by the fishery agencies. He was also instrumental in designing the PIT-tag studies that proved survival through reservoirs was far higher than commonly supposed. His response:

> "On multiple occasions, we have invited CBFWA personnel to attend presentations, seminars and workshops—and they have refused. We have tried to work with the [Fish Passage Center] personnel: we have asked to see their alleged predictive approaches and when given the opportunity, to

compare methods head-to-head. We have shown in our 1994 BPA annual report how their methods have an error rate many times that of the PIT-forecaster. We have yet to see any documentation or any post-season evaluation of their capabilities."

"The bottom line is that we have demonstrated the accuracy and precision of our run timing predictions over the last three years. The greater issue is whether we as a community want informed resource decisions based on the best available science or politics to govern the stewardship of Pacific salmon." [106]

State and tribal harvest managers, wasting funds from the Bonneville Power Administration, continue to produce reams of useless computer projections. Typically they support the state and tribal policy positions, and on the rare occasions when they don't, they are simply ignored. The state and tribal community of fishery managers has made its choice: politics must not only govern the stewardship of Pacific salmon, but also the scientific process.

Flow Theorists Take Over the National Marine Fisheries Service

In the early 1980s the National Marine Fisheries Service abandoned any further efforts to document a link between river flow and survival. But in the 1990s, with salmon listed as endangered, the Sims and Ossiander data enjoyed an unprecedented revival despite its fatal flaws.

Reviewing the efforts of the National Marine Fisheries Service to assist salmon through flow augmentation, Drs. Chapman and Giorgi complained that

"Unquestioning reliance on the Sims and Ossiander (1981) data and lack of willingness to even consider the possibility that more recent data better reflect current reality is most dismaying. It may mean that the Sims and Ossiander data are preferred because they rationalize higher flows and drawdown. It may exemplify the observations of cognitive science that truth never catches up with false information, i.e., remove or disprove the premises of a long-held belief and, paradoxically, some people will inappropriately continue to believe the long-held belief is warranted." [107]

"Some people" unfortunately includes nearly all Northwest salmon policymakers.

NMFS appointed a blue-ribbon panel, the Snake River Salmon Recovery Team, to craft a recovery plan for endangered Snake River Salmon. The Team took months of public testimony and met with scientists from all over the Region. They approached the problem like the academics most of them were. The Chairman, the late Don Bevan, former Dean of the School of Fisheries at the University of Washington, more than once characterized the state and tribal fishery scientists pushing increased spring flow augmentation as akin to students who could not defend their thesis. The Team thought that most of the water that was being flushed down the river in the spring was wasted.

By 1995, the National Marine Fisheries Service was defensive about making reliance on flow augmentation the cornerstone of its endangered salmon strategy. Alone among all the dozens of scientific issues relevant to salmon recovery, the Proposed Recovery Plan has page after page of graphs designed to support the Plan's emphasis on flow augmentation. The entire Appendix F is called "Basis for Minimum Flow Ranges for Operation of the Federal Columbia River Power System". And the Biological Opinion for 1995 and Future Years which, as a practical matter, governs operation of the mainstem dams along the Columbia and Snake Rivers, was released with an accompanying paper purporting to provide the bases for the flow targets set by NMFS.

The Service's website, providing a selective set of materials on the salmon problem, suggests that "it seems likely that reductions in flows and turbidity in the spring have not only increased the smolts' travel time, but also added to their risk of predation on their way to the estuary. Reductions in flow have also decreased the size of the river plume extending into the ocean (an environmental factor which offers the smolts some concealment from predators when they first reach the ocean)."[108]

Right now, the "river plume" theory is *en vogue* among the conservation biologists, including the Northwest Power Planning Council's Independent Science Group.[109] In all likelihood, research will eventually prove this theory as bogus as all the other asserted bases for flow augmentation. After all, just how much more turbid can we make the estuary by releasing water from Montana and Idaho? Or removing upriver dams? Enough to make a difference in predation rates?

Further Attempts to Halt Useful PIT-tag Research

By 1997, the state and tribal harvest managers were recognizing that scientific testing using PIT-tags was not showing the enormous effects of dams that they all believed in. While continuing to fight a rear guard action against the studies, they resurrected a theory of "delayed hydrosystem mortality". Under this theory, the fish that migrate through the hydrosystem are marked for death by processes that are hypothesized (like "stress"), but unproven.

To try and prove that such effects existed, the harvest managers are pushing studies comparing smolt-to-adult survival ratios for upriver and downriver hatchery stocks. The NMFS/University of Washington scientists have been harshly critical of this approach, and for good reason. As one report by University of Washington researchers John Skalski and Richard Townsend pointed out, it was a necessary condition for the statistical validity of such studies that the upriver and downriver stocks be equally mixed in the ocean, yet they could identify no stocks meeting such a test. The choice of comparison stocks "had dramatic effect on results and inferences"—"select a stock, select an answer".[110]

Recognizing a need to silence the pesky scientists in Seattle once and for all, the state and tribal harvest managers are in the process of slowly attempting to take over the most critical salmon research in the Columbia Basin: the efforts to measure survival through the river using PIT-tags. Just six months after they had completed a comprehensive prioritization of salmon research and recovery programs, which was rubber-stamped by the Northwest Power Planning Council, they emerged with an unprioritized proposal to PIT-tag hundreds of thousands of fish at Snake River hatcheries and build PIT-tag detectors at the hatcheries. (Presumably, they still continued to oppose constructing PIT-tag detectors at Bonneville Dam, so that measurements of in-river survival could be made.)

Their proposal triggered criticism from NMFS scientists and University of Washington scientists. The NMFS scientists pointed out that at least 40% of the PIT-tags would be lost before the first dam because the smolts would die upriver, and that ongoing NMFS research based on marking at the dams would probably "provide a more complete and cost-effective analysis".[111]

Dr. Anderson reported to BPA, which sought his advice, that the "proposal lacks an ecological framework, ignores biological mechanisms, mathematical formalism, and hypothesis testing". Beyond the lack of scientific merit, Dr. Anderson had the temerity to observe that the experiment was "beyond the capabilities of the Fish Passage Center", the ostensible project manager. Indeed, he noted that the principal investigator, Michele DeHart, "has no track record in research".[112]

The state and tribal response to Dr. Anderson betrayed a characteristic biological ignorance. Dr. Anderson was advised to "cut back on his bile intake" (bile is produced by an organ in the digestive system, not ingested), and was accused of making a "rabid dog attack".[113] But Dr. Anderson was not the only critic. Others observed that it would be at least "unusual" for Ms. DeHart to be the principal investigator "because she does not have an advanced degree or a history of peer-reviewed research".[114]

The Council's Independent Science Advisory Board told the Council that we might get useful information from tagging fish, but that the study design "would need substantial revision to achieve a degree of scientific rigor sufficient for the ISAB to endorse it . . ."[115] Pressured by the States of Oregon and Idaho, the Power Planning Council members gave the go-ahead to start tagging the fish, letting the states and tribes make up the study as they went along.

The old saying is that the fish rots first at the head. The head of the federal environmental effort is Vice President Gore, who has written that optimistic environmental studies should be ignored because they "undermine the effort to build a solid base of support for the difficult actions we must soon take".[116] When the official policy of the federal government is to ignore and discredit scientists whose research reveals the small significance the mainstem dams have for salmon survival, there is little hope that we are going to get good decisions on what to do with those dams.

NOTES TO CHAPTER 7

[1] Dr. Peacock is or was the Chairman of Surgery, University of Arizona, College of Medicine, quoted in Med. World News, Sept. 1, 1974, at 45.

[2] T. Sowell, *The Vision of the Anointed: Self-Congratulation as a Basis for Social Policy* 2 (Basic Books 1995).

[3] T. Sowell, *Visions of the Anointed* 31.

[4] R. Fox, quoted in "Science Under Scrutiny", *Harvard Magazine* 27 (Mar.-April 1997).

[5] Ms. Fox suggests that "sociologists are just plain used to *social* facts—that's what they study—and may be constitutionally unable to distinguish the other kind". *Id.* at 23.

[6] M Landolt, *Fisheries Forum* 3(2), at 1 (May 1995).

[7] Letter, G. Heath to N. Dicks, July 21, 1994.

[8] M. Landholt, *Fisheries Forum* 3(2), at 1 (May 1995).

[9] J. Pinkerton, "Enviromanticism: The Poetry of Nature as a Political Force", *Foreign Affairs*, May/June 1997, at 5.

[10] *See, e.g., Sierra Club v. Marita*, 46 F.3d 606 (7th Cir 1995).

[11] *See, e.g.,* Open Letter to Sen. Chafee and Cong. Saxton, July 23, 1996 (attacking proposed "no surprises" policy for landowners) (http://darwin.eeb.uconn.edu/Documents/esa-letter.html).

[12] R. Noss, "Some Principles of Conservation Biology as They Apply to Environmental Law", 69 Chicago-Kent L. Rev. 893, 895 (1994).

[13] R. Keiter, "Conservation Biology and the Law: Assessing the Challenges Ahead", 69 Chicago-Kent L. Rev. 911 (1994).

[14] J. Cone, *A Common Fate* 24.

[15] *See generally* J. Cone, *A Common Fate* 25-28, 34-38.

[16] *Id.* at 41.

[17] While the group is centered in Portland, there are also members in other states, including Ed Bowles and Steve Pettit of the Idaho Department of Fish and Game, and James Nielsen and Olaf Langesson of the Washington Department of Fish and Wildlife.

[18] These quotes appear in B. Harden, *A River Lost* (at p. 214), attributed to consultant and utility lobbyist Al Wright.

[19] ISG, *Return to the River* xv.

[20] Quoted in G. Easterbrook, *A Moment on the Earth* 63.

[21] NRC, *Upstream* at 194 (Prepub. ed.) (Figure 9-1).

[22] *Id.* at 193.

[23] *PNGC v. Brown*, 822 F. Supp. at 1487.

[24] *Id.* n.16.

[25] H. Raymond, "Effects of Dams and Impoundments on migrations of juvenile chinook salmon and steelhead from the Snake River, 1966 to 1975". Trans. Am. Fish. Soc. 108:505-29 (1979).

[26] C. Sims & F. Ossiander, "Migrations of juvenile chinook and steelhead trout in the Snake River from 1973 to 1979, a research summary". Final Report to U.S. Army Corps of Engineers (NMFS N.W. Fish. Sci. Cent. 1981).

[27] Data from C. Steward, "Assessment of the Flow-Survival Relationship Obtained by Sims & Ossiander (1981) for Snake River Spring/Summer Chinook Salmon Smolts", Final Report, BPA Contract No. DE-AM79-93BP99654, at 5 (April 1994) (reprinting Sims & Ossiander's 1981 data).

[28] J. Williams & G. Matthews, "A review of flow/survival relationships for juvenile salmonids in the Columbia River Basin", manuscript submitted to *Fishery Bulletin* (NMFS CZESD March 1994), at 12.

[29] C. Steward, "Assessment of the Flow-Survival Relationship Obtained by Sims & Ossiander (1981) for Snake River Spring/Summer Chinook Salmon Smolts", Final Report, BPA Contract No. DE-AM79-93BP99654, at iv (April 1994)

[30] J. Williams & G. Matthews, "A review of flow/survival relationships for juvenile salmonids in the Columbia River Basin", manuscript submitted to *Fishery Bulletin* (NMFS CZESD March 1994), at 20.

[31] *Id.* at 24.

[32] C. Steward, "Assessment of the Flow-Survival Relationship Obtained by Sims & Ossiander (1981) for Snake River Spring/Summer Chinook Salmon Smolts", Final Report, BPA Contract No. DE-AM79-93BP99654, at vii (April 1994)

[33] R. Hilborn *et al.*, "The Relationship Between River Flow and Survival for Columbia River Chinook Salmon", U. Wash. Draft Report WH-10 (1993).

[34] D. Chapman & A. Giorgi, "Comments on Work of Biological and FCPRS Alternative Work Groups", at 10 n.8 (1994).

[35] D. Chapman & A. Giorgi, "Comments on National Marine Fisheries Service Draft Biological Opinion on FCRPS Operations", at 7 (1995).

[36] Letter, Snake River Salmon Recovery Team to J. Etchart, April 17, 1997, at 7-8; *see also* D. Chapman & A. Giorgi, "Comments on Work of Biological and FCPRS Alternative Work Groups", at 9 (1994) ("Preliminary data from the 1993 smolt migration show no relationship between detection rate [presumed to be a surrogate for survival] and either travel time or Snake River discharge . . .").

[37] NMFS, 1996 Annual Report to the Oregon Department of Environmental Quality, Jan. 24, 1997, at 8 (emphasis added).

[38] S. Smith *et al.*, "Survival Estimates for the Passage of Juvenile Salmonids Through Snake River Dams and Reservoirs, 1996", at 50 (DOE Contract DE-AI79-93BP10891) (Sept. 1997) (review draft).

[39] From K. Whitty, "Migration Responses of Juvenile Salmonids to Pulses in Flow" (Figure 3) (1994).

[40] K. Casavant, "New thinking about Columbia salmon", *Seattle Times,* Jan. 30, 1997.

[41] SEIS at 4-11.

[42] W. McNeil, "Water Velocity and Migration of Juvenile Chinook Salmon in the Columbia River", Sept. 26, 1994, at 9 (paper prepared for *Hydro Review;* later published).

[43] SEIS App. H, at H-10.

[44] *Id.*

[45] ISG, *Return to the River,* at 55.

[46] H. Raymond, "Effects of dams and impoundments on migration of juvenile chinook salmon and steelhead from the Snake River, 1966 to 1975", *Trans. Am. Fish. Soc.* 108: 505-529 (1979).

[47] W. McNeil, "Water Velocity and Migration of Juvenile Chinook Salmon in the Columbia River", Sept. 26, 1994, at 5 (paper prepared for *Hydro Review;* later published).

[48] *Id.* at 6.

[49] *Id.*

[50] S. Smith *et al.*, "Survival Estimates for the Passage of Juvenile Salmonids Through Snake River Dams and Reservoirs, 1996", at 35.

[51] *Id.* at 34. Flow did explain about 30 percent of the variance in travel time in a regression based on a different set of data derived from groups released at Lower Granite Dam.

[52] W. McNeil, "Water Velocity and Migration of Juvenile Chinook Salmon in the Columbia River", at 8.

[53] F. Seufert, *Return to the River* at 145 (emphasis added).

[54] ISG, *Return to the River* 231.

[55] B. Harden, *A River Lost* 71-72.

[56] *See also,* NMFS, 1995 Biological Opinion on FCRPS Operations, Mar. 2, 1995, at 72 ("In his review on smolt transformation, Hoar (1976) provided clear evidence that juvenile fall chinook salmon once they begin to migrate are likely in a state of maturation that would allow a gradual (and possibly sharp) transition to full-strength seawater").

[57] *See, e.g.,* J. Cone, *A Common Fate* 119; B. Harden, *A River Lost* 71-72; K. Petersen, *River of Life, Channel of Death* 107 ("young salmon do not swim to the sea").

[58] ISG, *Return to the River* 198.

[59] A. Giorgi *et al* "Migratory Behavior and adult contribution of summer outmigrating subyearling chinook salmon in John Day Reservoir", NMFS Final Report to BPA under Contract No. DE-A179-83BP39645 (1990); D. Chapman *et al.*, "Status of Snake River chinool salmon, Report to PNUCC (1991); *but cf.* D. Rondorf & W. Miller, Identification of the spawning, rearing and migratory requirements of fall chinook salmon in the Columbia River Basin, BPA Annual Report, Contract No. DE-A179-91BP21708-2 (1994).

[60] ISG, *Return to the River* 208.

[61] *See, e.g.*, D. Chapman *et al.*, "Status of summer/fall chinook salmon in the mid-Columbia region", Feb. 28, 1994, at 114 (D. Chapman Consultants) ("Travel times for median arrival at McNary Dam for wild and hatchery fish, respectively, were about 39 days in 1991 and 24 days in 1992. Thus survival should have been considerably greater in 1992 than in 1991. Recovery percentages show that it was not.").

[62] A. Giorgi *et al.*, "Factors that Influence the Downstream Migration Rates of Juvenile Salmon and Steelhead through the Hydroelectric System in the Mid-Columbia River Basin", *North American Journal of Fisheries Management*, 17:268-82 (1997), at 278.

[63] *Id.* at 280.

[64] ISG, *Return to the River* 235.

[65] *Id.* at 220.

[66] *Id.* at 222.

[67] *Id.* at 223.

[68] SOR, Final EIS, at 4-99.

[69] NRC, *Upstream* 210 (Prepub. ed.).

[70] R. Shively, T. Poe, & S. Sauter, "Feeding Response by Northern Squawfish to a Hatchery Release of Juvenile Salmonids in the Clearwater River, Idaho", *Trans. Am. Fish. Soc.* 125:3230-236 (1996).

[71] *See* J. Anderson & R. Hinrichson, "A Life History Approach to Managing the Columbia River Hydrosystem for the Benefit of Salmon Populations", Oct. 28, 1994, at 1-2.

[72] NRC, *Upstream* at 199 (Prepub. ed.).

[73] ISG, *Return to the River* 280.

[74] O. Bullard, *Crisis on the Columbia* 111 (Touchstone Press 1968) (reporting comments of unidentified Oregon State Fish Commission biologists).

[75] U.S. Army Corps of Engineers, "Interim Status Report", at 9-38.

[76] U.S. Army Corps of Engineers, "Interim Status Report", at 2-4.

[77] ISG, *Return to the River* 461.

[78] C. Simenstad, L. Small & C. Intyre, *Consumption Processes and Food Web Structure in the Columbia River Estuary*, 25 Progressive Oceanography 271 (1990), *cited in* U.S. Army Corps of Engineers, "Interim Status Report", at 2-7 to 2-8.

[79] ISG, *Return to the River* at 460.

[80] ISG, *Return to the River* 458.

[81] *Our Promised Land* 130-31

[82] *The Oregonian*, Sept. 24, 1995. Jeff Ohman, the cartoonist, graciously agreed to let me reprint his work

[83] I. Martin, *Legacy and Testament: The Story of the Columbia River Gillnetters* 25 (WSU Press 1994).

[84] W. McNeil, "Timing of Passage of Adult Salmon and Steelhead at Columbia Basin Dams", May 17, 1993, at 6.

[85] *Id.* at 2.

[86] *Id.* at 6-7.

[87] J. Cone, *A Common Fate* 127 (citing unspecified assertions of the "Fisheries Service").

[88] U.S. Army Corps of Engineers, "Interim Status Report", at ES-13.

[89] *See, e.g.,* ISG, *Return to the River* 265.

[90] Section 4(h)(6)(E)(ii) of the Northwest Power Act; *see also* 16 U.S.C. § 839.

[91] K. Lee & J. Lawrence, "Adaptive Management: Learning from the Columbia River Basin Fish and Wildlife Program", 16 Envt'l Law 431, 445-46 (1986).

[92] *See* NMFS, 1995 Biological Opinion on FCRPS Operations, Mar. 2, 1995, at 96 (comparing Endangered Species Act program requirements as applied to "the drought years of 1992-94").

[93] ISG, *Return to the River* xxii.

[94] *Id.* at 46.

[95] *Id.* at 266-67.

[96] *Upstream* at 209 (Prepub. ed.).

[97] J. Anderson, "FLUSH and PAM models: A critique of concepts and calibrations", Oct. 28, 1994.

[98] *Id.* Dr. Anderson informed me early in 1997 that the FLUSH modelers had revised the model so that it no longer predicts greater than 100% survival at high flows.

[99] Letter, E. Bloch to J. Buchal, Feb. 13, 1994 ("It is our strong position that, in several respects, Dr. Anderson's analysis indeed violates the terms of the protective order, and therefore may not be presented to the EQC, NMFS or any other body at any time. . . . I want to be clear that in the event you go forward with your effort to submit this analysis, we will seek a contempt order against your clients.").

[100] NMFS, Biological Opinion, "Impacts on Listed Snake River Salmon by Fisheries Conducted Pursuant to the 1996-1998 Management Agreement for Upper Columbia River Fall Chinook", July 31, 1996, at 14.

[101] J. McGinnis, "Courtroom Arguments", *The Wall Street Journal,* Feb. 4, 1997, at A16 (reviewing *A Matter of Interpretation* by Antonin Scalia).

[102] E-mail, P. Poe to S. Cramer, Aug. 8, 1996.

[103] *Id.*

[104] Memo, S. Pettit, J. Nielsen, R. Boyce, M. Yoshinaka, and R. Heineth to C. Henriksen, Aug. 2, 1996, at 5.

[105] E-mail, J. Anderson to C. Henricksen, August 6, 1996.

[106] Reprinted in *Clearing Up,* Aug. 12, 1996, at 7.

[107] D. Chapman & A. Giorgi, "Comments on Work of Biological and FCPRS Alternative Work Groups", at 9 n.4 (1994).

[108] http://kingfish.ssp.nmfs.gov/tmcintyr/fish/nwsalmon.html (accessed 12/14/96).

[109] *See, e.g.,* ISG, *Return to the River* 58.

[110] J. Skalski & R. Townsend, "Lessons Learned for the Upriver-Downriver Analysis of Priest Rapids Hatchery Returns", overheads presented to the ISAB, Dec. 17, 1996.

[111] Memorandum cited in B. Rudolph, "Huge PIT-Tag Study Planned by Long-Time Critics; NMFS Has Doubts", *Clearing Up*, Dec. 23, 1996, at 6.

[112] Memo, Dr. Anderson to BPA (attn. J. Geiselman) & NMFS (attn. J. Williams), Dec. 16, 1996.

[113] Memo, O. Langeness to J. Geiselman, Dec. 25, 1996.

[114] B. Rudolph, "Huge PIT-Tag Study Planned by Long-Term Critics; NMFS has Doubts", *Clearing Up*, Dec. 23, 1996, at 5.

[115] Letter, ISAB to J. Etchart, Jan. 14, 1997, at 1.

[116] Quoted in G. Easterbrook, *A Moment on the Earth* 561.

195

CHAPTER 8: THE PUSH FOR DAM REMOVAL OR "NATURAL RIVER DRAWDOWN"

> "Decisionmakers ought to view skeptically those critics of mitigation measures based on study designs with minor imperfections, who at the same time espouse other mitigative measures that have little or no reliable data to support them. The best example of this double-standard problem is seen in detailed critical treatment of transportation as a mitigation tool on the one hand, and the uncritical acceptance of drawdown as a mitigative tool on the other." Drs. Don Chapman & Al Giorgi (1994).[1]

> "I would like to be the first Secretary of the Interior in history to tear down a really large dam." Bruce Babbitt (1994).[2]

As we have seen, it was and is an article of faith among the flow theorists that the most important thing that salmon need is high velocity in the Columbia and Snake Rivers. There are two ways to increase the velocity of a river: move more water past the same point, or move the same quantity of water through a smaller river. The smaller the cross-sectional area of a river, the higher the velocity must be to get the same quantity of water through.

The mainstem dams on the Columbia and Snake Rivers offer an obvious way to decrease the cross-section of the river: simply lower the level of the reservoir. The critical dispute in salmon recovery today is whether the Pacific Northwest should draw down reservoir levels to assist salmon, or instead rely on transportation and continuing passage improvements at the dams.

Governor Andrus Gives Snake River Drawdown a Boost

Former Idaho Governor Cecil Andrus was one of cleverest politicians west of the Mississippi. He knew that Idaho irrigators, primarily potato farmers, were removing millions of acre-feet of water from the Snake River. The flow advocates in the Idaho Department of Fish and Game told him that the problem for Idaho salmon was insufficient river velocity. Governor Andrus feared that the federal government would try to increase velocity in the Snake River by taking water from the farmers and releasing it downstream.

The Idaho Department of Fish and Game told him that a drawdown strategy could save the potato farmers, albeit at the expense of Northern Idaho interests that wanted to maintain a navigable river to the port of Lewiston,

Idaho. They explained to Governor Andrus how reservoir drawdowns could produce higher river velocity with the same amount of water.

In April 1993, Governor Andrus' office put out a glossy brochure, which is a textbook example of propaganda promoting the Great Salmon Hoax.[3] This single brochure, which was widely distributed at public expense, contains all the key elements of the Hoax. Blasting the dams as "deadly" and the "principal killers", Governor Andrus claimed that "[y]oung salmon stalled in the slack water reservoirs lose their urge to migrate, become easy prey for predator fish, or perish from stress-related causes".[4]

According to Governor Andrus: "The remedy is known. The dams must be modified so reservoirs periodically can be drawn down to speed water and young salmon to the Columbia River and thence to the ocean."[5] This was to be contrasted with the option of releasing water from upstream reservoirs like the ones Idaho irrigators relied on. That "won't fix the problem", said Governor Andrus, because "[i]n a typical low flow year, it would take more stored water than exists to flush young salmon through four full reservoirs on the lower Snake River".[6]

Besides, he said, "[d]raining upstream reservoirs would destroy many agricultural economies and communities, devastate resident fish and wildlife populations, and force building expensive coal-fired or nuclear power plants".[7] Draining the four Lower Snake reservoirs in Eastern Washington would have the same effects on Eastern Washington communities (and also require building power plants), but that wasn't Governor Andrus' concern. After all, he was the Governor of Idaho, not Washington. Governor Andrus even had the state buy billboard space in Washington to advertise his slogan: "Idaho salmon should not be dammed!"[8]

Dam removal efforts have tended to focus on the four lower Snake River Dams, Ice Harbor, Lower Monumental, Little Goose and Lower Granite. Few people remember that when those dams were authorized, the U.S. Army Corps of Engineers made "an all-out effort to convince Congress to authorize the Lower Snake River Fish and Wildlife Compensation Plan, the largest in the nation at the time".[9] By the end of 1996, Northwest electric ratepayers had invested $215,696,000 in the Plan.[10] People also tend to forget that at the same time Lower Granite was completed in 1975, Congress also created the Hell's Canyon National Recreation Area, and deauthorized the last major dam planned for the Snake River.[11]

Governor Andrus' aggressive promotion of the drawdown plan for salmon recovery caused a split between Northern and Southern Idaho interests that persists to this day. Northern Idahoans fought for 50 years to get out from under the rail monopolies and have river navigation from Lewiston, Idaho to the sea. Governor Andrus' answer: while waterway transportation would be "temporarily interrupted", ports and shippers "did not create this problem, and should not have to pay for fixing it. Their costs should be mitigated as part of the overall solution."[12] No one has ever bothered to estimate how much it would cost to build new rail lines; the existing lines are crowded enough that shippers experience frequent delays.

The Northwest Power Planning Council's First Step Towards Drawdown

As explained in Chapter 9, the United States Court of Appeals for the Ninth Circuit issued an extraordinary opinion in 1994 declaring that the Northwest Power Planning Council had failed to explain its rejection of state and tribal fishery agency proposals to increase flows for salmon. The state and tribal fishery agencies stepped up pressure on the Council to rewrite the fish and wildlife program and adopt their recommendations.

The Council staff hastily cobbled together a new fish and wildlife program giving the state and tribal fishery agencies what they asked for—at least to the extent that it was technically feasible to do so. The proposed program called for very significant increases in river flows, and significant steps toward drawdown. In particular, the Council concluded that an immediate drawdown of John Day Reservoir to Minimum Operating Pool was necessary.

Computer modeling evidence suggested that the effect of large scale drawdowns would almost certainly be negative on endangered salmon, particularly the scarcer endangered Snake River fall chinook salmon. At our request, Dr. James Anderson prepared a paper using the CRiSP and SLCM computer models to compare the effects of a transportation-based salmon strategy vs. a drawdown strategy, which he forwarded to the Council. His cover letter to the Council summarized the findings:

> "What is vital for the Council to understand is that salmon survival decreases under a drawdown-based strategy, and increases, in some cases substantially, under a maximum transportation strategy. The lifecycle model runs presented in the paper illustrate dramatically that the Council's apparent path poses a risk of causing the rapid extinction of fall chinook in particular . . ."[13]

Dr. Anderson also warned the Council that the state and tribal computer models on which its staff relied "ignore much of the available data, substantially overstate the benefits of increasing river velocity, and substantially understate the benefits of smolt transportation."[14]

The entire Northwest Senatorial Delegation wrote to the Council on the eve of the vote to urge the Council to reject drawdown, but the Council staff withheld the letter from the Council on the grounds that the time period for public comment had expired.

On December 15, 1994, the state and tribal drawdown proposal came up for a vote. Because both Montana members opposed drawdown, the unanimous votes of all other members would be required to adopt it. Pro-drawdown forces had to force a vote quickly because a new governor had been elected in Idaho, Phil Batt, who was not expected to support drawdown. One of the Idaho representatives appointed by Govenor Andrus, Jay Webb, resigned on principle rather than support the proposal. Governor Andrus quickly appointed a new member from his staff, Andy Brunelle, to vote as directed.

The final vote was 6-2 in favor of the proposal, with the both Montana members rejecting the program in an eloquent dissent. They faulted the Council for its hasty adoption of measures whose effects were unknown, and probably harmful to the salmon. Washington's Dr. Ken Casavant was perceived as the "swing vote", and Eastern Washington agricultural interests never forgave him for it. As of 1997, they are still trying to get rid of him.

Congress got the last word, however, because Congress had to appropriate the funds necessary to do drawdown. As the Conference Committee Report for the 1996 Energy and Water Appropriations bill (H.R. 1905) stated:

> "The conferees share the concern of both the Senate and the House regarding the costs and justification for the John Day drawdown as an effective method for salmon recovery. To date, the conferees have not been provided with any scientific evidence supporting the drawdown; therefore the Administration is directed to provide scientific justification of the project as an effective means of salmon recovery along with any further requests for funding. Considering the extraordinary cost of completing this project, if the Administration does not find significant benefits, the proposal should be abandoned altogether."

On November 28, 1995, General Fuhrman of the U.S. Army Corps of Engineers punted the question of scientific justification to the National Marine

Fisheries Service, which did not respond for more than a year. When Regional Director Stelle finally responded, he claimed that the new information supporting drawdown included the ISG's *Return to the River* report; he also said that NMFS now "believes that a deeper drawdown of John Day, possibly to natural river levels, should also be studied".[15]

Different Species of Drawdown

There are four main species of drawdown, ranging in severity. Reservoirs have, by engineering design, a variable operational range, from full to minimum operating pool. Minimum operating pool, or MOP for short, is the lowest water level at which the dams were expected to operate. Both fish and commerce require dams, at least in their present configuration, to be run at MOP. The fish passage facilities will not generally work below MOP, and barges will run aground.

As of 1997, the reservoir behind John Day Dam, Lake Umatilla, is the focus of efforts to reduce reservoir levels to MOP. Irrigation interests in the area would prefer to operate at minimum irrigation pool (MIP), which is the lowest level at which they can pump water out of the reservoir without installing new pumping facilities. In Lake Umatilla, MIP is about five feet higher than MOP. New pumping facilities would cost $25 million.

The effects on salmon from reducing the water level by five feet are essentially unknown. We do know that if the entrances to fish ladders are not deep enough, adult passage suffers.[16] There is evidence that the ladders are substantially less effective at MOP than at higher reservoir levels because of reductions in orifice passage efficiency,[17] but fishery managers have never bothered to quantify the adverse effects on adults from MOP operation. Drawdown proponents point to a slight increase in water particle travel time as a supposed benefit to salmon.

Under threats of litigation from the states and tribes, the National Marine Fisheries Service included a recommendation for MOP drawdown of Lake Umatilla in its 1995 Biological Opinion on Federal Columbia River Power System operations. In 1997, NMFS' Donna Darm admitted that the only reason the MOP drawdown was still on the table was that to withdraw the recommendation would require a lengthy and "unwieldy process".[18]

Promoters of the Great Salmon Hoax, like former Congressman and Northwest Power Planning Council member Mike Kreidler, proclaim the John Day drawdown as "the mainstay of salmon recovery", and urge its immediate adoption.[19] Kreidler's continued support for the MOP drawdown provoked his irrigation constituents to label his statements "totally false, irresponsible, and a political embarrassment to the new administration being formed by Governor Locke in Washington State".[20]

Most of the pressure, however, particularly at the four dams on the lower Snake River, is for deeper drawdowns. The next level down is "spillway crest" drawdown. Drawing down the dams below the top of the spillway would force all migrating juvenile salmon through turbines. Thus fish advocates have pressed for drawdown to spillway crest as an intermediate step before total dam removal. Spillway crest drawdown is typically 35-50 feet below MOP, depending on the dam. With a spillway crest drawdown, the length of the typical reservoir would be reduced by about one-third, river-borne navigation would cease, and no adults could pass upstream at all without expensive modifications to the fish ladders. Juvenile bypass systems would be completely inoperative because the entrance orifices would be out of water. Power production would not be feasible.[21]

Ken Casavant, the Chairman of the Northwest Power Planning Council's Fish and Wildlife Committee, persists in promoting the Hoax that spillway crest drawdown "could allow for continued barge transportation through the reservoir".[22] As in many statements offered by leading promoters of the Great Salmon Hoax, there is a tiny kernel of truth to what he says. Before the dam was constructed, there was a seven foot channel used by steam boats and other shallow draft vessels. But none of the commercial barges and tugs operating today could make it upriver through a seven foot channel; they draw up to fourteen feet of water. A huge dredging program, coupled with a complete reconstruction of the locks at John Day Dam, might permit navigation to continue with a spillway crest drawdown. It could cost another half a billion dollars, or more if channels had to be blasted through the solid basalt that forms the riverbed in some places.

To mitigate adverse effects on the economy, spillway crest drawdown is usually discussed as a "seasonal" alternative. The idea is that every year, during some portion of the salmon migration season, the reservoirs would drop down, and then refill later. No one has bothered to make a comprehensive estimate of the total costs of spillway crest drawdown. The U.S. Army Corps estimates the construction costs to modify the four lower Snake River dams as $1.033 billion, with an estimated time to implementation of ten years.[23] That is probably a substantial underestimate.

By 1996, few in the Pacific Northwest other than flow zealots seriously defended the concept of seasonal drawdowns; they defended it only as a tactical step on the way to natural river drawdown. Parties ranging from the National Research Council[24] to the state and tribal scientists leading the "Plan for Analyzing and Testing Hypotheses" (PATH),[25] all recognized that drawdowns short of "natural river" level—removing the dam, in effect—were unlikely to have much effect on salmon.

Natural-river drawdown involves the most drastic alteration, reducing reservoir levels about 100 feet below MOP.[26] There are a variety of engineering schemes for natural-river drawdown, most of which involve digging a channel around or through the existing dams. No one proposes to remove them; they would continue to stand idle as the water rushed by.

As a matter of engineering, a permanent natural river drawdown has the lowest construction costs (other than drawdown to MOP) of the drawdown alternatives, because the dams would be simply decommissioned.

Unlike seasonal drawdown, there would be no need to construct new means of passing fish and commerce by the dams during periods of seasonal refill. Commerce would cease, and the fish would be left to make it around the dams as in natural rapids.

The U.S. Army Corps of Engineers has concluded that the construction costs for bringing the four lower Snake River dams to "natural river" level" would be about $533 million, and the project would take about five years.[27] This number is widely believed to be fanciful. Among other things, it was based on multiplying by four the cost of building a channel around a dam built on dirt. Two of the Lower Snake dams are set in sold rock, and it will cost far more to build a channel around them. Compared to the cost of the concrete for building the dams, however, dynamite is cheap.

Benefits to Salmon from Destroying the Reservoir Ecosystems

Environmentalists hate reservoirs, focusing on the loss of habitat when the reservoirs were flooded. But new habitat is created, which is, in essence, quite similar to habitat in a natural lake. As a Canadian official involved in hydropower development in Quebec put it: "People think the reservoir is a liquid desert. Nobody ever says that about a lake. If you propose draining a lake, environmentalists would say that would cause a shocking loss of valuable habitat. But if you propose making a reservoir, which is a lake, they say the reverse."[28]

Profound effects on salmon, both positive and negative, would arise from a natural-river drawdown. The most significant negative effect of a natural-river drawdown would be to remove three points at which most juvenile Snake River salmon are collected and transported downstream: Lower Granite, Little Goose, and Lower Monumental Dams. If the water no longer flows through bypass and collection systems, the salmon can no longer be transported. And the barges carrying salmon could not longer make it down the river.

The Snake River Salmon Recovery Team observed that "the drawdown alternatives are highly uncertain, and even the most optimistic juvenile passage assumptions associated with a four pool drawdown fail to improve survival values of Snake River stocks beyond what is achievable with juvenile transportation".[29] Computer modeling suggests that the reduced survival associated with reduced transportation would offset all positive effects of drawdown, because "[e]ven drawdowns to a natural river do not give survivals equal to current levels".[30]

The original motive for drawdown was to avoid "lethal slackwater pools". When the first data showing high reservoir survival became available in 1993 and 1994, NMFS researchers warned the NMFS Regional Director, Will Stelle, Jr., that reservoir survival was already so high that drawdown did not seem to be a useful tool for generating more salmon.[31] He ignored them.

Given consistent evidence of high reservoir survival, most drawdown advocates now stress increases in river velocity as the primary benefit to drawdown. They blithely skip over the premises that that water particle travel time is a surrogate for fish travel time, and that reducing fish travel time increases survival.

Drs. Chapman and Giorgi suggest that removal of the four lower Snake Dams would decrease juvenile travel time by about 13%,[32] but this estimate is based on Raymond's 1979 paper, which erroneously assumed that the time sample groups were released had no effect on travel time. Even so, they conclude that "we consider the gain from dam removal as modest at best" and warn that "[n]o one should expect a quick fix from dam removal".[33] The U.S. Army Corps of Engineers has reported that the travel time of spring chinook would be reduced by eight to fifteen days, depending on the amount of natural flow.[34]

The travel time for adult salmon would be increased, probably by 10-30%, because of the increased water velocity.[35] No one has bothered to try and figure out whether adverse effects on adults would outweigh benefits believed to accrue to juveniles. One of the most important pieces of computer modeling that has yet to be completed is the upstream passage model which will permit policymakers to balance positive effects on juveniles against negative effects on adults. Without increased funding, such a model will not be completed any time soon. Until the model is available, policymakers have no quantitative basis for assessing the effects of structural or operational changes to the dams.

Under drawdown, the predators in the existing reservoir could actually be "concentrated . . . in the relatively small channel volume".[36] This could increase the "mortality per mile" suffered by the juvenile population as it moves downstream, thus offsetting any supposed gains from speeding the juveniles through those river miles. In addition, salmon predators could lose alternate prey, such as crayfish, and could increase their attention on juvenile salmon, at least until the new environment was formed.[37]

The Northwest Power Planning Council's Independent Science Group has also warned that drawdowns could drive non-native fish, like shad, from mainstem habitats into tributaries. "The result could be temporary if not permanently increased interaction between wild salmonids and non-native fishes in tributary environments that have so far remained mostly free of dominance by non-native fishes."[38]

Major transition effects would occur. Not only would passage facilities fail to operate as planned, forcing more fish through turbines, but turbine efficiencies would fall, and total dissolved gas supersaturation levels would rise. And because of the more than 20 years of siltation since the reservoirs filled, there could be possibly lethal levels of sediment in the river during the entire decommissioning process.[39]

Following "normative" demands for high spring flows could have negative effects on salmon in the Columbia River Basin. As explained in Chapter 1, the single largest source of mortality to salmon eggs in the spawning grounds is floods. The Independent Science Group has not attempted to explain how manipulating reservoirs to provide "scouring flows" for salmon would not wipe out the salmon redds.

And since no one is talking about removing many dams downstream, like Bonneville Dam (since that is where large numbers of urban voters live), most of the sediment that is "scoured out" won't be able to get to the sea, but will get stuck at the next dam down. Some biologists, like John Pizzimenti of Harza Consultants, worry that the sediments contain pollutants that ought to be left alone.

Another negative effect is the loss of rearing habitat for endangered Snake River fall chinook and other fall chinook, like the healthy runs in the Hanford reach. Because fall chinook feed as they migrate downstream, they may have a comparative advantage in the Columbia and Snake reservoirs, which tend to have higher levels of food than the free-flowing rivers would.

Drawdown proponents claim this effect would be overshadowed by an increase in the spawning habitat for adult fall chinook, but no data are available to confirm whether spawning in "natural rivers" would be greater or lesser than in reservoirs. There is substantial evidence that fall chinook now spawn in reservoirs, particularly in the tailraces of the dams. This phenomenon was discovered accidentally when chinook eggs and fry showed up while the Corps of Engineers was dredging the tailrace of Lower Monumental Dam; subsequent surveys have confirmed tailrace spawning in the Lower Granite and Little Goose tailrace areas.[40] Drs. Chapman and Giorgi concluded in 1994 that "[e]very time we look for tailrace spawning we seem to find it".[41] The Northwest Power Planning Council's *Return to the River* push for drawdown asserts that "[m]ost fall chinook populations spawning in the mainstem reaches of the Columbia and Snake River have been driven extinct",[42] but the Independent Science Group does not consider the significance of tailrace and other reservoir spawning.[43]

The most dramatic and immediate effect of the drawdowns would be to destroy the ecology that has developed since the reservoirs were filled. Many resident fish species spawn in the reservoir pools and tributaries feeding into the reservoirs, and all this spawning habitat would be lost.[44] This, of course, may be counted as an advantage by the salmon partisans.

Nothwithstanding the enormous uncertainty, the Northwest media has begun to build support for drawdown, reiterating the refrain that "the science is now here".[45] In reality, the science has been suppressed nearly out of existence.

The Northwest Power Planning Council's Second Try, the "Normative River"

By 1996, the hypothesis that flow releases would decrease travel time, decrease in-river mortality, and decrease mortality associated with salmon migration had little life left. Because it was possible to *measure* changes in flow, travel time and survival, the hypothesis could be, and was, disproved.

But that did not stop the conservation biologists. Under pressure to provide some sort of scientific basis for its salmon programs, the Northwest Power Planning Council staff assembled a group of conservation biologists led by Dr. Rick Williams, a prototypical "bearded environmentalist" from Idaho with a degree in genetics. By the fall of 1996, as the Independent Science Group, they produced the most recent in a series of 500-page reports on salmon recovery in the Pacific Northwest.

206

But this report was different. Rather than start by reviewing science, the Group began by inventing the concept of the "normative river" "as a way to describe the central processes of the Columbia River salmonid ecosystem".[46] Then, the Group made the time-honored assumption (contrary to fact) that the most significant feature of the Columbia River ecosystem from the perspective of salmon survival was the spring freshet of water. Thus the Group speculated that the most important means to restore salmon is to restore their ecosystem by enormous increases in river velocity during the spring, through drawdowns or flow augmentation.

Leading promoters of the Great Salmon Hoax, like Northwest Power Planning Council Member Ken Casavant, lauded the ISG for freeing them from the straitjacket of science:

> "... this ISG report is so refreshing. It tells us to step outside, get away from expensive and contradictory computer modeling. Kick some dirt, look at places like the Hanford Reach, understand why the habitat there is so good, then try to let nature recreate those conditions in other parts of the river system."[47]

Others, like Idaho Council Member Mike Field, are working hard on public relations efforts to help "underscore [the report's] credibility and its contribution to scientific understanding of fish survival ... in the Columbia River Basin".[48]

Most Northwest media outlets, incapable of discerning science from speculation, advise readers that the ISG report represents the verdict of science. As for policymakers whining about "contradictory computer modeling", no one reports that one model fits the data and one is hard-wired to promote flow and drawdown without regard to the data.

Dr. Williams and his fellow advocates have many new theories for why flow matters besides the "surfing" theory discussed in Chapter 7. According to them, we must "allow spring flows that are high enough to restructure the riverine habitat, to make pools and eddies, clear out old sediment and deposit new ..."[49] But as Dr. Ernest Brannon has pointed out,

> "Chinook salmon are bulldozers and I have regularly seen their redds over three feet deep in stream substrate. Chinook will plow up their own gravel. Chinook in British Columbia often use lake outlets for spawning because of the flow and temperature stability such sites provide. These circumstances are far more gravel-deficient that the river below the dams on

the Elwha, and chinook do very well under these circumstances."[50]

While Dr. Brannon was discussing the spawning grounds below dams on the Elwha River, his remarks suggest that chinook do not require the sort of habitat restructuring sought by normative river theorists.

Moreover, as the Snake River Salmon Recovery Team has pointed out, unless new gravel can come in from upstream, restructuring would not work at all—even if flows could somehow be elevated enough to reshape the river bed without wiping out whole communities through floods. As the Team succinctly points out, "scientific evidence that this proposal would in fact benefit endangered species is not presented by the ISG".[51] Scientists like Don Chapman also warn that "[d]rawdown has no history of empirical data obtained with scientific method".[52]

The Clinton/Gore Administration did conduct one experiment on the benefits of moving dirt and gravel from one part of a river to another, launching a massive media campaign to announce the program. Glen Canyon Dam has regulated flow into the Grand Canyon for decades, creating clean electric power for Southwest citizens. Bruce Babbitt appeared on national television to open the gates and release a flood of water downstream, and teams of biologists were dispatched by the Interior Department to measure the results.

The experiment was immediately proclaimed an enormous success. Debris was moved around, new sand bars were formed, and the once clear river ran muddy—a process called "flush[ing] nutrient-rich matter into the river".[53] (Water quality standards preventing excessive turbidity would stop a private entity from ever getting a permit to do something like this.) No one ever asked whether the changes were worth the millions of dollars spent to achieve them. It is hard to quantify the value of moving dirt around at the bottom of the Grand Canyon.

Six months later, it appeared that high natural spring flows would undo nearly all the supposed positive effects of the experiment.[54] And the non-native fish species and large invading shoreline plants that were targeted by the releases were "scarcely affected".[55] But Bruce Babbitt isn't going on television to talk about that. Instead, the Clinton/Gore Administration inches toward removal of the Glen Canyon Dam.[56]

Science seems powerless in the face of a good political slogan. The "normative river" has, like "family values", already taken its place in the jargon of politicians eager to please environmentalists and the media. It is an especially useful phrase for politicians because it has no fixed meaning. Thus Idaho's Governor Phil Batt could tell reporters with a straight face that drawing down John Day Reservoir by five feet "has to be an option under consideration" because it can "achieve a more normative river".[57] He also says that "large scale flow augmentation" using water from Idaho irrigators is "inconsistent with the normative approach", while "efforts to recreate a natural hydrograph would be an action consistent with the normative approach".[58] No reporter has had the wit to ask him how to "recreate a natural hydrograph" in the Snake River without taking the water away from the irrigators.

The Hanford Reach Fad, and Other Drawdown "Science"

The Hanford Reach of the mid-Columbia River supports the single largest naturally-spawning run of chinook salmon in the Columbia River Basin. In 1986, the run peaked at over 200,000 fish. The ISG report pointed to the Hanford Reach run of salmon as an example of what "natural conditions" can accomplish. Environmental advocates claim that the Reach is "the only free-flowing stretch of the Columbia River unaffected by reservoirs",[59] and imply that salmon runs everywhere would be like the Hanford Reach runs if we just removed the dams.

The Hanford Reach is not "free-flowing". It is regulated by several upstream dams, and it is regulated in particular to maximize salmon production by maintaining higher-than-natural (pre-dam) flows to protect salmon redds at critical times. Indeed, there is a formal agreement among the dam operators and fishery managers to do this, called the Vernita Bar Agreement.[60]

The river regulation has other beneficial effects. As Dr. Don Chapman has pointed out, winter flows are now higher from storage releases, and probably warmer as well, with positive effects on salmon from the elimination of freezing conditions on redds in the shallows and improved conditions for the incubation of juveniles.[61] And, of course, the regulation of the reach prevents massive flooding that would scour out salmon redds.

Gregg Easterbrook has pointed out that with water regulation rules in place to protect salmon, "rivers of the Northwest Northwest may become more friendly toward salmon than before genus *Homo*, as humanity's dams and reservoirs smooth out the swings of natural flood and drought."[62] In the case of the Hanford Reach, that has already happened. There is every reason to believe that thanks to human development, the Hanford Reach now has *better-than-natural* conditions for salmon.

One of the things that the Mid-Columbia dam operators did not agree to do was prevent daily fluctuations of river levels associated with changes in electric power generation. Dr. Williams, in his lectures promoting the *Return to the River* report, shows slides of juvenile salmon trapped in the gravel by receding water below these dams, blaming power generation. He does not mention the extensive studies below the lowermost dam, Priest Rapids, showing little or no effect on fall chinook spawning or abundance from such changes in flows.[63]

There is some possibility that lower fishing pressure could explain the abundance of the Hanford Reach stock. The harvest managers express no interest in examining this hypothesis; Dr. Al Giorgi has suggested that the stocks "may differ in locations of their ocean residence, which could affect overall population success".[64]

In the late 1950s, before the John Day and McNary pools were filled, the Hanford Reach was estimated to provide spawning habitat for only about 15,000 fish.[65] Some biologists believe that when the John Day and McNary pools were filled, groups of salmon gradually moved up to the Hanford Reach.[66] The Hanford reach run did not increase for many, many years, and suddenly shot up in the 1980s, along with most other salmon runs in the Columbia River Basin.

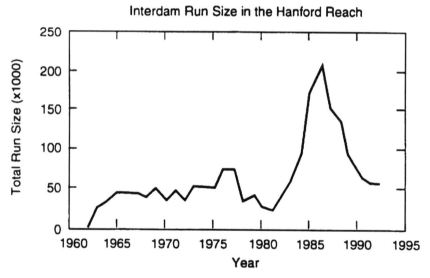

Figure 22: Interdam Run Size in the Hanford Reach[67]

At one time, this rise in population was proclaimed to be an accomplishment of the Northwest Power Planning Council's programs. The fishery scientists do not really understand why the populations increased, and to what extent "natural" conditions had anything to do with it.

In fact, it is possible that the population rebounds on the Hanford reach are really a story of hatchery success. A 1988 report by two University of Washington biologists states that "[a]ttempts to artificially enhance the production of chinook salmon in the Hanford Reach have gone on for over twenty years—first as a spawning channel that apparently failed and now as a hatchery that is apparently succeeding".[68] The operators of the Priest Rapids Hatchery believe that its success has something to do with rebounds in wild Hanford Reach fall chinook.[69] Sam Penney of the Nez Perce Tribe claims that "the supplementation projects being developed by his tribe 'are really the same as what is being accomplished at Vernita Bar on the Columbia River—a place, Penney said, that the Council's own science panel 'likes so much'."[70]

The current fascination with the Hanford Reach runs is best understood as a fad. Conservation biologists such as those on the Council's Independent Science Group like the Hanford Reach because they think it is "more natural" than a reservoir. Since there are lots of salmon returning to the Hanford Reach, they assert that if we drain reservoirs to produce more "natural" conditions, we can have lots of salmon where we drain the reservoirs.

Conservation biologists are so eager to promote drawdown using the Hanford Reach example that they even propose to take action that could well destroy the productivity of the Hanford Reach. Consider the following line of reasoning:

> ". . . the Hanford fall chinook spawn only in the upper two-thirds of the reach, probably because interstitial flow pathways are nonfunctional in the lower third of the reach due to the elevated water table created by virtual continual maintenance of the full pool elevation of McNary Reservoir. Lowering McNary pool likely *would lower the water table in the alluvial reaches upstream*, significantly increasing the size of the river reach at Hanford containing both surface and ground water habitat components."[71]

But lowering the water table in the most productive spawning ground around might have some adverse effects, like reducing the subsurface flow that is critical to keep chinook eggs alive. The very same conservation biologists criticize irrigation for reducing water tables and destroying spawning grounds in the Yakima and other rivers, yet they want to reduce the water table in the most productive part of the Hanford Reach.

Drawing down John Day and McNary pools might cause the salmon to tend to move back down the River. But the net gains from this process could be zero—or less than zero. We could wind up reducing the Hanford Reach populations without restoring them in John Day and McNary pools.

Another major question posed by the "normative river" theory is why the regulated reach below the mid-Columbia dams is so productive, while the regulated reach below the Hell's Canyon Complex isn't. If, as some believe, "[p]roductive populations spawning in large alluvial mainstem reaches may have functioned as critical core populations",[72] it may be impossible to increase abundance of endangered Snake River fall chinook salmon without a core population in the mainstem reach below the Hell's Canyon Complex.

Of course, it is always possible that the gravel reaches within Hell's Canyon were never particularly good spawning habitat, which is consistent with the idea that the Snake River chinook stocks have always been variable. It is awfully hot there. Archaelogical evidence from Hell's Canyon shows that salmon bones make up only 7-8% of the remains, with the balance coming from suckers and other warm water fishes.[73]

Yet another problem with the "normative river" theory is that some research suggests salmon may do worse in the more "complex" or "normative" habitat that the ISG would purportedly promote through dam removal. Juvenile Snake River fall chinook get trapped in a series of sloughs and wetlands on the Snake River side of the Columbia River that last for about 10 miles downstream from the confluence of the Snake and Columbia. The ISG speculates that this phenomenon "could be responsible for a disproportionate loss of Snake River fall chinook at this point compared with the Hanford stock coming down the Columbia channel at the same time".[74] Sometimes more complex habitat helps salmon; sometimes it kills them. The ISG offers no reason that "complex" habitat in reservoirs would be any worse for salmon than "complex" habitat in a more natural river.

One of the main lines of reasoning supporting the "normative river" theory is that reservoir shorelines tend to be eroded soil or rock, with little vegetation, while the shorelines of the Hanford reach (and other natural rivers) have more vegetation. The ISG theorizes at one point in its report that rising spring river waters flood vegetation and promote insect populations, which they suggest are an important food source for migrating juveniles.[75] They call for additional research into the question of how juvenile fish migrating seaward feed in the reservoirs, and whether they have enough food.

Figure 23: The Mainstem Snake Before Dams (ca. 1890)[76]

The ISG report is now commonly cited for the proposition that the dams destroyed "riparian cover for resting and predator avoidance".[77] In fact, there was very little such habitat along the lower Snake. The most comprehensive assessment of habitat along the Snake River was prepared in connection with the Lower Snake River Compensation Plan. The U.S. Army Corps of Engineers reported that "riparian habitat existed as scattered, narrow strips along the river". Most of the inundated area "consisted of rocky cliffs and rather steep hillsides covered mostly with sagebrush and dryland grasses". There was only "about 1,123 acres of brush and tree-type vegetation backed by fertile bottom lands" along the river shore.[78] Destroying four huge dams to bring back 1,123 acres of property seems senseless. It should also be remembered that the Corps acquired 24,124 acres in "mitigation" for the lost 1,123 acres.[79]

Older fisheries scientists like Dr. Chapman remember what the riverbanks looked like back in the 1950s, before McNary Dam was built. He remembers the edges of the river as being "mostly rock rubble and gravel, with some sandbars". He thinks "the stream fluctuated so much from freshet to low flow that scouring took away seedlings of willow and other edge species in most margins that juvenile fall chinook might use".[80] The conservation biologists, however, have no institutional memory, and are untethered by historical facts.

Historical photographs of the Snake River reaches now inundated by the reservoirs do not show rich vegetation. They show desert scrub, mud and rock. The ISG recognized that pre-dam photos of the mainstem Columbia "show large sand dunes along the river".[81] How these sand dunes were supposed to produce a large food supply for migrating fish is not explained.

Ultimately, the ISG simply transplanted research findings on the "ecology of regulated *streams*" to the mainstem Columbia and Snake Rivers based on the assertion that "principles" from the stream literature "directly apply" to one of the larger rivers in the world running through desert country.[82]

One member of the ISG, Dr. Charles Coutant from Oak Ridge National Laboratory, promotes the idea that reservoirs are so short of food that migrating juvenile salmon starve to death. This hypothesis is not supported by either theory or data.

The ISG report stretched to cite a master's thesis of an Idaho Fish and Game employee, Tom Curet, as data for the notion that fall chinook smolts were starving in the reservoirs.[83] When contacted by Bill Rudolph, a reporter trying to track down the source of the new "starving fish" theory of dam harm, Mr. Curet was reportedly "surprised" to see his work cited by the ISG, since it represented only two years of data.[84] Mr. Rudolph even had the perspicacity to contact Mr. Curet's thesis advisor, who said that "there is no lack of food in

214

[their] stomachs" and that fall chinook had five or six different species of food to choose from in Lower Granite Reservoir.[85]

Other studies confirm that migrating salmon are not starving. Measuring stomach contents on a scale from 1 (empty) to 7 (distended) at Lower Granite, McNary, and Bonneville Dams, researchers Bill Muir and Travis Coley found averages of 2-3 at Lower Granite and 3-5 at the other two dams.[86] One would not expect wild fish to have full stomachs all the time—like any wild animals, they spend a lot of time looking for food. The two researchers suggested that increased hatchery production, coupled with the tendency of migrating fish to delay in the forebay of Lower Granite Dam (where there is not much food), may have accounted for the results at Lower Granite. Muir and Coley suspect that Lower Granite, being the first of the mainstem reservoirs, has finer sediments that reduce feeding opportunities by reducing the diversity of food sources; downstream reservoirs have coarser sediments.[87] So much for data showing that juvenile salmon are starving.

As for theory, reservoirs have a larger surface area than rivers, and thus absorb more solar radiation and breed greater quantities of algae. The lower velocity of reservoirs also encourages algae growth. These algae in turn feed larger organisms up the food chain. These points have recently been emphasized by Portland State University researcher Ralph Vaca and the Montana Department of Fish and Game, seeking to prevent destructive drawdowns of Montana reservoirs. The ISG does acknowledge that as some sources of food for salmon have declined, other species of salmon food originally native to the lower river estuary have become established further and further upstream.[88] However, they speculate that these newer species are not as nutritious.

In short, conventional wisdom on feeding and reservoirs appears to be dead wrong. Studies on the mid-Columbia River have found that the mean size of subyearlings juvenile chinook sampled in the 1980s were substantially larger than the mean sizes in the 1960s, when reservoirs there were either nonexistent or new, so that food chains in them had not fully developed. Nine biologists, including Don Chapman, who reviewed the evidence in the course of an exhaustive review of the status of summer and fall chinook, believe that subyearling chinook may be "achieving more rapid growth in reservoirs".[89]

Indeed, they speculate that the reservoirs may be compensating for the lost of estuarine habitat, so that any delay in reservoirs may provide a net benefit for subyearling chinook.[90] If that is true, then draining reservoirs will positively injure fall chinook salmon—the result predicted by computer models, albeit for different reasons.

Notwithstanding the work of Muir, Coley, and Chapman, the media has begun to broadcast starving juveniles in the reservoirs as the newest aspect of the Great Salmon Hoax.

Yet another claim promoted by the Independent Science Group is that draining reservoirs will increase the amount of spawning habitat available in reservoirs. But no one measured how much spawning habitat there was before the dams were constructed. And no one measures how many salmon spawn there now.

To the extent that "groundwater upwelling areas" in the mainstem were used by salmon,[91] it is possible that such areas persist inside the reservoirs and are still used by salmon to spawn. It is also possible that the "complex island, point and eddy reattachment bars composed of sand, gravel and cobble" whose inundation is cited by the ISG[92] may have been useless without adequate subsurface flows of water.

Like all elements of the Great Salmon Hoax, it requires careful deconstruction to discover the origin of claims of lost spawning habitat. The Independent Science Group now claims that the "second largest" group of fall chinook salmon, some 34,000 strong, "spawned in the mainstem Columbia River in the area now inundated by John Day Dam.[93] This number comes from a single 1968 article prepared by biologist Leonard Fulton for the U.S. Fish and Wildlife Service in 1968.[94] I first heard about the Fulton Report when a reporter told me that federal fishery biologists had told him that the 34,000 number was a "wild-assed guess", made by someone trying to count underwater salmon redds from planes.

Sitting down to read the report, I became somewhat suspicious of Mr. Fulton when, following a brief reference to overfishing, he attributed all reductions in upriver spring and summer chinook runs to dam construction.[95] Mr. Fulton informs us that

> "The areas below the confluence of the Snake River [including the area inundated by John Day Dam] are more turbid, and it has been difficult to distinguish redds and spawning salmon in this reach of the Columbia River. Evidence indicates, however, that a large population of fall chinook spawns in the 160 km. stretch of river below McNary Dam".[96]

What is the evidence? Reading further to Table 5, the reference listed is "unpublished information".[97] The ISG reports that the original quantitative data has all been lost by the fishery agencies, and all that remains is "summaries

216

or brief, qualitative accounts".[98] Reading further, one comes to a Table 8, called "Average number of fall-run chinook salmon entering sections of the Columbia River and its tributaries", and there is the claimed number: 34,000 fish entered the section of the Columbia River from "John Day damsite to McNary Dam".[99] Note that Mr. Fulton does not claim that 34,000 fish spawned there; that is an invention of the ISG.

There is a footnote to the 34,000 number, which claims that "[e]stimates of population using this reach are based on aerial surveys".[100] In other words, even though the water is so turbid that seeing fish or their nests is hard from the ground, these counts are made by *airplane*. Right.

Then, on the very same page, the 34,000 number appears again, in another context. According to Fulton, "[a]verage counts of fall chinook salmon at Bonneville, The Dalles, and McNary Dams were 163,000, 90,000 and 56,000, respectively, for 1957-60".[101]

34,000 just happens to be the difference between 90,000 and 56,000. It is a remarkable coincidence that the total number of fish disappearing in this reach just happen to be the exact same number of fish that the ISG claims were spawning in the reach now inundated by John Day Dam. In other words, every fall chinook salmon that disappeared after being counted at The Dalles Dam, as measured by the lower counts at McNary (the reach that includes John Day Dam), is supposed to be a salmon spawning above the John Day damsite.

If that were true, we would have to assume that no fall chinook salmon stopped before the John Day damsite to spawn. We would have to assume that none turned out of the mainstem Columbia River at the Deschutes River, John Day River, Willow Creek, the Umatilla River, or any of the other tributaries of the mainstem in that reach.[102] We would have to assume that no fall chinook salmon were caught by fishermen, or died of any other causes.

By the same logic, we could calculate the number of fall chinook salmon supposedly spawning today in the *reservoir* behind Bonneville Dam by subtracting counts at The Dalles Dam from counts at Bonneville Dam: 163,000 minus 90,000 or 73,000 fish. But that would be wrong.

Just for fun, I compared more recent fall chinook dam counts at The Dalles and McNary for 1991-93. The results: an average 98,000 fall chinook were counted at The Dalles and 70,000 were counted at McNary.[103] The difference? 28,000 fish. This number is probably low by a couple thousand fish because the McNary counts include jacks and The Dalles counts don't.

Thus the evidence suggests that before and after the construction of John Day Dam, roughly 30,000 adult fall chinook salmon vanished in that reach, for reasons that remain essentially unknown. The net effect from construction of John Day Dam on spawning habitat for fall chinook salmon? Surely salmon spawned there, and perhaps fewer spawn there now. Perhaps the reason that 30,000 salmon now disappear has to do with the rise of the tribal gillnet fishery in the John Day reservoir. But there is not really any scientific *evidence* to support the claim of a large lost spawning ground.

Yet the Fulton report is cited over and over again by the ISG and others to support the claim that "[s]ome of the most valuable spawning areas were in the mainstem of the Columbia River, nearly all of which were inundated by construction of dams".[104] This is a leading argument for drawdown, but it is not based on scientific data. Maybe the truth is that "inundating" spawning areas doesn't bother the salmon much. They spawn in the tailraces of dams; they can probably spawn in "inundated" gravel as well. After all, they live underwater.

The same sort of claims about inundated spawning habitat were made more than twenty years ago when fisheries agencies complained about the inundation of habitat alleged to support 5,000 spawning chinook in the Snake River below the mouth of the Clearwater River. The Corps of Engineers pointed out that "accurate counts of the actual numbers of fish spawning in this stretch of river have not been made because the water was too turbid . . . Estimates appear to have been made, at least in part, on the basis of early surveys to catalog areas possessing necessary spawning ground requirements such as gravel availability and proper depths, water velocities, and temperatures."[105]

But we now know that chinook salmon never use most of what looks to human beings like suitable habitat, instead sniffing out the few areas where water flows in and under the gravel. Without actually counting salmon redds, biologists have no idea whether valuable habitat has been lost or not.

The ISG also claims that ". . . riparian forest canopy, undercut banks, and large woody debris accumulations in the vicinity of spawning habitat can be critical for survival and successful reproduction of migratory salmonids . . .".[106] There certainly wasn't much of that along the mainstem Columbia and Snake Rivers as compared to headwaters tributaries. Ultimately, the ISG admits that "[i]t is unknown to what extent reservoirs replace the ecological functions of these lost riverine habitats . . ."—but this is not what they tell the media.[107]

It is surely true that when John Day Dam was constructed, fishery biologists believed that spawning grounds would be lost. The decision was made to enlarge Spring Creek and Bonneville Hatcheries to compensate for the loss,[108] and those hatcheries have been highly successful at producing large quantities of fish for harvest. As far as I know, no one has even tried to figure out whether that enlarged production compensated for alleged losses in the John Day pool. The question is simply ignored.

If we want more spawning grounds in the vicinity of the reservoirs behind John Day and McNary Dams, another approach is simply to dig artificial spawning channels adequately irrigated with cool water and lined with gravel. At one time, before spawning channels fell from favor, they provided 42 percent of the summer chinook juvenile outmigrants in the Columbia River Basin.[109] I have heard that some of the channels failed because the operators failed to consider the importance of subsurface water flow, but have seen no data one way or the other. Some irrigators and I were once talking about this, and all agreed that it was worth trying to run drainpipes off the bottom of irrigation dams, burying them in a load of gravel, and creating artificially-irrigated spawning beds with perfect upwelling for salmon.

Spawning channels may not be "natural", but neither are birdhouses. They may represent a reasonable compromise between hatcheries and natural production; hatcheries might serve to seed the channels for greater consistency of returns. This kind of "supplementation" probably wouldn't interfere at all with traits needed for survival in the wild. Hatching channel operators would be able to select from adults to improve the size and fecundity of the breed, and seed the gravel with the results; the emerging juveniles would have to learn to fend for themselves. Unfortunately, these sort of solutions are no longer politically-correct. With a decentralized approach to habitat restoration and hatchery management, communities in the Columbia River Basin that wanted salmon to return could experiment with approaches like this.

Pros and Cons of Dam Removal

The most obvious problems with dam removal are not biological, but economic. Biologists generally agree that a river without dams is likely to improve the survival of salmon as they migrate upstream and downstream. They have no hard evidence of this, but they have a seemingly powerful intuitive argument on their side: these are the conditions under which the salmon evolved, so it certainly seems reasonable that the salmon would prosper by restoring those conditions. As noted above, however, only those in grips of Darwin's "deeply-seated error" give primacy to habitat in assessing the reasons for species abundance.

Natural rivers are not necessarily better for salmon, for two important reasons. First, as we have seen, the salmon that evolved to strive upstream

219

through Cascade Rapids and over Celilo Falls no longer exist. Salmon now mature faster, and are much smaller. For all we know, today's salmon would be disadvantaged by removing reservoirs that are probably easier for them to navigate than the pre-dam obstacles to upstream passage.

More generally, just because a species evolved under one set of conditions does not mean that those conditions are optimal for the species. Cockroaches evolved in the jungle, but parts of New York City probably have a higher density of cockroaches per square foot than many jungles. Shad did not evolve in the Pacific Northwest at all, yet they thrive in the Columbia River. And fall chinook may do better in reservoirs.

Most biologists, even the members of the ISG, will admit to policymakers that there are no guarantees that removing dams will bring back the salmon. The Chair of the Snake River Salmon Recovery Team, Dr. Don Bevan, has said that the Recovery "Team doesn't really see it as a good recovery method, but we're willing to try a drawdown experiment if we can see a design that will provide some useful information. As yet, we haven't seen an experimental design."[110] Since the death of Dr. Bevan, the Region continues to march toward drawdown with no idea how to measure whether it works or not.

Nor have any of the fishery agencies now trying to remove the dams attempted to assess what was achieved through the Lower Snake River Compensation Plan. The nine hatcheries included as part of that Plan have provided salmon, steelhead and other fish to mitigate for, and probably overmitigate for, the effects of dam construction. It seems doubtful whether removing the dams would generate as many fish as the hatcheries. But presumably the fishery agencies wish to have their cake and eat it too, by taking out the dams and running the hatcheries.

Removing the dams would impose large costs on the Pacific Northwest, with benefits that are utterly speculative. The entire upriver shipping industry, carrying billions of dollars of freight from as far up river as Lewiston, Idaho, would die at once. One-quarter of America's feed grain and 35% of its wheat move down the river now.[111] Indeed, 80% of the shipping is wheat, with each barge the equivalent of 33 rail cars or 144 tractor-trailer rigs.[112] Forest products come in second.[113] Most of the shipping is for export, contributing to the reduction of America's trade deficit. As China and other developing countries import more and more grain, the Northwest is expected to become a major supplier through the Port of Portland.

Before the dams were put in, shipping rates were abominably high. As one historian explained:

"By the early 1930s products went by barge for 50 cents a ton from Duluth, Minnesota to Buffalo, New York, a distance of about a thousand miles. Boats towed freight from Kansas City to Chicago—approximately 550 miles—for $1.94 per ton. At the same time, farmers in the interior Northwest paid railroads $4.80 a ton to ship wheat to Portland or Seattle, a distance of less than four hundred miles."[114]

It is no wonder that inland leaders fought for decades to get barge transportation up the Snake River.

And just as hydropower is one of the most environmentally-benign forms of energy generation, so too is barging one of the most environmentally-benign forms of shipping, using less energy per ton of freight moved than any other method. In addition to the barges, the reservoirs are used by a large fleet of recreational boaters. Recreational losses from drawing down the lower Snake reservoirs are estimated at $59 million a year.[115]

Although navigation interests have appeared before the Northwest Power Planning Council to explain that any drawdown would destroy their industry, the Council does not seem to be listening. Joyce Cohen, representing the State of Oregon, told them: "I would urge you all to continue this dialog, go back to your religion and figure out how much you can tithe without losing your fifteen percent margin . . .".[116] It was a perfect metaphor, because salmon worship has become a sort of state religion in the Northwest; drawdown is, like transubstantiation, to be accepted on faith. Promoters of the Great Salmon Hoax like Ms. Cohen can see nothing wrong in declaring that "a whole lot of folks are going to have to go back to the church and figure out what they can give".[117] Presumably, they would be horrified at aggressive state promotion of more conventional religions.

Many human communities depend upon the dams for their water supplies. Lower Snake Reservoirs irrigate 35,000 acres of land, and supply 16 facilities with municipal or industrial water supplies.[118] The land along the Snake River is unique. "Geologists call this wind-deposited silt 'loess', and it forms an icing over the lava, a sensuous curving landscape of incredible fertility, topsoil over two hundred feet deep in places, some of the richest on earth."[119] Irrigation has turned the loess into highly productive farmland. Northwest citizens whose lives are largely invisible to the urban majorities in Seattle, Olympia, Portland, and Salem live and work on farms that will be destroyed if drawdown plans pass. And John Day Reservoir is "our last line of defense for flood control" downstream.[120]

As this book is being written, the fisheries bureaucrats are solidly behind the march towards drawdown. In its proposed Snake River Salmon Recovery Plan, the National Marine Fisheries Services declares that it "supports the 'normative river' concept", and regards "'technological solutions'" for salmon recovery as only an "interim" approach.[121]

The Governors of Oregon and Washington have their troops in legal battles promoting drawdown. Prodded by Oregon's appointees to the Northwest Power Planning Council, the Council has just "upped the ante" by calling for a study of drawing down the reservoir behind McNary Dam, which until March 1997 had never been formally proposed in any state or federal salmon recovery plan.[122] At a meeting with federal and tribal officials on June 20, 1997, Oregon Governor Kitzhaber's chief salmon advisor, Roy Hemmingway, declared: "The key question here is how much of the hydroelectric system do we need to dismantle to restore fish and wildlife."[123] Governor Kitzhaber shares his views, stating later in 1997 that "money would be better spent dealing with the economic dislocation caused by drawdown . . . That's where we've got to get."[124]

Oregon Senator Gordon Smith and Washington Senator Slade Gorton are perhaps the only political leaders willing to take a strong stand against drawing down reservoirs as the one true path to salmon recovery. Senator Smith stands behind his Eastern Oregon constituents and is one of the few Northwest public officials to publicly state his opposition to dam removal.[125] Senator Gorton warns that "[l]egislation may well be needed in this area to assure that the multiple purposes of the Federal power system are protected together with the public benefits they bring".[126]

Montana politicians have pursued a strategy aimed at putting Montana reservoirs off-limits for flow augmentation, and appear willing to let Oregon and Washington take the lead on what happens to the reservoirs in their states.

Idaho's Governor Phil Batt, under heavy pressure from Southern Idaho interests eager to make the drawdown deal, says "everything is on the table",[127] but tells his Northern Idaho supporters that Lewiston, Idaho ought to remain a port. Under Governor Batt's stewardship, the Idaho Department of Fish and Game remains perhaps the single most aggressive promoter of dam removal efforts. Reporters constantly quote Idaho Fish and Game officials for the proposition that dam removal is "biologically, a no-brainer".[128]

The Committee of Nine, formed in 1919 to settle water disputes among Idaho irrigators, is one of the most potent groups influencing Idaho policy.[129] Unfortunately, the Committee seems to persist in the foolish belief that by sacrificing dams downriver, environmentalists in Idaho can be held at bay. Idaho Power Company, another major influence in Idaho policy, has managed to arrange things so that downriver ratepayers pay its Endangered Species Act compliance costs. Idaho Power Company has no quarrel with the drawdown strategy, which has successfully deflected attention from its Hell's Canyon Complex.

In March 1997, the environmentalists served notice of their intention to bring suit under the Endangered Species Act to challenge operations of the Hell's Canyon Complex and irrigation reservoirs in the upper Snake River, which may finally cause Idaho to recognize that its anti-science, anti-technology approach to salmon recovery could be counterproductive.

Promoters of the Great Salmon Hoax have begun to mount appeals outside the Pacific Northwest for dam removal, echoed in the Eastern media, asserting that "[t]he Northwest is paralyzed by big money . . . It would be nice if the rest of the country would save us from ourselves."[130] After the *Idaho Statesman* ran a series of editorials in support of breaching the four Lower Snake dams,[131] the *Washington Post* proclaimed that the editorials "left some very large footprints and may have fundamentally altered the Pacific Northwest's ongoing debate over salmon".[132] One newspaper closer to the dams had a different view: "Bad science. Bad economics. Bad timing. Bad politics. Bad neighbors. Bad stewardship. Bad biology."[133]

If the Northwest Establishment lines up behind dam removal, Congress will probably go along with it. It will be another $10 billion mistake, and it won't bring salmon back. But people taken in by the Great Salmon Hoax will think progress is being made. And given the media's bias, most people would never even remember that it didn't work.

In most areas of the country, people might rely on the courts to stop irrational government conduct. When the Federal Energy Regulatory Commission and the Interior Department ordered the owners of a small hydroelectric dam in Maine to install fishways despite the absence of credible evidence that they would have much impact on fish populations. Judge Silberman of the United States Court of Appeals for the District of Columbia wrote:

> "Interior is quite open about its policy view that it prefers fishways to alternative escapement remedies. It is, of course, entitled to a good deal of deference concerning its policy choice. That does not mean that Interior is not obliged to show some reasonable support for its determination to insist on that requirement in this case. *It will not do to present only a 'Field of Dreams' justification ('If you build it, they will come.')*"[134]

There is little chance, however, that the United States Court of Appeals for the Ninth Circuit, the most-reversed court among the federal courts of appeals, will do anything to stop the Northwest policymakers from pursuing their Field of Dreams: the normative river.

NOTES TO CHAPTER 8

[1] D. Chapman & A. Giorgi, "Comments on Work of Biological and FCRPS Alternative Work Groups", at 4 (footnotes omitted).

[2] Quoted in K. Petersen, *River of Life, Channel of Death* 248.

[3] C. Andrus, "Snake River Salmon: National treasure at risk of extinction", April 1993 (Office of the Governor).

[4] *Id.* at 6.

[5] *Id.* at 7.

[6] *Id.* at 8.

[7] *Id.*

[8] *See* J. Cone & S. Ridlington, *The Northwest Salmon Crisis* 319 (reprinting a picture of a billboard in Clarkston, Washington).

[9] K Petersen, *River of Life, Channel of Death* 18

[10] Interim Report, "Lower Snake River Fish and Wildlife Plan, Lower Snake River, Washington and Idaho", at 26 (USACE Walla Walla District April 1996).

[11] *Id.* at 5.

[12] C. Andrus, "Snake River Salmon: National treasure at risk of extinction", April 1993, at 8 (Office of the Governor).

[13] Letter, Dr. J. Anderson to A. Duncan and W. Stelle, Jr., Dec. 13, 1994, at 2.

[14] *Id.* at 1.

[15] Letter, W. Stelle, Jr., to R. Griffin, Dec. 23, 1996.

[16] NMFS, Biological Opinion on FCRPS Operations, Mar. 2, 1995, at 114.

[17] W. Ebel, pers. comm. (May 5, 1997).

[18] B. Rudolph, "NMFS to Army Corps of Engineers: Study Deep Drawdowns", *NW Fishletter*, Jan. 21, 1997.

[19] M. Kreidler, quoted in "John Day Plan Left Off Budget, *Tri-City Herald*, Feb. 7, 1997.

[20] Memo, Columbia Snake Irrigators Association Board of Directors to Mike Kreidler, Feb. 10, 1997, at 1.

[21] U.S. Army Corps of Engineers, "Interim Status Report", at ES-4 to ES-5.

[22] K. Casavant, "New Thinking about Columbia salmon", *Seattle Times*, Jan. 30, 1997.

[23] U.S. Army Corps of Engineers, "Interim Status Report", at ES-7.

[24] NRC, *Upstream* 211 (Prepub. ed.).

[25] *See Clearing Up*, Jan. 13, 1997, at 8 (PATH preliminary conclusions).

[26] U.S Army Corps of Engineers, "Interim Status Report", at ES-5.

[27] U.S. Army Corps of Engineers, "Interim Status Report", at ES-12.

[28] Gaetan Hayeur, quoted in G. Easterbrook, *A Moment on the Earth* 339.

[29] Quoted in NRC, *Upstream* 211 (Prepub. ed.).

[30] J. Anderson, "Comparison of Mainstem Recovery Options Recover-1 and DFOP", Dec. 13, 1994, at 1.

[31] M. Schiewe, "Preliminary survival estimates for passage of juvenile salmonids through Lower Granite reservoir and Lower Granite dam", NMFS Internal Memo, Aug. 5, 1994.

[32] D. Chapman & A. Giorgi, "Comments on Work of Biological and FCRPS Alternative Work Groups", at 12 (1994).

[33] *Id.*

[34] U.S. Army Corps of Engineers, "Interim Status Report", at ES-13.

[35] U.S. Army Corps of Engineers, "Interim Status Report", at ES-13.

[36] NRC, *Upstream* 211 (Prepub. ed.).

[37] U.S. Army Corps of Engineers, "Interim Status Report", at ES-13.

[38] ISG, *Return to the River* 151.

[39] U.S. Army Corps of Engineers, "Interim Status Report", at ES-14.

[40] U.S. Army Corps of Engineers, "Interim Status Report", at 9-38.

[41] D. Chapman & A. Giorgi, "Comments on NMFS Draft Biological Opinion on FCRPS Operations", at 11 (1994).

[42] ISG, *Return to the River* 79.

[43] *Id.* at 204 (acknowledging research showing "small groups that spawn in the tailwaters of Snake River dams").

[44] NRC, *Upstream* 211 (Prepub. ed.).

[45] K. Casavant, "New thinking about Columbia salmon", Jan. 30, 1997.

[46] "Interview: Rick Williams", *Northwest Energy News*, Summer 1996, at 8 (NWPPC). Informed sources stated that he Council staff was careful to conceal the genuinely radical nature of Dr. Williams' views through careful editing of this interview.

[47] K. Casavant, "New thinking about Columbia salmon", *Seattle Times*, Jan. 30, 1997.

[48] Memo, M. Field & M. Walker (the NWPPC Public Affairs Director) to Council Members, Feb. 20, 1997, at 1.

[49] "Interview: Rick Williams", *Northwest Energy News*, Summer 1996, at 8.

[50] Quoted in Rescue Elwha Area Lakes report dated April 5, 1996. The author writes: "We learned that the main argument used by the other side—that the dams were ruining the river for salmon spawning by starving it for gravel—*is a hoax* . . . We have the written opinions of two biologists, both holding Phd's from the University of Washington, that there is no truth to the 'gravel starvation' theory."

[51] Letter, Snake River Salmon Recovery Team to J. Etchart, April 17, 1997, at 15.

[52] D. Chapman & A. Giorgi, "Comments on Work of Biological and FCPRS Alternative Workgroups", at 4 n.2 (1994).

[53] "Man-made flood in Grand Canyon revives river, banks", *The Oregonian*, Oct. 9, 1996, at A7. This article is typical of what passes for reporting on environmental issues, representing uncritical regurgitation of government-supplied "news".

[54] T. Kenworthy, "Nature may undo human work in Grand Canyon", *The Oregonian*, Feb. 17, 1997.

[55] W. Stevens, "Grand Canyon roars again as ecological clock is turned back", Feb. 25, 1997.

[56] See D. Beard, "Dams Aren't Forever", New York Times, Oct. 6, 1997. Daniel Beard was Clinton's first Commissioner of the U.S. Bureau of Reclamation and is now a senior vice president of the National Audubon Society.

[57] M. Wickline, "Batt says port has nothing to worry about; Governor says that if John Day is drawn down to help steelhead, he doesn't want it to go lower than minimum pool", *Lewiston Tribune Online*, Jan. 29, 1997.

[58] "Measures to Enhance Salmon and Steelhead Migration Success During 1997", March 25, 1997, at 2 n.1 (Idaho Governor's Office).

[59] *Big River News* (Fall 1996), at 13.

[60] ISG, *Return to the River* 205.

[61] D. Chapman (pers. comm.)

[62] G. Easterbrook, *A Moment on the Earth* 565.

[63] NRC, *Upstream* at 195. (Prepub. ed.).

[64] Cited in *id.* at 211.

[65] B. Rudolph, "NMFS to Army Corps of Engineers: Study Deep Drawdowns", *NW Fishletter*, Jan. 21, 1997.

[66] *Id.*

[67] From ISG, *Return to the River*, at 31A (Figure 2.6)

[68] D. Rogers & R. Hilborn, "Impact of Redd Loss at Vernita Bar on Hanford Reach Chinook Salmon Production", Final Report 1988, BPA Contract No. DE-AM79-87BP35885, at 3 (Oct. 1988).

[69] *See* Letter, D. Godard (Manager of PUD No. 2 of Grant County) to M. Walker, April 15, 1997.

[70] Quoted in B. Rudolph, "Tribes Complain about Upcoming Project Scrutiny", *NW Fishletter*, Oct. 14, 1997.

[71] ISG, *Return to the River* 268 (emphasis added).

[72] ISG, *Return to the River* 77.

[73] B. Rudolph, "Archaelogist takes long look at salmon recovery", *NW Fishletter*, Jan. 29, 1997.

[74] ISG, *Return to the River*, at 212.

[75] *Id.* at 211.

[76] This picture, by a photographer named Towne, shows a grain chute running from the hills down to a dockside warehouse, and is from the collection of the Oregon Historical Society (#OrHi 1727). A collection of pictures with other pre-dam views of the Snake River can be found in *Steamboat Days on the Rivers* (Oregon Hist. Soc. 1969).

[77] *See, e.g.*, "Measures to Enhance Salmon and Steelhead Migration Success During 1997", at 4 (Idaho Governor's Office Mar. 25, 1997).

[78] "Special Report: Lower Snake River Fish and Wildlife Compensation Plan, Lower Snake River, Washington and Idaho", at 66-67 (USACE Walla Walla Dist. June 1975).

[79] "Interim Report, Supplement to Special Report, Lower Snake River Fish and Wildlife Compensation Plan, Lower Snake River, Washington and Idaho, June 1975", at 8 (USACE Walla Walla Dist. April 1996).

[80] D. Chapman (pers. comm.)

[81] ISG, *Return to the River*, at 130.

[82] ISG, *Return to the River*, at 147 (emphasis added).

[83] *Id.* at 157.

[84] Quoted in B. Rudolph, "Snake River Chinook far from starved, scientists say", *Clearing Up*, Dec. 9, 1996, at 6.

[85] *Id.*

[86] W. Muir & T. Coley, "Diet of Yearling Chinook Salmon and Feeding Success During Downstream Migration in the Snake and Columbia Rivers", *Northwest Science* 70(4) (1996) (Figure 4).

[87] *Id.*

[88] ISG, *Return to the River* 155-57.

[89] D. Chapman *et al.*, "Status of summer/fall chinook salmon in the mid-Columbia region", Feb. 28, 1994, at 85 (D. Chapman Consultants).

[90] *Id.*

[91] ISG, *Return to the River* 136-37.

[92] *Id.* at 147.

[93] *Id.* at 91.

[94] L. Fulton, Spawning areas and abundance of chinook salmon (*Oncorhynchus tshawytscha*) in the Columbia Basin—past and present", USFWS Spec. Sci. Rpt.—Fisheries No. 571 (1968).

[95] *Id.* at 4.

[96] *Id.* at 16.

[97] *Id.* at 19.

[98] ISG, *Return to the River* 431.

[99] L. Fulton, Spawning areas and abundance of chinook salmon (*Oncorhynchus tshawytscha*) in the Columbia Basin—past and present", USFWS Spec. Sci. Rpt.—Fisheries No. 571, at 22 (1968).

[100] *Id.*

[101] *Id.*

[102] Fulton's report contains estimates for fall chinook turning out of the mainstem river into tributaries between Bonneville Dam and The Dalles Dam, but simply ignores the tributaries between The Dalles and McNary. It may well be true that fall chinook have never been a significant presence in these tributaries.

[103] USACE, "Annual Fish Passage Report 1993" (Table 40 (The Dalles); Table 67 (McNary))

[104] ISG, *Return to the River* 91; *see also id.* at 147.

[105] "Special Report: Lower Snake River Compensation Plan, Lower Snake River, Washington and Idaho", at 18 (USACE Walla Walla Dist. June 1975).

[106] *Id.* at 135.

[107] *Id.* at 147-48 (the ISG speculates that the status and trend of fish populations suggests that reservoirs do not replace lost riverine habitats).

[108] J. Kincheloe, "Panel 8: Compensation for Fishery Resource Damage`: The Federal Background", in E. Schwiebert (ed.), *Columbia Basin Salmon and Steelhead* 166, Spec. Pub. No. 10 (Am. Fish. Soc. 1977).

[109] This tantalizing fact is reported in "Compilation of Salmon and Steelhead Losses in the Columbia River Basin", at 212, with no further explanation.

[110] Interview, *Fisheries Forum* Vol. 3(2), at 6 (May 1995).

[111] B. Harden, *A River Lost* 25.

[112] L. Mapes, "Dams key to area shipping", *The Spokesman-Review*, Dec. 23, 1996; cf. T. Palmer, *The Snake River* 218 (110 rail cars)

[113] *Id.*

[114] K. Petersen, *River of Life, Channel of Death* 79.

[115] *Id.*

[116] Quoted in B. Rudolph, "Drawdowns Will Sink Barge Business, Council Hears", *Clearing Up*, April 7, 1997, at 7.

[117] *Id.*

[118] L. Mapes, "Dams key to area shipping", *The Spokesman-Review*, Dec. 23, 1996.

[119] K. Petersen, *River of Life, Channel of Death* 33.

[120] J. Noland, "Exceptional Water Year Could Mean Trouble, Corps Warns", *Clearing Up*, Mar. 10, 1997, at 9.

[121] NMFS, Draft Snake River Salmon Recovery Plan, at 66 (copy obtained October 1997).

[122] USACE fisheries planning manager Witt Anderson, quoted in J. Brinckman, "Dam reservoir study proposed", Mar. 14, 1997.

[123] Quoted in "'Sovereigns' lobby for official role on Columbia-Snake", PNWA Nor'Wester, August 1997, at 3.

[124] Quoted in J. Brinckman, "Salmon failure forces a hard look at dams", July 28, 1997.

[125] *See* J. Mapes, "Smith tells City Club he'll fight to keep Columbia dams", *The Oregonian*, Dec. 14, 1996.

[126] 105 Cong. Rec. S12439 (Nov. 10, 1997) (daily ed.).

[127] Quoted in L. Mapes, "Plan leaves 4 dams high and dry", *The Spokesman-Review*, Dec. 22, 1996.

[128] Ed Bowles is the most frequent source for this quote. *See, e.g.,* L. Mapes, "Plan leaves 4 dams high and dry", *The Spokesman-Review*, Dec. 22, 1996. Other IDFG dam removal advocates include Dave Cannamela. *See* L. Mapes, *The Spokesman-Review*, Sunday, July 28, 1996, at H10.

[129] *See* T. Palmer, *The Snake River* 22.

[130] Reed Burkholder, quoted in "New Plan for Rescuing the Salmon", *The New York Times*, April 27, 1997.

[131] *See, e.g.,* "Lower Snake dams killing salmon, Idaho's economy", *Idaho Statesman*, July 20, 1997.

[132] T. Kenworthy, "Salmon's New Ally Is Quite a Catch", *Washington Post*, Oct. 14, 1997, at A6.

[133] The *Tri-City Herald* (Pasco, WA), quoted in *id.*

[134] *Bangor Hydroelectric Co. v. FERC*, 78 F.3d 659, 664 (D.C. Cir. 1996).

CHAPTER 9: ENVIRONMENTAL LAW AGAINST THE DAMS

Many people are under the impression that the federal courts have examined efforts to protect endangered salmon protection by the agencies that operate dams on the Columbia and Snake River and found them wanting. Although many cases have been filed seeking such holdings, only two cases (so far) have reached this result.

In both cases, the courts did not hear a single witness, and reached their conclusions because they relied on the unsupported and erroneous assertions by lawyers, not witnesses. One decision, by United States District Judge Malcolm Marsh, was later vacated. The second opinion, which relied, in part, upon Judge Marsh's subsequently-vacated "findings", is best understood as abuse of the federal judicial power by the United States Court of Appeals for the Ninth Circuit.

The First Shot from the Environmentalists and their Backers: the Commercial Salmon Harvesters

In 1992, the Sierra Club Legal Defense Fund, representing a group of commercial fishermen and environmentalists, filed suit in the United States District Court for the Western District of Washington. The group sought, among other things, a declaration that operation of the dams and reservoirs comprising the Federal Columbia River Power System were jeopardizing the continued existence of endangered Snake River salmon.

At that time, I had just moved to Oregon from New York City. I knew almost nothing about salmon. All I knew was that the law firm for which I worked represented a group of companies that purchased enormous quantities of electricity from the Bonneville Power Administration (BPA). These companies, called the Direct Service Industries or DSIs, made aluminum and other products in electro-chemical processes highly dependent upon electricity. The Sierra Club plaintiffs sought to get an injunction banning BPA from entering into any new power sales contracts. At the time, the DSIs were beginning to think about new contracts with BPA, so they were concerned about the suit.

Two years before I had arrived in Oregon, Jeff Ring, the senior lawyer for the DSIs responsible for environmental issues, had pushed the DSIs to get involved in decisions concerning salmon recovery. Mr. Ring believed that the anti-dam plans pushed by self-styled salmon advocates could not withstand scientific scrutiny, and that salmon populations in the Columbia River Basin would never recover so long as the primary focus of salmon recovery efforts was the dams. He thought that the interests of the salmon could be consistent with those of the DSIs. Among other things, the DSIs used electric power in a manner that caused smooth releases of water from the dams, rather than large day and night shifts. The DSIs had considerable incentive to make sure that the dams did not end up as scapegoats for salmon decline while other problems faded from public attention.

Jeff was ably assisted by Gary Firestone, a former Oregon Supreme Court clerk who was keenly aware of the failures of salmon management, and the salmon agencies' misinterpretations of the environmental laws. At the DSI office, Nanci Tester, a former Bonneville Power Administration employee with a degree in biology, supervised our efforts.

The environmentalists sued under § 7 of the Endangered Species Act, a provision that declares that every federal agency must avoid taking action that would "jeopardize the continued existence of" a listed species. Section 7 tells every federal agency taking action that may affect endangered species to consult with the federal fish and wildlife agency responsible for those species.

In the case of endangered salmon, the responsible agency is the National Marine Fisheries Service (NMFS). Under § 7, NMFS is to render a "biological opinion" as to whether the proposed action would be likely to "jeopardize the continued existence of the species". In 1992, the very first year after the salmon were listed, BPA, the Corps and the Bureau had prepared an enormous "biological assessment" showing the effect of their planned operations on salmon. NMFS reviewed the document, conducted additional analyses, and concluded that the operations planned in 1992 were not likely to jeopardize the continued existence of Snake River salmon.

The fishermen and environmentalists disagreed. In their view, the dams stood as the sole obstacle to healthy salmon runs, and they sought a court decision to invalidate NMFS' biological opinions and the resulting BPA, Corps and Bureau decision to go ahead with their operational plans. At the outset, their lawsuit ran into a procedural problem, for they had sued BPA together with NMFS, the Corps and the Bureau, and BPA cannot be sued in district court. BPA can (with very limited exceptions) only be sued in the United States Court of Appeals for the Ninth Circuit.

Throughout the fall of 1992, the lawsuit was mired in procedural wrangling. Paul Murphy, the senior partner representing the DSIs, had been litigating against BPA for almost a decade. He knew the laws governing BPA inside and out. He convinced Jeff and me that there was no way that a suit against BPA could go forward in District Court, and we waited and watched. The District Court dismissed the suit. The environmentalists and fishermen appealed. They lost. As expected, the Ninth Circuit followed several of its prior decisions and concluded that the case should be dismissed.

Our First Attempt to Get Salmon Bureaucrats to Look Beyond the Dams

All of us could see that other federal agencies had not begun to approach the enormous efforts of BPA, the Corps and the Bureau to comply with the Endangered Species Act. Most of them had yet to begin the consultation process required by § 7 of the Endangered Species Act. There was considerable doubt as to whether some agencies, like the Bureau of Land Management, ever would. As we interviewed government employees to get a handle on the situation, we found that they would point the finger at other agencies, giving us further leads.

After a considerable amount of investigation, I drafted a broadly-based complaint that focused on the federal government's failure to reform harvest, habitat management and hatchery management. We filed it in the United States District Court for the District of Oregon. It was assigned to Judge Malcolm Marsh.

We were joined in our efforts by Erick Johnson, Bill Masters and Dan Lindahl, lawyers representing the Pacific Northwest Generating Cooperative, a cooperative providing generation and transmission service for 29 rural electric cooperatives. They filed their own complaint, adding a claim that the government had failed to pursue a comprehensive approach to analysis of effects on salmon, and thereby erred in its application of the Endangered Species Act to hydropower operations. Greg Minor and Cynthia Rutzick represented the Public Power Council, a non-profit corporation representing 114 public power entities in the Pacific Northwest. They also filed a separate complaint. All three complaints were consolidated under the name *PNGC v. Brown*.

Judge Marsh had presided for several years over another salmon case: *United States v. Oregon*, where states and tribes had long fought, sometimes bitterly, over the allocation of salmon harvested from the Columbia River. Initially, we were hopeful that Judge Marsh's experience with *United States v. Oregon* would give him a useful familiarity with salmon issues. As time passed, we were more and more discouraged to discover he was not merely familiar with the issues, but also appeared to have absorbed from the fishery interests an anti-dam and pro-harvest dogma.

How Administrative Law Destroys Justice in Suits Against the Government

One of the bedrock principles of our system of justice is that litigants should have an opportunity to "discover" the facts of a case that are in the possession of their opponents. Another bedrock principle is that litigants should have an opportunity to question witnesses whose testimony is used against them. Anyone can appreciate the injustice of making judicial decisions based solely on what lawyers (rather than witnesses) tell the judge.

Even if the lawyer resists the temptation to shade the testimony, the lawyer writing an affidavit is obviously only focused on one side of the issue. Without cross-examination of the actual witness, which has been characterized as "the greatest engine for the discovery of truth ever invented", one can never be sure what has been left out of affidavits.

Most people would be surprised to learn that, generally speaking, both of these bedrock principles are thrown out the window when it comes to citizens litigating against their government. Over the past century, the Supreme Court has gradually staked out the position that in litigation against the government, the universe of relevant facts is to be limited to something called the "administrative record."

The theory for limiting the evidence in cases against the government is conceptually appealing. A court or jury is supposed to limit its consideration to facts that are presented in court through the testimony of witnesses—"facts of record". In most cases, a jury's verdict will be set aside if it wanders off to do its own investigation, unknown to the parties in the case.

In some administrative agencies, hearings are conducted that resemble, in many respects, trial before a court or before a jury. There is a definable set of evidence that is presented by testimony, with cross-examination of witnesses, and a formal record is made. The Supreme Court reasoned that it didn't make a lot of sense for a court to go look for other facts to see whether the agency decision was lawful. Letting parties start all over again in court could gum up the works.

Unfortunately most administrative decisions—including nearly *all* decisions under the Endangered Species Act—are made without any type of formal process whatsoever. Generally, a responsible official is presented with alternatives by his or her staff, hears objections from the outsiders involved (if they even know about the decision) and makes a decision. Without looking through the government's files and questioning the officials who make decisions, no one can never really know what facts they used to make decisions, or whether they were right or wrong.

Yet, as a general matter, no one is allowed to do this. Instead, the courts pretend that there is such a thing as an administrative record. In our first salmon case, before the government learned it could put in affidavits from witnesses without letting us question the witnesses, the government let us take the deposition of J. Gary Smith of the National Marine Fisheries Service.

Mr. Smith confirmed that what really happens is that while the government is making an Endangered Species Act decision, documents accumulate in the files, which decisionmakers might or might not read.[1] Later, after the decision is made, the government's lawyers look through the files and decide in a "collaborative process" with agency officials what documents will be designated for inclusion in the fictitious administrative record.[2] As counsel for the government put it, "the administrative record is really only relevant in the context of judicial review".[3]

In other words, the only evidence ordinarily allowed is whatever the government's lawyers edit and select. How can this possibly lead to justice in disputes between citizens and the government? It cannot.

Worse still, many of the most highly relevant documents in the agency's possession can be lawfully excluded from the administrative record on the ground that they are "privileged". They remain a secret from the litigants and the public at large. The Freedom of Information Act is no use, because it exempts documents protected by an "administrative deliberative process privilege" invented by the courts and then endorsed by Congress.

In the case of the salmon, the National Marine Fisheries Service adopted a formal policy of identifying scores of relevant documents as "predecisional ESA decision documents". These documents, which occasionally leak out, may be withheld entirely from the public.

Thus the law has created a situation in which the real documents that would show the basis of an official decision are often withheld as "privileged", while scores of documents of lesser importance are produced and represented to be the bases of the decision.

The idea that a government may have documents concerning endangered salmon that are "privileged" from disclosure to its citizens *because they expose the deliberative process of government* is one I have never understood. The theory seems to be that public officials will not make the "right" decisions if the public can see what they are doing, apparently because they will be too embarrassed, or subjected to public pressure. The unstated premise seems to be that pressure from the public is improper; pressure from those privileged to know what is going on is not.

There may be legitimate claims of privilege in the endangered species context, such as documents that would, for example, reflect the location of some of the few remaining salmon redds, which might be used by those who wish to injure the salmon. Those were not the documents we sought. We sought documents that would reflect the agency's beliefs and misconceptions, and would be highly relevant in rendering any reasoned appraisal of the agency's action. Indeed, such documents often contain information that is embarrassing to the government, because they flatly contradict the final decision made.

But in the view of the courts, avoiding embarrassment to the government is more important than allowing citizens to find out what is really going on. Given that courts invented this rule, only new judges or some sort of amendment to the Constitution can really cure the problem. And from what I can tell, courts aren't too eager to enforce the Constitution against the government either.

Jeff and I were a little surprised to find out that our clients were not particularly eager to bring affirmative claims against the government for overlooking other causes of salmon decline. Large corporations have a visceral distaste for bringing claims against other sectors of economic activity, and there are many forums in which such conduct is criticized. Some legitimately fear retribution from the government.

But we recognized that the "blame the dams" strategy was going to be a perfect success so long as all the other causes of decline were essentially ignored. The unholy alliance of commercial fisherman and environmentalists meant that at least two of the three main human-induced causes of decline, harvest and hatcheries, would go essentially untouched.

We convinced the clients to allow us to file a complaint that targeted not only harvest and hatcheries, but also certain activities on federal land, including federal grazing and mining permits and timber contracts. We quickly ran afoul of another strange development in environmental law. Our complaint set forth the specific activities on federal land causing harm to salmon. We knew that the government had lists of particular timber sales that had potential salmon problems, and lists of grazing allotments with an assessment of their effects on important salmon tributaries.

But the government refused to produce the lists. We moved to compel production of the lists, and Judge Marsh refused. Worse still, Judge Marsh threatened to dismiss the complaint unless we could file a "bill of particulars" (a device sometimes used to make prosecutors specify their charges against criminal defendants) identifying the particular areas we were concerned about.

So we hired a biologist to go to the BLM and Forest Service offices in Idaho and Eastern Oregon and Washington. The Justice Department quickly tried to close the files that had heretofore been open to the public, but our people got in before the word got around to all the offices, so we were able to get enough information to file the requested "bill of particulars". Over and over again, I have seen the government's lawyers tell employees not to talk to us or our representatives. Over and over again, by restricting citizens' access to public documents and public employees, government justice departments promote injustice.

Most environmental groups bringing Endangered Species Act suits avoid the problem of actually identifying the particular actions injuring salmon by challenging a general planning document, such as a Forest Plan, instead. In our view, this did not make a lot of sense, since the planning document just outlines general principles that are supposed to guide specific administrative decisions.

Dozens of Supreme Court precedents have counseled that the federal courts are supposed to review only specific administrative decisions that have an "immediate and concrete impact" on the litigant. But the United States Court of Appeals for the Ninth Circuit has repeatedly allowed challenges to the most general of plans whose impact on any particular citizen is minimal at best.

Even the Clinton/Gore Administration took issue with the Ninth Circuit's 1995 decision in the *Pacific Rivers Council* case.[4] There Judges Reinhardt, Tang and Wright held that the Forest Service could not lawfully proceed to manage an Idaho forest—allowing logging to proceed—unless they conducted consultations with the Forest Service on a forest plan made several years before the Endangered Species Act listing of spotted owls. The Forest Service protested that each and every individual timber sale had been reviewed for effects on endangered species and were "not likely to adversely affect" listed salmon within the meaning of the Endangered Species Act and the governing federal regulations. The Court held that that did not matter. All activities in the forest that might affect salmon were enjoined until another paper addressing the effects of the obsolete planning document could be produced.

Judge Marsh Gets Hoaxed

Judge Marsh is a good man, trying to do justice in his own way, but his ideas about salmon and what was causing the problems with salmon were all given to him by the propagators of the Great Salmon Hoax. When it came time for him to write an opinion, he repeated all of them.

Relying in part on what he candidly characterized as "semi-historical" background information,[5] Judge Marsh began by stating, as if it were undisputed fact, that "the most significant 'stress' upon the river resource is industrial and commercial electric usage which rely upon the dams and hydropower operations".[6] He repeated the Northwest Power Planning Council's politically-driven and scientifically-unsupportable conclusion (discussed in Chapter 13), that hydropower development caused 80% of the salmon losses.[7] He suggested that harvest effects on the endangered salmon were minimal in part because of the Columbia River Fish Management Plan (CRFMP) he pushed the parties in *United States v. Oregon* to create.[8]

He then declared that "to permit non-parties to interfere with this carefully balanced process"—the CRFMP—would cause "chaos", and revealed that

> "it was with a continuing desire to avoid both confusion and chaos and to preserve what I feel is an essential 'big picture' perspective, that the case management committee and the Chief Judge of this district determined that cases which may impact the CRFMP, and which related to salmon harvest activities on the Columbia, be brought before me, as the judge presiding in *United States v. Oregon*."[9]

Judges are normally assigned at random, to assure fairness. This assignment decision, which we learned about for the first time when Judge Marsh issued his opinion throwing us out of court, meant that we would never escape Judge Marsh's efforts to preserve his "essential 'big picture' perspective"—a perspective generated by the anti-dam advocates that had appeared before him for years in *United States v. Oregon*. It always seemed as if he regarded us as the agents of chaos.

But it was really the Endangered Species Act that was the bringer of chaos. As former Northwest Power Planning Council member Kai Lee of Washington had warned in 1991, "a stock-based plan virtually requires measures to control the impact of mixed-stock fisheries, broadening the attack on the hydropower operators to an internecine struggle among fisheries".[10] Professor Lee did not foresee that the courts would refuse to enforce the Act against salmon harvest, avoiding the "internecine struggle" from implementing stock-based management, and instead align themselves with the harvest managers in the "attack on the hydropower operators".

Others aligned with the harvest managers included the States of Oregon and Washington, which promptly intervened in the action, along with "Salmon for All", representing gillnetters, and the Northwest Resource Information Center (Ed Chaney). Six tribes and the State of Idaho sought and obtained the right to file briefs without being bound by the results of the case, as "friends of the court"—*amicus curiae*.

Closing the Courthouse Door to Wise Use of Natural Resources: Judge-Made Standing Doctrine

In November 1992, the federal government (later joined by the State of Oregon) filed a motion to dismiss our complaint for lack of "standing". In simple terms, the government asserted that the Pacific Northwest Generating Cooperative (PNGC), the Public Power Council (PPC), and my clients the direct service industries (DSIs) had no legitimate interest in salmon. According to the government, these parties were unworthy plaintiffs to bring suit under the Endangered Species Act because they sought to protect their economic interests.

Of course, the government couldn't make this argument if review were limited to the "administrative record". The courts have invented an exception to the "administrative record" rule that allows the government to question plaintiffs before trial to gather facts for a challenge to "standing". In this case, the government took the deposition of Steve Waddington, Deputy Director of the DSI office.

We, however, were unable to gather the corresponding facts from the government. When the government's lawyers filed an affidavit from BPA's Walt Pollock, and we sought to take his deposition to question him about the bases for his testimony, Judge Marsh refused to allow the deposition to go forward. He justified this by saying the evidence was not needed, because "I am assuming that there is a link between harvest reductions and BPA expenditures".[11] "Plaintiffs have adequately demonstrated that an increase in their power rates is as inevitable as death and taxes and that a portion of that increase will be attributed to endangered species protection measures".[12]

Then, however, Judge Marsh consulted his expert in a different harvest allocation case, Dr. Howard Horton, to obtain data which he concluded demonstrated that even if we prevailed on our harvest claims, we would get "at best, a 20.6% reduction in adult Snake River fall chinook mortality".[13] This, he declared, was "simply too tenuous a connection with the lower power rates and power stability sought by plaintiffs".[14]

This calculation, which we learned about for the first time when we read his opinion, ignored the fact that the principles we sought to establish would achieve far greater mortality reductions. It ignored the evidence that even a 20 percent reduction in mortality would, according to the computer models, produce rising (instead of falling) salmon populations. Federal judges are not supposed to make these sorts of calculations on their own, without even holding a trial. Under the Federal Rules of Civil Procedure, "summary" judgment must be denied if there are any disputes of fact. Disputes of fact are supposed to be resolved by presenting evidence in open court, at a trial.

Having found that there was no sufficient link between the overfishing cited in our complaint and increased power rates, Judge Marsh then declared that Article III of the U.S. Constitution prevented the federal judiciary from even considering the merits of our claims. He relied primarily on a U.S. Supreme Court case where environmentalists attempted to challenge the construction of a water project in Egypt because they might someday want to go there, and the water project might someday reduce the populations of endangered crocodiles that they might someday want to observe.[15]

The DSIs, PPC and PNGC were not going to be injured someday. They were already paying, just by themselves, most of the Bonneville Power Administration's fish and wildlife costs through their electric power purchases, and the link between overfishing and increased fish costs was so clear that the Judge had assumed it to be true in order to deny them the right to question Mr. Pollock.

Judge Marsh went on to declare that even if the Constitution did not bar the Courts from considering their claims, they could not sue because they had a "conflict of interest". In what became the "sound bite" for the case, Judge Marsh declared:

> "To permit these plaintiffs to proceed with their claims under
> the ESA would be akin to permitting the fox to complain that
> the chickens have not been fed—sure, he has an interest in
> seeing that the chickens are well fed, but it's just not the same
> interest the farmer has, nor is it an interest shared by the
> chickens."[16]

Righteous environmentalists crowed that Judge Marsh had "scornfully questioned the motives of the industries".[17]

Judge Marsh's attitude toward the fishermen was far different. According to him, their "central interest is the fish".[18] Lost in all this rhetoric was the "interests of the chickens" or the salmon themselves. In elevating those who seek to kill and eat the fish over those who seek to generate electricity, and minimize adverse impacts on fish in a sensible fashion, Judge Marsh fashioned a law of standing that bore no resemblance to the law passed by Congress.

That law is simple. Under the Endangered Species Act, "any person" may file suit to enjoin the federal government from violating the Act.[19] Many courts have said this means what it says: anyone, even a corporation (specifically defined as a "person" by the Act[20]), can bring a suit under the ESA.

On appeal, the United States Court of Appeals for the Ninth Circuit reversed Judge Marsh's standing ruling. After noting that Judge Marsh was "highly knowledgeable in these matters from his former judicial experience", Judges Browning, Kozinski and Noonan relied upon all of his findings, including his recitation of the elements of the Great Salmon Hoax.[21] They ignored our objections to his finding facts without a trial, and declared that it was "far from obvious that the benefit to the species [from the relief sought] will be of sufficient magnitude to require the Bonneville Power Administration to change the spill and flow requirements designed to aid the species or lower the rates it must charge in order to finance conservation of the species".[22]

They did reject the fox/chicken coop analogy, noting that "a narrow or cynical understanding of economic interest is not decisive". They recognized that "under the regulatory system governing these hydropower users, they may actually derive some benefit from the health of the rivers and the fish within them. The plaintiffs may thus be partners in the preservation of the species."[23] Accordingly, they decided that our clients had a right to ensure that the procedures required by the Endangered Species Act were followed, even if they could see no direct link to BPA electricity prices.

Our success in reversing Judge Marsh was one of the very few times commercial interests have gotten standing to sue under environmental laws in the Ninth Circuit. Other panels of that Court have continued to deny standing to commercial groups. Perhaps the low point in Ninth Circuit jurisprudence was reached in August 1995, when one of the Court's most prominent liberals, Judge Reinhardt, issued an opinion in *Bennett v. Plenert*. The plaintiffs were "two ranchers and two irrigation districts located in" Oregon. They challenged the Bureau of Reclamation's decision "that the water level in two reservoirs should be maintained at a particular minimum level in order to preserve two species of fish". The plaintiffs claimed that "there is no evidence to support the [government's] conclusion that the long-term operation of the [reservoirs] would adversely affect" the fish. *The Court never reviewed the accuracy of plaintiffs' claims.*

Instead, the Court decided to act as if the claim were true: that there really was no evidence that the water the government was taking away from the irrigators was needed to preserve the fish. The Court then held that Congress did not really mean "any person" could sue when it passed the Endangered Species Act. Congress, said the Court, meant any person "whose interest was arguably within the zone of interests sought to be protected by the statute". And the courts would decide whether any particular interests were in that "zone of interests". The ranchers and irrigation districts were not in the zone of interests, because *"only plaintiffs who allege an interest in the preservation of endangered species" could ever sue.*

In short, according to the Ninth Circuit, when administrative agencies violate the Endangered Species Act, and interpret it far more broadly than Congress ever intended, the judiciary is not supposed to stop them. Many people see nothing wrong with that, but they have never had their property or livelihoods threatened by lawless government action. The Ninth Circuit's opinion emboldens federal agencies (and the political appointees who control them) to violate the law. They think that no one can stop them—a fact that both government attorneys and government employees have told me more than once during the progress of the salmon cases.

Fortunately, on March 19, 1997, the United States Supreme Court reversed the Ninth Circuit's *Bennett v. Plenart* decision in a unanimous opinion. The Court quickly dismissed the argument that the irrigators lacked standing, writing that "[i]t is difficult to understand how the Ninth Circuit could have failed to see [how to interpret the Supreme Court's standing cases]".[24] Responding to the notion that the law only allowed suits that would be protective of endangered species, and not protective of economic interests, the Court explained:

> "The obvious purpose of the requirement that each agency 'use the best scientific and commercial evidence available' is to ensure that the ESA not be implemented haphazardly, on the basis of speculation or surmise. While this no doubt serves to advance the ESA's overall goal of species preservation, we think it readily apparent that another objective (if not indeed the primary one) is to avoid needless economic dislocation produced by agency officials zealously but unintelligently pursuing their environmental objectives."[25]

Over time, this opinion could begin to improve the quality of Endangered Species Act decisions in the courts, because someone besides environmentalists might be bringing the suits. But economic interests will probably still have to fight to get standing to invoke other environmental laws, like the National Environmental Policy Act, that would prevent some of the irrational decisionmaking now going on.

The larger problem is that law itself, and the Endangered Species Act in particular, remains too vague and ambiguous. When there is no law, endangered species themselves can easily become tools exploited to achieve other policy objectives, typically the environmentalist objective of limiting growth. When environmentalists sue to save a particular species, it is nearly always because there is some other goal, and even when the government invokes the Endangered Species Act, there is often another goal. As set forth in Chapter 13, below, an overriding goal for fish and wildlife agencies in the Pacific Northwest is obtaining funding for their programs and personnel. By pushing their anti-dam agenda for decades, they have concealed their own mismanagement, extracted funding for the largest fish and wildlife program in the world, and wasted nearly all of the money.

Misuse of the Mootness Doctrine

When justice department attorneys cannot throw citizens out of court for lack of "standing", they have an additional powerful weapon in their arsenal: claims of "mootness". The idea behind mootness is a simple one. The Supreme Court long ago decided, based on language in the Constitution declaring that the federal judicial power extends to resolving "cases or controversies", that the Court should not and would not be in the business of giving federal officials advisory opinions on the lawfulness of their actions. That would be left to the government's lawyers.

From this acorn of a decision against advisory opinions, a mighty oak tree of doctrine grew to the point where most of the legal arguments we have advanced to challenge federal salmon decisions have never been resolved. Almost every time we would make a claim, the federal government would declare that it was too late to provide effective relief, because conditions had changed.

In the endangered species context, the government often issues decisions that cover only a year's worth of harvest, hatchery operations, grazing, or whatever. This means that by the time a court is ready to reach the merits of the claim, the year is usually already over. Endangered Species Act decisions are typically not published in the Federal Register, and citizens generally find out about them after the fact, unless they are intimately involved in the decisionmaking. After that, the Act requires a two-month notice and waiting period before suit can be filed.[26] Then the government has two more months to answer the complaint. The government will then typically seek extensive delays for the preparation of the "administrative record". By 1997, the government has taken as long as a year just to come forth with the "administrative record".

In *PNGC v. Brown*, we had sued about events concerning the federal government's decisions in 1992. Judge Marsh did not make his decision until April 1, 1993. We had complained that hatchery releases had proceeded in 1992 despite a failure to conduct *any* analyses of harm to endangered salmon, as required by § 7 of the Act. For example, juvenile hatchery steelhead have an unfortunate tendency to eat endangered juvenile chinook salmon, because the steelhead are much larger, a phenomenon that biologists observing the salmon call a "common sight".[27] We thought that if the fish and wildlife agencies really wanted to comply with the Endangered Species Act, they might bother to at least figure out how many endangered fish were lost through hatchery releases in § 7 consultations. They never have, and unless someone sues them again, they probably never will.

In response to our hatchery claims, the government lawyers told Judge Marsh that they were going to do a hatchery analysis next year. Ignoring Supreme Court authority stating that a promise is not enough, Judge Marsh declared that because the government was now starting the required analyses, the claim was moot.[28] The Ninth Circuit affirmed his decision with a single sentence. They didn't discuss the Supreme Court precedent either.

As for the government's failure to do the § 7 analyses for grazing permits and other activities on federally-managed land, Judge Marsh complained that "because these plaintiffs have relied upon generalized claims . . . it is impossible to tell if the generalized failures are of such short duration that they may evade review."[29] He did not address the highly specific "bill of particulars" he had required us to prepare. Thus with no trial and no discovery, the habitat claims were thrown out, apparently because it was not enough to prove that the government had violated the law, so long as the government promised to do better.

How then, do environmentalists manage to win their lawsuits? The mootness doctrine contains an exception for "extraordinary cases" that are "capable of repetition yet evading review". This means whatever the courts want it to mean. Abortion cases are nearly always decided, because it takes more than nine months to get the Court of Appeals, and the case would evade

242

review. Salmon cases are sometimes decided and sometimes not, even though it takes more than a year to get to the Court of Appeals, and by the time you get there, the government has probably issued a new salmon decision.

One of our worst experiences with mootness came in a case where we sued BPA in the Ninth Circuit. BPA Administrator Randy Hardy had, over the objections of his staff, decided to cave into National Marine Fisheries Service demands for operational changes at the dams, which were expressed in a 1993 biological opinion issued pursuant to § 7 of the Endangered Species Act. In particular, Mr. Hardy directed BPA to expand significantly the flow augmentation strategy for salmon recovery.

For purposes of the National Environmental Policy Act (NEPA), Administrator Hardy's formal Record of Decision was supported by the same Supplemental Environmental Impact Statement (SEIS) that the environmentalists had indirectly challenged in the District Court before Judge Marsh in their transportation lawsuit.

We decided to challenge the adequacy of the SEIS—albeit for quite different reasons than the environmentalists. We thought that the National Environmental Policy Act required BPA and other agencies to consider the environmental impact of major reductions in clean and renewable hydropower. Increases in flow augmentation in the 1990s have cut BPA's firm load carrying capability by anywhere from 2,000 to 5,550 average *megawatts* of electricity.[30] That's as much electricity as would be generated by two large nuclear plants or dozens of combustion turbines. Deciding to buy that much power, instead of letting water run through the turbines at the dams, is a decision with very significant consequences to the environment. Nearly all of that electricity comes from burning fossil fuels; some comes from nuclear plants. You have to burn a lot of something to make that much electricity.

The SEIS contained virtually no analysis about the environmental impacts from generating increased electricity from fossil and nuclear fuel. The SEIS dismisses the consequences as "difficult to assess" and says that the effect of increased pollution "is considered to be small".[31] The language is carefully chosen. It means that the government is not willing to actually figure out the effects of generating as much pollution as four power plants.

Fergus Pilon, the General Manager of the Columbia River People's Utility District, has calculated that building enough of the cleanest power plants—combustion turbines burning natural gas—to replace electricity lost by removing the four Lower Snake dams would, each year, generate 222 tons of particulates, 148 tons of SO_2, 518 tons of NOx, 148 tons of CO, and 2,588,000 tons of CO_2. If John Day Dam were removed as well, these figures would roughly double.[32] One estimate suggests that the resulting pollution would be "equivalent to about 3,300,000 more cars traveling 11,000 miles [a year] at 20 miles per gallon".[33]

It is especially ironic that the Clinton/Gore attack on hydropower is going hand in hand with aggressive efforts to promote global warming theories. Some recent reports suggest that if present trends continue, the earth could be almost five degrees warmer by the year 2100.[34] That would move most of the salmon populations north, entirely out of the continental United States. Only Alaska would have salmon left.

Hydropower is the only large-scale method of generating electric power (other than nuclear power) that does not promote CO_2 buildup. Other than effects on anadromous fish, it is a clean and renewable resource. Yet because the Clinton/Gore administration opposes hydropower, we have shut down gigawatts of power and spewed forth huge quantities of air pollution, with no benefit to salmon runs.

Before commercial salmon harvest interests co-opted Northwest environmentalists, hydropower used to be seen as the best way to generate electric power. Even the citizens of the imaginary Pacific Northwest environmental paradise *Ecotopia* continued to use hydroelectric dams, albeit while developing solar and other cleaner technologies.[35]

On October 22, 1993, we filed a petition in the Ninth Circuit for review of the Record of Decision. We fully briefed the case, explaining how BPA had violated NEPA (and several other federal statutes). A week or so before oral argument, the government came out with a new biological opinion. The new opinion also contained no analysis of the effects of decreased hydropower production. Nevertheless, the Court dismissed our challenge as moot.

In theory we could start from scratch and bring a whole new lawsuit to raise exactly the same questions. As you might imagine, our clients had a difficult time understanding the logic of this decision.

At the same time, the environmentalist and fishermen's anti-transportation case against the National Marine Fisheries Service and the Corps of Engineers was before the Ninth Circuit. The cases were argued the same day, in front of the same judges. The enviro/harvester coalition had, ironically, made the very same claim we had: they too thought the SEIS was inadequate, because it did not include environmental analysis of the effects of smolt transportation.

The Court decided, for reasons that remain a mystery to me, that the environmentalist challenges to the SEIS were not moot. However, the environmentalists lost too, because although the Court at least considered their claims, it rejected them on the merits.

The *Idaho Fish and Game* Case: "One Person's Train Wreck is Another Person's Little Engine that Could"

As explained above, Governor Andrus believed that drawdowns of the Lower Snake dams offered the best hope for protecting irrigators. Governor Andrus instructed his Attorney General to file suit in federal court in the District of Idaho, challenging NMFS' conclusion that hydropower operations, as modified by NMFS, would not jeopardize the continued existence of Snake River salmon. The suit was filed in early 1993, and assigned to Judge Ryan, who was too ill to preside. Over both Idaho's and our strenuous objections, the case was transferred out of Idaho to Judge Marsh.

Idaho never came forward and admitted that what it was after was drawdown. Formally, the suit sought an order setting aside NMFS' 1993 biological opinion as arbitrary, capricious, and contrary to law. Idaho obtained affidavits from experts who believed that when salmon populations reached low levels, an "extinction vortex" could occur. These experts claimed that the "extinction vortex" would cause more rapid extinction than the government had considered in its review of hydropower operations. Idaho also complained that NMFS' use of computer modeling was inadequately explained.

Applied to a genuine species, where the number of potential breeders was extraordinarily low (like the finches on Darwin's islands), there was at least theoretical merit to "extinction vortex" theory. Applied to a context where the species numbered in the millions, the theory was junk science. The particular population model used by Idaho, the "Dennis model", has been criticized as "too simplistic to be of use except under rather limited circumstances".[36]

Given our prior experience with Judge Marsh, we didn't think Idaho was likely to succeed by putting in affidavits of supposed experts who disagreed with NMFS. In *PNGC v. Brown*, we had put in expert affidavits taking the position that NMFS was wrong when it concluded that continuing to harvest endangered salmon would not jeopardize their continued existence. Citing a prior decision of the Ninth Circuit called *Mt. Graham Red Squirrel*, Judge Marsh had declared that because our experts and the government's experts disagreed—indeed, had "sharply conflicting views"—"the agencies then have the discretion to rely upon whichever reasonable opinions they choose".[37] Going further, Judge Marsh had stated: "I do *not* see how, even if they had standing under the ESA to challenge harvest activities, plaintiffs could succeed on such a 'technical difference of opinion' which was soundly rejected by the Ninth Circuit in *Mt. Graham Red Squirrel*."[38]

The rule of the *Mt. Graham Red Squirrel* case means that even if citizens can somehow persuade federal courts to reach the merits of their claims, they will nearly always lose. As Ted Strong of the Columbia River Inter-Tribal Fish Commission has complained, this rule "allows the federal agencies to pick whatever science they like best, no matter how improbable and untested".[39] The whole idea that two experts can render contrary scientific opinions, that both are deemed "reasonable", and that the courts should be unwilling to figure out which expert is is right is peculiar. Imagine the outcry that would arise if courts declared that in lawsuits between individuals and corporations where scientific questions are at issue, the corporations would always win.

Idaho's lawsuit, which was essentially premised on dueling scientific testimony, should have failed under the rule of *Mt. Graham Red Squirrel*. Unfortunately, like many of the judge-made rules for review of government action, the rule is frequently honored in the breach.

Our first indication of how Judge Marsh would approach the scientific issues came in the oral argument of Idaho's motion for summary judgment. Judge Marsh passed out a list of four questions, and, instead of taking scientific evidence from experts, decided to poll the attorneys of the parties on their views.

Three of the four questions amounted to overly simple statements of the fundamental scientific differences of opinion at issue in the case. Judge Marsh questioned the attorneys for each party as to their answer to the questions. The federal government quickly agreed with the representatives of the state and tribal fishery agencies on each question. The other industry intervenors and I disagreed.

After the skirmishing over salmon science, Judge Marsh asked the parties to address what was the critical issue in the case from our perspective: whether the National Marine Fisheries Service had correctly applied § 7 of the Endangered Species Act to dam operations.

There are federal regulations specifying how to apply § 7 of the Endangered Species Act in exhaustive detail: the agency is supposed to determine whether the proposed action "reduces appreciably both the survival and recovery of the listed species".

In its biological opinion, NMFS had simply ignored the federal regulations, and adopted a two-step process: (1) comparing the effects of agency action to a "base period" from 1986 to 1990; and (2) assessing "combined effects" of the dam operations with a number of other actions. This standard was, in our view, carefully crafted to protect commercial harvest, because 1986 to 1990 were extraordinarily high harvest years, and because the "combined effects" analysis required dam operators to offset the effects of continued overfishing. Idaho's chief gripe was with the dates selected for the "base period".

As soon as I got my chance to address the question, the following exchange took place:

> "Mr. Buchal: We disagree.   We think that there are regulations here.   We think that it's remarkable that the agencies did not even purport to apply the regulations, and we think that this thing that they have invented, this base period analysis, combined effect analysis, is seriously flawed for a number of reasons.   It's inconsistent with the statutory purposes, and it was an agency rule [of] general application promulgated in violation of the Administrative Procedure Act.
>
> "Mr. Disheroon [the Justice Department lawyer]:   May I respond, Your Honor?   These parties are here as intervenors with the understanding, at least to date, they are not supposed to raise new issues. . . . I know that they have filed a proposed counterclaim.   Our time to respond has not yet run.   We have standing issues and other things.
>
> "Judge Marsh: I'm glad you raised that, because I'm not going to allow the counterclaim for the same reasons I didn't [allow] the standing in the previous case [*PNGC v. Brown*].   You need not respond to it.   You are in here as intervenors and on the issues that are here.
>
> "Mr. Buchal: May I ask a question?
>
> "Judge Marsh: Yes.
>
> "Mr. Buchal: Is it an issue that is *here* whether or not the base period analysis and combined effect analysis can be applied consistent with law?   Are we allowed to argue that here?
>
> "Judge Marsh: Well, I think you just did.   And I am going to consider that a little later, but I want to stay with this methodology [*i.e.*, the base period and combined effects analysis] for a little while . . ."[40]

In substance, Judge Marsh had declared that as intervenors (who under federal law are generally entitled to all the rights of a party), we could make no claims of our own, even if neither the government nor the plaintiffs were focusing on the correct provisions of law. In particular, the National Marine Fisheries Service could concoct a special interpretation of the Endangered Species Act to blame dams, the plaintiffs could complain it didn't blame the dams enough, and we couldn't get NMFS to follow the rules it should have been following.

From our perspective, perhaps the most critical issue in the case concerned what "effects of the action" were supposed to be analyzed under § 7—a subject covered in the controlling federal regulations.[41] Section 7 is supposed to keep federal agencies from exterminating endangered species based on discretionary decisions that they have yet to make. Decisions already made, like the decisions to build the dams decades ago, are not something that is supposed to be revisited in § 7 consultations because the dam operators don't have the discretionary authority to remove the dams.

The biological opinion ostensibly addressed the effect of the 1993 plans for hydropower operations. But the National Marine Fisheries Service had never clearly specified the effect of *operations*. Instead, NMFS had simply pretended that each and every fish that died in the Columbia and Snake Rivers died because of the 1993 operational plans challenged in the lawsuit. This led to the following exchange with Judge Marsh:

> "Judge Marsh: I realize you want to make that division between the construction—that which is sitting across the river and that [which] is how it operates. That distinction was not made by NMFS in its analysis under the biological opinion, was it?
>
> "Mr. Buchal: They did not expressly use that term, but the whole analysis where you run the juvenile passage models and you change the flows and you see what happens, that *is* estimating the effect of the operational changes, that little piece of [mortality]. Then [there] is the big piece. The big piece is the 70-90 percent [mortality] that is existing and that is natural mortality. These things are in the record.
>
> "Judge Marsh: Not your distinction.
>
> "Mr. Buchal: Not with my distinction.
>
> "Judge Marsh: Okay. Does the government think that is an accurate distinction to make between the fact, what I understand the DSI, PPC and PNGC to say to us is that the

dams are irrelevant; the fact they are there is irrelevant? They are just as if we were looking at a bend in the river. That is their on[ly] relevance, and how we operate them is the sole purpose that we are examining.

"Mr. Disheroon: No, Your Honor, the government does not make that distinction. NMFS spelled out in their opinion they believe they need to look at all the mortality attributable to passing through the system. We have been in arguments about angels dancing on the head of a pin. . ."[42]

In my view, the government threw the case with this and other statements at oral argument. We pointed out that the government had made this very distinction in the briefs they filed,[43] but to no avail. Once you pretended that the effect of the discretionary 1993 operational plans was to kill 70-90 percent of the fish in the river, there was no way that the government was going to win.

On March 28, 1994, almost exactly a year after the *PNGC v. Brown* decision, Judge Marsh issued his opinion in the *Idaho Fish and Game* case. Judge Marsh decided that the questions involving the "extinction vortex" were a "mixed question of policy, law and science and, therefore, must be distinguished from the more typical scientific differences of opinion discussed in *Mt. Graham Red Squirrel*".[44] Judge Marsh then proceeded to hold that NMFS "arbitrarily and capriciously discounted low range assumptions without well-reasoned analysis and without considering the full range of risk assumptions."[45] NMFS would have to "consider and address" state and tribal computer modeling, hardwired to produce lower survivals and underestimate the benefits of transportation and overestimate the importance of flow.

But Judge Marsh went further than merely identifying matters that NMFS should have considered. Apparently assuming that NMFS was flat out wrong when it concluded that hydropower operations (as modified pursuant to NMFS demands during the consultation process) would not jeopardize the continued existence of the salmon, Judge Marsh explained that once "jeopardy" was found, NMFS had a duty to consider "reasonable and prudent alternatives" to dam operations.

The worst aspect of Judge Marsh's opinion, from our perspective, was the fact that he had swallowed the Great Salmon Hoax whole and rebroadcast it in a series of sound bites that swept through the media in an anti-dam tidal wave. According to Judge Marsh, "[i]nstead of looking for what *can* be done to protect the species in jeopardy, NMFS and the action agencies have narrowly focused their attention on what the establishment is capable of handling with minimal disruption." This was not a finding based on evidence, for there had been no such *evidence* in the case.

The Justice Department refused to appeal Judge Marsh's ruling. With the White House driving the decisions, the Justice Department lawyers told the Judge that the government would not appeal, and would help the plaintiffs avoid mootness problems by putting aside the 1993 Biological Opinion, and meeting with the plaintiffs and other sovereign parties to the lawsuit to renegotiate the current 1994-98 Biological Opinion.

One recurring error of government officials is their foolish attempt to strike bargains with conservation biologists. They don't understand that the conservation biologists reject the very concept of a compromise as illegitimate, and that all bargains are merely a device to extract concessions while continuing to agitate for more.[46] As Michele DeHart of the Fish Passage Center says, "it's true what they say, we always want more".[47]

The federal officials went off to a fancy resort on Mt. Hood with the state and tribal officials to try and hammer out some sort of deal. We were, of course, not invited. To encourage the federal defendants in their negotiations with the state agencies and tribes, Judge Marsh sent a postcard with a picture of a steam engine on it to the resort, writing: "To the parties: One Person's train wreck is another person's Little Engine that Could. Best Wishes, Malcolm Marsh". The federal attorneys expressed some surprise that Judge Marsh would sent out such a communication to some, but not all, the parties in a lawsuit, and showed me the postcard; I grabbed it and ran to a photocopier. Here it is:

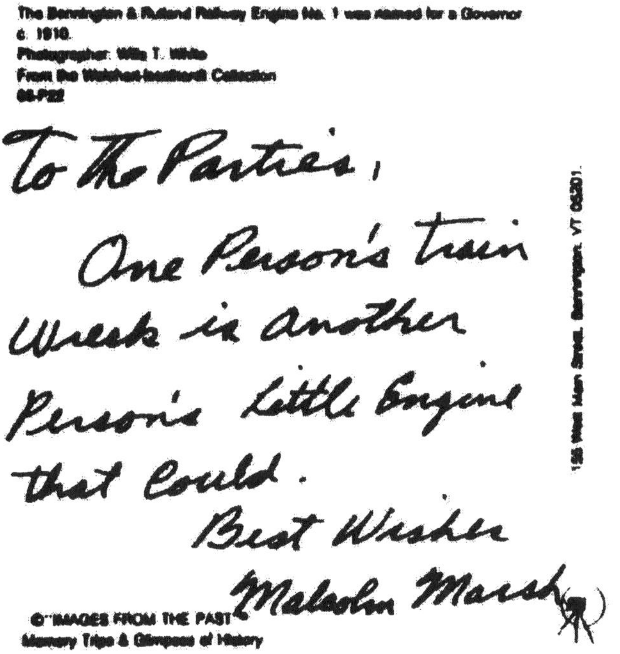

The Bennington & Rutland Railway Engine No. 1 was named for a Governor
c. 1910.
Photographer: Wm. T. White
From the Walshan-Inscharett Collection
68-P22

To the Parties,

One Person's train
Wreck is another
Person's Little Engine
that Could.
    Best Wishes
        Malcolm Marsh

© IMAGES FROM THE PAST
Memory Trips & Glimpses of History

Figure 24: Judge Marsh's Postcard

I could not help but see the postcard as further evidence that Judge Marsh's primary goal was to facilitate a settlement that he thought would protect fish, rather than decide a case based on evidence.

We did appeal the case, prompting the government to argue that the case could not be appealed without its consent. During the oral argument of the appeal, Ninth Circuit Judge Pamela Rhymer questioned how Judge Marsh could have found that NMFS should have considered alternatives to the operational plans. After all, "alternatives" must only be examined after a determination that the plan would jeopardize the continued existence of an endangered species. According to Judge Marsh, NMFS had to correct its analysis to determine or not the original plans jeopardized the salmon.

Unfortunately, the Ninth Circuit panel decided to dismiss the case on mootness grounds and did not discuss Judge Marsh's rulings, other than to direct that the judgment be "vacated". Under the rules for citation of judicial opinions, vacated decisions are void and entitled to no precedential value whatsoever. But those rules don't apply to the media. Quotes from Judge Marsh's decision continue to appear in popular accounts of salmon recovery.[48]

The Pacific Northwest Power Electric Power Planning and Conservation Act

No one can deny that dams have had adverse effects on salmon. The real question is what, if anything, to do about the *present* effects in the face of much larger and much more important things that are currently causing an adverse effect on salmon, and whether the benefits of the dams outweigh the remaining costs to salmon runs. That is the question Congress grappled with when it passed the Pacific Northwest Electric Power Planning and Conservation Act (often called the "Northwest Power Act" for short). Congress sought to balance the goals of providing "adequate, efficient, economical and reliable" electric power from the dams with "protecting, mitigating and enhancing" fish and wildlife in the Columbia River Basin.[49]

The Act created the Northwest Power Planning Council, and charged it to develop a power plan for the Northwest, including a fish and wildlife program, which is supposed to guide the federal agencies who actually run the dams and sell the power. The Act was actually written by an "Ad Hoc Committee" that represented both fish and power interests. The idea was to get more coordinated operations of the separate projects. The House Committee on the Interior confirmed in adopting the work of the Ad Hoc Committee that "this approach is not intended to create any new obligations with respect to fish and wildlife".[50]

Certainly Congress did not intend fishery agencies to strike the planning balance between optimizing dam operations for power and for salmon. That task was delegated to the Council itself, as an interstate compact of Oregon, Washington, Alaska and Montana. Indeed, it would make no sense to put fish agencies solely in charge of striking the balance between fish and power, but that is just what the Ninth Circuit did in one of its more far-fetched environmental law decisions.

A peculiar thing about the Northwest Power Act is that it ultimately produces nothing more than a piece of paper: here called the "Fish and Wildlife Program". The Council has no authority to implement its plan. The federal agencies that actually conduct dam operations are not expressly required to *follow* the plan; there is a general requirement to protect fish and wildlife "in a manner consistent with the plan".[51]

But none of them consistently do, and the Council itself routinely ignores the plan. For example, the plan calls for a Fish Operations Executive Committee to resolve disputes about dam operations for fish. The Power Act requires the Council to put ratepayer representatives on its committees. Using threats of litigation, we got the Council to add a ratepayer seat on the

252

Committee. So the Council simply stopped holding meetings of the Committee. They ignore their own program in more substantive ways as well.

It remains unclear just how much legal authority the Council has. The question came before the Ninth Circuit, when litigants claimed that the Council was a violation of the Appointments Clause of the U.S. Constitution. According to the United States Supreme Court, "any appointee exercising significant authority pursuant to the laws of the United States is an 'Officer of the United States' and must therefore be appointed by the President".[52] This provision tends to provide centralized authority and accountability for federal actions.

Unfortunately, the Ninth Circuit, in a 2-1 decision, once again stretched the law to uphold what it characterized as "an innovative system of cooperative federalism".[53] A federal law had created the Council, and the Council had veto power over some federal decisions (outside the fish and wildlife context). Nevertheless, Judges Goodwin and Schroeder concluded that because the Northwest states passed state legislation to implement the Council, the Council members were not exercising significant authority pursuant to federal law.

Judge Beezer dissented, noting that the United States had conceded that the Northwest Power Act could give the Council "significant" authority under federal law. As for the idea that the Council should be upheld as "an innovative system of cooperative federalism", Judge Beezer responded that this "position lacks a basis in the text of the Constitution". The Constitution expressly provides that "Congress may by Law vest the Appointment of such inferior Officers, as they think proper, in the President alone, in the Courts of Law, or in the Heads of Departments".[54] It simply does not empower Congress to let Northwest Governors appoint what are, in effect, federal officials.

The drafters of the Northwest Act had recognized a serious risk that it would be held unconstitutional and provided that it would be established as a federal agency if that happened.[55] Had the Ninth Circuit decision gone the right way, and the Council held unconstitutional, salmon decisionmaking would have been more centralized and accountable. The buck would have stopped at the President's desk. But this is just one of the many legal errors that has helped render salmon policy a quagmire. Years after the decision holding the Council constitutional, the Clinton/Gore Justice Department formally adopted the view that the Ninth Circuit was right, "disavowing" contrary legal opinions of prior Administrations.[56]

The Ninth Circuit Neuters the Council

In 1992, environmentalists, state fishery agencies and tribes got the Council to issue a "Strategy for Salmon", adding literally hundreds of millions of dollars of costs to electric power bills. Yet they remained unsatisfied with the Council's fish and wildlife program. Wisely, the Council had declined to insist on directing the federal agencies to not generate power in the winter, saving even more water to be dumped down the river in the spring.

Thus several tribes and groups of environmentalists sued the Council (and not dam operators), charging that the Council had failed to give "due weight" to their recommendations in fashioning a fish and wildlife program. The case was called *Northwest Resource Information Center v. Northwest Power Planning Council.*

It was clear from the record before the Council that the program sought by the fishery interests was in fact impossible to implement, because there was not enough water to meet the flow targets. Indeed, at the oral argument of the case, one judge questioned Tim Weaver, the attorney for the Yakima Indian Nation, as to how the Council was supposed to get all this water. He responded that it was not his problem to figure out how to get the water.

Professor Michael Blum, who has crusaded against the dams for years from his pulpit at the Northwestern School of Law of Lewis & Clark College, walked out of the oral argument before the Ninth Circuit thinking his allies had lost. Luckily for him, the Court did not do the hard work of focusing on the facts before it, and instead used his many law review articles to form a warped and outdated view of the facts.

In an opinion that received a huge degree of media coverage, the Ninth Circuit spent page after page proclaiming the virtues of the flow-based fishery agency program, and excoriating the Council for declining to adopt the program. The opinion by the late Judge Tang (joined by Judges Wiggins and Henderson[57]), is one of the more remarkable pieces of judicial overreaching ever to emanate from the Ninth Circuit.

The Court's opinion begins with a highly-biased factual summary, reaching back to a 1979 report of the General Accounting Office, which the the Court quotes at length, for evidence of the adverse effects of dams.[58] Ignoring the decades of research discussed above, the Court summarily concludes that 15-20%, or even 30% of juvenile salmon are lost per project. Many facts are not cited to any source at all. On other occasions, the Court points to sources that it grossly misapprehends.[59]

After the decision came out, the lead environmentalist attorney would brag before a forum at Lewis and Clark law school that his and the tribes' strategy of painting a simple political picture of a Council controlled by power interests had overcome the facts—the long "string-cites" in the Council's briefs.[60] The Court did not just use the "facts" about salmon and dams from the law review articles. It adopted the political rhetoric of the articles as well, accusing the Council of "sacrificing the Act's fish and wildlife goals for . . . the lowest common denominator acceptable to power interests and DSIs".[61]

This was dead wrong. The Council lobbied hard for bypass systems that solved most problems at the dams and had started a huge flow augmentation program—the 3.5 million acre-foot "water budget", which was expanded to perhaps 8 million acre-feet in the very decision challenged. The Council had gone against the wishes of the power interests every time they raised flow targets on the river.

Power interests and other river users believed that the flow augmentation schemes were a waste of energy and money, and consistently opposed them. Sometimes, they swallowed hard and said nothing. They never made much of effort to win the hearts and minds of the Council or its Staff. Academics and environmentalists did.

Led by Professor Blum, the Ninth Circuit judges reinterpreted the Act as requiring all sorts of bold new initiatives asserted to help salmon—even the every measures the fishery advocates disavowed before Congress at the time (like increased spill). John Volkman, the lead lawyer for the Council, later remarked: "I was surprised that the Court pretty much adopted Mike [Blum]'s entire opus—I do not think the opinion misses a single point."[62]

We later learned that Ninth Circuit judges and their clerks had attended classes taught by Professor Blum, presumably indoctrinating them in his views about salmon law. When we tried to find out which judges and clerks had attended the classes, and what they had been taught, the law school said it had lost the records. Judge Marsh has also educated the Ninth Circuit judges, giving a speech on salmon issues to them at a gathering in Troutdale, Oregon even as appeals of his own decisions were pending before the Ninth Circuit.

In any event, after its outdated and biased recitation of the facts, the Court turned to the legislative history of the Northwest Power Act. Normally, one interprets a statute by reading it, and focusing on the meaning of the statutory language. Here, however, the statutory language could not get the Court anywhere near where it wanted to go. The provision of law upon which the environmentalists and tribes relied was § 4(h) of the Act, which told the Council how to create a fish and wildlife protection program.

Specifically, the Council was charged to develop a program based on "recommendations, supporting documents and information obtained through public comment and participation, and consultation with the [federal and the region's state fish and wildlife] agencies, tribes and customers . . ."[63] The Council was also charged to

> "determine whether each recommendation received is consistent with the purposes of this Act. In the event such recommendations are inconsistent with each other, the Council, in consultation with appropriate entities, shall resolve such inconsistency in the program giving *due weight* to the recommendations, expertise, and legal rights and responsibilities of the federal and the region's state fish and wildlife agencies and appropriate Indian tribes. If the Council does not adopt any recommendations of the fish and wildlife agencies and Indian tribes as part of the program . . . it shall explain in writing, as part of the program, the basis for its finding that the adoption of the program would be [inconsistent with other provisions of the Act]".[64]

The environmentalists and the tribes focused on the words "due weight", which they interpreted to mean that the Council should adopt the recommendations from fish interests notwithstanding objections by power interests that the recommendations would do nothing for fish, and cost a great deal of money.

The Ninth Circuit found that the Council had not adequately explained its decisions on the flow-based proposals of the fishery interests. That aspect of the opinion was correct; from our perspective, the Council had not explained why it had adopted a flow-based program absent any credible scientific evidence that the program would have any measurable effect on salmon.

But then the Court went on to give the Council some additional advice about how to do its job, and engaged in a remarkable effort to demonstrate that the words "due weight" in the statute really meant a "high degree of deference". The Court made it unmistakably clear that, in its view, the Council ought to do nothing more than give the state fishery agencies and tribes what they wanted, repeating the phrase "a high degree of deference" over and over again in the opinion.

To reach this result, the Court focused heavily on statements by Representative John Dingell and his House Commerce Committee as the authoritative background for the bill. But power interests had opposed Dingell's Commerce Committee bill precisely because it suggested that the Council would have little discretion to reject recommendations proposed by fishery managers.[65] The Act had originated in the Senate; Dingell's House Commerce Committee had added fishery provisions objectionable to power interests and then, to save the legislation, an Ad Hoc Committee of fishery and power interests had together drafted revised fish and wildlife provisions.

The House Interior Committee then adopted those revised provisions, and wrote its own report explaining them.[66] Indeed, it was only after the Northwest Power Act left the Commerce Committee that the Act was modified to provide the Council with clear authority to reject or modify fishery agency recommendations.[67] A former member of the Council recounts that "[w]hen the Act passed, a lobbyist for the state of Oregon called his governor and announced, 'The good news is, we got what we wanted. The bad news is, so did everybody else.'"[68]

But what the power interest groups got from Congress, the Ninth Circuit could take away. Citing Representative Dingell and the Commerce Committee for the meaning of the Northwest Power Act, after it was removed from Dingell's jurisdiction, was as gross a misuse of legislative history as one sees in the law books. It is would be like looking to 1964 statements by Jesse Helms to interpret the meaning of the Civil Rights Act. In effect, the Ninth Circuit was interpreting an earlier bill that never passed, and ignoring what Congress (and the President) had actually agreed upon.

The DSIs had also sued the Council, because the Council had not made any effort to comply with the Act's requirement that its program "utilize, where equally effective alternative means of achieving the same biological objective exist, the alternative with the minimum economic cost".[69] The Court agreed with the DSIs and other petitioners that the Council had failed adequately to define biological objectives.

But the Council had also failed to assess the cost of any of its measures. Indeed, the only economic analysis in the hundreds of pages of the Strategy for Salmon was a single paragraph asserting that adoption of the Program as a whole would "only" cause electricity rates to go up 4%. The Council made no attempt to determine what benefits, if any, would accrue from this Region-wide rate increase.

The Court found nothing wrong with this, and recognized that the record was inadequate to determine whether the Council had, in fact, chosen alternatives "with the minimum economic cost". Relying again on the Commerce Committee and Dingell legislative history, the Court emphasized that "a fish and wildlife measure cannot be rejected [by the Council] solely because it will result in power losses and economic costs".[70] (It was only after the bill left the Commerce Committee that the word "economical" was added to the Council's duty to provide an "adequate, efficient, economical and reliable power supply".) After we all read the opinion, we wondered why have a Council at all, if Congress really intended it to rubber-stamp harvest agency recommendations without regard to their cost?

The direct service industries and another industry group, the Pacific Northwest Generating Cooperative, filed a Petition for Rehearing urging the Ninth Circuit to reconsider its "due weight" ruling. The industry groups explained that Congress had empowered the Council to balance fish and power considerations, and that requiring a "high degree of deference" to one side of the balance would inevitably lead to unbalanced results. The DSIs also took issue with the factual "holdings" of the opinion. We pointed out, in a lengthy factual appendix, that nearly all of the Court's factual assumptions were simply wrong. The Ninth Circuit denied the Petition for Rehearing without opinion.

The Pacific Northwest Generating Cooperative petitioned for the Supreme Court review. The DSIs, preferring to keep their powder dry for another fight, did not. The Supreme Court ultimately rejected the petition for review, giving no reasons, as is customary.

Courts are still somewhat reluctant to admit to second-guessing administrative decisions. There are too many Supreme Court cases telling them not to do this. So they issue opinions that tell agencies what to do, and disguising the real message in complaints about the agency's explanation of what it did. Here, the Ninth Circuit even went so far as to adopt the clever trick of quoting Judge Marsh, lauded as "experienced in these particular matters", in his call for a "major overhaul" of the hydropower system. The Ninth Circuit did not see fit to disclose, consistent with ordinary rules of legal citation, that Judge Marsh's opinion was under appeal (it was not vacated until later).[71]

The media do not get tangled up in the niceties of judicial review of agency action. They simply reported that the Ninth Circuit, like Judge Marsh, had ordered a "major overhaul" of the system. Others more accurately describe what happened as the Court "rebuking" the Council.[72]

But courts are not supposed to be in the business of offering "rebukes" to government agencies. They are supposed to provide directives about how those agencies must conform themselves to the law established by

258

the Legislative Branch. Their whole institutional legitimacy depends on the idea that they are interpreting the law, not running amok as self-appointed czars of natural resource development. In my view, the United States Court of Appeals for the Ninth Circuit has lost legitimacy through its misguided, results-oriented approach to interpreting the environmental laws.

The Struggle Continues: the *American Rivers* Case

One of the reasons the environmentalists and salmon harvesters have made so much bad law is that they never give up. They bring the same lawsuits over and over again. On March 14, 1996, they filed a suit against the 1995 biological opinion on Federal Columbia River Power System operations. Like all the other salmon cases, it was reassigned away from the judge randomly picked to hear it, and assigned to Judge Marsh.

After an abortive run at obtaining a preliminary injunction in the summer of 1996, the plaintiffs filed a motion seeking to have Judge Marsh set aside the new biological opinion as arbitrary and capricious. The plaintiffs' complaint was, in substance, that the National Marine Fisheries Service issued a "no-jeopardy" opinion (after requiring significant changes in dam operations) even though some computer modeling showed that salmon stocks were unlikely to reach recovery targets.

Representing the Columbia River Alliance, I told the Court that there were a lot of reasons computer modeling showed that the salmon would not recover. First, because dams were not the major problem, fixing dams wasn't going to fix the problems with salmon. Second, the computer models cited by the environmentalists were hard-wired to downplay the benefits of operational improvements at the dams, and assumed continued heavy harvest of endangered salmon.

The environmentalists also had some new arguments, focusing on the failure to meet the flow targets set forth in the biological opinion. Whether the targets had been met depended on whether they were to be interpreted as seasonal averages or daily constraints. Notwithstanding plain language in the biological opinion to the contrary, the environmentalists insisted that the targets had to be met every day.

I pointed out that the summer targets (the focus of the environmentalists' claims) were higher than river flows before any dams were built, and *could never be achieved.* Flow targets have become a critical part of the Great Salmon Hoax, because newspapers repeatedly report that the targets are "missed", never mentioning that they cannot physically be achieved.[73]

259

Repeating its performance in the *Idaho Fish and Game* case, the State of Oregon joined the environmentalists as a plaintiff, and filed its own motion for summary judgment echoing the complaints of the environmentalists. Other states and tribes intervened as well.

In March, the Regional Director of the National Marine Fisheries Service, Will Stelle, Jr., paid a visit to the Governor of Oregon. The Service was threatening to list Oregon coastal coho as endangered, which Governor Kitzhaber did not want. No one reported on what happened in that meeting, but shortly afterwards, the State of Oregon commenced secret settlement negotiations with the federal defendants in the case. When the environmentalists found out about them, they wrote letters to the Justice Department protesting their exclusion from the talks. One of the Justice Department lawyers sent me a copy of the letter and said, "well, at least you can be happy that you're all getting the same treatment". Less than a week later, the federal government began secret settlement negotiations with the environmentalists and fishermen (but not my clients).

On March 31, 1997, the parties gathered before Judge Marsh for oral argument of the motions for summary judgment filed by the environmentalist/harvester alliance and the State of Oregon. The State of Oregon tried to persuade Judge Marsh to defer a ruling, because of supposed progress toward settlement, but the Judge refused.

On April 3, 1997, the Judge issued his opinion, which, to our relief, denied the plaintiffs' motions. He specifically affirmed the authority of the National Marine Fisheries Service and other federal agencies to adopt a "flexible" approach to meeting flow targets,[74] and to make their own judgments as to what constituted "jeopardizing the continued existence" of endangered salmon.[75]

While denying the motions was the right result, Judge Marsh continued to reiterate the same elements of the Great Salmon Hoax we had fought about for years. Judge Marsh again reported that "80% of historical salmon losses are attributable to hydropower development and operation".[76] He declared that "[a]nticipated impacts of proposed [Federal Columbia River Power System] operations on the listed species" would be, among other things, "62-99% for juvenile fall chinook".[77] By now, I thought to myself, he should have known that these things were not true.

Judge Marsh noted with approval that the National Marine Fisheries Service had "incorporate[d] nearly all of the . . . recommendations" of the state and tribal "Biological Requirements Work Group", including ("most critical" to Judge Marsh) the decision to extend Endangered Species Act protection to

260

39 subunits of the "distinct population unit", and adoption of the Group's "recommended threshold survival levels".[78]

Those of us who knew what the Group had actually done knew that the Group's approach was both misleading and arbitrary. Among other things, the Group had presented data for only six of the 39 stocks, and then discarded the one stock that consistently exceeded the thresholds as unrepresentative. As explained in Chapter 13, the Group operated in violation of a federal law designed to prevent biased and secret recommendations to federal agencies.

Finally, Judge Marsh declared that "[a]s a long-time observer and examiner of this process, I cannot help but question the soundness of the selected level of risk acceptance . . ."[79] What this "sound-bite" seemed to mean was that it was not enough for Judge Marsh that the National Marine Fisheries Service had tried to assure a 70% chance that endangered salmon would fully recover through the device of dictating changes in dam operations.

One might quarrel with the 70% chance if the lawsuit addressed a recovery plan under § 4 of the Endangered Species Act. But NMFS had issued a biological opinion under § 7 as to whether the dam operators had avoided *jeopardizing the continued existence of* the salmon by their proposed action. Congress never authorized NMFS to declare that a federal agency action must be halted or modified because that single agency action does not *assure recovery of* endangered species. However, NMFS, backed by the White House, asserts and exercises the power to do so.

NOTES TO CHAPTER 9

[1] Deposition of J. Gary Smith, taken in Case Nos. 92-1260-MA, 92-1164-MA, & 92-973-MA, Jan. 7, 1993, at 132.

[2] *Id.* at 134.

[3] *Id.* at 135-36.

[4] *Pacific Rivers Council v. Thomas*, 30 F.3d 1050 (9th Cir. 1995), *cert. denied*, ___ U.S. ___ (1995).

[5] *PNGC v. Brown*, 822 F. Supp. at 1484 (discussing "genetic pollution" from hatcheries based on B. Brown, *Mountain in the Clouds* (1982)).

[6] *Id.* at 1485.

[7] *Id.*

[8] *Id.*

[9] *PNGC v. Brown*, 822 F. Supp. at 1486.

[10] K. Lee, "Rebuilding Confidence: Salmon, Science, and Law in the Columbia Basin", 21 Envt'l Law 745, 797 (1991).

[11] *PNGC v. Brown*, 822 F. Supp. at 1502 n.53.

[12] *Id.* at 1502.

[13] *Id.* at 1503.

[14] *Id.*

[15] *Lujan v. Defenders of Wildlife*, 112 S. Ct. 2130 (1992).

[16] *PNGC v. Brown*, 822 F. Supp. at 1504.

[17] J. Cone, *A Common Fate* 276.

[18] *Id.*

[19] 16 U.S.C. § 1540(g)(5).

[20] 16 U.S.C. § 1531.

[21] *PNGC v. Brown*, 38 F.3d at 1060.

[22] *Id.*

[23] *Id.* at 1065.

[24] *Bennett v. Spear*, No. 95-813 (Mar. 19, 1997).

[25] *Id.*

[26] 16 U.S.C. § 1540(g).

[27] B. Harden, *A River Lost* 227.

[28] *PNGC v. Brown*, 822 F. Supp. at 1507.

[29] *PNGC v. Brown*, 822 F. Supp. at 1507.

[30] *See* M. Schultz & A. Chilingerian, "Impact of Draft Biological Opinions on the Northwest Electric Power System and Facilities", Report to PNUCC, Feb. 9, 1995, at 12.

[31] SEIS at 4-105; SEIS at H-75.

[32] Letter, Fergus Pilon to Sen. Wyden, Aug. 26, 1997, at 2.

[33] M. Eldridge, Testimony to the House Committee on Resources, May 31, 1997, at 2 (mimeo). Mr. Eldridge is the General Manager of the Umatilla Electric Cooperative.

[34] *See, e.g.,* "1995 Captures Record as Warmest Year Yet", Science News, Vol. 149, Jan. 13, 1996, at 23. There is another side to the global warming debate, based on satellite temperature measurements that do not show such rapid increases. I have frankly never invested the time to try and figure out what accounts for this discrepancy.

[35] E. Callenbach, *Ecotopia: The Notebooks and Reports of William Weston* 103 (Banyan Tree Books 1975) ("Ecotopia also took over numerous hydroelectric installations at dams in its great mountain ranges. However, these are regarded as temporary expedients too, since they tend to silt up after a few generations, and have unfortunate effects on salmon and other wildlife.")

[36] J. Emlen, "Population Viability of the Snake River Chinook Salmon (*Onchorynchus tshawytscha*), at 5.

[37] *PNGC v. Brown*, 822 F. Supp. at 1505.

[38] *Id.*

[39] T. Strong, "Endangered Species Act won't save these salmon", *Seattle Post-Intelligencer*, May 23, 1997 (Mr. Strong's complaints are ironic since the "improbable and untested" "science" employed to date by the federal government—such as anti-transporrtation dogma—has been employed at the behest of the tribes).

[40] *IDFG v. NMFS*, No. 92-1603-MA, Hrng. Tr. 29-31 (Mar. 18, 1994) (emphasis added).

[41] *See* 50 C.F.R. Part 402.02 *et seq.*

[42] *IDFG v.* NMFS, 3/18/94 Tr. at 44-45.

[43] *Id.* at 50.

[44] *IDFG v. NMFS*, 850 F. Supp. at 898.

[45] *Id.* at 898-99.

[46] As one writer explained, environmentalists object to finding "balance" in negotiations over salmon because "that seemed always to mean that the balancing began right now, with the chips everyone had *then*. But the fish advocates saw the time frame differently." J. Cone, *A Common Fate* 90-91.

[47] Quoted in B. Harden, *A River Lost* 215.

[48] *See, e.g.,* J. Cone, *A Common Fate* 299;

[49] 16 U.S.C. § 839.

[50] H. Rep. No. 96-976, Pt. II, 96th Cong., 2d Sess. 37 (Sept. 16, 1980); *see also* Ad Hoc Pacific Northwest Power/Fisheries Committee, "Section-by-Section Analysis of Fisheries Provisions of the Northwest Regional Power Bill (S. 885) if Amended in Accordance with the Ad Hoc Committee Proposals", at 4 (Aug. 22, 1980).

[51] 16 U.S.C. § 839b(h)(10)(A).

[52] *Buckley v. Valeo*, 424 U.S.1, 126 (1976).

[53] *Seattle Master Builders Ass'n v. Pacific Northwest Electric Power Planning and Conservation Council*, 786 F.2d 1359, 1366 (9th Cir. 1986).

[54] U.S. Const. Art. II, §2.

[55] 16 U.S.C. § 839b(b)(1)(A).

[56] W. Dellinger, "The Constitutional Separation of Powers between the President and Congress", Memorandum for the General Counsels of the Federal Government, at 20 n.53 (U.S. Department of Justice May 7, 1996.

[57] Judge Thelton Henderson would later achieve fame by enjoining the implementation of the California Civil Rights Initiative, believing that the United States Constitution forbid Californians from declaring that their state government should not practice discrimination, even for a "benign" purpose.

[58] *Northwest Resources Information Center v. Northwest Power Planning Council*, 35 F.3d 1371, 1376 (9th Cir. 1994). I first heard of this report when it showed up in a brief filed by the State of Oregon. No library in Portland had it, so I called to ask the State's attorney for it. She didn't have it either. She had just cited it without reviewing it.

[59] For example, the opinion claims that "the Supreme Court told the tribes: 'The paper [the treaty] secures your fish.'" *NRIC v. NWPPC*, 35 F.3d at 1376 n.6. In fact, the quotation is from recorded remarks in the 1850s attributed to territorial Governor Stevens. The opinion also suggests that three statutes "recognize a relationship between smolt travel time and survival in state statutes protecting minimum instream flows". *NRIC v. NWPPC*, 35 F3d. at 1382 n.24. The statutes make no mention of smolt travel time, and, in any event, there is no relationship between smolt travel time and survival that can be influenced by flow augmentation.

[60] *See* A. Berger, "An Insider's Perspective on *NRIC v. NWPPC*", 25 Env'tl Law 369, 372-373 (1995).

[61] *NRIC v. NWPPC*, 35 F.3d at 1395.

[62] J. Volkman, "Steering by Dicta", 25 Env'tl Law 385 (1995).

[63] Section 4(h)(5) of the Act, 16 U.S.C. § 839b(h)(5).

[64] Section 4(h)(7) of the Act, 16 U.S.C. § 839b(h)(7) (emphasis added).

[65] *See generally*, M. Early & E. Krogh, *Balancing Power Costs and Fisheries Values Under the Northwest Power Act*, 13 U. Puget Sound L. Rev. 281, 303 (1990).

[66] H. Rep. No. 96-976, pt. II, 96th Cong., 2d Sess. (1980).

[67] *See generally* M. Early & E. Krogh, *Balancing Power Costs and Fisheries Values Under the Northwest Power Act*, 13 U. Puget Sound L. Rev. 281, 306 (1990).

[68] K Lee, "Rebuilding Confidence: Salmon, Science and Law in the Columbia Basin", 21 Envt'l Law 745, 772 n.100 (1991).

[69] 16 U.S.C. § 839b(h)(6)(C).

[70] *NRIC v. NWPPC*, 35 F.3d at 1394.

[71] *NRIC v. NWPPC*, 35 F3d at 1390-91.

[72] K Petersen, *River of Life, Channel of Death* 5.

[73] *See, e.g.*, J. Brinckman, "$3 billion later, Columbia Basin salmon dwindle", July 27, 1997.

[74] *American Rivers v. NMFS*, No. 96-384-MA, slip op. at 26-30 (D. Or. April 3, 1997)

[75] *Id.* at 26.

[76] *Id.* at 12.

[77] *Id.*

[78] *Id.* at 25.

[79] *Id.* at 26.

CHAPTER 10: LAWLESSNESS IN THE MANAGEMENT SALMON HARVEST

"Power tends to corrupt, and absolute power corrupts absolutely." Lord Acton

While the courts have been willing to distort environmental laws to limit the use of federal land and water projects in the West, they have not been willing even to apply those laws in order to limit destructive mixed-stock salmon harvest practices. The failure of the judicial branch to redress violations of law in the harvest context is perhaps the greatest human failure in salmon recovery. If the same laws that restricted logging in the Pacific Northwest had been applied to salmon fishing, there would be a lot more salmon running in the rivers of the Pacific Northwest.

By the time the federal, state, and tribal fishery managers had gotten through the cases discussed in this chapter, their lawyers were advising them—and telling me privately—that there was nothing they couldn't do, at least as long as we were the only people complaining about it.

Impacts of Continuing Commercial Harvest of Endangered Columbia Basin Salmon

Large numbers of endangered Snake River fall chinook are caught in a large number of commercial fisheries protected and supported by federal, state and tribal fishery managers. Even among those managers, however, there seems to be a consensus that harvest rates on endangered Snake River fall chinook salmon are too high. Independent scientists have prepared papers demonstrating that harvest rates on endangered Snake River fall chinook are significantly understated because they are based on questionable assumptions.

Yet the most recent biological opinion issued by the National Marine Fisheries Service authorizes an in-river harvest of ranging from 24.4% to 29.4%.[1] The Idaho Department of Fish and Game reports that current guidelines permit a cumulative harvest rate for all fisheries on endangered fall chinook of 47-52%, a harvest rate they admit is "excessive".[2] The true harvest ratios are doubtless higher. Even the proposed Recovery Plan published by the National Marine Fisheries Service would permit continued commercial harvest of endangered Snake River fall chinook salmon at rates of around 50%.

In 1997, the Pacific Fishery Management Council finally trimmed ocean salmon harvest on account of listed Snake River stocks, admitting candidly that "[f]or the first time, impacts of Council-area fisheries on the endangered Snake River fall chinook stock have played a critical role in the season-setting process".[3] This, coming years after the listings, was no great victory for the salmon. The Council's proposed regulations called for *increased* chinook harvests for the third year in a row—albeit to a level below that which had prevailed years ago.[4]

Total ocean harvest of endangered Snake River fall chinook salmon was expected to remain at 70% of 1988-1993 levels.[5] From 1988 to 1993, the average harvest rate on endangered Snake River fall chinook salmon was 63%.[6] Tribal harvest in 1996 took 367 chinook, leaving only about 600 to make it all the way back above Lower Granite Dam.[7]

Interestingly, some of the entities advocating measures to save endangered Snake River salmon will privately discuss "writing off" the fall chinook salmon, including the National Marine Fisheries Service and the State of Idaho. Yet the fall chinook apparently have the easiest time of any of the chinook navigating dams and reservoirs, and by 1996 were at the highest levels in nearly ten years, despite the highest official harvest rate of any of the endangered salmon species. "Writing off" the fall chinook would be a tragic mistake, because they may be a more viable salmon population in warmer, slower rivers.

There is a consensus among fishery managers that harvest rates on endangered Snake River spring/summer chinook salmon are *not* too high. As of 1996, the National Marine Fisheries Service had issued an "incidental take statement" that allows in-river harvest rates from 9.1 to 11.1 percent of the run.[8] This, of course, is the amount of *legal* harvest in the river. There are many, many fisherman who are out on the river in the springtime. Many can't tell a chinook from a steelhead. Many of them, if they catch a spring chinook will keep it. There are occasional estimates of illegal harvest, but the legal harvests have not been limited because of total (legal and illegal) harvest impacts.

The endangered Snake River spring/summer chinook salmon are also caught in the ocean. NMFS' official position is that "there is little evidence that [endangered spring/summer and sockeye salmon are] affected significantly in ocean fisheries".[9] This is largely because the fishery agencies do not collect the data that one would need in order to make any reasonable estimate of the harvest impacts.

One of the positive contributions of the conservation biologists' *Return to the River* manifesto was a frank discussion of this problem. The Independent Science Group warned that the "impact of ocean fisheries on spring chinook salmon is uncertain due to an almost complete lack of information on stock composition of undersized chinook or chinook incidentally killed in the Pacific

Ocean fisheries".[10] "It is therefore not inconsistent with available data", they say, "to postulate that substantial numbers of immature spring chinook salmon of Columbia Basin origin could be killed each year in the Pacific Ocean fisheries".[11] I have spoken to a prominent fisheries scientist, who would only speak off the record, who is convinced that harvest rates on endangered Snake River spring chinook are very significantly understated. When I asked him whether he would be willing to prepare a scientific paper on this question for my clients, he refused. It would, he said, terminate his consulting career with the fisheries agencies.

The ISG also pointed out that NMFS estimates the catch of endangered spring/summer salmon through Coded Wire Tag recoveries in fish landed in selected ocean fisheries. They suggested that if one took account of the fish that were caught but not landed, it was possible that the additional "annual loss in adult equivalents to the Columbia River basin would be 1,500 to 3,000" stream-type fish.[12]

Some biologists now believe that it is possible that endangered Snake River spring/summer chinook are now turning south at the mouth of the Columbia, exposing them to fisheries (and warmer ocean conditions with increased predation) where they were previously not thought to exist.

As of 1997, the Pacific Fishery Management Council maintains that ocean harvest has a small effect on upriver spring chinook stocks, but candidly notes that its Salmon Technical Team still "has not undertaken a review or assessment of the abundance estimation methodologies for these stocks".[13]

There are computer models using the available data on salmon harvest. Even though the data understate harvest impacts, the models readily predict positive effects of reducing harvest on populations of endangered species. During the *Idaho Fish and Game* case, we arranged for Dr. Anderson to come down to Portland with his laptop and a projector and use computer modeling to demonstrate the effect of harvest cuts. He pressed the buttons for a 25% harvest cut on fall chinook, and the population trends turned from down to up. But the harvest managers were not impressed. They continue to tell gullible journalists that the effect of stopping all fishing "would be very small and would not reduce the downward trend".[14]

Ignoring the Plain Language of the Endangered Species Act to Protect Salmon Harvest

Although the focus of the *PNGC v. Brown* court decision was on standing, it was not our objective to set precedents on questions of procedure. The first motion we filed was a claim for summary judgment on two *substantive* claims alleging that the Endangered Species Act prohibited commercial harvest of endangered Snake River salmon. Both of these claims, if successful, would have shut down salmon harvest wherever it took an appreciable percentage of endangered salmon along with the non-endangered salmon. There is not a doubt in my mind but that if we had won this lawsuit, it would have had a greater positive impact on salmon populations than anything the federal government has yet accomplished.

The first claim was that under the Endangered Species Act, a hunting season on endangered animals cannot be authorized at all. The focus of the Act is, of course, on conserving endangered species, not killing them. The Act even defines "conservation" with the idea that one would never "conserve" endangered species by catching and killing them except "in the extraordinary case where population pressures within a given ecosystem cannot be otherwise relieved".[15] Nobody thinks that we have a salmon overpopulation problem in the Columbia River Basin.

The precise language we relied on in the Act was the prohibition against "taking" any endangered species.[16] Under § 7 of the Act, when the National Marine Fisheries Service reviews agency action (including its own action of authorizing commercial salmon harvests), it has the power to allow "the taking of an endangered species or a threatened species *incidental* to the agency action".[17] The regulations define the concept of an "incidental take": "*Incidental take* refers to takings that result from, but are not the purpose of, carrying out an otherwise lawful activity . . ."[18] No one disputes, for example, that if a salmon is hit by a turbine blade and killed, that is an incidental taking of salmon.

We thought that when the gillnetters dropped their nets in the water, knowing that the population was (in the in-river case) as much as 10-15% endangered, catching endangered fish was not "incidental" to the activity. It was the whole idea. The government had two answers to this.

First, the government asserted, contrary to its own documents, that there was really no proof that endangered salmon would be caught. We therefore questioned the government's witnesses, getting nowhere:

"Q. Sitting here today, do you have any doubt whatsoever that members of the listed species were caught in the ocean and in in-river fisheries in 1992?

"MR. DISHEROON: I object to asking his opinion, this matter is covered by the administrative record.

"Q. Go ahead.

"MR. DISHEROON: He's not here to give expert opinion testimony. He won't answer the question. . . ."

Q. Hold on a second. In your opinion, Mr. Smith, does one have to be an expert to know whether or not any of the listed species were caught in the ocean or in the river in 1992?

"MR. DISHEROON: I have the same instruction [not to answer]."[19]

Notwithstanding the government's obstructionism, the courts gave short shrift to the "it's not happening" defense.

The second defense was that there was no fishing season on endangered fish. The government claimed that the fishing season was "targeted at" the non-endangered fish, and that it was only by accident that endangered ones were caught.

The concept of catching endangered fish "by accident" was new to fisheries management. Fisheries managers are trained in Fisheries Management 101, so to speak, that mixed-stock fisheries are harmful to weak stocks. But they were always called "mixed-stock" fisheries, with no one pretending that the harvesters weren't trying to catch every fish they could. There was such a thing as accidental catch, which had a technical term for it: "bycatch". But "bycatch" is used to describe what happens when you are out fishing for one kind of seafood and catch another, like the bycatch of salmon by shrimp trawlers, or the bycatch of salmon in groundfisheries.

While the fishermen could claim that they really didn't want to catch endangered salmon, courts had refused to allow this defense in criminal prosecutions under the Endangered Species Act. For example, cases had established that anyone charged with "taking" an endangered sea turtle, punishable by imprisonment, is guilty whether or not he or she knew that the particular turtle was endangered. All the person had to know was that he or she was in possession of a turtle.[20] Here, there was no dispute that the fishermen were trying to catch *Onchorychus tshawystcha*—the chinook salmon species. They denied that they were trying to catch the ones that would later swim up the Snake River, but that shouldn't have made any difference given the turtle decisions.

Judge Marsh quickly rejected this attack on the salmon harvest. After first declaring that the fishermen had an interest in "harvest of genetically superior listed wild stocks", Judge Marsh declared that none of the fisheries were "'directed at' listed species". Our affidavit from a fishery expert who averred that the fisheries *were* directed at listed stocks was simply ignored.

269

Because summary judgment was granted, the case was decided on the papers, without any cross-examination of the government's experts.

On appeal, the Ninth Circuit agreed with Judge Marsh, declaring that "it cannot be believed that Congress intended to ban all salmon fishing in the Columbia and Snake Rivers and in the Pacific Ocean whenever one salmon stock, indistinguishable by sight, became endangered."[21] While this may have some intuitive appeal, it is not consistent with prior Endangered Species Act decisions. For example, Congress didn't intend to stop logging merely because owls, one of many species in the forest, became endangered, but the Ninth Circuit stopped the logging anyway. Congress didn't intend to stop construction of the Tellico Dam in Tennessee merely because the snail darters became endangered (and passed appropriations for the dam knowing about the snail darter problem), but the Supreme Court stopped the dam construction. As far as I know, this is the first time and only time the "Congress didn't intend it" defense ever worked in the Endangered Species Act context.

But the Endangered Species Act contained even stronger language that should have stopped fishermen from harvesting endangered salmon. Under the ESA, there is an absolute ban on trade or commerce in endangered species.[22] NMFS cannot issue a permit to get around that.

We asked the court to rule that the federal government could not issue a permit allowing a commercial harvest when everyone knew the result would be the sale of lots of endangered salmon. Here we cited cases where other courts had said that the federal government could not blind itself to the consequences of its actions. By virtue of the government's approval, there was (and still is), commerce in endangered salmon. In the fish markets of the great cities (which prize highly the gillnetted spring chinook salmon), you can, as in the movie *The Freshman*, dine on endangered species. But you'll never know whether the particular salmon you are eating is endangered, so you shouldn't pay any premium for that reason (as in the movie).

The judges made short work of this claim. Judge Marsh refused to enforce the provision because, according to him, Congress had obviously intended to allow "incidental take" of salmon and the prohibition on commerce in endangered species would interfere with NMFS's ability to allow "incidental take". The Ninth Circuit disposed of the claim with two sentences:

> "To these contentions the defendants make a short answer: it is impossible to enforce the trade or transport law as to the few forbidden fish harvested in the ocean or rivers. Impossibility in our view is sufficient answer. It was not the intention of the statute to ban all salmon fishing or to place

upon the federal defendants an enforcement burden that no one could accomplish." [23]

Again, under this logic, the federal government could have defended continued old growth logging by saying it was impossible to enforce measures to protect spotted owls, because it was impossible to tell whether they were nesting in the trees or not.

After getting the Ninth Circuit's decision, we filed a petition for rehearing, trying to explain to the judges that enforcing the plain language of the law would not shut down all salmon fishing, just destructive mixed-stock harvests. The Ninth Circuit offered no response to the petition for rehearing. Unfortunately, my clients determined not to appeal the case to the Supreme Court; as a statistical matter, the vast majority of cases are not accepted for review.

As a result, more than five years after the Snake River salmon were supposedly under the protection of the Endangered Species Act, none of the government's formal harvest management plans really address the problem of harvesting Snake River salmon. The Columbia River Fish Management Plan doesn't use abundance of Snake River salmon as a guideline for managing in-river harvest. The elaborate formal models and stock-by-stock accounting by the Pacific Fisheries Management Council (responsible for ocean harvest off the coast of Oregon, Washington and California) do not manage by abundance of endangered Snake River salmon.[24] Things are no better up in Alaska, where the federal regulators have simply abdicated their role to the state.

No other Circuit Court has addressed this question, and it seems likely that some might resolve it differently. For a while, we talked about bringing a second action in the United States Court of Appeals for the District of Columbia, but we never found anyone who wanted to do it. Perhaps someone will call someday and we can give this another try.

The State of Oregon has its own Endangered Species Act modeled on the federal Act. Lawyers working for the Oregon Department of Fish and Wildlife decided that our arguments in federal court would support an injunction against harvest under the state statute in state court, and convinced Oregon's Attorney General to issue an opinion so stating.[25] Indeed, they concluded that even if the harvest were authorized by federal law, Oregon law would forbid it if listed fish were taken. Needless to say, they didn't tell us about the opinion.

The Oregon Department of Fish and Wildlife circulated the Attorney General's opinion among fishermen and their legislators to mobilize support for amending Oregon's Endangered Species Act to allow the harvest of endangered species. In a process regrettably typical for Oregon, the Act was amended so quickly we never even heard about it until after it had passed. As far as I know, this significant weakening of environmental laws in order to promote commercial harvest of endangered fish was not reported in a single Oregon newspaper.

Fishing Without Permits: Mootness Strikes Again

> ". . . there is no method, in good conscience, by which any commercial harvests of upriver spring chinook or steelhead, at present run levels, can be be tolerated." J. Greenley, Idaho Department of Fish and Game (1976).

More than twenty years later, with significantly lower runs, the National Marine Fisheries Service continues to authorize commercial harvest of the now-endangered upriver spring chinook.

Our next effort to apply the Endangered Species Act to salmon harvest involved § 10 of the Act, which declares that anyone who captures endangered species must have a permit to do so. The permit application process allows for public comment; it is not easy to get permits. If the law were applied to salmon harvest as to all other areas of human endeavor, each fisherman likely to harvest endangered salmon would need a permit to do so. That has never happened.

In some cases, states have applied for § 10 permits designed to clear their fishing seasons (and protect all the fishermen). That wasn't happening either. Instead, the States of Oregon and Washington determined fishing seasons as part of process supervised by Judge Marsh, in committees with federal, state and tribal members.

The National Marine Fisheries Service issued opinions to itself, the U.S. Fish and Wildlife Service, and the U.S. Bureau of Indian Affairs, determining that pursuant to § 7 of the Endangered Species Act, the federal involvement in salmon harvest was not sufficient to jeopardize the continued existence of Snake River salmon. These opinions typically declared that some single, arbitrary, total harvest percentage in the Columbia River would not jeopardize the salmon. But without more specific permits and permit conditions, no one could really tell whether the "no-jeopardy" conditions in the federal § 7 opinion would be met.

As the spring 1995 gillnetting season was about to start, once again there were no § 10 permits. Indeed, there wasn't even a § 7 biological opinion. For several years, the government waited until the day before the scheduled fishing season was supposed to start before issuing the biological opinion.

This did the fishermen no favors, because they were not sure the opinion would authorize the requested season (although it usually did, albeit sometimes with minor modifications). And this also did us no favors, because by the time one could mount an effective legal challenge to the opinion, the season would be over.

On February 11, 1994, the National Marine Fisheries Service issued its biological opinion authorizing federal participation in setting the spring gillnetting season. The season was a mixed-stock harvest; among the several stocks that would be harvested were endangered Snake River spring chinook salmon, which would comprise about 13% of the total fish to be harvested. This, the National Marine Fisheries Service declared, would not jeopardize the continued existence of the salmon.

So on February 15, 1994, I filed a complaint and motion for a temporary restraining order against the opening of the spring chinook season, which was to occur at noon that day. The gist of our argument was that no one had applied for any permits to kill 13% of the endangered fish in a public process required by § 10 of the Endangered Species Act. We argued that the States of Oregon and Washington were not parties to the § 7 consultations between the federal agencies. The plain language of the Endangered Species Act required that they, or even the fishermen, get a permit in a public process before they could kill endangered species.

Although the whole idea of a temporary restraining order is to get immediate relief, on February 16th the case was reassigned to Judge Marsh, who was then in California. He scheduled a hearing for Friday afternoon, February 18th. He was not happy with my legal arguments, and accused me of "tak[ing] a lot of the Court's time trying to figure out what you are really talking about".[26] But once he had figured out the argument, he lost no time in disposing of it:

> "The problem we've got here, and taking it more critically, I don't know when this train wreck is going to occur, but I can see from the many other cases that are coming into this court ... I have often said that is going to make the spotted owl look like a chickadee.
>
> "Now, ... since the predominance of these cases before me, I cannot look at any of them in a vacuum. I have to look at them all collectively, and I have to make sure that when I pull the string one way, I don't unravel something in another case or vice versa. And it is a critical problem that I'm extremely serious about."[27]

Judge Marsh then made it clear which case he was worried about "unraveling": *United States v. Oregon.*

> "Now once before in this court there was an injunction against the State of Oregon and the State of Washington issued by a State of Oregon court. And suffering all of the despair of comity, state, federal relation, I found it necessary to enjoin the State Court of Oregon. When I did that, I made this statement: The absolute need for coordinated and centralized management of fishery [re]source management in the Columbia River to protect fish and the balance between treaty Indians and non-Treaty Indians and fisheries, if compact members or nonparties are permitted to interfere with this carefully balanced process by seeking an eleventh hour restraining order from judges unfamiliar with the cases and its background, that state fishery management agency would be confronted with confusion and chaos."[28]

I could not help but feel that the most important factor for Judge Marsh was not the protection of endangered salmon, but the protection of fishery management agencies from "confusion and chaos".

Having explained his motivations, Judge Marsh then held that the setting of fishing seasons by the States of Oregon and Washington "does qualify as [federal] agency action under § 7 and does qualify to ask for the conference through NMFS to see whether or not the operations of the compact plan and fish management plan as adjusted year to year is going to affect the listed species".[29]

Judge Marsh did not explain how actions by *states*, even two states acting together in an interstate compact, could constitute "federal agency action" subject to § 7, or how the states could obtain the protection of § 7 consultations when they did not apply for such protection or, indeed, have any formal status in the consultations whatsoever. At my request, and with the consent of all parties, he deemed the hearing to be called a hearing on a preliminary injunction (which typically follows a hearing on a temporary restraining order), so as to facilitate an immediate appeal.[30]

The United States Court of Appeals for the Ninth Circuit, however, was less cooperative. We filed the appeal on February 22nd, along with an emergency motion to have the appeal heard immediately, since the fishing season was half over. Judges Schroeder and Wiggins immediately denied the motion, but did agree to grant the appeal expedited status, so that it would be heard by the Court in May, long after the harvest was over.[31]

Then another panel of Judges, Alarcon, Norris and Leavy, declared that the action was moot, and that the appeal must be dismissed. In our briefs on appeal, we had cited no fewer than three prior appeals from fishing seasons on the Columbia River that had not been dismissed as moot.[32] The Ninth Circuit opinion did not even mention these cases, which formed the most relevant authority on the question of mootness. Once again, the Ninth Circuit had told us to go back and present exactly the same claim all over again.

Jim Ramsey's Attack on the Gillnetters: the Promise of the National Environmental Policy Act (NEPA)

"The fundamental goal of the NEPA is to provide high quality scientific analysis *before* decisions are made. Existing harvest management agreements and incidental take statements were made in violation of this principle . . ." Idaho Department of Fish and Game (1997).[33]

James Ramsey is a retired manager for Northwest Aluminum in The Dalles. He has lived there for decades. He has fished all his life, and even in his 70s takes frequent fishing trips. He remembered back in the 1960s fishing for salmon in the river, and listening to the old-timers talk about how increasing numbers of gillnetters downriver were going to wipe out the salmon. He watched as they put in The Dalles Dam, and how the salmon learned to swim around it on their way upstream.

For our next salmon lawsuit, we decided to focus on harvest, and to file suit along with Mr. Ramsey to avoid possible standing problems. We brought the suit in Seattle, the location of the regional headquarters of the National Marine Fisheries Service, the primary defendant, in an effort to try to get away from Judge Marsh. The suit was assigned to Judge Dwyer, the same federal judge who was instrumental in shutting down logging on National Forest Service land to protect the spotted owl.

The government, sensing in Judge Marsh a friendly forum for claims protective of salmon harvest, immediately moved to transfer the case to Judge Marsh. They stressed his experience in salmon cases, and claimed that this new action involved the very same issues as were pending in Portland. That was only partly true, since this case focused on a different federal statute, but Judge Dwyer went ahead and transferred the case over our objections.

Our claim was simple, but broad in scope. It challenged the salmon harvests in the Columbia River, on the Pacific Ocean off the coasts of Oregon, Washington and California, and the harvest off the coast of Alaska in the Exclusive Economic Zone subject to federal regulation. The primary claim was that these salmon harvests constituted "major federal actions" within the meaning of the National Environmental Policy Act (NEPA). NEPA requires that the federal goverment prepare an "environmental assessment" or "environmental impact statement" assessing the effects of major federal action.

The federal Council on Environmental Quality has declared that the "heart" of these analyses is the consideration of alternatives to the proposed action. Our main goal was to require the federal government to begin to look at alternatives to harvesting endangered salmon. In particular, we stressed that fish could be marked, caught alive, and the endangered and other wild fish thrown back alive. NEPA also requires consideration of the full range of environmental impacts arising from major federal action. In our view, the overriding imperative to continue harvesting endangered fish was causing impacts throughout the Columbia River Basin as fishery agencies shut down or modify logging, grazing, mining, recreational boating, and, of course, hydroelectric power generation.

Because the fishery agencies manipulate the Endangered Species Act to protect harvest at the expense of other economic sectors, it seemed logical to conclude that the environmental impact of their harvest decisions range as far as propelling the construction of new power plants.

In the case of the Alaska and Columbia River harvest, the federal agencies ignored NEPA entirely. They did, of course, offer excuses. As to the Alaska harvest, they pointed out that the federal officials had delegated responsibility for managing the harvest to the Alaska Department of Fish and Game, a bureaucracy regarded in some circles as a wholly-owned subsidiary of a powerful fishermen's lobby group, the Alaska Trawlers' Association.

As to the Columbia River harvest, the federal agencies claimed that the harvests did not constitute federal action, because the harvest proceeded in accordance with state or tribal fishing regulations. While that was true, the harvest was also reviewed by the National Marine Fisheries Service, the U.S. Fish and Wildlife Service, and the Bureau of Indian Affairs. Indeed, NMFS issued an "incidental take statement" under the Endangered Species Act, reviewed in our spring gillnetting season case, declaring that the commercial harvest of endangered salmon under those regulations was a lawful "taking" of endangered species.

We thought that our new claims would put Judge Marsh on the horns of a dilemma. Having already ruled in the spring gillnetting case that the state harvests were sufficiently "federal" so that no one had to apply for permits to kill endangered salmon, we thought he would have a difficult time holding that they were now "state" action for purposes of the National Environmental Policy Act.

Judge Marsh proved inventive, however. He suggested that the in-river harvest constituted "judicial action" exempt from NEPA because he had approved a Consent Decree years before under which the federal, state and tribal officials continued to negotiate to set harvest levels. The federal government did not attempt to defend this ruling on appeal. Judge Marsh then held that the Alaska harvest was, as the Justice Department claimed, a state action with no federal involvement—even though the Director of NMFS' Alaska office reviewed and approved the state's decisions.

As to the Pacific Ocean harvest, Judge Marsh declared that because harvest levels had been cut since 1993, the issue was now moot. Once again, mootness allowed unlawful action to evade review. We tried to explain that the federal defendants were refusing again to consider selective harvest methods or broader environmental impacts, but Judge Marsh ignored those claims.

Reviewing Judge Marsh's decision, the Ninth Circuit affirmed the finding of mootness, but could not affirm the rest of it. Obviously reluctant to rule in favor of Mr. Ramsey and the DSIs, the panel declared it was "compelled to conclude" that the Alaska and in-river harvests violated NEPA.

On January 22, 1997, the federal government announced that it would prepare a single EIS to consider the environmental impacts of all West Coast fisheries that might affect not only the endangered Snake River salmon, but also the steelhead, coho and sea-run cutthroat trout "species" that had been listed under the Endangered Species Act (or were proposed for listing).

The government also agreed to include a study of alternatives, including substantial reductions or elimination of harvest, and various means of selective harvest that would avoid capture of listed stocks.

As of 1997, we are all pretty skeptical that the EIS will consider any meaningful reforms to salmon harvest practices. The first thing that the National Marine Fisheries Service did was put Joseph Blum, the former director of the American Factory Trawler Association, in charge of preparing the EIS.[34]

NOTES TO CHAPTER 10

[1] NMFS, "Biological Opinion on Impacts on Listed Snake River Salmon by Fisheries Conducted Pursuant to the 1996-98 Management Agreement for Upper Columbia River Fall Chinook", July 31, 1996, at 14; *see also* Letter, R. Holt (NMFS) to M. Spear (USFWS), Sept. 23, 1996, at 3.

[2] Letter, S. Huffaker (Chief, Bureau of Fisheries) to J. Blum (NMFS), Feb. 27, 1997, at 1.

[3] PFMC, *Council News*, Vol. 21, No. 2, at 1 (April 8-11, 1997 Meeting Summary).

[4] *Id.* at 4 (Chinook harvest, in numbers of salmon, was 31,700 for 1997; 12,600 for 1996; and 9,700 for 1995; harvest levels averaged 334,700 from 1976 to 1980).

[5] *Id.* at 12 & 13 n.f.

[6] NMFS, "Biological Opinion on Impacts on Listed Snake River Salmon by Fisheries Conducted Pursuant to the 1996-98 Management Agreement for Upper Columbia River Fall Chinook", July 31, 1996, at 7.

[7] B. Rudolph, "Fall Harvest Cuts Pay Small Dividend to Northwest Fishers", *Clearing Up*, Dec. 16, 1996, at 7.

[8] NMFS, "Biological Opinion on Impacts of the 1996-98 Management Agreement for upper Columbia River spring chinook, summer chinook and sockeye on listed Snake River salmon", Feb. 16, 1996, at 8.

[9] *Id.*

[10] ISG, *Return to the River* 63.

[11] *Id.* at 64.

[12] ISG, *Return to the River* 365 (Pre-pub. ed. 1996)

[13] PFMC, "Preseason Report I: Stock Abundance Analysis for 1997 Ocean Salmon Fisheries", at II-15 (Feb. 1997).

[14] Jim Coon, who works for the Pacific Fishery Management Council, quoted in B. Harden, *A River Lost* 219.

[15] 16 U.S.C. § 1532(3).

[16] 16 U.S.C. § 1538(a)(1)(B).

[17] 16 U.S.C. § 1536(b)(4)(B) (emphasis added).

[18] 50 C.F.R. § 402.02.

[19] Deposition of J. Gary Smith, Jan. 7, 1993, at 140-41.

[20] *See, e.g., United States v. Nguyen*, 916 F.2d 1016 (5th Cir. 1990); *see also United States v. Ivey*, 949 F.2d 759, 766 (5th Cir. 1991), *cert. denied*, 113 S. Ct. 64 (1992).

[21] *PNGC v. Brown*, 38 F.3d at 1067-68.

[22] 16 U.S.C. § 1538(a)(1)(E)-(F).

[23] *PNGC v. Brown*, 38 F.3d at 1068.

[24] *See, e.g.,* PFMC, "Preseason Report I: Stock Abundance Analysis for 1997 Ocean Salmon Fisheries", at II-18 to II-19 (Feb. 1997). This report contains detailed projections and indices for five distinct stocks of fall chinook salmon, but not endangered Snake River fall chinook salmon. Simple estimates of abundance for endangered stocks are prepared for submission to NMFS, but are not really used in planning harvests.

[25] T. Kulongoski, Opinion dated Feb. 21, 1995.

[26] *Peterson v. Washington*, No. 94-167-MA, Hrng. Tr. at 44 (D. Or. Feb. 18, 1994).

[27] *Id.* at 44-45.

[28] *Id.* at 46.

[29] *Id.* at 48.

[30] *Id.* at 54.

[31] *Peterson v. Washington*, No. 94-35160, Order at 1 (9th Cir. Feb. 22, 1994); *Peterson v. Washington*, No. 94-35160, Order at 1 (9th Cir. Feb. 24, 1994).

[32] *United States v. Oregon*, 657 F.2d 1009, 1012 n.7 (9th Cir. 1981); *United States v. Oregon*, 718 F.2d 299, 302 (9th Cir. 1983); *United States v. Oregon*, 769 F.2d 1410, 1414 (9th Cir. 1985).

[33] Letter, S. Huffaker (Chief, Bureau of Fisheries) to J. Blum (NMFS), Feb. 27, 1997, at 4.

[34] J. van Amerongen, "Feds Probe Impact of Salmon Fishing", *Alaska Fisherman's Journal*, March 1997.

CHAPTER 11: THE OROFINO COMMUNITY'S STRUGGLE OVER DWORSHAK DAM

The Great Salmon Hoax is invisible to most Northwesterners. They may be paying a 20% tax in their electric bills, but the tax isn't visible. But many communities in the Northwest have suffered much greater impacts. Each community has its own story, and this book would be overlong if I tried to tell them all. As the Great Salmon Hoax proceeds, more and more communities will suffer the same fate.

Fish Kills in the Steelhead Capital of the World

In Lewiston, Idaho the Clearwater River joins the Snake. An hour's drive up the Clearwater River is the town of Orofino, Idaho. Orofino is Idaho's sacrificial lamb to the jealous gods of salmon recovery. Orofino is home to Dworshak dam and the huge reservoir behind it, with hundreds of miles of shoreline filled with beautiful camping sites. For much of the summer now, the reservoir is empty and in place of the beautiful shoreline are steep cliffs of mud and mudflats littered with an occasional dead and rotting elk. The reservoir has been turned into a storage tank for salmon flow augmentation and huge gushes of water are released at the whim of bureaucrats in Portland.

The houseboat business is dead, the marina has gone out of business, the small bait and tackle shops that supplied the hundreds of recreational fishermen and boaters who would show up at Orofino every summer are boarded up. In the bars of Orofino, angry residents talk about armed takeovers of the dam, and hanging Idaho politicians in effigy. Most of them don't know how far science and law was twisted to shut down their community.

On June 20, 1994, the U.S. Army Corps of Engineers advised the City of Orofino of its plans to lower the Reservoir levels eighty feet for the ostensible benefit of Snake River fall chinook salmon. The Corps gave the City 48 hours to comment on the plan, enough time for the Mayor, Roy Clay, to fire off a letter listing the many reasons the proposal made no sense and complaining that given that the releases would start on June 21st, "[o]bviously, no real consideration for a valid comment period was intended, thereby eliminating any public input into our government process".[1]

On July 1, 1994, the National Marine Fisheries Service issued a press release repeating the myth that "ninety percent of the fall chinook, which have to traverse 900 miles and eight dams, are expected to die on their way to the ocean." But, claimed the Service, "the additional water provided by federal water agencies will help the fish better negotiate their trip and reduce the death rate".[2] This was the beginning of a public relations campaign that has continued ever since to try and claim that the damage to the Orofino community serves some useful purpose.

The community leaders looked to the Columbia River Alliance for assistance. Dennis Harper, a local chiropractor, was an avid recreational fisherman and boater, and one of the most active in fighting to save the reservoir. He was joined by Nick Chenoweth, a leading lawyer in Orofino and James Grunke, the Executive Director of the Orofino Chamber of Commerce.

They petitioned Bruce Lovelin, Executive Director of the Columbia River Alliance, to help them fight the federal agencies. Bruce and I went to Orofino to assess the problem. Mr. Chenoweth arranged with Jimmy Dodge, a local fisherman, to give us a ride in a power boat up to the base of the dam. As we lowered the boat into the water we saw dozens of small dead kokanee lining the banks of the river. Jimmy explained that the force of the releases was expelling untold numbers of kokanee through the dam and out in the river. Many of them were broken in two from the force of their explosive emergence from the dam.

The massive releases, 15,000 cubic feet per second, were blowing out of the ports on the dam wall like giant waterfalls. Below, in the body of the dam, another 10,000 cubic feet per second of water turned turbine blades. The dam was constructed with bays for additional turbines, which would permit greater water releases without wasting the stored energy, but plans to add the additional turbines had been abandoned in the face of environmentalist opposition. It was truly an impressive sight standing on top of the reservoir and watching the thundering water.

I marveled at the engineers' capacity to harness all this power. Later I was amused to read one environmentalist's account that the "noise, the vibration, and the height of the dam scared" him.[3] There is a Continental Divide between those who fear technology and those who see it as useful.

As we motored up the river, Mr. Dodge expressed his indignation that the Idaho Department of Fish and Game refused to set a salvage season to allow the residents to pick up the fish. If they authorized the salvage season, it would draw attention to the fish kill. Jimmy was an expert in smoking and pickling kokanee and provided us with some samples of his efforts, which he gave to some of the older folk in the town.

As we got closer to the dam the water became almost effervescent and took on a deep blue-green color laced with millions of tiny bubbles of gas mixed into the water when it plunged from the dam. As we motored along

Jimmy pointed out a road that the Corps of Engineers had built which he told us had destroyed a huge area of fall chinook spawning beds. We took pictures of the dead kokanee along the banks of the river.

A mile down the river is the Dworshak National Fish Hatchery. We visited the Hatchery and discovered that they were having problems because their water intake screens were becoming clogged with dead kokanee. We talked to the engineer in charge of the water system at the Hatchery, David Owsley. He told us that they were finding 40-50 dead kokanee a day on the screens, which withdraw 134 cubic feet of water per second. Assuming that the kokanee were evenly distributed in the water, this meant that about 4,500 kokanee a day were being killed, or about 135,000 if the operation continued for 30 days. Mr. Owsley thought this was likely to be an underestimate, because not all the fish stuck to the screens, and many of them were eaten by birds before they got to the hatchery.[4]

Based on the science set forth in Chapter 7, it was pretty clear that the release of all of this water in June wasn't going to do any good for salmon. I hadn't previously realized the harm it was doing. In addition to killing hundreds of thousands of kokanee, the cold water releases were altering the entire ecosystem of the Clearwater River.

Dworshak Dam was specifically designed with expensive selector gates, the goal being to release water from the dam at temperatures corresponding to those which prevailed in pre-dam conditions. Now every summer there are huge blasts of cold water thrown down the river which have displaced the warm water fish populations and retarded the development of the fish indigenous to that stretch of the river, including chinook and steelhead.

Most of the people in Orofino believe that the National Marine Fisheries Services' ill-conceived plans to assist salmon are injuring the steelhead. Mr. Dodge later testified: "Normally, water is released from Dworshak in the fall which lowers the temperature of the North Fork of the Clearwater River, causing the adult steelhead to migrate up the river. Because of the summer releases from Dworshak, less water has been available for releases in the fall, and fewer steelhead have been returning in the fall."[5] In 1997, the steelhead were listed under the Endangered Species Act; they were perhaps the first species put on that list, in part, by ill-conceived efforts to protect another species already on the list.

Dworshak National Fish Hatchery, an important source of returning steelhead, was especially hard hit by the cold water releases, which stunted the growth of the juveniles in the raceways. Because hatchery juvenile survival drops sharply if the fish are released at smaller sizes, hatchery managers complained about the cold water releases since they began. As of late 1996, the proposed solution is to spend $1.25 million on a giant boiler to warm up water that could have been released at the right temperature through the selector gates that now stand idle.[6]

The massive spill from the reservoir also caused total dissolved gas levels in the Clearwater River to rise well above the Idaho State Water quality standard of 110% of normal saturation to 121%; even 40 miles down the river, the total dissolved gas levels were measured at 117% of normal. An important part of the Great Salmon Hoax is the purposeful violation of these standards, established to protect salmon, by the fishery agencies pushing flow augmentation and spill schemes; that subject is explored at greater length in Chapter 12.

The Orofino Community Seeks Legal Protection

Like most lawyers who do not specialize in environmental law, Nick Chenoweth thought that the law ought to provide a remedy for Orofino. He asked for our assistance in drafting a complaint to stop the releases. We met with the Clearwater County Board of Supervisors and the supervisors agreed that it was an appropriate matter for the county to pursue. Thus began the case of *Clearwater County, Idaho vs. U.S. Army Corps of Engineers*.

There were two claims in the case. Orofino residents had been involved with the federal government's attempt to comply with the National Environmental Policy Act ("NEPA"), as it applied to water releases from Dworshak, and found the effort utterly inadequate. The NEPA analysis coverage for the releases consisted of a page or two in two larger documents called the "Columbia River Salmon Flow Measures Options Analysis Environmental Impact Statement" (OA/EIS) and the "Interim Columbia and Snake Rivers Flow Improvement Measures for Salmon Supplemental Environmental Impact Analysis" (SEIS). In these documents, the U.S. Army Corps of Engineers, Bonneville Power Administration and the Bureau of Reclamation had agreed to analyze the environmental impact of various schemes to increase river flows sought by the state fishery agencies and tribes.

In doing this, they got off on the wrong foot with respect to NEPA because the most important part of NEPA is the requirement that the government study alternatives to the proposed action. Obviously, there are more sensible ways to attempt to manufacture salmon than manipulating river flows. By shutting down fishing for a matter of days a larger effect on salmon populations could be achieved than 10 years of flow manipulation. But the federal government refused to expand the scope of the NEPA analysis to include consideration of more sensible means of manufacturing salmon.

NEPA also requires that the federal government analyze the socioeconomic impact from its proposed course of action. The government's attempt to do this in the SEIS had enraged the citizens of Orofino. According to the federal bureaucrats, adoption of the reservoir releases would, under a median range of assumptions, trigger a loss for the community of approximately $7,854.[7]

Residents of Orofino knew that this was less than the loss of one of the many businesses that had failed in the wake of the drawdowns, and their own evidence suggested adverse impacts on the order of a million dollars or more. Thus, we prepared an affidavit of Mr. Grunke identifying the inadequacies in the government's NEPA analysis. He pointed out that "the lost revenue from a single houseboat rental season may exceed $7,854". He listed several of the small businesses that had failed in the wake of the releases, any one of which "would have had annual receipts in excess of $7,854". [8]

NEPA analysis also requires that the government achieve a fairly full understanding of the adverse environmental impacts on its decisions. While there were references in the 1,000 page SEIS to possible harm to kokanee, the magnitude of the resulting fish kill was never anticipated by the drafters of the SEIS.

The second claim was directly under the Endangered Species Act and amounted to a suggestion that the reservoir releases were not necessary to help the salmon (see Chapter 7) and, by the government's own admission, could injure them.

The third claim was more subtle, but more important. Judicial decisions in the early part of this century rationalized the creation of administrative agencies under the theory that the discretion of the agencies was limited by law, so that courts would always be able to review the actions of administrative agencies to confirm that they had acted within parameters set by Congress. So long as the actions of the officials could be reviewed by reference to a standard set by Congress, there could be no objection that the establishment of the agencies represented an unconstitutional delegation of legislative power.

Unfortunately, Congress seldom does a very good job of establishing clear standards to guide administrative officials. Indeed, the orthodox view is that limiting the discretion of administrative officials limits their ability to "do good" and should be discouraged. The U.S. Army Corps of Engineers operates under a number of extraordinarily vague laws. In particular, the law authorizing the Corps to construct Dworshak dam merely suggests that the Corps is "authorized to construct the project . . . for recreation and other purposes consistent with the program described in House Document 403". A review of that document confirms that one of the primary purposes of the dam was to enable increase logging of the Clearwater National Forest. Logging roads are expensive, but log rafts are cheap.

By creating a reservoir hundreds of miles long extending deep into the Clearwater National Forest and state forests as well, Congress intended to facilitate the logging of all this area and specifically authorized the Corps to construct log handling facilities. The log handling facilities only work when the reservoir is full or nearly full. The Orofino citizens, including a local logging company, stressed in the lawsuit that the drawdowns had essentially nullified a critical purpose of Congress in constructing the reservoir. Congress had relied on the Corp's representations of substantial income to the local population from logging activities and improving the reservoir; the Corps had now shut down the logging by removing any ability to get the logs out.

We thought it likely that the Corps could not, as a matter of law, simply decline to pursue one of the critical purposes for which the reservoir was constructed. It would be as is Congress authorized the construction of a highway bridge and the Corps constructed a railway bridge instead. Dworshak had been converted from a reservoir that was full for log rafting and boating, to a giant water tank for flow augmentation experiments. In addition to completely nullifying Congress's ideal of facilitating log transportation, the drawdowns also rendered recreational boating nearly impossible. Most of the boat ramps simply did not extend down to water level during the summer season anymore. Only by backing down a single half-mile ramp, causing enormous delays for those few boaters willing to go, could boaters get their boats in the reservoir.

For many years, a lodestone of federal management of natural resources has been multiple use. Multiple use means what is says: when the federal government owns a resource, multiple uses of that resource should be encouraged in order to maximize the benefit to society that comes from ownership of that resource. In the case of the U.S. Army Corps of Engineers, this goal has been formalized since the 1950s through regulations that require the Corps to account to Congress for the expected benefits from public works projects.

The Fate of the First Orofino Lawsuit: Mootness Strikes Again

Bruce Lovelin and I worked around the clock to prepare the legal papers to support an injunction against the releases. Mr. Owsley provided a sworn statement which later nearly got him fired from his job at the fish hatchery. Dennis Harper and Jimmy Dodge testified that the reservoir releases were not only killing kokanee, but also destroying the spawning beds for

286

resident bass by exposing them and drying them out. They also explained how, in earlier years, the Corps of Engineers had released bursts of water from the Reservoir in the winter to break the ice, saving large numbers of elk and white-tailed deer which would otherwise try and cross the Reservoir, fall through, and drown. The National Marine Fisheries Service objected to this, saying that the water had to be saved for salmon, which killed substantial numbers of elk and white-tailed deer.[9]

The manager of the Dworshak State Park testified that he personally believed there was a significant adverse effect on fish and wildlife in and around the Reservoir. He explained that the lack of water had virtually halted recreational use at the Park, the campgrounds were empty, and he was required to lay off Park workers.[10]

Neither the Orofino community nor the Columbia River Alliance could afford to hire a fish biologist to testify concerning the National Marine Fisheries Service's claims of benefit for the salmon. Luckily, the Columbia River Alliance had an economist on retainer who understood the Service's use and misuse of salmon statistics, Dr. Darryll Olsen of the Pacific Northwest Project. He analyzed the materials accompanying the Service's press release, which claimed that by increasing river flows from 37 to 43 thousand cubic feet per second, a 40% improvement in survival would result.

The government relied heavily upon the only study ever to find a significant relationship between flow and travel time for subyearling chinook salmon, in this case endangered Snake River fall chinook salmon. This 1993 study, by Thomas Berggren and Margaret Filardo, has been the subject of heavy criticism and is contrary to at least five other studies. In reviewing the literature as a whole, the Northwest Power Planning Council's Independent Science Group, recently offered the face-saving gesture toward Berggren and Filardo that the relationship they purported to identify "might appear at very low flows" with "essentially no current".[11]

Dr. Olsen testified that the Service was misrepresenting its own Biological Opinion by equating changes in detections (the data in the Biological Opinion) with changes in survival (the claims in the press release)—a trick soon to be repeated by the U.S. Fish and Wildlife Service. He pointed out that there was no way, as a matter of simple mathematics, that a slight change in flow could lead to a huge change in survival; he also pointed out that the National Marine Fisheries Service had access to sophisticated computer models that would predict only a 4% change in survival—giving every benefit of the doubt to the flow theorists.[12]

Having prepared the necessary papers and affidavits, Bruce and I turned them over to Nick and caught the plane back to Portland. The Idaho

U.S. Attorney's Office managed to delay the action by refusing to accept service of the papers at their Moscow, Idaho office. Then the court's clerk raised questions about a bonding issue addressed in the papers, which the clerk had apparently not read.

By the time Nick overcame these hurdles, and Judge Lodge finally heard the matter, on July 29, 1994, the reservoir releases were in their last day. The Corps of Engineers' witness testified that the releases could not possibly be halted before midnight, and the Judge indicated that there was no point in resolving the issues. The next day the newspapers reported that the Corps has decided to end the releases early, an impossibility according to the sworn testimony of its representatives. Months later, the Judge issued a written order denying the motion to stop the releases "based upon testimony that the Corps of Engineers was going to terminate the drawdown in question immediately, [so that] the motion for a preliminary injunction terminating the drawdown is unnecessary".[13]

How Judge Lodge Ignored the Facts to Deny Any Relief to Orofino

The citizens of Orofino continued to gather information on the adverse impacts of the reservoir drawdowns and eventually engaged the Mountain States Legal Foundation to assist them in prosecuting their claims. Like most of the victims of the Clinton/Gore administration's salmon programs, the Orofino residents could not afford to hire lawyers, and had to rely on public interest organizations to represent them. The following spring Bruce and I returned to Orofino to bring Paul Seby from the Defense Fund up to speed. Mr. Seby, a bright young environmental lawyer from Denver, worked frantically to get the case heard on a more expedited basis. This time, thanks to the Idaho Farm Bureau, which had sent a film crew up to the reservoir to film the adverse impacts of the drawdowns, we had a videotape to show the judge.

Mr. Seby and I worked to prepare a second round of affidavits, updating the prior year's affidavits and adding more from area residents. Mr. Irby, who was responsible for a local lumber mill's operations, explained how the drawdowns had destroyed all possibility of using the reservoir to transport logs cut from the forests surrounding the Reservoir. He also pointed out that log rafting was the most environmentally-benign method of moving the logs, since fewer roads needed to be constructed, and less energy spent moving the logs.[14]

Mr. Grunke reported that the Corps had finally conducted a survey of the losses resulting from the drawdown, which disclosed that the community had suffered losses of over $15 million, including the loss of 135 jobs, as a direct result of draining the Reservoir. At the same time, the Corps' environmental analysis pursuant to the National Environmental Policy Act continued to report only a "slightly negative" effect.[15]

On July 20, 1995, a second hearing was held before Judge Lodge. Mr. Seby presented several witnesses, who amplified on the testimony they had given in their sworn statements. Dr. Harper testified that the recreational value of the Reservoir had been destroyed. James Grunke testified about the enormous economic losses to the community. The Manager of the Dworshak State Park testified that Park visits had dropped sharply. Alex Irby confirmed that it was now impossible to transport logs through the reservoir, as the log handling facilities were left high and dry. Lindsay Nothern of the Idaho Farm Bureau Federation played the Farm Bureau's videotape showing dead and rotting elk littering mud flats in the reservoir, and others testified that no one would go near the Reservoir when water levels dropped to the lowest levels. Indeed, he testified that most of the footage "was too graphic to be used in a regular news story".[16]

Mr. Nothern also tried to testify about the Idaho Department of Fish and Game's efforts to cover up the problems by removing the elk carcasses before anyone found them. Unfortunately, the U.S. Attorney was well prepared, and fired off an objection before Mr. Nothern could even start that story.[17] It was peripheral to the claims.

The government presented testimony from National Marine Fisheries Service fishery scientist Chris Toole, who confidently asserted for the U.S. Attorney that "granting of this injunction would cause instant mortality to downstream migrating juvenile fall chinook salmon".[18] He was, however, unable to quantify any benefits achieved from the releases, instead offering speculation based on the changes in PIT-tag detections from a low flow year (1993) that survival might double.[19] No analysis or evidence was offered on the effect of adding additional water in an average water year, like 1995, because none existed (or yet exists).

David Ponganis from the Corps of Engineers explained how the Corps had conducted its NEPA analyses. He confirmed that the NEPA analysis "does not cover summer releases out of Dworshak".[20] Normally, if the federal government takes an action without subjecting it to NEPA analysis that has an adverse effect on the environment, the action will be enjoined.

Russell George was the hapless witness from the Corps assigned to defend the idea that the Corps had authority to drain the reservoir in the summer. Mr. Seby conducted an effective cross-examination, first getting Mr. George to admit that the discretion of the Corps "and its scope with limits is set forth in the Corps of Engineers Regulations".[21] Mr. Seby then read a regulation stating that further Congressional authoritization was not required to revise reservoir operating plans "if the related revisions in the plan would not significantly affect operation of the project for the originally authorized purposes".[22] Mr. George began to quibble with the word "significant", insinuating that there was no significant difference between having the reservoir full in the summer vs. empty in the summer, and claiming ignorance as to the purposes of the reservoir.

Judge Lodge expressed frustration: "You get the witness here telling the Court that he does not know what the original purpose is, and while he may be only one individual out of a team . . . certainly a witness knows whether or not it was one of the original purposes, this flow augmentation for the movement of fish."[23] Of course it wasn't one of the original purposes of Dworshak Dam to be a storage tank for flow augmentation purposes.

Mr. Seby was optimistic after the hearing. Observers from the Idaho Attorney General's Office reported that the federal government had put on a terrible case. This was not surprising, since this was the first and only time that the government has ever had to present witnesses and evidence (apart from the "administrative record") in court to defend its flow augmentation plans.

But when it came time to write his opinion, Judge Lodge invoked all of the pernicious doctrines we have seen before to deny any relief. He declared that even if Dworshak Reservoir were being operated inconsistently with Congress' authorizing legislation, "plaintiffs have failed to establish any legally protected right or interest under applicable law that enables them to bring such a challenge".[24] He seemed to believe that even if the federal officials were violating the law, and injuring local residents, the law provided no remedy.

As for the NEPA claims, Judge Lodge declared that the citizens of Orofino were seeking to prevent "commercial losses", and that "whether such losses will actually be sustained is highly speculative at this point".[25] In light of the economic devastation documented in the record, this finding was simply incredible.

Recognizing that Dr. Harper and others also claimed the loss of the ability to fish, a "recreational" interest clearly protected under NEPA, Judge Lodge found that "plaintiffs have not established that they have any legally protected right under NEPA or any other statute, including the authorizing statute for this project, to use that reservoir for recreational purposes . . ."[26] Except for my experience with Judge Marsh, I would have thought that this was a truly remarkable opinion. Who would expect a federal judge to declare that citizens have no "legally protected right" to use a Reservoir that was sold to them on the promise that they would be able to use it for recreation?

All of Judge Lodge's findings are variants of the "standing" excuse for refusing to hear cases. According to Judge Lodge, the government can violate the law, wiping you out financially in the process, and as far as the federal judiciary is concerned, you can do nothing about it. It may be unfair to single out Judge Lodge since this doctrine is now well-rooted in Ninth Circuit jurisprudence.

Judge Lodge went on to hold that Mr. Toole's testimony "demonstrates that there is a compelling need for additional water to enhance the survival of juvenile fall chinook", and that asking the Corps to prepare additional environmental analysis pursuant to NEPA "would itself likely be contrary to the requirements of the [Endangered Species Act] and would likely cause great harm to the listed species".[27] In short, the government had once again succeeded in demonstrating that if it merely asserts that it does something "for" an endangered species, it can violate any other law in the process.

The U.S. Fish and Wildlife Service Press Machine

Notwithstanding a lack of legal success, Orofino's efforts put pressure on the fishery agencies to cobble up some sort of claimed benefit from the Dworshak releases. Thus on August 30, 1995, the United States Fish and Wildlife Service, led by one of the leading progenitors of the Great Salmon Hoax, Fred Olney, put out a press release declaring that releases from Dworshak Reservoir in July and August 1995 had produced a "dramatic increase in survival of endangered fall chinook salmon smolts in the Snake River". [28] The Service announced "minimum survival figures" of 47-55% for summer 1995, over and above a rate of 7% for 1992.[29] The Service corralled the sheepish agency scientists in a room and presented them to reporters to discuss the findings.

Alerted to the press conference by a friendly agency source, we worked hard to educate the media that these claims were bogus. The news media did manage to report some criticism of these findings, including Bruce Lovelin's observation that "the big difference between the two years is not the amount of water released from the reservoir, but the fact that natural river conditions are much better this year".[30] August of 1995 was, in the words of one local observer, "the coldest, wettest August in the past ten years".

At the press conference, it became apparent that the numbers reported were not estimates of survival at all, but changes in the percentage of fish detected at Lower Granite Dam after tagging further upstream.

There are several logical problems with assuming that because detections were higher, survival was higher. Much of the effect could have been accounted for by temperature differences between 1992 and 1995. When river temperatures are high (as in 1992), juvenile salmon tend to be found lower in the water column. Fish lower in the water column are less likely to be swept into the bypass system, so the cooler weather by itself produced higher detections.

It is true that the releases of cold water from Dworshak Reservoir were large enough to lower the water temperature downstream in Lower Granite Reservoir. There may well be some benefit to anadromous fish from lowering water temperatures, but because of the misdirected attention to supposed flow effects, no one has tried to figure out how much benefit can be obtained from reducing temperatures—and determining whether such benefits offset the adverse effects of colder temperature on smolt growth rates.

The detection devices had also changed significantly between 1992 and 1995. In 1994, extended length traveling screens were installed at Lower Granite Dam. Although the screens had only been installed on one turbine unit, it was a turbine unit in the center of the dam where most of the fish were concentrated. It is these screens that collect most of the fish and direct them through the detectors.

The extended length traveling screens are a subject of extensive scientific research. At this point, there is no conclusive study concerning their efficiency at sweeping fish into the bypass system. Preliminary data, however, indicates that they are perhaps twice as effective as the conventional screens. This too accounted for the increase in detections at Lower Granite Dam.

Finally, there was a critical variable known as fish condition. The premise of these studies is that one selects a group of fish, injects them with the PIT tags and looks to see how many are detected downriver at the first dam. However, juvenile salmon suffer a known amount of handling mortality. This is one of the principal excuses that the states and tribes have always used to try and shut down PIT tag research when it began to show evidence that their strongly-held beliefs on smolt migration were invalid.[31]

In warmer water temperatures, the effects of handling mortality are larger. Thus, in a cooler year, more of the fish will tend to survive the handling experience quite apart from any change in survival as they migrate through the reservoir. None of these facts were brought out at the press conference. A few reporters had the wit to ask how much of this change actually had to do with the claimed operation. The responses from the scientists were equivocal.

In the wake of the press conference, James Grunke called up the Fish and Wildlife Service Field Office in Idaho. He was shocked to discover that there was no "study" at all. What had happened was that the fish advocates occupying "policy" positions in the service had learned of the preliminary data showing that detections were up. They seized upon the data and claimed that it was the result of the operation they had promoted. The scientists would draw no such conclusions. They stressed to Mr. Grunke that all that was available was raw data.

Nevertheless, from the standpoint of the Orofino community, the damage was done. Yet another effort to promote the Great Salmon Hoax had succeeded.

Several months later, after Steve Cramer released the results of his study (discussed in Chapter 12) showing that PIT-tag detections at McNary Dam had dropped by nearly half after excessive spill caused high levels of gas supersaturation, the very same individuals who had proclaimed the success of Orofino releases based on PIT tag detections now loudly proclaimed that Cramer's study was meaningless, because it only showed the results of detections, not true survival.

And in 1996, we learned that the 1995 rise in summer detections was apparently a local effect at Lower Granite Dam only, and was not present at Snake River dams further downriver.[32] No one seems very interested in pinning down the phenomenon. For all we know, the PIT-tag detectors at Lower Granite were malfunctioning for a while.

Judge Lodge Declares that the Corps Can Nullify the Purposes for Which Dworshak Was Constructed

Mr. Seby knew that a preliminary injunction is an extraordinary remedy, and that sometimes a judge will ultimately grant relief even after a preliminary injunction is denied. So Mountain States Legal Defense Fund moved for summary judgment on the claim concerning the Corps' statutory authority. Mootness had struck again to shut down judicial review of the NEPA claims, for the federal agencies had prepared yet another NEPA analysis, and Orofino would have to start all over again to challenge that document.

This time, the decision got even worse. After reiterating his earlier holdings, Judge Lodge baldly declared that the Corps was "providing for the multiple uses, including recreation and log transport at Dworshak".[33] After all, said the Judge, recreation was not "eliminated". People could still come and look at the mud flats that used to be a beautiful reservoir. In a footnote, the Judge blamed problems in transporting logs on the Forest Service (which has nothing to do with the operation of Dworshak Dam); the fact that loggers would not buy timber on the basis that someday they might be able to get it to market; and "the inability to guarantee a certain level of water above minimum pool during summer months".[34]

By the end of 1996, the kokanee population in the Reservoir had fallen from 1,300,000 to about 37,000, a drop that even the Idaho Department of Fish and Game called "alarming".[35]

Undaunted by the legal setbacks, Mr. Grunke has kept up the fight to keep Dworshak full in the summer, shifting his focus to the political arena. But Northern Idaho is not the center of political power in the State of Idaho. The power center is the State's capital, Boise, and the most powerful interests are well-organized farmers dependent on irrigated water and the Idaho Power Company.

Mr. Grunke continued to exert pressure on the Boise politicians, continually reminding them of Governor Phil Batt's campaign promise to help the Orofino community. He recognized that the federal Clean Water Act gave states authority to regulate water quality, even water quality problems produced by federal agencies, and sought to get the State of Idaho to tighten up water quality regulations in the North Fork of the Clearwater River immediately below the Dam.

By limiting total dissolved gas and below-natural water temperatures, the water quality regulators could limit releases from the Dam. Mr. Grunke got the Clearwater Basin Advisory Group to recommend adoption of such measures, but the state water quality regulators were directed by the Governor's office to ignore the request. Governor Batt had forged a shaky alliance with Idaho environmentalists and never really tried anything that might work to help the Orofino community.

The community continues to fight, and the government continues to find excuses to drain the Reservoir. In December 1996, the U.S. Army Corps of Engineers announced that it would have to be drained in the summer of 1997 to grout some leaks at the bottom. The Corps visited the community and announced that the problem was a "maintenance issue, not a safety issue".

Once again, James Grunke went on the offensive, recognizing that the grouting plan was probably a subterfuge for draining the reservoir without taking the heat for wasteful salmon efforts. He asked why the grouting could not be rescheduled for some time other than the peak summer recreation season. He got some support in the Governor's office. But then the Corps reversed its position, announced that the grouting was a safety issue after all, and Grunke gave up on efforts to keep the Reservoir full in 1997. Orofino's struggle continues.

NOTES TO CHAPTER 11

[1] Letter, Mayor Clay to Lt. Colonel James Weller, June 21, 1994. In fairness to the Corps, the representatives had showed up in Orofino earlier and told the community leaders of the release plans, telling the Orofino citizens that the releases were required by Endangered Species Act and that there was nothing that they could do about it.

[2] United States Department of Commerce News, "Federal Agencies Agree to Provide Additional Water Flows for Threatened Salmon", July 1, 1994, at 1.

[3] B. Harden, *A River Lost* 89 (describing a visit to Grand Coulee Dam with his father).

[4] *See generally* Declaration of David Owsley, July 19, 1994, filed in Civ. No. 94-0030-N-EJL (D. Idaho).

[5] Declaration of James Dodge, July 19, 1994, filed in Civ. No. 94-0330-N-EJL (D. Idaho).

[6] Columbia River Alliance, *Alliance Alert*, Nov. 8, 1996, at 2.

[7] SEIS at 4-132.

[8] Affidavit of James Grunke, July 19, 1994, filed in *Clearwater County v. U.S. Army Corps of Engineers*, No. 94-0330-N-ELJ (D. Idaho).

[9] *See generally* Declarations of Dennis Harper and James Dodge, July 19, 1994, filed in Civ. No. 94-0330-N-EJL (D. Idaho).

[10] Declaration of Mike McElhatton, July 21, 1994, filed in Civ. No. 94-0330-N-EJL (D. Idaho).

[11] ISG, *Return to the River* 209.

[12] Declaration Darryll Olsen, July 20, 1994, filed in Civ. No. 94-0030-N-EJL (D. Idaho).

[13] Order, Dec. 22, 1994, Civ. No. 94-0330-N-EJL (D. Idaho).

[14] Declaration of Alex Irby, July 1995, filed in Civ. No. 04-0330-N-EJL (D. Idaho).

[15] Second Declaration of James Grunke, July 1995, filed in Civ. No. 94-0330-N-EJL (D. Idaho.

[16] *Clearwater County v. U.S. Army Corps of Engineers*, No. 94-0330, Hrng Tr. at 36 (D. Idaho July 20, 1995).

[17] *Id.* at 32.

[18] *Id.* at 279.

[19] *Id.* at 285-88.

[20] *Id.* at 226.

[21] *Id.* at 195.

[22] *Id.* at 196.

[23] *Id.* at 208-09.

[24] Memorandum Opinion and Order, Civ. No. 94-0330-N-EJL (D. Idaho), July 1995, at 7.

[25] *Id.* at 9.

[26] *Id..* at 10.

[27] *Id.* at 13.

[28] "Craig calls FWS Dworshak smolts study 'Giant Leap of Faith'", *Clearwater Tribune*, Sept. 7, 1995.

[29] M. Wickline, "Drawdowns aiding smolts, agency claims", *Lewiston Tribune*, Aug. 31, 1996.

[30] *Id.*

[31] *See, e.g.,* Memorandum, M. DeHart to Fish Passage Advisory Committee Members Liaison Group, "FPAC recommendations to reduce smolt handling and marking and concerns regarding the PIT Tag workshop", Sept. 23, 1994; Letter, D. DeHart to NMFS, April 1994, *cited in* B. Rudolph, "Huge PIT-Tag Study Planned by Long-Time Critics; NMFS Has Doubts", *Clearing Up*, Dec. 23, 1996, at 6.

[32] ISG, *Return to the River* 222.

[33] *Clearwater County v. U.S. Army Corps of Engineers*, No. 94-0330-N-ELJ (D. Idaho Nov. 1, 1996), at 13.

[34] *Id.* at 13 n.7.

[35] M. Maiolie & S. Elam, Dworshak Research Summary, Oct., Nov. & Dec. 1996, at 1.

CHAPTER 12: THE FIGHT FOR MORE SPILL AT HYDROELECTRIC PROJECTS

> "The results are horrible and deadly. In a heavily afflicted fish, bubbles of free nitrogen appear under the skin and in the fins, tail and roof of the mouth. Eyes protrude or hemorrhage, and in extreme cases they are actually blown out of the head. Fish blinded in this dreadful manner have been known to live long enough to beat themselves to death against the concrete barrier of a dam they can no longer see." *Outdoor Life* (1972).[1]

Untold numbers of salmon and other fish in the Columbia and Snake Rivers died in the 1970s because water at the federal dams, then under construction, was directed over the top of the dams, through spillways, causing levels of dissolved gas in the river to rise to supersaturated levels. Absorbed into the bodies of migrating salmon, the supersaturated water produced horrifying symptoms, akin to a severe case of "the bends" in humans.

An entire generation of fishery biologists in the Columbia River Basin fought to make the dams safer for salmon by limiting excessive spill and dissolved gas. The U.S. Environmental Protection Agency produced a national water quality guideline intended to limit excessive dissolved gas from spill. Legislative history during passage of the Northwest Power Act reflects some consensus that spill was something to be avoided.

To the power engineers who designed the federal projects in the Columbia Basin, spilling water over dams instead of generating electricity with it was something to be avoided for reasons entirely independent of salmon. Spill was economic waste, pure and simple. At a single large dam with available turbines, spilling can cost tens and even hundreds of thousands of dollars a day in lost revenues. Ultimately, as more and more turbines were installed, less water had to be diverted through the spillways, and the spill problem of the 1970s went away.

Today, harvest managers have generally forgotten the lessons of the 1970s, and push for spill as an unquestioned good. The question of spill has become entirely politicized, and all the fine points—whether and to what extent more spill might help salmon—have been lost in an overriding political imperative for more spill, whatever the cost to salmon, or humans.

The Superficial Appeal of Spill

Superficially, spill over hydroelectric projects seems to be a sensible way to pass fish over dams. Spill proponents point to several studies showing spillway mortality to be negligible—2% or even less. The problem is that spill at every hydroelectric project is different. It works at some projects and not at others, depending on the configuration of the water and concrete. Sometimes the results are dramatically different at various spillways in a single dam. The results also vary among species.

Juvenile steelhead may have problems with spill. An older study showed mortality as high as 27.5% for steelhead passing over Lower Monumental Dam when the fish went over dams without spill deflectors, called "flip lips".[2] The fishery agencies disregard that study as unrepresentative, but have no coherent criticism of its design or execution. More recent research at Little Goose Dam showed steelhead survival close to 100%, except in spillways with spill deflectors, installed, where survival feel to a range of 93-97%[3]—within the range of direct turbine mortality.

Spill can also have adverse effects at dams like The Dalles, where spill dumps juvenile fish in an area of shallows and islands where they suffer higher predation than the fish emerging from turbines.[4] U.S. Army Corps of Engineers modeling suggests that "40% spill is the maximum that could occur without subjecting passing juveniles to excessive predation risk".[5] Yet the National Marine Fisheries Service has required 64% spill at The Dalles.[6] Preliminary data collected on coho salmon during 1997 showed losses of approximately 12% when spill volumes were at the required 64% level— probably significantly higher than turbine losses—and 6% losses for juvenile fall chinook.[7]

Spill at The Dalles also dumps the smolts onto "energy dissipators" which may cause direct physical injuries to the fish. In 1995 studies using balloon tags, five percent of the fish released above the spilllway were not recovered at all, suggesting high levels of physical stress on spilled fish.[8]

The Bonneville Power Administration has been trying for quite some time to get the fisheries agencies to do some dam-specific work to see what spill survival really is, and how it is affected by particular structures over which the water flows. Unfortunately, the states and tribes continue to veto the research. When the National Marine Fisheries Service finally proposed to study spillway survival at The Dalles in the summer of 1997, the Executive Director of the Columbia River Inter-Tribal Fish Commission declared that the proposed study was "unacceptable" and threatened to bring the matter before Judge Marsh under his continuing jurisdiction in *United States v. Oregon* harvest allocation case, purportedly because of tiny losses to hatchery coho salmon from tagging them for study purposes.[9]

The pro-spill bias is so overwhelming that all problems with spill are minimized. As is the case with turbine mortality, there is a single, politically-correct number for losses from spill: 0-2%. And high spill is required at all projects, even when it is counterproductive.

The most widely-known problem with spill (apart from its cost) is the 1970s problem: spilling water from 60 feet or more over the top of dams tends to dissolve a lot of atmospheric gases in the water. This phenomenon is known as dissolved gas supersaturation, and results in the water becoming like soda water full of gas, which gradually comes out as bubbles. When these bubbles come out inside of a fish, they can kill it. Tiny bubbles forming in the gills of fish can quickly asphyxiate them; larger bubbles can cause blindness and loss of physical control. The same phenomenon happens to human divers when they come up too rapidly from the deep: the nitrogen gas bubbles cause "the bends", a condition which is often fatal.

In the late 1960s and early 1970s, there were huge quantities of spill at federal projects on the Columbia and Snake River, primarily because all of the turbine units had not yet been installed. Large quantities of fish began showing up dead, with then-mysterious symptoms. Federal fish biologists, led by Dr. Wes Ebel at NMFS, began a crusade to identify the problem and cure it.

Laboratory experiments soon proved that salmon and steelhead were acutely sensitive to dissolved gas. Early experiments putting juvenile salmonids in water saturated at levels above 110% of normal killed large proportions of the fish; results varied by species with steelhead being more susceptible than salmon.[10] More refined experiments indicated that fish in deeper tanks could tolerate higher saturation levels. Still, at 124% and 127% saturation, juvenile chinook salmon suffered 67% and 97% mortality in water 2.5 meters deep.[11] Fish deeper than three to four meters are generally safe. The United States Environmental Protection Agency eventually established a national water quality criterion of 110% as the maximum allowable level of dissolved gas. One of the key considerations in establishing the standard was the effects on salmon. The studies by Dr. Ebel and others on the Columbia River achieved national significance.

Under the federal Clean Water Act, the states were permitted to adopt a more rigorous standard. Oregon adopted the 110% standard, setting a more stringent standard of 105% for waters used by salmon hatcheries. At the time, L.B. Day, the first director of Oregon's Department of Environmental Quality, said that he would have preferred a 105% standard. Since then, only the politics of spill have changed, not the science.

One of the first big battles to gain more spill was fought before the Northwest Power Planning Council in the middle 1980s. Former Council member Kai Lee of Washington has pointed out that in 1985, fishery advocates were complaining that is was not a good year for fish because there was not enough spill. Yet adult returns soared for the following three years.

> "Of course, much happens to salmonids after they leave the Columbia Basin, and these data do not show that 1985 was a good year after all. They do illustrate the shaky underpinnings of the fishery managers' experience, which is usually offered without explanation *ex cathedra*.[12] . . .

> "By 1986, the Council's impatience with unreliable statements of inscrutable experience had grown to the point that a recommendation for improved spill operations failed on a vote of four to four. The Council's rationale . . . was that there were no significant biological benefits from increasing spill. More precisely, the support for the fishery managers' claim of biologically significant benefit had fallen below a bare majority."[13]

A decade later, "unreliable statements of inscrutable experience" on spill continue to fill decisionmaking forums in the Pacific Northwest. The 1994 Ninth Circuit decision discussed in Chapter 9 even went so far as to declare that the Northwest Power Act "requires only the best available scientific *knowledge*, not *data*"[14] in arguing that the Northwest Power Planning Council must give a "high degree of deference" to the fishery managers. Fishery managers now tell the Council that their "unreliable statements of inscrutable experience" must be followed as a matter of law.

From the perspective of my clients, the main problem with spill was simple: its cost. Luckily, since the juvenile salmon tend to migrate at night, spill levels tend to be higher at night, when electric power demand is less. When experts told my clients that, in addition to wasting money, the spill would not help salmon, and probably injure them, they thought there was some chance that they could stop increases in spill. They were wrong.

Fish Passage Efficiency and Fish Survival

For several years, salmon advocates have advocated that the federal projects be run so as to achieve 80% "Fish Passage Efficiency". Most people think this means that the project passes 80% of the fish, or, conversely, that 20% never make it past the dam and die. Luckily, that isn't what Fish Passage Efficiency means.

300

One of the clever tactics used by the salmon advocates is the adoption of terminology that is misleading. "Fish Passage Efficiency" is one of the "best" of these ploys. Fish Passage Efficiency means *the percentage of fish that pass by a project by a means other than through the turbines.* Thus, a Fish Passage Efficiency (FPE) of 80% would mean that 20% of the salmon die *only if 100% of the fish died in the turbines.*

As set forth in Chapter 4, the most recent studies suggest that turbines only cause about 5% direct mortality. Even if the turbines killed 10% of the fish, which is doubtful, survival through a dam would be 98% at 80% FPE. At 70% FPE, survival would be 97%. The misleading "Fish Passage Efficiency" terminology, however, produces media accounts of "high death rates" because media representatives assume that FPE is the "percent of migrating smolts to safely traverse each dam".[15]

What matters to salmon, however, is survival, not FPE. The relationship between FPE and survival is not simple, and varies project by project. Here is a graph prepared with the CRiSP computer model for Little Goose Dam that shows the relationship between the percent of fish spilled, the percent transported, Fish Passage Efficiency, and ultimate percent survival:

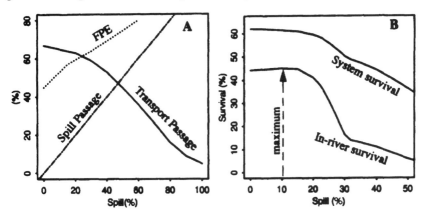

Figure 25: FPE vs. Survival[16]

It is clear that pursuing increased FPE does not make much sense as a goal in itself, since both system survival (transported and untransported fish) and in-river survival drop with higher FPE. Even though fewer fish go through the turbines with higher FPE, more are lost to the gas supersaturation and other injuries associated with spill, including decreased transportation.

Higher FPE, however, is the formal goal of federal, state and tribal harvest managers, not higher survival. The Bonneville Power Administration continues to advise the fishery managers that "survival across the concrete may be a better criterion than FPE",[17] and the fishery managers continue to ignore BPA.

Unless you were trying to reduce power production for the sake of reducing power production, why wouldn't you simply adopt a goal of maximizing survival? I don't know, but I do know that fish advocates used to have a goal of improving survival; after it was largely met, they began to focus on goals that seem to have no purpose but to make dams uneconomical.

FPE is a highly politicized number. The Corps of Engineers has spent hundreds of millions of dollars putting in traveling screens in front of the turbine intake to guide fish away from the turbines. The Corps continually evaluates their efficacy. The most recent studies have suggested that travelling screens on the Snake projects can guide 80% of the yearling juveniles away from the turbines. Thus, a project can have 80% FPE with no spill at all. Dam opponents cite older studies showing that FPEs, based on older configurations, were much lower.

Beginning in the late 1980s, the Corps of Engineers had pursued fish passage goals that aimed for 70% FPE. Higher FPE targets required more spill, which would cause levels of total dissolved gas to rise too high. Beginning in the 1990s, the state fishery agencies and tribes no longer worried about dissolved gas.

Their basic rationale was that years with high flow and spill tended to be associated with more returning adults. Thus spill must be good. No one pointed out that the fishery managers were already claiming that the flow itself caused higher survival, through reduced travel time, or some other means they could never really explain. No one challenged the fishery managers to distinguish positive effects of spill from other factors associated with high flow and spill years, such as better ocean conditions.

The 1994 Spill Attack

Flushed with success at their victory in *Idaho Department of Fish and Game v. NMFS*, the state fishery agencies and tribes demanded that the Corps commence a spill program to meet their proposed 80% FPE target. The most immediate obstacle to this plan was the states' own water quality standards. Initially, federal biologists at BPA and the Corps fought the plan. In their view, spill had already been increased to the maximum extent possible without serious problems from dissolved gas.

The dispute circulated all the way to the White House, where the state agencies, aided by the tribes, the U.S. Fish and Wildlife Service, and political appointees at NMFS, convinced the Vice President and the White House office of Environmental Policy that they knew better about spill. The state proponents assured the White House that the state laws ostensibly prohibiting excessive spill would be no problem, for waivers could be obtained.

A lot of the problems in the salmon area stem from the enormous influence in the Clinton/Gore Administration of former staffers of Vice President Gore. Gore's political theology elevates consensus-based environmentalism above reason. According to Gore, "[w]e must make the rescue of the environment the central organizing principle for civilization".[18]

Over and over again, Gore's people, including Doug Hall, the Undersecretary of Commerce, Katie McGinty, the Director of the White House Office of Environmental Policy, and Will Stelle, the Northwest Regional Director of NMFS, have ignored government scientists in favor of the unscientific assertions of environmentalists and Indian tribes.

As the political forces began to assemble behind the proposition that spill was an unmitigated good, we consulted several salmon experts and became convinced that the fishery agencies were about to embark on a plan that would *decrease* salmon abundance. All of the experts we consulted had substantial experience in assessing the effects of dissolved gas on salmonids, and published work on the subject.

We consulted Dr. Larry Fidler, a Canadian biologist who was involved in setting water quality standards for Canadian rivers. We consulted Wes Ebel, a former NMFS scientist who, as noted above, was instrumental in establishing the 110% total dissolved gas standard. We consulted Don Weitkamp, who had published the leading literature review in the field. We consulted Dr. Jerry Bouck, a retired biologist who had worked for the U.S. Department of Fish and Wildlife and the Bonneville Power Administration. And we consulted Dr. Anderson, whose computer models of salmon survival have consistently predicted decreased survival from increases in the spill program.[19]

The contrast between these experts, who supported the current water quality standard, and those who would set it aside, was striking. Dr. Bouck was moved to state that the Oregon Department of Environmental Quality "and those agencies and tribal representatives who propose raising the [total dissolved gas level] have inadequate specific training and experience with gas bubble disease and supersaturation to evaluate this highly specialized subject."[20]

All of these experts presented testimony to the Oregon Department of Environmental Quality and the Washington Department of Ecology, charged to evaluate the fishery managers' requests to set aside the gas supersaturation standards to promote spill. Drs. Fidler and Bouck would not even take our money to testify, because they thought it would taint them. As events turned out, that didn't matter. Both the paid and unpaid experts were ignored.

The fishery managers put considerable effort into preparing a "Risk Analysis" of the costs and benefits of spill, concluding that the water quality standard should be loosened to 125% total gas supersaturation. Independent scientists who reviewed the Risk Analysis declared that it was fatally flawed. So did NMFS' scientists in Seattle. Perhaps as a result of this, NMFS only half-heartedly embraced the Risk Analysis, and, under threats of litigation from the states and tribes, agreed to seek an increase to "only" 120%.

One of the problems with the Risk Assessment was that it did not contain any quantitative assessment of effects on adults. Dr. Ebel advised us that dams were constructed to operate with limited spill, and were finely tuned over decades to attract as many fish as possible to the fish ladders. Excessive spill generates currents that confuse the adults searching for the fish ladders. The adult salmon also tend to swim about laterally in the tailrace area where gas concentrations are highest before ascending the fish ladders.[21] As a BPA spokeman pointed out in 1997: "We have always found high spill to impede adult passage . . . [and since the vast majority of juveniles were avoiding turbines at lower spill levels] the status quo [of high spill] doesn't make a lot of sense."[22] High levels of spill also cause adults to "fall back" over the top of the dam, measurably reducing spawning success.[23]

While the BPA representative did not say so, it was entirely possible that radical increases in spill were killing many adults and saving comparatively few juveniles (at least as measured in adult equivalents). This could have a strong negative effect on the population, since the death of adults about to spawn can be devastating for a weak population. Rather than respond to BPA's evidence, though, fishery interests have merely "scoffed at BPA 'arguing for fish benefits'".[24]

Dr. Ebel also tipped us off to a fundamental computational error in the state and tribal calculation of Fish Passage Efficiency. The states and tribes assumed a one-to-one relationship between the quantity of water spilled and the percentage of fish passing over the dam in that water. Thus, for example, they would require a 40% increase in the amount of spill to credit dam operators for directing 40% more fish away from the turbines.

In fact, studies at Lower Granite Dam demonstrated that the relationship was not one-to-one. The first 20% of spill passed perhaps 40% of the fish; the first 40%, perhaps 60% of the fish. Studies at other projects have shown similar numbers. Some limited data from 1996 studies at The Dalles Dam indicates that increasing the percentage of spill from 30% to 64%

produced no measurable change in the proportion of smolts passing over the spillway.[25]

By abandoning the one-to-one assumption, the quantity of spill could be reduced from the amounts assumed by the fisheries managers, and still meet the 80% Fish Passage Efficiency target. This would cost less, and cause less gas supersaturation. The fishery managers were (and are) not interested in using the Lower Granite and other data. They insisted on the one-to-one assumption. This was yet another position that convinced us that their real goal was to destroy the economics of the dams, rather than protect fish.

The states and tribes quickly rolled over any skeptics in the state water quality departments. To further justify setting aside the very water quality standards that had been established to protect salmon, the Oregon Department of Justice assured the Oregon Department of Environmental Quality that granting the gas waiver was essential to avoid conflict with a federal court order.

Judge Marsh had issued no such order. I filed papers with Judge Marsh pointing out that the federal agencies and states were initiating a program that would do more harm than good, and asserting that he was requiring it. Counsel for Oregon and the other parties were quick to deny that they had said any such thing (although it is evident in the record of the Commission's proceedings). Judge Marsh declined to issue any ruling with respect to the spill program, declaring that he was not going to get involved in "scientific disputes" and that the matter was "not properly before him."

The spill proponents convinced the Oregon Department of Environmental Quality to issue a waiver to allow the spill program to go forward. They promised the Department to conduct a careful and extensive monitoring program to assure that no adverse effects would result from the spill. John Colt, a consultant hired by BPA to review the monitoring plans, reported that the monitoring program was riddled with inconsistent and faulty procedures. Even the limited data that was collected was not distributed in a fashion that would permit anyone to make decisions using it. He concluded: "The study team was unable to clearly document the time history of what data was distributed and what data (if any) was not published... there is a perception by some agencies that the Fish Passage Center is withholding data."[26] As events continued to unfold over the next several years, Mr. Colt's recommendations for improvement went unheeded.

From our perspective, there was only one bright spot in the 1994 spill program. Researchers at Bonneville and other dams using ninety-power microscopes to examine tiny, two-inch juvenile steelhead found that a very high percentage of fish had gas bubbles in their gills, leading the National Marine Fisheries Service to reduce the amount of spill in mid-season.

Unfortunately, the fishery managers fixed that problem the next year by taking away the ninety-power microscopes in favor of lower-powered instruments so that no symptoms could be seen.[27] They also terminated any analysis of the gill filaments of juvenile salmonids, even though experts told them "examination of excised gill filaments can detect evidence of GBD that is not detected using stereoscopic methods of examination of fins, lateral line and intact gill filaments".[28]

This was sufficiently outrageous conduct to provoke a Congressional hearing, during which Idaho Senator Dirk Kempthorne suggested that it was possible "that NMFS has designed a program so that it is ignoring this gas bubble trauma situation".[29] The media ignored the hearing, and Senator Kempthorne gave up trying to fix the problem. Later, some at NMFS (not the scientists in Seattle) began to claim that the researchers had never even seen gas bubbles at all, but had seen tiny globules of fat, probably a biological impossibility.

The 1995 Spill Program

Dr. Fidler was sufficiently outraged by the proposal to set aside the 110% standard again in 1995 that he wrote to Bob Baumgartner of the Oregon Department of Environmental Quality, warning that "with anadromous fish populations in their present state, it is possible that by allowing dissolved gas levels in these rivers to rise above the U.S. E.P.A. guideline, some populations might be lost entirely."[30]

Mr. Baumgartner reviewed the evidence for and against spill, and wrote a number of memoranda questioning the reasoning and data of the state and tribal spill advocates. This was the only time we ever saw a government employee fresh to the salmon problem take an unbiased look at it. He was promptly removed from his position of reviewing the spill waivers and "promoted" to a new position. We were later told that Oregon Governor Kitzhaber's office had intervened to accomplish this. Perhaps chastened by these events, his new, junior replacement never put much effort into critical review of the claims of spill proponents.

On March 1, 1995, the *Oregonian* reported that as many as forty thousand juvenile salmon held in net pens below Willamette Falls on the Willamette River died as a result of total dissolved gas supersaturation.[31] The net pens were eight feet deep, and the gas levels were under the newly-minted 120% standard when the salmon began dying. We hoped that the death of these salmon would serve as a wakeup call for the Oregon Department of Fish and Wildlife and the Oregon Department of Environmental Quality.

As soon as he read the *Oregonian* article, Erick Johnson, the lawyer for the Pacific Northwest Generating Cooperative, sprang into action, asking that day "to inspect and obtain copies of all public records relating to any lethal or sublethal effects observed in juvenile spring chinook salmon on the lower Willamette River".[32] I called him up to congratulate him on beating me to punch with a request for the documents. He was enthusiastic, hoping that the State would wake up and look at this evidence.

Unfortunately, as soon as the Willamette River incident occurred, Oregon Department of Fish and Wildlife also sprang into action, producing a report which declared, among other things, that the saturometers used to measure the total dissolved gas supersaturation at the net pen site were somehow in error because there was a "temperature effect" that could not be captured by the saturometers. Lapsing into pseudoscientific babbling, the report suggested that there was some sort of mysterious kinetic energy of the gas particles that had an adverse effect on the fish that could not be detected by gas supersaturation detection technology.

Dr. Larry Fidler laughed when he heard this claim. In a letter to the Oregon water quality regulators, Dr. Fidler acidly noted that the National Bureau of Standards and every other scientific organization involved in measuring the effects of gas supersaturation on aquatic life would not use saturometers if they were not capable of accounting for changes in temperature.

Undaunted, the Oregon Department of Fish and Wildlife switched tactics. Now it claimed, through means it did not attempt to explain, that the net pens were riding several feet out of the water so that they were not really eight feet deep, but were perhaps only two or three feet deep. We contacted the Department's biologist in charge of running the net pens, who acknowledged that the pens were nearly entirely *in* the water. Unfortunately, citizens typically cannot subpoena witnesses to bring the truth into administrative proceedings like the proceedings the Oregon Department of Environmental Quality was holding on the spill waiver, so we could only assert what we had been told.

Ultimately, the deaths of the Willamette salmon served no purpose. Acting in reliance on the misinformation and distortions produced by the Oregon Department of Fish and Wildlife, the Oregon Environmental Quality Commission again approved a waiver of the total dissolved gas limits. The staff prepared a report swallowing the Oregon Department of Fish and Wildlife's fish story hook, line and sinker, saying the "fish in the [Willamette] net pens were likely restricted to depths of much less than eight feet".[33] They were a little harder on the federal agencies, characterizing the U.S. Fish and Wildlife Service's review of the science supposed to support the waiver as "a remarkably limited evaluation of available literature".[34]

After several weeks of steadily increasing spill, juvenile fall chinook salmon placed in net pens below Ice Harbor Dam on the Snake River in Eastern Washington began to die from gas bubble disease. All the fish confined to a shallow one-meter-deep pen were found dead after only four days of exposure. Bruce Lovelin, Executive Director of the Columbia River Alliance, took the lead in publicizing the deaths in the net pens.

Once again the spill advocates sprang into action, declaring that these deaths were "irrelevant" and that conditions in the net pens had nothing to do with the real world conditions in the river. Northwest Power Planning Council members Ken Casavant and Mike Kreidler publicly accused Bruce Lovelin of "fear mongering" and "dishonesty" for daring to raise questions about spill, and Idaho environmentalists accused him of "fabricating" a claim that spill was harming salmon.[35] Others proclaimed that the net pen deaths were "meaningless" because the fish confined to the net pens could not dive to avoid the effects of gas supersaturation.

State and tribal spill proponents claimed that juvenile salmon could sense the presence of excessive levels of total dissolved gas in the water and dive to avoid the adverse effects. One government scientist, amused and disgusted by the whole proceedings, declared "the idea that fish can sense and dive to avoid total dissolved gas supersaturation is silly. Human beings who get the bends suffer nitrogen narcosis and cannot tell themselves whether they are the victims of gas bubbles in the blood. It seems unlikely that tiny fish less than two inches long can do so." NMFS was later to conduct an exhaustive review of the "diving" theory to conclude that there was "no evidence that fish can 'sense' TDG supersaturated water and deliberately sound to compensate".[36]

The kernel of truth behind the state and tribal position is that the symptoms of gas bubble disease are avoided at greater depths because the pressure keeps the bubbles from forming. This fact set off a festival of misrepresentations about the depth distribution of juvenile salmon. Unfortunately for the salmon, "[m]ost studies of salmon migration in rivers and reservoirs have indicated a surface orientation during movement".[37] But the states and tribes ignore the evidence, instead pointing to measurements in the forebays of dams, where fish both (1) rest at deeper levels in holding patterns; and (2) are attracted deep below the surface by turbine currents.

After the net pen deaths, the U.S. Army Corps of Engineers insisted on taking some measures to reduce dissolved gas concentrations below Ice

Harbor Dam. They reduced upstream reservoir releases for flow augmentation, and also lowered reservoir levels above Ice Harbor Dam. Each step was opposed by all the fishery agencies, with NMFS, the Oregon Department of Fish and Wildlife and the Fish Passage Center leading the opposition.

The Corps refused, however, to reduce spill levels at projects upstream of Ice Harbor Dam. Here they assumed, erroneously, that only the gas levels immediately below Ice Harbor Dam were causing a problem. Because the amount of gas produced in the water below Ice Harbor did not depend very significantly on the gas level in the water coming into Ice Harbor, they thought that upstream spill did not matter. Later, analysis would reveal that fish died below Ice Harbor much faster if they had also been exposed to higher gas levels upstream.

As all this was going on, I noticed a startling fact. Although the number of juvenile salmon entering Lower Granite Dam was well above the 10 year average, the number of fish making it five dams downstream to McNary Dam was significantly below that average. I brought this up in a meeting of the Technical Management Team, charged to manage river operations on a week-to-week basis to optimize conditions for migrating salmon. They had no idea why it was happening. None of them had noticed. They promised to look into the matter and ultimately offered explanations which, except for one, did not make sense. The sensible one was that the Fish Passage Center's projections of fish expected at McNary were worthless to begin with.

I also pointed out that the PIT-tag technology permitted a nearly instantaneous means of assessing the effects of spill on salmon, for it was possible to track the progress of each individual salmon downstream, dam by dam, and compute the percentage of release groups that survived during the spill experiment. In May, I requested the National Marine Fisheries Service, in writing, to analyze this data, but they declined to do so.

My clients were willing to engage S. P. Cramer and Associates to conduct the PIT-tag analysis the government should have been doing. Cramer and his analysts found, consistent with the massive mortality in the net pens, that salmon mortality had increased sharply just as the mortality in the net pens began to show up.

The reaction of the states and tribes was typical. When the National Marine Fisheries Service later conducted analyses similar to those conducted by Cramer, Stephen Pettit of the Idaho Department of Fish and Game and Michelle DeHart of the Fish Passage Center wrote to NMFS to complain that "analyses by some consultants have forced the NMFS to begin analyzing their data in a way that is not supportable by the original study design".[38]

This criticism is nonsense. Of course the analysis is not supported by the original study design. The data was originally gathered to provide survival estimates, not estimates of the effect of spill. But it is the very ideal of science to take data gathered and learn everything you can from it—whether or not anyone had the wit to think of each and every possible use of the data before they are collected. To promoters of the Great Salmon Hoax, like Pettit and DeHart, unapproved use of data is subversive.

In the meantime, the Oregon Department of Environmental Quality's staff had become concerned that notwithstanding the promises of the federal agencies and the state fishery agencies, even the excessive gas levels that they had authorized were being routinely exceeded. One Department staffer confided to me that he had attended a meeting with representatives of the Corps of Engineers and National Marine Fisheries Service and inquired about the fact that adult salmon had begun to show up at Lower Granite Dam with "headburns", a symptom that seems to correlate with spill in the dam system (and leads to increased prespawning mortality among the few remaining adults). He was shocked when the National Marine Fisheries Service person at the meeting denied that any such thing had occurred, leading the Corps of Engineers person to pull out a National Marines Fisheries Service report to the contrary. "It was at that moment I realized," he said, "that this program was based on ideology and not science."

The EQC Strikes Out

The 1996 request for a waiver of Oregon water quality standards constituted the Commission's third opportunity to bring some common sense to the question of salmon recovery. Arriving at the hearing, I picked up and read the staff memorandum and was disappointed to see that it contained an unqualified endorsement of NMFS' spill proposal. Contrary to the staff's assurances the day before, it would not be Brian Brown of NMFS and I in a two-member panel debating the propriety of the waiver. Instead, there would be three proponents of the spill program, Mark Schneider, Fred Olney, and Brian Brown, as supplemented by Gary Fredericks and other policy analysts in the audience. The room was full.

After a good deal of preliminary banter among the commissioners, Russell Harding, the lead DEQ staff person, announced the procedure to be followed: first, the spill proponents would make their presentation and then there would be a panel of two "experts" (Brian Brown and I). The panel was supposed to answer questions from the commission. The spill proponents gave their presentation, which, among the three of them, lasted nearly 35 minutes. It was punctuated by sharp questioning from one member of the panel, Henry Lorenzen. I was pleased to see that Commissioner Lorenzen was still playing an active role. That morning an extraordinarily harsh piece had appeared in the opinion page of *The Oregonian*, which all but accused Commissioner Lorenzen of a betrayal of the public trust for daring to question the spill program. Luckily, he hadn't seen it.

Finally, it was my turn to speak. Having previously tried the theme that "the emperor has no clothes" (when the fish began dying in the net pens in 1995), I told the Commission my new theme was "where's the beef". I presented the results of Cramer's work and emphasized that the only scientific quarrel was over whether and to what extent the spill program had decreased salmon survival, *there being no evidence at all that it had increased salmon survival as promised.*

I then addressed the monitoring program and asked the commission to consider how they would deal with me if I represented the Amalgamated Toxic Sludge Company, and proposed the following: The company wished to dump large quantities of chlorine into a stream. They were confident that this would not harm the fish. To prove it, they proposed the following: a tube would be inserted into the stream. Any fish that swam up it would be put in a tank containing a material that absorbed chlorine. The fish would be allowed to heal for a while (and any fish that died would be removed). Then, technicians would examine the surviving, healed fish. The Company fully expected that no signs of environmental damage would be found.

This is a fairly precise analogy to the internal workings of the current smolt monitoring program. Russell Harding all but admitted this before the Commission, stating, however, that the difference was that no possible good could come from putting chlorine into the river, whereas some possible good could come from the spill that was putting dissolved nitrogen and other gases into the river.

Responding to my presentation, Brian Brown told the Commission that he was sorry if they had previously gained the impression that anyone from the Fisheries Service would be able to measure the benefits of what they were trying to do. This provoked an angry response from Commissioner Whipple, who said she felt misled by the fisheries agencies; that this was the third year in a row that they had come in seeking a waiver of the water quality laws; and now it was becoming apparent that they had no idea whether it was going to do any good or not. She said she would vote against the waiver, provoking a gasp from the audience.

Commissioner Van Vliet, recently appointed to the Commission by Governor Kitzhaber, attempted to characterize the situation as one of imperfect information where one didn't really know what the right thing to do was and maybe had to take a chance. He drew upon his personal experience to give an analogy of how it had taken ten years to build a computer model showing the effects of some other environmental decision. I quickly told him that the region had already spent the ten years building the computer model, the computer model said this wouldn't work and that was why the National Marine Fisheries Service had showed up that morning with a one-page spreadsheet that they had cobbled together trying to demonstrate some sort of benefits.

As the fishery representatives realized that their credibility was collapsing, particularly on the issue of smolt monitoring, they began to invoke a draft executive summary of NMFS' expert panel on spill. I was angered to hear this because I knew that the expert panel had not yet issued a report. I also knew about how a similar report last year had been "spun" by Dr. Coutant, much to the annoyance of the other panel members.

According to NMFS, the draft executive summary of the Expert Panel's report said that there was basically "no problem" with the smolt monitoring program. At this point, Commissioner Lorenzen, who had spoken to the chairman of the Snake River Salmon Recovery Team, and had reason to believe that this might not be accurate, announced that he proposed to split the spill program into two parts. First, he would deal with the March spill requested for hatchery fish, because the Commission had to make a decision, but the decision concerning the larger program, which would not begin until late April, would be deferred.

The hatchery program was ludicrous. Fred Olney, the U.S. Fish and Wildlife Service representative promoting this waiver, told the commission that increasing the survival of a group of hatchery fish (at a cost of $1 to 2 million) would help the endangered fish by reducing harvest pressure on them.

No one was permitted to tell the Commission that, in fact, the entire premise of the recovery plan for endangered Snake River salmon was to *curtail* hatchery production. Indeed, when NMFS listed the Snake River salmon, it warned that hatchery releases, like the Spring Creek hatchery release then at issue, could "result in competition for limited food and habitat . . . and, therefore, contribute further to the decline of wild Snake River fall chinook salmon".[39]

Mr. Olney said that some 330 more fish might be caught as a result of the spill program and suggested that this was vitally important for endangered fish, because it would reducing fishing pressure on endangered salmon. Unfortunately, Commissioner Castle, who had openly ridiculed this notion the year before, was no longer on the panel. No one on the Commission challenged Olney's assertions.

312

My presentation had lasted less than 10 minutes. As the meeting went on, I tried to correct the gross misrepresentations that emanated from the fishery managers, but Chairman Wessinger would not recognize me. Finally, after about an hour and a half of misinformation from the spill proponents, I asked him for permission to speak on the ground that the proponents had been talking for nearly 30 straight minutes and had said many things that weren't true. I told him that it would be a good thing for the Commission to know what the misrepresentations were. He angrily refused. The other commissioners looked askance at him, but did not overturn his decision to silence me.

This is typical of how policy is set in administrative proceedings in the Pacific Northwest. Administrative agencies stage meetings before their governing bodies. By picking who is allowed to talk to the governing body, and for how long, the staff of the agency can very significantly influence the outcome. Ordinary citizens can come and speak for five minutes or so during a "public comment" period—and have no hope of overcoming hours of misinformation and outright misrepresentations by the preferred witnesses. It is the same story in Congress. Most of the witnesses at Congressional hearings are carefully-selected agency officials or lobbyists. The judiciary is the only branch where citizens can, in theory, get equal airtime, but for the doctrines of administrative law (discussed in Chapter 9) that disenfranchise them there, too.

As the Chairman called for a vote on the hatchery program, Commissioners Whipple and Lorenzen voted against it. Commissioner McMahan, who had also declared that she felt misled by fishery agencies, voted for the plan, but only because she said she thought it would help endangered salmon. Chairman Wessinger and Commissioner Van Vliet voted for the program without comment. Thus it came to pass that the State of Oregon's official policy was to spend $2,000 per fish to make hatchery fish survive to compete with endangered fish.

As for the proposal to spend tens of millions of dollars by spilling all spring and summer, the Commission agreed to defer resolution of it, awaiting the final report of the expert panel. Returning to the office, I made some inquiries of the expert panel members to find out what was going on. They were enraged. Apparently, the first thing the expert panel had done this year, given their prior experience with Dr. Coutant, was to adopt a resolution that no written materials would be issued without the approval of all the members of the panel, and to adopt Roberts' Rules of Order.

The 1996 Spill Program Gets Underway

1996 was shaping up to be one of the wettest years in recent memory. As early as January, the early bird forecast of the Corps of Engineers showed expected precipitation well above 100% of normal. Notwithstanding the total dissolved gas problems at Ice Harbor the year before, and notwithstanding the warnings they had received from us and others about the inadvisability of augmenting flows, NMFS continued to insist that BPA buy high-priced replacement power all winter instead of generating electricity with the water sitting behind the dams. As it became clearer and clearer that the spring was going to get wetter and wetter, the analysts at BPA and the Corps were the first to realize that 1996 was going to be a year of serious total dissolved gas problems at the dams.

Early estimates by Bonneville Power Administration suggested that the river would sustain an average dissolved gas level of about 125% over its entire length for the duration of the entire migration season—and that was if the melting snow and run-off came perfectly and smoothly. If there were warm spells or storms or anything else that caused spikes in the run-off, the gas levels would be far, far higher.

Stung by the criticism of their spill management in 1995, the fish agencies quickly realized that the appropriate response in 1996 was to point the finger at the Corps of Engineers. As the spill season mounted, the weekly report of the Fish Passage Center announced every week that no spill was being requested on behalf of the fishery managers and that it was all "involuntary." Asked whether NMFS cared if the State of Oregon issued the total dissolved gas waiver, Donna Darm said it would not make any difference anyway because all of the spill was going to be involuntary.

A lot of the spill was involuntary, but a lot of it was not. In the meantime, the Oregon DEQ waited patiently for NMFS to provide the report of its Expert Panel. Throughout the month of March they waited, but the report did not come. The Panel was deeply split.

Every member of the Panel who worked for a state, federal, or tribal fishery agency seemed predisposed to downplay the significance of total dissolved gas. In fact, some members of the Panel had serious conflicts of interest. For example, Tom Bachman served on the Panel, yet was also in charge of a $500,000 spill monitoring and research program that was the very subject of the Panel's scrutiny. The Panel members who were not government employees, many of whom had formerly worked for the government, took an extremely dim view of the program and grumbled privately that Bachman seemed to be defending every inadequacy of it.

314

The report was finally issued, although the Panel members never got to see the final draft before it went out. The Report concluded that there was simply no way to tell whether the 1995 monitoring program or the program proposed for 1996 had any ability to detect problems arising from total dissolved gas in the river. In essence, there were seven critical uncertainties, any one of which could destroy the efficacy of the program. Although the private Expert Panel members essentially recommended that the program be abolished, the government majority of the Panel thought that it would have some value to consider the Program and a set of recommendations was made in the report to try and improve upon the existing Program.

In the meantime, we had provided the Oregon Department of Environmental Quality with some proposed conditions that we felt should be attached to their waiver—although we firmly believed that the only appropriate course would be for the Commission to deny the waiver altogether. The Department staff, who we hoped (wrongly) were slowly overcoming their prejudice against aluminum companies and in favor of their fellow civil servants, embraced the idea of requiring conditions. That way, they could issue the waiver, but still have some sense that they were doing their job by bringing about better monitoring and reporting. In particular, they called for a comprehensive report to be issued by the end of the year that would (in theory) provide answers to many of the questions that had remained unanswered through three years of the program.

About four days before the Commission meeting to approve the waiver, NMFS finally released the Expert Panel report. The DEQ staff amended their conditions to include a requirement that the agencies adopt the suggestions made by the Expert Panel. That never happened.

After the order was issued, the fishery agencies reacted with outrage. They could brook no interference in their program and began to tell the Department staffers that the conditions were unreasonable or could not be met for one reason or another. They also complained to everyone who would listen that my clients had had far too much influence in the process.

The conditions required that the fishery agencies install a net pen below Bonneville Dam, put juvenile salmon in it and monitor the effect on them. But the fishery agencies had already decided that, since the data from 1995 was "misused" (death of salmon in the river was inferred to suggest a problem with the program), there would be no salmon put into net pens during 1996. As the states and tribes put it, "[t]he premise . . . that signs of GBD [gas bubble disease] on fish in supersaturated water in net pens can be assessed and related directly to mortality from DGS [dissolved gas supersaturation] is not acceptable to the SFATs [state fishery agencies and tribes]".[40] Under the prevailing political regimes, a premise unacceptable to the SFATS cannot even be the subject of scientific experimentation, while their unproven premises govern dam operations.

From our perspective, failing to put net pens full of salmon into the river to monitor effects of the spill program was but one of many problems. The biggest problem, and worst decision, was to turn off the transportation system that had been installed at enormous ratepayer expense to protect the salmon. In particular, machines had been installed at McNary Dam to collect salmon before they went through the turbines. They would then be put into a bypass facility, where they could be transferred into transport barges. Because the water in the transport barges is degassed, transport was a safe means downstream even during an extremely high total dissolved gas conditions. We had recognized this early on, and Bruce Lovelin wrote to many government officials questioning this decision. They ignored him.

On May 10, 1996, Oregon Senator Mark Hatfield wrote to Will Stelle questioning the decision to turn off transportation in favor of spill. "With dissolved gas levels in the river at such extremely high levels, and your agency's own experts urging that smolt transportation be increased, I am curious about the logic behind the decision not to take at least some fish out of the river and barge them around the dams."[41] Mr. Stelle did not deign to respond to the letter until the migration season was over. As conditions on the river grew worse and worse, the Corps of Engineers began to point out that the facilities that would protect the salmon from these conditions were lying unused. Every week tens of thousands of salmon were collected for safekeeping and then put back into the river.

In the meantime, my clients re-engaged Steve Cramer and Associates to conduct further analysis of the effects of the spill program. We soon received his first analysis which, as expected, showed that survival rates in the river were substantially lower than in 1995 and took an especially sharp drop for a week or two in April when total dissolved gas conditions were extremely high.

Dr. Fidler had told us when we first engaged him that because the Smolt Monitoring Program sampled principally fish that had been collected deep below the dams, the resulting data were worthless: the tell-tale bubbles disappear at the greater depths, and frequently do not reappear when the fish surface. His conclusions had been confirmed by a firm BPA hired to review the monitoring program; its report warned that "pressurization to 100 feet for 5 minutes resulted in significant reduction in the clinical signals of GBT" and that "the current smolt monitoring program may be underestimating the prevalence of GBT in the Snake and Columbia Rivers".[42] Dr. Fidler and the consultants were all ignored; lab tests, said the state fishery agencies and tribes, were unrepresentative of conditions on the river.

By late April, observers noticed that one of the stations in the Smolt Monitoring Program was reporting substantial signs of symptoms: the Rocky Reach facility. This dam, on the mid-Columbia River, is a "low-head" dam. The water only rises a few feet before being pushed through the turbines to generate power. As a result, fish that were diverted away from the turbine by the bypass system did not have to dive 60 feet or more, as on the Snake River projects, but only about 20 feet or so. Despite relatively nominal gas levels at the dam (about 116%), fish at Rocky Reach were showing up with huge percentages of symptoms, out of all proportion of anything that was being observed at any of the other Smolt Monitoring Program sites.

Naturally, we were excited by the Rocky Reach results, which we thought might finally convince observers that the Smolt Monitoring Program was simply not working. Again we were wrong. At a weekly TMT meeting in April, the Fish Passage Center representative, Margaret Filardo, suggested that perhaps the holding tanks at Rocky Reach were too shallow and thought that perhaps the gas levels were really in the range of 142%. That was false. Ultimately, the fishery agency position came to be that there must have been something upriver of Rocky Reach Dam causing the high measurements, though no one could explain exactly what it was or provide any measurements that substantiated it.

By early May, conditions on the river were so bad that one member of the Expert Panel, Dr. Bouck, was moved to collect his colleagues to write to Senator Hatfield and explain that the McNary transport really ought to be turned on. Six of the nine members of the Panel signed the letter. Dr. Dawley, a NMFS employee with a reasonably objective approach to science, initially promised to sign the letter, but changed his mind after his boss, Dr. Schiewe, advised against it. The letter went to Senator Hatfield, who used to pay some attention to the details of these matters, and the Senator sent a letter to Mr. Stelle asking him to explain what was going on. Mr. Stelle never did.

During November 20-21, 1996, NMFS assembled most of the characters in the gas bubble drama for a conference to review the latest developments. Steve Cramer and Steve Smith both presented evidence of a decline in survival, and a marked negative correlation between flow and survival.

Tom Backman was supposed to be sampling fish in the reservoirs to confirm that they were experiencing no symptoms of gas bubble disease, but he did not bother to measure the gas levels where he caught the fish, instead calling up the nearest dam to get measurements there. He and his research crew caught about 6,000 fish and found only 0.6% with signs of GBD—at a time when even the defective monitoring program at the dams was detecting levels of about 3.3%.

One biologist told us that Backman had left many fish in pails for hours before examining them, so that the symptoms were gone by the time they were examined. BPA consultants had warned the fishery agencies of the "necessity to analyze fish very quickly once they are captured" because "[s]mall spherical bubbles from intact fish dissipated in less than two minutes while elongated bubbles dissipated in three to eight minutes".[43]

In fairness, Backman was not the only one who failed to conduct the research under the exacting standards required to detect any symptoms. No one did. Even at the dams, fish were held in a "collection tank up to 24 hours prior to examination".[44]

Backman concluded his presentation with slides of tribal fishing at Celilo Falls. This mixture of poor science and pro-tribal propaganda led many in attendence to conclude that it was one of the most embarassing presentations they had ever witnessed at a scientific seminar. For this effort, Bonneville Power Administration paid about $500,000.

There was by now enough doubt about the usefulness of spill that even the Council's Independent Science Group was willing to conclude in September of 1996 that "[f]ield tests of critical assumptions regarding mechanisms and locations of reservoir mortalities, along with reach mortality estimates, are needed before spill can be relied upon as the most desirable means of passing the juvenile emigrants of all species and life history types through the hydroelectric system".[45] They also acknowledged that the monitoring program "may be inadequate (usually underestimate effects) because of changes in signs in bypasses, loss of debilitated fish in reservoirs between dams, and other untested critical assumptions".[46]

The Future of Spill: 1997 and Beyond

By the end of the 1996 spill season, Steven Cramer had assembled convincing evidence, based on PIT-tag counts of fish, that survival had dropped from 1995 to 1996, and the worst drops were in the periods of highest gas. As flow and spill rose over the course of the season, survival dropped (rising temperatures could have played a role too):

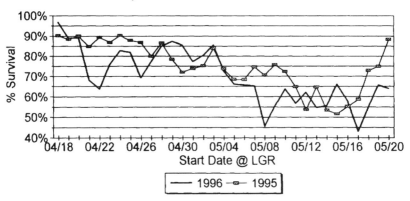

Chinook Smolt Survival - LGR to MCN
Comparison of 1995 and 1996

Figure 26: 1995 and 1996 In-River Survival, Lower Granite Dam to McNary Dam[47]

The National Marine Fishery Service's analysis of the 1996 PIT-tag data confirmed Cramer's work, although it used a different method of calculation. According to NMFS, survival measured from Lower Granite Dam to McNary Dam, fell from 66.7% in 1995 to 58.7% in 1996.[48] Large increases in flow and spill had produced a 12-13% decrease in salmon survival. Because no one could measure what was happening below McNary Dam, the true losses may have been much higher.

In January 1997, Oregon's Environmental Quality Commission held a meeting to allow the fishery agencies to present their report. The Commission did not offer opponents of the spill program an opportunity to present their views, which was the first sign that all of our efforts would prove unavailing. Dr. Mark Schneider of NMFS, who had evolved into NMFS' hatchet man on spill, and Dr. Margret Filardo of the Fish Passage Center downplayed the contents of the draft Annual Report. They claimed that they were not worried about the PIT-tag data because survival was generally up (a false claim) and the Smolt Monitoring Program had not detected any problems (for reasons discussed above).

Dr. Filardo went so far as to claim that new research, not yet written up, suggested that the smolt bypass systems had no effect on symptoms, so there was reason to have confidence in the Smolt Monitoring Program results. I wrote to her asking what research she was talking about, and she referred me to NMFS' Earl Dawley.

Mr. Dawley sent me a copy of the abstract of his research. The abstract had precisely the opposite results from those claimed by Dr. Filardo: "Data obtained in 1996 identified a decrease in prevalence and severity of GBD signs in steelhead released 0.5 km upstream from the dam. A smaller decrease in prevalence and severity was observed in fish held in a 5-m deep net-pen".[49] In other words, fewer symptoms were measured after fish went deep below the dam for collection, just as lab tests had predicted.

Mr. Dawley refused to tell me what the numbers were. He thought that the experimental design was defective, so it didn't really prove anything— the standard response by fishery officials when their own experiments, that they design, produce results inconsistent with the party line. Bruce Lovelin sent Mr. Dawley's abstract to the Commission as an example of why the Commission ought to "look beyond the testimony of Fish Passage Center representatives and other fishery agency managers with no particular expertise in the effects of gas bubble disease on fish".[50]

In the meantime, the upper level bureaucrats at NMFS carefully edited out all the controversial passages that the scientists had written in the draft Annual Report. No longer were drops in survival attributed to gas bubble disease.

One of the saddest facts about bureaucracies, is that once someone rises to the level of making decisions of real importance, they are too busy to learn the details. They must trust their subordinates to summarize complicated issues in a single page or two. In this case, that trust was sadly misplaced.

The Commission staff went all out to support the fishery agencies. Their memo to the Commission made the preposterous claim that some 288,000 fish would be generated by ten days of spill at Bonneville Dam.[51] The "right" number—giving the benefit of the doubt as to positive effects of spill—was about 237.[52] That's the difference between spending a thousand dollars a fish, or a dollar a fish. Given the current economics of salmon recovery, a dollar a fish would be a bargain, and no one would complain.

The staff discounted the scores of violations of the Commission's 1996 waiver by accepting the claim that the spill "was not specifically requested for fish passage"[53]—as if having enshrined the request in a biological opinion and sought and obtained a waiver to allow it, the harvest agencies could disavow all responsibility for it. Although the harvest managers had numerous opportunities to reduce spill and try and get gas levels down within the water quality guidelines, the violations were ignored because, said the staff, "[t]he spill management objective during the spring migration was directed toward meeting the total dissolved gas waiver . . ."

The PIT-tag-measured evidence of survival decreases was discounted as the possible result of other factors. The idea that spilling at collector projects removed hundreds of thousands of salmon from barges that could have doubled their survival was denied on the basis that transportation studies had produced "equivocal" results.[54] The staff even echoed harvest manager testimony that adding more hatchery fish would somehow reduce harvest pressure on endangered Snake River salmon.

The staff did disclose numbers from Mr. Dawley's study he had been unwilling to disclose to me. More than half the fish sampled after passage through the bypass systems had no signs of gas bubble disease at all, while the control groups in the net pens showed "a progressive loss of signs".[55] Like Mr. Dawley, however, the staff argued that the data was inconclusive and could not be generalized to other salmonid stocks.

On February 28, 1997, the Commission met to consider the fourth annual request for a waiver. My clients' lobbyists gave advice that it was better not to be confrontational with the Commissioners. My "emperor has no clothes" and "where's the beef" speeches were not appreciated. Lobbyists think it is far better to deliver a set speech than to contradict opponents to the point where their credibility is openly questioned. They fight to keep details out of the realm of public policy, and are a significant reason the legislatures pass laws that grow more and more vague. So I wasn't invited to speak at the meeting.

Despite advice from the Bruce Lovelin of the Columbia River Alliance that the Spring Creek hatchery spill program would cost electric ratepayers from $1,500 to $3,000 per harvestable adult salmon (if it had any positive effect at all), the Commission voted 3-1 to approve a waiver designed to allow spill for ten days. Only Chairman Lorenzen voted no.

After the meeting, reporter Bill Rudolph called up the assistant hatchery manager at Spring Creek, who was "puzzled by the duration of the 10-day March spill at Bonneville since most [of] the smolts made the 20-mile trip in 'eighteen to twenty-four hours'".[56] When Rudolph asked Commissioner Lorenzen about this, he responded that "state fishery managers assured the Commission that it took ten days for the fall chinook to make the passage".[57] As the Commission (and everyone else) continues to let the fishery managers get away with their misrepresentations, the misrepresentations get more and more extravagant.

Rudolph also interviewed a NMFS scientist, Gary Fredericks, who told him that 7.5 million fish to be released from Spring Creek hatchery represented "pre-production thinning", because the U.S. Fish and Wildlife Service raises too many fish so as to cushion for the possible effects of a disease outbreak.[58]

Survival for these fish would be much higher if they were released later. The bottom line: citizens of the Pacific Northwest were taxed more than $1 million to enhance the survival of fish that probably never should have been produced in the first place.

The dam operators initially agreed to provide the spill for only seven days. At a meeting of the "Technical Management Team" for river operations on March 19, 1997, representatives of the U.S. Fish and Wildlife Service demanded an extension of the spill to ten days. Their request was supported by Ron Boyce of the Oregon Department of Fish and Wildlife and Bob Heineth of the Columbia River Intertribal Fish Commission.

The U.S. Fish and Wildlife representative acknowledged that most of the smolts would have passed Bonneville Dam within the first twenty-four hours, and that, based on 1996 data, 99.8% of the smolts would have passed by the dam in the first seven days.[59] When representatives of Bonneville Power objected to the cost, the response from the fish managers, was, in substance, that BPA had already agreed that changes in operations to benefit fish would not be credited against fish program spending (see Chapter 13). Fishery managers see absolutely nothing wrong with spending virtually any amount of BPA's money to make fish, even hatchery fish. The bottom line is that they proposed to spend $300,000 to improve the survival of 0.2% of the fish by 0.3%—or about $150,000 per adult salmon (again giving the spill proponents the benefit of the doubt as to positive effects).

By the time the Commission met to approve the waiver of total dissolved gas standards for the balance of 1997, any pretense of actually measuring the effects of the waiver on salmon and other fish and wildlife collapsed. The Commission dutifully issued the waiver, watering down its 1996 conditions *so that there was no longer any requirement that the fishery agencies even measure changes in survival of salmon from the spill program.* The troublesome PIT-tag studies that had shown a 13% drop in survival from 1996 to 1997 would not have to be conducted at all. Instead of measuring effects on fish, the fishery agencies would be permitted to use their one-page spreadsheet model that ignores gas effects, SIMPAS, to predict survival.[60] The Commission even ratified the abandonment of net pen research.[61]

The staff of the Department is eager to get out of the business of reviewing the harvest managers' demands for waivers. Thus the staff is promoting a scheme whereby the Oregon Department of Environmental Quality, the Washington Department of Ecology, and the U.S. Army Corps of Engineers would enter into a "Memorandum of Understanding" that would obligate the Corps to "fix" the dams so that they would no longer generate high levels of dissolved gas. In exchange, the state water quality agencies would grant a long term waiver of the water quality standards.

Some within the Corps object to this approach, since "we're several years away from knowing what th[e gas reduction] strategy will be, and how it will be paid for".[62] As the Corps' Doug Arndt has explained, "you can't guarantee meeting the 110% standard under any and all conditions without spending billions".[63] The state fishery agencies, notwithstanding their insistence that dissolved gas levels of 120% or more are harmless when seeking spill, insist that "meeting the 110% total dissolved gas (TDG) standard should be used as a 'hard constraint' in evaluating gas abatement alternatives".[64]

The harvest managers are so eager to avoid continuing public scrutiny of their spill programs through state water quality review that they have mobilized all available political power to attempt to force the execution of such a Memorandum of Understanding. The White House has directed the United States Environmental Protection Agency to work with the states and tribes to this end.

The EPA has a carrot to offer the states: in exchange for going along with the White House efforts to re-engineer the hydrosystem, the state water quality agencies may get relief from federal requirements that they prepare "Total Maximum Daily Load" (TMDL) listings for the Columbia River system.[65] This is a recurring pattern in the environmental law context: federal officials threaten an enormous, invasive and unnecessary expansion of federal authority, and then back off in exchange for policy concessions by state officials in other areas.

Oregon Representative Elizabeth Furse and Idaho Representative Mike Crapo, the anti-transportation leaders of the Northwest Congressional delegation, went so far as to demand that gas abatement structures "be completed at all mainstem projects by March 1, 1997"—three months after they issued their demand.[66] That was utterly impossible, and probably would have been illegal, since Congress has yet to appropriate money for gas abatement construction.

Chairman Lorenzen still tells the press that the Commission "strive[s] to apply the same scientific standards to anyone who comes before them".[67] If the Commission strives, it certainly fails miserably. No private citizen could get a water quality standard set aside by showing up in front of the Commission unable to answer the simplest questions.

NOTES TO CHAPTER 12

[1] Reprinted in K. Petersen, *River of Life, Channel of Death* 139.

[2] C. Long, F. Ossiander, T. Ruehle & G. Matthews, "Survival of Coho Salmon Fingerlings Passing through Operating Turbines with and without Perforated Bulkheads and of Steelhead Trout Fingerlings Passing Through Spillways with and without a Flow Deflector", NMFS NW Fish. Sci. Center. (1975).

[3] B. Rudolph, "Latest Survival Research Highlighted at IT Meeting", *NW Fishletter*, Nov. 11, 1997; *see also* BPA, "Interim Research Monitoring, and Evaluation Program to Support the FCRPS Biological Opinion and Recovery Plan", at 23 (Nov. 15, 1995 draft) (similar results elsewhere).

[4] NMFS, Biological Opinion on FCRPS Operations, Mar. 2, 1995, at 109.

[5] Memo, J. Ruff & B. Hevlin to Implementation Team, April 22, 1997, Attachment (3), at 1.

[6] NMFS, Biological Opinion on FCRPS Operations, Mar. 2, 1995, at 106.

[7] USACE, Memorandum for the Record, Aug. 15, 1997, at 2 (CENWP-PE-E (1146)) (Review of "Relative Survival of Juvenile Salmon Passing Through the Spillway and Ice and Trash Sluiceway of The Dalles Dam", Admin. Code MPE-P-92-2).

[8] Memo, J. Ruff & B. Hevlin to Implementation Team, April 22, 1997, Attachment (3), at 1.

[9] Letter, T. Strong to W. Stelle, Jr., Mar. 14, 1997, at 3.

[10] *See generally*, D. Weitkamp & M. Katz, "A Review of Dissolved Gas Supersaturation Literature", *Trans. of the Am. Fish. Soc.* 109:659-702 (1980).

[11] *Id.* at 675.

[12] This phrase was originally applied to the decisions of the popes from their *cathedra*, or chair.

[13] K. Lee, "Rebuilding Confidence: Salmon, Science, and Law in the Columbia Basin", 21 Envt'l Law 745, 795 (1991) (footnotes omitted).

[14] *Northwest Resource Information Center v. Northwest Power Planning Council*, 35 F.3d 1371, 1391 (9th Cir. 1994). This case is the subject of extensive commentary in Chapter 9.

[15] *See, e.g.,* "Fish passage projects under scrutiny", *The Northwest Salmon Recovery Report*, Oct. 24, 1997, at 10. This article, in a newsletter focused on salmon recovery, actually confuses FGE (Fish Guidance Efficiency) with Fish Passage Efficiency (FPE). FGE is the percentage of smolts that a particular bypass system, like screens, will catch. It has even less of a relationship to survival than FPE does.

[16] From J. Anderson, "Impact of 1995 River Operations on Smolt Survival", Sept. 7, 1995, at 7 (Figure 7).

[17] BPA, "Interim Research, Monitoring, and Evaluation Program to Support the FCRPS Biological Opinion and Recovery Plan", at 29 n.5 (Nov. 15, 1995 Draft).

[18] A. Gore, *Earth in the Balance.*

[19] *See, e.g.,* J. Anderson, "The Impacts of a Spill Program", Jan. 12, 1995.

[20] Letter, G. Bouck to R. Baumgartner, Dec. 22, 1994, at 1.

[21] NMFS, Biological Opinion on FCRPS Operations, Mar. 2, 1995, at 107.

[22] Quoted in B. Rudolph, "TMT Wrestles with Questions of Barging and Spill", *Clearing Up*, May 19, 1997, at 9.

[23] The most recent study of this phenomenon is T. Bjornn *et al.*, "Passage of Adult Chinook Salmon and Steelhead Past Dams and Through Reservoirs in the Lower Snake River and into Tributaries", conducted for the U.S. Army Corps of Engineers and BPA.

[24] *Id.* (quoting R. Heineth of the Columbia River Inter-Tribal Fish Commission).

[25] Memo, J. Ruff to B. Hevlin, April 22, 1997, Attachment (3), at 1.

[26] Montgomery Watson, Report for Contract No. DE-AC79-93BP66208, "Task 5—Review of Monitoring Plans for Gas Bubble Disease Signs and Gas Supersaturation Levels on the Columbia and Snake Rivers", at 48 (Oct. 18, 1994).

[27] *See generally* Salmon Spill Policy on the Columbia and Snake Rivers, Hearings before the Senate Subcommittee on Drinking Water, Fisheries and Wildlife of the Committee on Environment and Public Works, S. Hrng. 104-291, June 22, 1995, at 33 (NMFS officials concede that more symptoms are visible at higher powers).

[28] "Comparison of Clinical Signs of Gas Bubble Disease in the Gills of Smolts Using both Compound and Dissecting Microscopes", Report for Contract No. DE-AC79-93B966208, at 9 (BPA Aug. 25, 1995).

[29] Salmon Spill Policy Hearing, June 22, 1995, at 33.

[30] Letter, L. Fidler to R. Baumgartner, Jan. 9, 1995, at 1.

[31] B. Monroe, "Nitrogen kills Willamette salmon", The Oregonian, March 1, 1995, at A15.

[32] Letter, R. Johnson to ODFW Custodian of Records, March 1, 1995.

[33] Memo, L. Taylor to EQC, Mar. 15, 1995, at B-12.

[34] *Id.* at B-3.

[35] Quoted in Letter, M. Sanchotena to B. Lovelin, May 30, 1995, at 1.

[36] 1995 BO, at 108.

[37] ISG, *Return to the River* 201.

[38] Letter, M. DeHart to M. Schneider, Dec. 20, 1996, at 1; Letter, S. Pettit to M. Schneider [undated], at 1.

[39] *See* 42 Fed. Reg. _____ (April 22, 1992) (referring to "large numbers of chinook salmon released from lower Columbia River hatcheries).

[40] Letter, J. Nielsen *et al.* to B. Brown, Mar. 25, 1996, at 3.

[41] Letter, M. Hatfield to W. Stelle, Jr., May 10, 1996, at 1.

[42] *See* "Bubble Reabsorption in a Simulated Smolt Bypass System -- Concept Assessment", Final Report, BPA Contract No. DE-AC79-93BP66208 (Aug. 7, 1995), p. ES-1.

[43] *Id.* at 6-1.

[44] J. McCann, "Results of 1995 GBT Juvenile Salmon Monitoring Program and 1996 Monitoring Proposal" (FPC Oct. 18, 1995), at 9 (concluding 1995 monitoring program a success).

[45] ISG, *Return to the River* 60.

[46] *Id.* at 323.

[47] S. Cramer, "Seasonal Changes During 1996 in Survival of Yearling Chinook Smolts Through the Snake River as Estimated from Detections of PIT Tags", Aug. 1996, at 1 (Figure 1).

[48] Chart presented to Implementation Team by John Williams, attached to Letter, B. Lovelin to H. Lorenzen *et al.*, Feb. 21, 1997.

[49] B. Monk, R. Absolon, & E. Dawley, "Changes in Gas Bubble Disease Signs and Survival of Migrating Juvenile Salmonids Experimentally Exposed to Supersaturated Gasses, 1996" (NMFS 1997).

[50] Letter, B. Lovelin to H. Lorenzen *et al.*, Feb. 21, 1997, at 5.

[51] Memo, L. Marsh to EQC, Feb. 28, 1997, at 1.

[52] B. Rudolph, "Oregon Will Grant NMFS Spill Waiver", *NW Fishletter*, Mar. 5, 1997, at 2 (citing NMFS calculation).

[53] Memo, L. Marsh to EQC, Feb. 28, 1997, at 3 (discussing April spill).

[54] *Id.* at 8.

[55] *Id.* at 10.

[56] B. Rudolph, "Oregon Will Grant NMFS Spill Waiver", *NW Fishletter*, Mar. 5, 1997, at 2.

[57] *Id.* at 3.

[58] *Id.* at 2.

[59] Spreadsheet by Gary Fredericks (NMFS), Feb. 11, 1997 (handed out at TMT meeting).

[60] EQC Order, April 18, 1997, Exhibit A, at 4.

[61] *Id.*

[62] R. Peters, quoted in Dissolved Gas Team Meeting Notes, Oct. 15, 1996, at 2.

[63] Quoted in Implementation Team Meeting Notes, Nov. 7, 1996, at 8.

[64] Letter, R. Boyce (ODFW) & M. Powelson (NWPPC) to B. Hevlin (NMFS) & J. Ruff (NWPPC), Sept. 9, 1997, at 2.

[65] *See* Dissolved Gas Team Meeting Notes, Oct. 15, 1996, at 2 (reporting comment by ODEQ's Russell Harding that "the MOU could very well substitute for a TMDL listing for the Columbia system").

[66] Letter, E. Furse and M. Crapo to R. Hardy *et al.*, Dec. 9, 1996, at 3.

[67] Reported in B. Rudolph, "Oregon Water Agency Wavers on NMFS Spill Waiver", *Clearing Up*, Mar. 10, 1997, at 8.

CHAPTER 13: WHY FUNDAMENTAL STRUCTURAL CHANGE IN SALMON REGULATION IS NECESSARY FOR RATIONAL SALMON RECOVERY PLANNING

> ". . . politics doesn't work. Look at the parts of America where the government has had the most power, where government has spent the most money. Look at those housing projects we've got the poor people in. Then say to yourself, 'What the government has done for folks in the inner cities, it can do *that* for spotted owls.'" P. J. O'Rourke, "Republicans Take Control of Congress"

> "A plain husband-man is more Prudent in the affaires of his own house, than a Privy Counselor in the affaires of other men". T. Hobbes, *Leviathan*

Every outside observer of salmon regulation has recognized for many years that the system is hopelessly broken. In 1983, a law review article pointed out that Congress and the courts "have unwittingly multiplied management authority to the point where the very institutions designed to protect the resource have now, by virtue of their numbers and their unwieldiness, become an additional threat."[1] As Judge Marsh observed, that was how things were before the salmon were listed under the Endangered Species Act, adding "yet *another* layer of regulatory restriction . . .".[2] By 1997, as Senator Gordon Smith recently pointed out, "[w]e have multi-layers of bureaucracy that are doing a lot of talking and stepping all over one another, but not saving any salmon."[3] State and tribal fishery managers are proliferating like the shad, their rise in numbers fueled by a river of money extorted from the Bonneville Power Administration.

The Fishery Agencies' Fundamental Conflict of Interest in Salmon Preservation

Putting fishery managers in charge of the administration of the Endangered Species Act for fish was a colossal mistake. Fishery managers see salmon not as an endangered wild animal to be protected but as a natural resource to be fully exploited. In this respect, fishery managers are the guardians of the salmon just as federal and state forestry agencies are guardians of the forest. And the results have been the same: overfishing is the analogue to the massive clearcutting (without replanting) that has characterized much forestry management, at least until recently.

The National Marine Fisheries Service in particular has a built-in conflict of interest when it comes to protecting salmon as wild animals. Congress has charged NMFS to "promote" commercial salmon harvest under the Magnuson Act.[4] Indeed, NMFS was formerly named the "Bureau of Commercial Fisheries".

NMFS has the authority, delegated from the Secretary of Commerce, to protect threatened and endangered salmon under the Endangered Species Act. The result is an endangered species program that is unique in the country: it is lawful to commercially harvest endangered salmon (NMFS issues so-called "incidental take statements" for commercial harvest), but unlawful to kill them by any other means. This has all the wisdom of the federal policy toward tobacco, which for many years subsidized its growth while at the same time discouraging its use.

Environmentalist and Oregon State University professor David Bella reportedly criticizes natural resource managers because "they tend to place first priority on their own survival"—"even if this means trouble for whatever or whomever they are supposed to protect. Organizations selectively produce and sustain information favorable to them . . . Contrary assessments tend to be systemmatically filtered out."[5] Although Professor Bella was talking about the resource agencies' treatment of his ecological concerns, he describes precisely what has happened to the scientific information presented in this book. It has been simply "filtered out" by harvest managers.

Over the years, the harvest agencies have become more and more blatant about using their authority under the Endangered Species Act to extract money from dam operators. In one of the first biological opinions NMFS issued concerning operation of the Federal Columbia River Power System, NMFS demanded from the Bonneville Power Administration a $40 million slush fund for unspecified salmon programs, as a condition of granting a "no jeopardy" biological opinion. BPA paid up. (Luckily, after the states and tribes accelerated their efforts to shut down useful scientific research, some of the slush fund money kept worthy projects going.)

By 1997, NMFS had expanded the shakedown to the Oregon State Legislature. After threatening to list the Oregon coastal coho as endangered, Regional Director Will Stelle appeared before the Oregon Legislature on February 11, 1997 to tell them that Oregon's plans to protect the coho needed a more solid financial base, and that they should raise taxes to pay for salmon recovery if they wanted to avoid an endangered species listing. Only one of the Oregon legislators, Sen. Ted Ferrioli of John Day, had the perspicacity to question Stelle's demands, calling the process "extortionary".[6]

328

Oregon's timber industry, anxious to avoid a federal shutdown of coastal timber harvest, has been quick to cave into the blackmail, offering to pledge $15 million to avoid an endangered species listing for Oregon coastal coho salmon—provided that the Oregon legislature matches their pledge. But money is not enough for NMFS. They want additional regulatory authority to improve salmon habitat too. Only then might NMFS stop threatening a coho listing.[7] But even after the timber industry and the Oregon legislature caved in, nothing stopped environmentalists from suing for a coho listing. As of 1997, the suit is pending.

Defining "Mitigation" for Hydropower Operations

Until recently, many measured society's commitment to salmon by the amount of money devoted to salmon recovery. Most of the money comes from citizens of the Pacific Northwest, collected through their payments for electricity, and funneled through public utilities to the Bonneville Power Administration. A spectacularly successful coalition of state and tribal fishery agencies, allied with environmentalists and the media, have extracted higher and higher payments from BPA since 1980. Unfortunately, after the general collapse of legal constraints on agency behavior, nothing assures that all this money is spent in any sensible way. It isn't.

The concept that the adverse effects of federal projects upon fish and wildlife should be mitigated is expressed in literally dozens of federal statutes and regulations. The concept is simple: a scientific effort is made to quantify the adverse effect, and then some sort of program is devised to offset that adverse effect. The U.S. Army Corps of Engineers, having the most experience in planning mitigation for the construction of federal water projects, has extensive regulations intended to produce a rational, cost-effective approach to fish and wildlife mitigation. They are all ignored.

The fish and wildlife statutes are so vague that Congress has essentially turned armies of fish bureaucrats loose to demand "mitigation" without any guidance whatsoever. Back before President Roosevelt's threats to pack the Supreme Court produced the "switch in time that saved nine", these sorts of statutes would have been held unconstitutional as "delegation run riot".

It is not an easy problem to figure out what it means to "mitigate" for dam construction and operations. The first problem is that no one really knows what the adverse effects of dam construction were. Nobody really knows how many salmon ran in the Columbia River before it was dammed. As far back as 1940, observers recognized this, reporting that at Bonneville Dam "391,595 ascending chinooks were counted. Is this number large or small? Who knows? The biologists do not. They have no basis of comparison; never before have the fish in a vast stream been counted at all."[8] In 1994, 400,000 chinook salmon entered the river.[9] A higher percentage are hatchery fish now, but no one really knows how much higher.

The Northwest Power Planning Council is charged in the Northwest Power Act to devise a plan to mitigate for the adverse impacts of hydropower development in the Columbia River Basin. Obviously, the scope of the plan depends on some assessment of how many salmon have been lost, and why. By the early 1980s, salmon advocates began to realize that they needed a benchmark against which to measure the progress in salmon restoration, a benchmark against which present efforts would fall far short. They convinced the Council to settle on the number of salmon that had run in the Columbia before it was dammed, ultimately inducing the Council to declare that historical salmon runs averaged 16 million fish.

Dr. Don Chapman reviewed the historical evidence and concluded that the Council's 16 million figure "cannot be supported by historical information and careful inference".[10] He reviewed the extensive data on historical catches of salmon and concluded that the total runs for all salmon and steelhead species probably ranged from 7.5 to 8.9 million fish.[11] The Pacific Fishery Management Council, using available habitat areas to estimate runs, came up with a similar estimate of 6.2 million for salmon species.[12]

This huge disparity between the Council's estimates and those of independent scientists continues to be noted in salmon recovery literature, with no resolution of which view is correct.[13] Even quasi-scientific reviews, like the Northwest Power Planning Council's *Return to the River* report, continue to cite the Council's political estimates as scientific fact.[14]

Salmon advocates then induced the Northwest Power Planning Council to declare that dams were responsible for about 80% of the decline from historic peaks. This figure, widely publicized by the Council and others, has been been cited by dam opponents over and over and over again.[15] Later, the figure was, by improper citation, recharacterized as an estimate of the National Marine Fisheries Service.[16] It is now repeatedly echoed in solemn judicial opinions as a finding of fact: "NMFS estimates that approximately 80% of historical salmon losses are attributable to hydropower development and operation".[17] This statistic, unquestioned in the courts, media or elsewhere, is utterly false and a key supporting element of the Great Salmon Hoax.

Here is how the Northwest Power Planning Council got the number. In Appendix E to the 1987 Columbia River Basin Fish and Wildlife Program, the Council staff provided two alternative means of computing "numerical estimates of hydropower-related losses". "Alternative 2", the more simple alternative, simply posited the equation:

Total loss * Percent hydropower purpose of dams = Hydropower-related losses

This produced a "resulting hydropower contribution range" from "about 5 million to 11 million fish".[18] Under this approach, the Council was to pretend that dams caused all salmon losses since 1850, and then was to use pre-existing estimates (prepared for federal accounting purposes) of the proportion of hydropower-related investment at the dams to reduce hydropower's share of the losses.

Alternative 1 was superficially more reasonable, but came to precisely the same result because of highly unreasonable assumptions. This approach attempted to estimate the ultimate survival of salmon with and without dams, going step by step through the stages of the salmon life cycle. The faulty assumptions were legion. To name just a few, the staff ignored pre-dam losses, assumed that each and every fish that died in the river died because of the dams, and ignored all beneficial effects of transportation and spill.[19]

The Council staff then proceeded on the "theory . . . that non-hydropower development effects (*e.g.*, irrigation, fishing, logging, mining, grazing, agriculture, urbanization, pollution and other effects) are largely reversible so hydropower caused all the mortalities that would occur if predevelopment run sizes existed".[20] They did not explain how removing dams would, by hypothesis, de-populate the Pacific Northwest and restore pristine conditions prevailing prior to 1850. The idea that salmon runs, but for dams, would be much higher than the runs *actually were* before the dams has long been a trick used by fishery agencies seeking mitigation funding.[21]

In the 1987 Columbia River Fish and Wildlife Program itself, the Council summarized these estimates, baldly asserting that "all reasonable approaches would result in loss estimates in this range".[22] The Council concluded that ". . . the salmon and steelhead run size has declined by more than 10 million from all causes. Of that 10 million, about 8 million can be attributed to the hydropower system."[23] The U.S. Army Corps of Engineers commented that "there [wa]s no sound factual basis" for the Council's conclusions, a view shared by all electric power interests at the time.[24] In its 1994 Fish and Wildlife Program, the Council reaffirmed the estimate.

Thus it is an article of faith among most Northwestern policymakers that the dams singlehandedly destroyed 80% of the salmon runs. No one questions the logic of taking the historic peak in salmon runs, decades before the first dam was ever built, long before the sustained development of a salmon canning industry that sent Columbia River salmon to dinner tables around the world, and arbitrarily attributing 80% of the decline to dams.

Lacking a statutory definition of "mitigation", everyone in the Columbia River Basin assumed for decades that replacing wild fish with hatchery fish was mitigation. The U.S. Army Corps of Engineers would figure out how many fish might be lost as a result of constructing a dam, and how many hatcheries would have to be built to replace them. This was a hugely successful, although expensive, effort.

Hatchery releases kept up total production for decades, even in the face of sustained or increasing fishing pressure. This has not made everyone happy. From the perspective of the tribes and upriver interests, what matters is the number of salmon they have been able to catch in the river. They look at the simple fact that the numbers of salmon they have been able to catch have dwindled as the number of dams has increased, and leap to the conclusion that the dams are responsible. They don't consider the effect of others who have intercepted the fish first.

It also seems as if fishery managers made conscious choices to favor commercial harvest interests by siting hatcheries in downriver locations. In 1986, the Council staff concluded that a "dramatic effect of mitigation activities for hydropower and for multipurpose developments has been to strengthen fish propagation in the lower Columbia River Basin without attempting to rebuild upriver runs. A related effect has been to increase the proportion of hatchery fish to the overall outmigration."[25]

For at least ten years, however, conservation biologists have been pushing to redefine "mitigation" to require the replacement of lost *natural* production of salmon.[26] This is an enormous shift in public policy, and one that has so far occurred without any democratic input whatsoever, in the form of laws or even policy guidance from Congress or other elected representatives. To fully replace lost natural production of salmon is impossible without evacuating the Pacific Northwest. Efforts to replace lost natural production inevitably have the effect of limiting and even reversing development of the Pacific Northwest. This serves all the goals of conservation biologists, but may not serve the public interest.

Special Obligations Owed to Native Americans

In 1855, Territorial Governor Isaac Ingalls Stevens signed peace treaties with the Yakama, Walla Walla, Cayuse, Nez Perce, Spokane and other tribes. The tribes relinquished claim to over 60,000 acres of land and moved to reservations, although the government did not, as in so many other horrific cases, force immediate relocations.[27]

The express promise in the Treaties concerning salmon was that the Native Americans would be guaranteed the right "to fish at their usual and accustomed grounds and stations . . . in common with the citizens of the Territory". The U.S. Indian Commissioner wrote in 1882 that this phrase was inserted "to give to the settlers there an equal privilege in that which heretofore had been exclusively enjoyed by the Indians".[28] The modern, politically-correct interpretation is that the tribes' right to go fishing means a right to catch fish, and even imposes an obligation on the federal government to supply fish to catch. (And maybe even to supply those fish by the restoration of historic environmental conditions.) Governor Stevens did make some extravagant promises to the tribes, telling one group of Indians gathered at Point-No-Point that "[t]his paper secures your fish. Does not a father give food to his children?".[29]

The States of Oregon and Washington for many years attempted to restrict tribal fishing rights under the Treaties. In a series of historic cases, the federal government finally stepped in to stop the state fishery managers from discriminating against the tribal fishermen. One Judge, Judge Boldt, actually spent three years hearing arguments and collecting live testimony—unlike salmon judges since. The state fishery managers argued that tribal harvests had to be curtailed to "conserve" fish, even as the non-tribal harvests expanded. Put to the test of actually presenting evidence, the state fishery managers failed. Judge Boldt observed that "the near total absence of substantive evidence to support these apparent falsehoods was a considerable surprise to this court".[30]

Judge Boldt interpreted the Treaties giving the tribes the right to fish "in common with" the white settlers as allowing the tribes half the available catch. While his decision was on appeal, the State of Washington and the commercial fishermen largely ignored the orders. The United States Court of Appeals for the Ninth Circuit noted that Judge Boldt "faced the most concerted effort to frustrate a decree of a federal court witnessed in this century"—with the exception of some desegregation cases.[31] The Washington State Supreme Court went so far as to declare that the State Department of Fisheries and Game could not enforce any aspect of Judge Boldt's ruling. Eventually, the United States Supreme Court affirmed Judge Boldt's ruling, and opposition died down. (To me, this lawlessness of fisheries agencies was the precedent for how they would apply the Endangered Species Act to the question of harvesting endangered salmon.)

Although media shills for the tribes report that "federal courts have ruled that longstanding treaties with the United States guarantee the availability of salmon for tribal harvest",[32] courts have not yet adopted this politically-correct view. In fact, the most recent case addressing that question, brought by the Nez Perce Tribe against Idaho Power Company, produced an opinion to the contrary:

> "... the 1855 treaty does not provide a guarantee that there will be no decline in the number of fish available to take. The only method that would guarantee such protection would be to prevent all types of development, whether or not discriminatory of Indian treaty rights. The Stevens treaties simply do not provide the Tribe with such assurance or protection."[33]

Notwithstanding their failure in this and other cases, the tribes continue to threaten to sue the United States for breach of the Treaties on account of decreased salmon runs, which they attribute to dam construction and operation.

It is reasonable to conclude that the United States breached the Treaties as the dams were built. The resulting reservoirs flooded many "usual and accustomed fishing places". The substitute shoreland conveyed to the tribes didn't measure up: nothing could replace Celilo Falls as a place to catch salmon with dipnets, although the tribes' switch to gillnets could in theory yield catches just as large. Most importantly, until recently, most mitigation hatcheries were generally built downriver, where they wouldn't do the tribes much good.

The federal government did pay the tribes damages for its breach of the Treaties. In the case of the historic fishery at Celilo Falls, the Oregon Fish Commission and U.S. Fish and Wildlife Service biologists concluded that the tribes had taken approximately 2,500,000 pounds of salmon annually, worth about $700,000. Accordingly, the federal government compensated the four tribes controlling the fishery with $23 million in government bonds bearing 3 percent interest (thus providing $690,000 annual interest).[34] The Corps of Engineers also agreed to construct 400 acres of fishing access sites to replace the ones innundated by the Dam.[35]

The Warm Springs Tribe, now one of the richest tribes, invested the money.[36] The Umatilla Tribe got $4,198,000, which was distributed in $3,494.61 per capita payments.[37] Bill Yallup, of the Yakama Tribe, says: "They gave people five thousand dollars apiece and I remember when I was growing up I could see a lot of those five-thousand-dollar cars in our yards. We played on them after they broke down and quit running."[38]

In the case of the Colville Tribe, whose much smaller fishery was destroyed by Grand Coulee Dam, the Tribe finally collected a lump sum settlement of $53 million in the 1990s, along with an annual payment of about $15 million.[39] In 1997, BPA spent $2.5 million to buy the Nez Perce Tribe a 10,300 acre cattle ranch in Northeastern Oregon.[40] There have been many, many other payments over the years.

The tribes have also collected enormous sums through BPA contracts designed to implement the Northwest Power Planning Council's Fish and Wildlife Program:[41]

BPA Contract Dollars Obligated to Tribes: 1978-1996

Yakama Indian Nation (Washington)	$20,996,065
Colville Confederated Tribes	18,836,714
Nez Perce Tribe (Idaho)	17,187,496
Umatilla Tribes (Oregon)	13,200,231
Shoshone-Bannock Tribes (Idaho)	10,717,202
Spokane Tribe (Washington)	7,856,919
Columbia River Intertribal Fish Comm'n	3,582,535
Kalispel Tribe (Washington)	3,786,661
Kootenai Tribe of Idaho	3,755,132
Warm Springs Tribes (Oregon)	3,549,801
Salish-Kootenai Tribes (Montana)	3,462,677
Coeur D'Alene Tribe of Idaho	2,245,969
Shoshone-Paiute Tribes (Nevada)	966,392

This list includes only contract obligations in BPA's Fish and Wildlife Division computer. The tribes have also collected monies from other Divisions, monies in legal settlements (e.g., the Colville's $53 million is not reflected above), and large sums from other federal agencies, particularly the U.S. Army Corps of Engineers.

There is no comprehensive record of all the compensation paid to the tribes over the years. There never will be unless and until some powerful person directs that such a record be prepared. In the Clinton/Gore Administration, no one perceives it useful to their careers to bring up the question. It is possible that the total payments to the tribes have exceeded the capitalized value of all salmon caught by the Native Americans that survived white settlement. In other words, it is entirely possible that although we breached the Treaties, we have already paid more than reasonable damages for the breach of those Treaties.

But as in science, the concept of actually measuring what we do is on the decline in law. Treating Native Americans as legally incompetent—like children—courts assert that federal agencies stand in a fiduciary relationship to

335

the tribes and have a "trust responsibility" to protect natural resources important to the tribes.[42] The irony of the tribes' status as both independent sovereigns (entitled by White House fiat to "nation-to-nation" consultations on salmon decisions), and children who must be taken care of, escapes the courts and commentators.

Many of the tribes have a straightforward and unabashed interest in shaking down federal bureaucracies and others for money, which they have developed to a high art. The Shoshone-Bannock Tribes in Idaho have been trying for years to get water rights so that they can sell the water to the Bonneville Power Administration.[43] As of 1997, the Nez Perce Tribe, which has claims pending in Idaho State Court for water rights to the entire flow of the Snake River, is trying to settle the claims in exchange for taking out the Lower Snake Dams. Their formal proposal to do this has circulated at the highest levels in the Clinton/Gore Interior Department and Justice Department. Federal officials refuse to release a copy of the proposal, however, claiming that it is "privileged".

Threats to the Golden Goose

The Bonneville Power Administration was charged to bring Columbia River electric power to the people at cost. Back then, the cost was well below the higher rates charged by private utilities. The Administrator employs an immense staff, which accounts for much of the cost of generating electricity. But for most of BPA's history, the largest cost was the cost of the dams. BPA was bound to repay the Federal Treasury for money borrowed to construct the dams.

The Administrator is directed to hold formal hearings and, based upon the record established in the hearings, set rates to recover those costs. Bonneville's customers, public and private utilities and direct service industrial customers, review BPA's accounting methods for compliance with the statutory rate setting directives. They argue about how costs should be allocated among the customers, and how costs can be controlled. They are the watchdogs who pay the most attention to BPA.

For decades, fish costs did not rise to a level sufficient to make much difference in BPA rates. In the early and middle 1980s, only the Pacific Northwest Utilities Conference Committee, led by Al Wright, paid a great deal of attention to fish and wildlife issues, occasionally providing BPA with white papers on accounting for fish costs. Most of the Great Salmon Hoax, including the flow-survival hypothesis, the Power Planning Council's blaming of dams for historic salmon losses, and the beginning of the attack on smolt transportation, arose during this period of time as BPA's customers slept.

336

As the fishery agencies and tribes began advancing more and more strident demands for flow-based programs, BPA's costs began to rise significantly. Under the statutory rate-setting directives, BPA's rates would collect every dollar of salmon costs from its customers. Many of BPA's wholesale customers depended upon BPA for all their electricity needs, and would pass BPA's rate increases along to their customers, the citizens of the Pacific Northwest. In the long run, every dollar that BPA costs increase for fish and wildlife programs is a dollar taxed from companies and individuals in the Pacific Northwest.

But the dams were not constructed merely for the generation of electric power. Congress specifically declared that half the reason to build Bonneville Dam was flood control. Each of the federal projects has a series of Congressionally-authorized purposes: hydroelectricity, flood control, navigation, recreation, etc. And the U.S. Army Corps of Engineers and U.S. Bureau of Reclamation, which operate the dams, have accounts that were established pursuant to a formal inter-agency memorandum, specifying how much of the cost at each dam is to be charged to each purpose.

Under the Northwest Power Act, fish and wildlife costs are supposed to be split between BPA and the other federal agencies on the basis of those accounts. But in the early 1980s, when BPA sought to enforce the law, the Reagan administration said no. By the 1990s, BPA had collected more than $325 million from electric ratepayers that was supposed to have been paid by the other agencies—in other words, by the U.S. Treasury. BPA has never refunded the money.

By 1994, profound pro-competitive changes that had been underway for some years in the structure of the electric power industry began to bear fruit, as wholesale power rates began an inexorable decline. (Retail power rates, propped up by state-granted monopolies, continued to drift steadily upward.) It became clear that BPA's expenses had risen to such extraordinary levels that one could build brand-new natural gas turbine generators and produce power that could be sold at prices below BPA's.

This was remarkable, because hydroelectric power has no fuel costs, and most of the capital costs were accumulated decades ago. Indeed, BPA's real cost to generate hydroelectric power is only about half a cent per kilowatt-hour. (Retail customers in the Northwest typically pay around five cents.) But on top of that half a cent per kilowatt-hour came a series of crushing burdens. First, prodded by environmentalists, Congress decreed that BPA promote "conservation", which in practice turned into a series of cash subsidies for a variety of ill-conceived ventures. For a time, BPA even handed out a $2,000 subsidy for each manufactured home built in the Northwest—provided that

337

they were "efficient" and all-electric. Thus BPA required manufacturers *not* to use gas heat, which, where available, is far more efficient.

Second, BPA, using dire threats of a power shortage based on projections of energy consumption that turned out to be fanciful, pushed utilities in the Pacific Northwest to build nuclear plants. None turned out well, particularly the five-plant scheme of the Washington Public Power Supply System (WPPSS). WPPSS issued bonds to raise money for the construction of the plants, and when a combination of gross mismanagement and Carter-era inflation caused huge cost overruns, WPPSS defaulted on the bonds.

When the bondholders sued WPPSS, the Supreme Court of Washington declared the bonds null and void. The bondholders sought review by the Supreme Court of the United States. Ducking its obligation to enforce the unfashionable Contracts Clause in the Constitution, as it has for decades, the Supreme Court refused to review the case.

Once again, politically-driven decisions by the legal system produced a mess: a multi-billion dollar obligation. The bondholders moved to federal court and charged fraud on the part of WPPSS and its participants, and eventually won a $600 million settlement. BPA volunteered to fund significant portions of the settlement and guarantee the remaining bonds. When ratepayers challenged BPA's generosity, the Ninth Circuit held that the Administrator had broad authority to settle disputes, and the courts would not second-guess the wisdom of his decisions. That is another textbook example of the mess that results when there is no real law to apply and Congress simply punts an issue to federal bureaucrats.

In any event, BPA's wholesale electric power rates consist primarily of three components: 1/2¢ for generating electricity, 1¢ for bailing out peddlers of bogus bonds and nuclear plant mismanagement, and 1/2¢ for salmon and wildlife protection and other "public purpose" programs (like conservation). Another way of looking at this is that but for the series of bad decisions by federal bureaucrats and judges, electric power rates for BPA customers could easily be far lower than they are.

Former Oregon Senator Mark Hatfield, who devoted his career to, among other things, protecting BPA, was one of the first to see that spiraling fish and wildlife costs posed a threat to BPA's future. He pushed hard for a solution. One of his former staffers, Jack Robertson, now at BPA, thought BPA's salmon problem could be solved like the striped bass problem in the Hudson River in New York. He proposed to create a trust fund for improvements in salmon habitat and other measures. What Robertson failed to appreciate is that the most critical element of the recovery of striped bass was simple: the commercial harvest of striped bass was shut down.

338

Robertson tirelessly promoted the idea of setting aside a portion of BPA revenues into a trust fund, but no one would settle for a fixed and bounded amount of salmon funding, and the idea never came to fruition. Instead of attempting to focus on what salmon needed, the fish advocates focused on extracting as much money as possible from BPA. The Trust Fund was one of the many casualties of a failure to define and limit "mitigation" obligations. As events later developed, only the potential collapse of BPA served to put any limit on salmon obligations.

By 1995, BPA was sounding the alarm that it could not continue to add salmon costs to its rates without losing sales. BPA's customers are not required to purchase power from BPA, although many have signed long-term contracts that limit their flexibility to switch suppliers quickly. Many other utilities have "captive" customers because they have state-sanctioned monopolies for the sale of electric power. If you want to buy electricity in most parts of Oregon, you have no choice but to buy from Pacific Power, or Portland General Electric, or the other local supplier. In Washington, there are no monopolies.

A utility without captive customers can experience a so-called "death spiral" as its costs rise. As customers switch to other suppliers, the cost per customer for the remaining customers goes up, more customers leave, and so on. BPA representative began to circulate charts showing that total revenues would decline as rates went further up, and began to sound alarms in Washington, D.C. If BPA revenues declined, BPA would be forced to stop making payments to the U.S. Treasury on the debts incurred to build the dams, and Congressional attention would be focused on BPA's profligate spending habits.

Senator Hatfield eventually persuaded the Clinton/Gore Administration that such a result was not in its interest. The Clinton/Gore Administration had enough sense not to want to kill the goose that is laying the golden eggs to distribute to its environmentalist and Native American constituencies in the Northwest.

In the fall of 1995, the Adminstration agreed to cap fish and wildlife expenditures by BPA at $435 million a year, a figure that was widely denounced as inadequate. Of that amount, somewhat more than half represented actual cash outlays, with the balance consisting of lost revenues and operational expenses to BPA from changes in hydropower operations (such as the cost of increased power purchases to cover power losses from spill and flow manipulation).

Roughly speaking, $130 million would go to "direct program expenses", mostly subsidies for the state and tribal fishery agencies. Around

$40 million would be handed out from BPA to other federal agencies. Capital expenditures for fish and wildlife would rise from $70 million to $156 million annually. And operational costs (including the lost revenues from spill and flow augmentation) were forecast to fall gradually from $195 million to $161 million.[44] Since the deal was struck, wet weather has significantly reduced the operational cost component.

In an attempt to blunt environmentalist criticism, the Administration agreed to take the $325 million in overpayments previously (and unlawfully) collected from ratepayers and to create a reserve fund for additional fish and wildlife spending. The Administration also agreed that other project purposes besides electricity would finally share in fish and wildlife costs, as required in the Northwest Power Act, to the tune of $40 to $60 million a year.

The Agreement was largely negotiated by National Marine Fisheries Service Regional Administrator Will Stelle, Jr., BPA Administrator Randy Hardy, and the then-Chairman of the Northwest Power Planning Council, Angus Duncan. Many of the other Council members were angered when they learned what Mr. Duncan had done; he had simply assumed the authority to act for the Council. In private meetings on Capitol Hill, Washington Senator Gorton told the Northwest representatives working on the Agreement, memorialized in a "Joint Statement", that none of the Senators thought that so much money was required. But the entire Delegation went along with the deal.

The Delegation blessed the Joint Statement negotiated by Duncan, Hardy and Stelle in a committee report accompanying an appropriations bill. The bill referred to the Joint Statement, setting overall spending guidelines and transforming broad spending limits into an affirmative mandate to spend the entire amount in accordance with detailed directives in the Joint Statement. The plan could be modified at will by the unanimous consent of BPA, NMFS and the Council.

The huge pot of money attracted flies from all over the Pacific Northwest. Legions of federal, state and tribal officials descended upon Washington to argue how the money should be spent. Fights over how to spend the money lasted for almost an entire year. The Interior Department and the tribes were particularly miffed to have been left out of the dealmaking, and wanted their projects funded as well. Throughout 1996, the tribes visited their Administration allies, presenting a message that "was harsh in tone and non-specific in the complaint department".[45] The White House delayed negotations for months by requiring the federal agencies to meet in "sovereign-to-sovereign" negotiations with each Tribe.

Like other Clinton/Gore Administration budget initiatives, the Memorandum of Agreement postponed the pain of budget limitations by borrowing for the present with the bills to come due after the year 2000. Under the agreement, over the six years it would be in effect (until 2001), BPA would essentially borrow another $800 million for capital expeditures.

As of 1997, the harvest managers in the Northwest are beginning to realize that if the $435 million per year spending level is extended after 2001, their share of spending is going to get cut way back by the need to repay the borrowing for the capital costs. The Vice Chairman of the Columbia River InterTribal Fish Commission, Wendell Harrigan, has been quoted as complaining that "the cap has already begun to strangle restoration efforts" and that extending the cap "will surely . . . provide the salmon with extinction certainty".[46]

As the states and tribes struggle to evade limits to spending, new schemes are emerging to protect BPA at the expense of electric ratepayers. There are proposals to *require* customers to buy BPA power no matter what the cost, proposals to extract monopoly profits using BPA's transmission lines, and a host of other means to keep BPA funding the Great Salmon Hoax. As this book goes to press, BPA has suggested that it might generate as much as $200 million a year through special transmission taxes, and negotiations are underway to send salmon spending correspondingly higher. No one is considering cutting wasteful expenditures on flow augmentation and spill as a means of funding other recovery measures.

The Lack of Fiscal Management in Existing Salmon Recovery Programs

A 1994 audit by the Inspector General of the U.S. Energy Department found that nearly all of the $300 million in fish and wildlife contracts awarded between 1990 and 1993 were awarded without competitive bidding. The audit also found that BPA didn't get what it paid for in three of the five specific contracts reviewed, worth $413,000, and in some cases paid twice for the same work.[47] This was the tip of the iceberg.

The audit did not move a single reporter in the Pacific Northwest to conduct further investigations. Not until 1996 did a reporter finally act. Linda Mapes works for the Spokane, Washington *Spokesman-Review,* and found a rich lode of material. Until others followed her lead with somewhat pale imitations of her work, she was the only reporter covering the story.

In addition to uncovering a total failure of management controls, she discovered extravagant spending that rivals the Pentagon and its legendary $200 toilet seats. She reported that BPA "pays for a four-state police force to patrol the Columbia and Snake for poachers and habitat vandals. It's a full time force of more than 35 officers, outfitted with state-of-the-art equipment, including an $85,000 fixed-wing airplane with $392,339 in heat-seeking radar equipment; night vision goggles at up to $5,011 a pair, $1,999 binoculars; infrared spotlights at $2,500 each; guns and body armor.

"Bonneville bought the troops a $127,999 three-bedroom house near Stanley, Idaho, and a $59,812 modular home. It also sprang for pickups; snowmobiles; all-terrain vehicles; a minivan; kayak; motorcycles; a $32,999 motor home; three $30,000 Zodiac boats; numerous chase boats and patrol boats with various outboard motors, radar and trailers; a $60,000 one-ton surveillance truck with covert intelligence equipment, and two horses for $3,400. The saddles and tack cost $4,600 and the horse trailer another $6,000.

"In 1995, the force spent $3.6 million, made 1,484 arrests and tracked down 139 illegally caught salmon."[48]

Ms. Mapes neglected to report that all this spending was not only wasteful, but also illegal. When it empowered BPA to spend money for fish and wildlife protection, Congress took care to specify that such expenditures "shall be in addition to, not in lieu of, other expenditures authorized or required from other entities under other agreements or provisions of law".[49] In other words, states should be taxing their own citizens to enforce their own fish and wildlife laws, not mooching off the electric ratepayers.

There is every reason to believe that is what they are doing. In February 1997, the Acting Chief of the State of Washington Department of Fish and Wildlife Enforcement Program, Ron Swatfigure, sent his officers a memo about "coding time" saying "I am sure that 6% of our time dedicated to habitat enforcement is not an accurate reflection of [the] reality of our time spent on this [reimburseable] issue".[50] Apparently that didn't work, because two days later he issued a directive that "all officers working the Columbia and Snake River system need to be coding **ALL** time to BPA".[51]

The festival of pork barrel spending on salmon has spread throughout the Columbia River Basin. The 1995 Annual Report of the Confederated Tribes of the Umatilla Indian Reservation boasts that "Salmon Corps" workers, in addition to restoring fish habitat, "cut and delivered 38 cords of firewood to tribal elders during 1995".[52]

Everyone involved with the process recognizes the problem, but no one has any real incentive to clean it up. One of the most vocal is Tom Vogel, a BPA biologist. He says "I don't see any accountability anywhere. I hate to see money go down a rat hole. . . . this is a crime. This thing has never gone anywhere because we don't know where we want to go. I can't tell what we are trying to achieve."[53] Witt Anderson of the Corps of Engineers is equally pessimistic: "I don't see us turning the corner anytime soon."[54]

Sometimes spending failures come from misconceptions as to what should be done to assist salmon. Environmentalists now claim that "[f]rom the 1940s into the 1970s fishery agencies viewed wood in streams as unnatural", so that "up to 90 percent of agency funds intended for fish habitat restoration were used for the removal of jammed debris".[55] While this is frequently cited as a criticism of early habitat efforts, there was some basis for the idea that debris was blocking access to salmon habitat. As with most things, details matter. Centralized directives to remove logs would not only remove debris that blocked access to spawning habitat, but also remove logs that were not blocking access, and creating small pools useful for juvenile salmon.

The saga of fishery agency efforts to remove woody debris, followed by the "back to nature" policy of leaving it there, is one of the many unexamined aspects of salmon recovery programs. Even the National Research Council couldn't come to a conclusion in its *Upstream* report, instead merely noting that while "removal and salvage logging of woody debris accumulations from streams w[as] encouraged and required", "[s]ince the early 1980s, the practice has largely been curtailed".[56] Did these early programs succeed? Are the new ones succeeding? No one bothers to measure the effects, and no one knows.

For many years, electric ratepayers have funded a program to repair and replace irrigation screens. These programs have never been tested. As the National Research Council pointed out, "[n]o study has balanced the net benefit of screens and comparison to the lost rearing habitat in irrigation canals and ditches downstream [*sic*] from the screens".[57] While they probably do some good, no one has tried to measure or quantify it.

Other failures have plagued habitat programs. Writer Joseph Cone cited one project to dump gravel in streams to replace habitat damaged by logging, where "the contractor had dumped the wrong size rocks into the stream. The rocks were the size of bowling balls, which . . . no chinook could move. Nevertheless, the project had been chalked up as 'completed successfully'."[58]

Investigating habitat spending, Linda Mapes of the Spokane, Washington *Spokesman-Review* found that

"BPA spent $938,990 to improve fish habitat along Oregon's Fifteenmile Creek near The Dalles from 1987 to 1989. The utility hired three independent scientists to review the project. Their 1993 study found no documented increase in returning fish, and said farmland erosion around the project and high water temperatures below it could wipe out any gains from the work. After that review, the utility spent another $1.7 million on the stream to continue the project . . ."[59]

Regrettably, Ms. Mapes never bothered to find out who was getting all this money, which probably would have made for an even better story. A similar project has been going on in the John Day River for nearly 20 years.[60]

The National Research Council concluded that "[d]espite the large amounts of time and money that have been devoted to habitat restoration and enhancement by federal agencies, state agencies, and others, few projects have been shown unequivocally to increase salmon populations".[61]

If BPA had an Administrator with any interest in discharging BPA's statutory responsibility to manage fish and wildlife spending, these sorts of problems might be remedied. But Congress gave BPA an excuse for mismanagement: BPA is supposed to act consistently with the fish and wildlife program proposed by the Northwest Power Planning Council, no matter how irrational that program is. The gubernatorial appointees to the Council typically think that their fish and wildlife program should include the pet projects of local politicians and agencies.

For a while, when Jim Luce was the head of Bonneville's Fish and Wildlife Division, he tried to put pressure on the fishery agencies to actually deliver results. As the son of a former Administrator of BPA, he had a long-term, responsible perspective for BPA. In early 1992, he could see the fishery program was getting out of control, with spiraling costs and no clear measurement of benefits. He got BPA's customers involved in a process called "Programs in Perspective", soliciting their input on critical policy questions. Those questions included: "To what extent have BPA ratepayers satisfied their obligation 'to protect, mitigate and enhance fish and wildlife', and how do we 'get credit' for their efforts?".[62] And "What is the appropriate responsibility of other federal and state agencies to assume financial responsibility for fish and wildlife recovery?"[63] He wondered whether BPA should commence a huge program for hatchery construction "before final decisions are made with respect to the appropriate mix of wild and hatchery fish".[64]

The result? The state and tribal harvest managers complained bitterly to the BPA Administrator. BPA's customers did not support Mr. Luce, and he was removed from his position. The Administrator hired a new Fish and Wildlife Division Head, Robert Lohn, who used to work for the Northwest Power Planning Council. Mr. Lohn seems to have adopted a formal policy of capitulation to the Council's pork barrel prioritization. According to him, questioning state and tribal spending involves "a balancing act of how to ask hard questions and maintain proper respect for other sovereigns".[65] His way of striking the balance is to never ask the hard questions, much less cut off the state and tribal programs that have wasted ratepayer money for years.

There is law that could allow private citizens to act directly to help clean up this mess: the False Claims Act. Successful litigants under the Act can get up to 30 percent of the amount the government recovers as a bounty. If you know of some outright fraud in the fish and wildlife spending, give me a call. I'll be glad to help you try and collect the bounty. Of course, the courts would probably decide that the Act cannot be applied to the state fishery agencies and tribes that are at the root of the problem. The Eleventh Amendment to the U.S. Constitution is supposed to prevent states from being sued in federal court, and the tribes are immune from suit. Law breaks down when the lawbreakers are government agencies and officials.

The Proliferation of Useless Committees and the Death of the Federal Advisory Committee Act

Lacking any clients who would testify to specific fraud in fish and wildlife contract, I focused on a different federal statute: the Federal Advisory Committee Act.

The billions of dollars expended on salmon recovery since 1980 have not produced much in the way of salmon, but they have produced an impressive salmon bureaucracy. Like the mythical hydra, the bureaucracy has many heads, which spend much of their time quarreling with one another. As a result, there is an incredible proliferation of committees established between and among federal agencies, state agencies, tribal authorities and other public and quasi public entities all of whom to purport to exercise some sort of jurisdiction over the salmon problem.

The Columbia Basin Fish and Wildlife Authority staff has prepared a diagram showing the linkages between all these committees. Here it is:

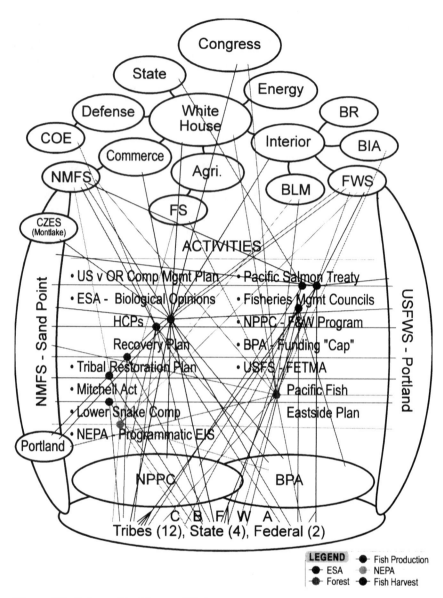

Figure 27: Salmon Entities and Roles

Looking at this diagram (which doesn't even include all the lines of communication), it is not hard to see that one of the principal obstacles to any success in the field of salmon recovery is the lack of any authority or accountability on the part of any agency for any aspect of the problem. Any single aspect of the salmon management has several agencies, all of whom, competing for funding and Washington, D.C.'s attention, tend to make inconsistent proposals. (After all, if they don't disagree, they have nothing to contribute to the meetings.) Any manager in private industry to came to his board of directors with a management structure like this would be told to fix it forthwith.

There is a federal law that was expressly designed to "prevent the proliferation of useless committees". It is the Federal Advisory Committee Act. The text of the law is simple. The Act regulates the use of any and all advisory committees by the President or any federal agency that are used to secure advice or recommendations for the President or federal officials (unless the committee is composed exclusively of federal employees). To limit the use of such committees, Congress required that each one be separately chartered with notice in the Federal Register. Congress could thus, in theory, keep its eyes on the problem of proliferating committees. The committees must also be balanced in terms of the points of view presented.

The Clinton/Gore Administration simply ignored this law when it came to salmon issues. The provision of the law that seemed to pose the most trouble for the Administration was the requirement that the committees be balanced in terms of the points of view presented and that their meetings be held open to the public, with opportunity for public participation.

The Administration's favored approach for resolving controversial and difficult policy issues seems to be to get together a group of its friends, who all share one point of view on an issue, and have the group labor at enormous expense in secrecy to come up with a set of recommendations which the Administration can then attempt to get enacted into law. This was the pattern established in the Administration's handling of health care reform, and it quickly extended to endangered species act questions as well.

When the question of whether to list the Alabama Sturgeon as endangered came to the attention of the Administration, the Administration quickly convened a group of scientists committed to the idea that the sturgeon should be listed. Groups opposed to the listing, who contended that there was no scientifically valid difference between the Alabama Sturgeon and any other of the more common sturgeon living in southern rivers, learned of the administration's plans and advised the Administration that the establishment of such a committee would violate FACA. The Justice Department quickly responded that the committee was not going to act as a committee. Rather, the individual scientists would present their own views, and there would be no collective group report.

Contrary to those representations, the scientists did produce a collective report, which recommended that the sturgeon be listed.

Accordingly, the Administration proposed to list the fish. Luckily, a federal district judge in Alabama was less than sympathetic to the Administration's plans. Finding that the Administration had violated FACA, he issued an order enjoining the Administration from listing the sturgeon based on the report. (The order did not prevent the Administration from conducting some other process in coming to the conclusion that the sturgeon should be listed, but merely forbid it from relying on the product of an illegal committee.) The United States Court of Appeals for the Eleventh Circuit affirmed the district court's decision, stating that this was the only remedy that could possibly stop the Administration from violating the law and that "anything less would be tantamount to nothing."

In April 1994, we began to hear that the administration was conducting secret meetings with representatives of the "sovereign" parties in the *Idaho Department of Fish and Game* case. Among other things, the participants in the meetings were trying to come up with a new way to implement § 7 of the Endangered Species Act in the salmon context. Under longstanding rules of administrative law, federal agencies are supposed to formulate new rules of general applicability in a public, rulemaking process, not by private meetings with affected parties.

We wrote to the Justice Department asking to be allowed to go to these meetings, as members of the public generally, and as litigants in that case. We received no response. We wrote again advising the Justice Department that these meetings violated FACA. We again received no response.

In the meantime, we sought through post-judgment motions in the *Idaho Department of Fish and Game* case to gain access to the meetings, but Judge Marsh would grant no such relief. Ostensibly, it was up to the federal defendants how to comply with his judgment; Judge Marsh did not appear disposed to micromanage that effort, beyond requiring periodic status reports.

On June 21, 1994, we filed a complaint in the federal district court alleging that these meetings violated FACA. The case was immediately assigned to Judge Marsh. We sought a temporary restraining order requiring the defendants to either open up the meetings to the public or to cease holding them. We also filed a motion for expedited discovery, asking the administration to identify who was attending the meetings and what was going on in them.

Lawyers for the Administration and the states that were attending the secret meetings assured Judge Marsh that nothing substantive was happening in the meetings at all. It was all about "process," said the lawyers. Judge Marsh refused to enter the requested injunctive relief. I asked him to rule on our request for discovery. He told me to work it out with the defendants. I told

348

him we could not work it out with the defendants because the defendants were asserting that they had a privilege to keep everything that was happening in the meetings secret. He still declined to rule on the request.

At this point, there was nothing left to do but file a formal motion to compel discovery. We did. Judge Marsh denied it. He declared that he would determine whether the secret meetings constituted "advisory committees" within the meaning of FACA by reading the government's status reports in *Idaho Department of Fish and Game* case.

We were outraged. Once again, we would have no opportunity to discover disputed facts critical to analyzing whether or not the groups were established or utilized by the federal agencies to secure advice or recommendations. We could only know what the government would tell us about the activities of the groups.

We asked the United States Court of Appeals for the Ninth Circuit to review Judge Marsh's decision immediately, through a writ of mandamus. And Justices Wiggins and Fernandez declined to do so. They said a writ of mandamus should only issue in extraordinary cases.

Since we were also in the middle of the *Idaho Department of Fish and Game* case, we again asked Judge Marsh to open up the meetings with the federal defendants, since he was ostensibly supervising them. This time, perhaps sensing that he had been misled by the government lawyers at the June 21st hearing, Judge Marsh issued an order declaring that meetings open to any party should be open to all parties.

When we showed up at the first meeting, the federal, state and tribal agencies shut down the meeting and asked Judge Marsh to reconsider his opinion. He called for a conference in his chambers. As I walked in, I noticed that there were two judges visiting from Eastern Europe, which turned out to be some kind of omen. Judge Marsh listened patiently as all the government attorneys explained why they could not allow us into the meetings. It would slow things down. It would be disruptive. Statements they made might be used against them later in litigation. (Later, the Sierra Club Legal Defense Fund did use events in these meetings, presumably leaked to them by allies in the states and tribes, in litigation against the federal agencies.)

An obsessive desire for secrecy has long been a characteristic of the fishery agencies. At the turn of the century in the State of Washington, cannery interests got legislation passed deeming the statistics of the Fish Commissioner to be "confidential", that they "shall not be open for inspection of the public", and were even immune from disclosure to other government agencies.[66]

To this day, harvest allocation decisions for the Columbia River are carried on behind closed doors in negotiations pursuant to a consent decree in *United States v. Oregon*. Even when the disputes boil over into Court, Judge Marsh has been known to take the parties in chambers, excluding interested observers and even the press. One of the lawyers who was called back in chambers with Judge Marsh during a 1995 dispute that arose in *United States v. Oregon* when NMFS tried to limit tribal harvest of endangered Snake River fall chinook salmon told me that they talked about progress in changing dam operations. As of 1997, the state fishery agencies (except Montana and Idaho) and tribes are pushing this closed-door model for all salmon recovery planning. Oregon's Governor Kitzhaber is leading the effort.

By September, it was time to go through the motions of briefing the case we already knew was to be decided on the government's version of the facts. The government claimed, falsely, that that every person involved in the secret meetings was an employee of a federal, state or tribal fishery agency.

Judge Marsh accepted everything the government said and ruled that the groups that were meeting did not constitute "advisory committees" within the meaning of FACA. To add insult to injury, he declared that even if the meetings did violate FACA, we had suffered no injury because he had protected us during the *Idaho Fish and Game* case, by requiring "separate but equal" meetings.

Months later, the government filed a final report in the *Idaho Fish and Game* case that revealed that its papers in the FACA case had been false. There were private consultants involved in the secret meetings. Far having "separate but equal" meetings, we had attended (and learned of) only a tiny fraction of the meetings underway.

So when we appealed Judge Marsh's decision to the Ninth Circuit, we were pretty confident that this was a salmon case we could win. How could the Court of Appeals possibly affirm the decision of a district court to resolve the facts based on "testimony" from government lawyers, deny all discovery, and declare, contrary to fact, that the federal government had neither established nor utilized "advisory committees"? You can read the resulting Court of Appeals decision, *ALCOA v. NMFS*, No. 95-35134 (9th Cir. Aug. 9, 1996), and see how.

The Court began by misconceiving what Judge Marsh had done in the *Idaho Department of Fish and Game* case. According to the Court, Judge Marsh "directed" the offending federal agencies to "take action" on the biological opinion for 1994-98. In fact, he had no jurisdiction over the 1994-98 opinion, because the plaintiffs in that case had sued on the 1993 biological opinion. Judge Marsh's judgment was that "the 1993 biological opinion and records of decision are set aside and remanded to federal defendants with instructions to review and reconsider them, or at their option, to review and reconsider the 1994-98 hydropower biological opinion".[67] The federal defendants had, instead of appealing Judge Marsh's decision, elected *voluntarily* to reconsider the 1994-98 biological opinion.

Having mischaracterized the entire context of the case, Judges Reinhardt and Fernandez then declared that the two advisory committees, the Biological Requirements Work Group and the Actions Work Group, "were not 'groups' formed by, at the prompting of, or solely for the federal government".

Then they declared that the District Court "had required 'the government to 'reinitiate consultation consistent with my findings'", perhaps assuming (erroneously) that the phrase consultation meant consultation with the parties in the two Groups. The District Court would have had no authority to order the federal defendants to consult with any non-federal parties; by statute, § 7 consultations are between federal agencies.

Judges Reinhardt and Fernandez also pointed out that the record before it—written by government lawyers—did not "show that the groups were funded by the federal government". In fact, some Group members were consultants paid for by the government. The Ninth Circuit could have, as Judge Marsh did, taken judicial notice of the fact that a very significant percentage of state (and nearly 100% of tribal) fish and wildlife spending—including the salaries of those that attended Group meetings—was paid by the Bonneville Power Administration.

The Federal Advisory Committee Act itself merely required us to prove that the federal agencies had "established or utilized" the Groups. Clearly the federal agencies had "established or utilized" the Groups under any common-sense definition of those words.

The two Judges also suggested that the Groups did not provide any "advice, except in the sense that one advises an opponent to mend its ways". The whole point of our lawsuit was to enjoin future reliance on a biased report that was a consensus product of the Biological Requirements Work Group. It was a consensus product of federal, state, and tribal members. It represented precisely the evil Congress was intending to avoid: a committee unbalanced in viewpoint, shielded from public scutiny, and working its will upon the federal government to the detriment of the public.

In formal comments to the National Marine Fisheries Service, BPA had confirmed that bias: "Most of the concerns with the recommended application of analytical methods and any discussion of alternative approaches raised by BPA and others were excluded from the BRWG by the state and tribal participants who performed the final report edits."[68]

Judges Reinhardt and Fernandez would not even acknowledge that Judge Marsh had refused to compel *any* discovery against the federal defendants. According to them, the District Court was "not convinced that there was more buried treasure to be dug out". The case was clear enough, they concluded, that the District Court could rule without *any* of what conventionally passes for evidence: the sworn testimony of witnesses that could be cross-examined.

The dissenting judge, Judge Kozinski, had no trouble realizing that the Groups in question were "actually created" by federal agencies, and that the federal government was trying to pull a fast one on the Court. One of the highlights of my career was watching him relentlessly question the government attorney before him who was attempting to misrepresent the record. To Judge Kozinski, the law was simple:

> "Where an agency sets up an advisory committee, the agency has 'established' that committee for purposes of FACA. If FACA does not apply in such a case, it never will."

It is that simple. The federal defendants violated FACA. Their Biological Requirements Work Group reports were the "product of an unlawful procedure" within the meaning of the Administrative Procedures Act. The federal government should have been enjoined from relying upon them.

"It never will" is a good epitaph for FACA. Congress tried to take aim at a specific problem and solve it, and the courts never gave it a chance. Judge Kozinski's epitaph came true, not just for us, but for the timber industry as well. The federal government's secret meetings to take care of the problem of "timber junkies", as the youthful Clinton/Gore staffers referred to rural Northwesterners, will remain secret forever. Lawyers for both the timber industry and environmentalists state that literally garbage bags full of documents were shredded to keep them secret from the public. According to the environmentalists' lawyers, it took four shredders to take care of all the evidence.

Government Management of Science

"Peer review" is a concept that used to have meaning in science. It arose quite apart from any government role in science, on the basis that scientific progress was reported in independent journals. The editors of these journals, after receiving a manuscript for publication, would identify some other researchers in the field and ask for their comments. The editors would then ask the researcher seeking publication to respond to the resulting critiques.

Promoters of the Great Salmon Hoax, such as Idaho Power Council member Mike Field of Idaho, claim that the *Return to the River* report issued by the Council's Independent Science Group was the subject of "traditional scientific peer review".[69] The ISG's "peer review" process consisted of the ISG itself selecting reviewers, receiving the comments, and deciding whether or not to address the comments received. When Bruce Lovelin tried to get the comments on the ISG's draft report in December 1996, the Power Planning Council's lawyer, John Volkman, wrote back and told him that the reports were privileged from disclosure.[70] The Freedom of Information Act did not apply, he said, because of an exemption said to encompass a "deliberative process" privilege. As we have seen, the government often invokes this "privilege" to keep fish and wildlife decisionmaking secret.

Unfortunately, review of the ISG report was consistent with the sort of "peer review" process commonly pursued in the government. Some Members of Congress, including Senator Dirk Kempthorne, are trying to reform the Endangered Species Act to get "good science" through requirements of "peer review", without defining what they mean by "peer review". That will not accomplish much.

In 1996, Senator Gorton, working with other members of the Northwest Congressional Delegation, secured passage of a new section to the Northwest Power Act. The new § 4(h)(10)(D) directs the Northwest Power Planning Council to appoint an "Independent Scientific Review Panel" to review projects proposed for funding as part of the Council's Fish and Wildlife Program.[71] The new law has had the salutary effect of giving the Council additional authority to reject fishery agency recommendations for its Program, undercutting (if not eliminating) the pernicious influence of the 1994 Ninth Circuit decision requiring a "high degree of deference" to the agencies. Given the degree to which fishery agency recommendations have lost a solid basis in science, allowing the Council to listen to scientists instead of fishery managers is an important first step in reform of the process.

Unfortunately, even before the bill was passed, fishery interests lobbied hard to scale back its effect. Instead of reviewing all the Council's fish and wildlife projects, as initially proposed, the Panel is to review merely "a sufficient number of projects to adequately assure that the list of prioritized projects recommended is consistent with the Council's program"—whatever that means. In November 1997, the Tribes, angry with the Panel's recommendation to defer funding of their hatchery projects, filed suit against the Council, arguing that their projects were unfairly singled out for cuts. No decision is expected for a year or more.

Section 4(h)(10)(D) also directs the Council to establish "Scientific Peer Review Groups" to assist the Panel. The members of these groups were supposed to be chosen from lists provided by the National Academy of Science. We were initially hopeful that this would bring some fresh, unbiased scientists into the picture.

After the bill was passed, however, the Council somehow co-opted the National Academy of Science, so that the list of scientists provided by the Academy was essentially pre-selected by the Council. Eight of the eleven members of the new Panel were the same conservation biologists composing the Independent Science Group, who continued to promote their "conceptual foundation" for back-to-nature salmon solutions.

Some believe that it is at least theoretically possible to establish a process to gather good science, even if the government funds the process. As the Director of the University of Washington's Fisheries Research Institute has pointed out,

> "Research conducted under the auspices of the National Science Foundation, the National Institutes of Health and certain other funding agencies is subjected to intense national competition and to review by persons who do not have a stake in the outcome. This process has produced a caliber of science that is respected worldwide. By contrast, much of the research that supports natural resource decisionmaking is weak or noncompetitive and is scrutinized only by the funding source. It may also be intensely political. As a consequence, the research may be dismissed after the fact as having been flawed in its hypothesis, experimental design, methodology or significance. We could save a considerable amount of time, money and credibility if topical, applied research was subjected to the same degree of competition and rigorous review as is basic science in this country."[72]

The key element here is competition. So long as research is dominated by harvest agencies that divert nearly all research funding to themselves, no progress can be made.

Others are more pessimistic. Three Canadian scientists reviewing the use of fisheries science in Canada recently published a controversial article entitled: "Is scientific inquiry incompatible with government information control?" Their conclusion:

"... the present framework for linking science with management can, and has, lead to abuses that threaten the ability of scientists to understand fully the causes of fish declines, to identify means of preventing fishery collapses from recurring, to incorporate scientific advice in management decisions, and to communicate research in a timely fashion to as wide an audience as possible."[73]

This succinctly describes the situation in the Pacific Northwest. The response of the Canadian government to the article also parallels the Northwest experience: the Deputy Minister of the Department of Fisheries and Oceans denounced the paper as "tabloid journalism" "based on innuendo and misrepresentation which have no place in a scientific journal".[74]

Experience above and below the U.S.-Canada border suggests that the more that government tries to manage the scientific process, the worse the problem will get.

NOTES TO CHAPTER 13

[1] Wilkinson & Conner, *Law of the Pacific Salmon Fishery*, 322 Kansas L. Rev. 17, 104 (1983).

[2] *PNGC v. Brown*, 822 F. Supp. at 1486 n.15.

[3] Quoted in *Northwest Salmon Recovery Report*, Vol. 1, No. 1, at 1 (Feb. 14, 1997).

[4] 16 U.S.C. § 1801(b)(3).

[5] Reported in J. Cone, *A Common Fate* 26.

[6] A. Green, "Plan to save coho must have plenty of fins, lawmakers told", *The Oregonian*, Feb. 12, 1997.

[7] *See generally* Editorial, "Rescuing a salmon plan", *The Oregonian*, Feb. 28, 1997, at B8.

[8] R. Neuberger, "The Great Salmon Mystery", Saturday Evening Post, Sept. 13, 1941.

[9] ISG, *Return to the River* 90.

[10] R. Neuberger, "The Great Salmon Mystery", Saturday Evening Post, Sept. 13, 1941.

[11] *Id.*.

[12] PFMC, "Freshwater habitat, salmon produced, and escapements for natural spawning along the Pacific Coast of the United States", Report of the Anadromous Salmonid Environmental Task Force (1979).

[13] *See, e.g.*, NRC, *Upstream* at 81 (Prepub. ed.).

[14] *See, e.g.*, ISG, *Return to the River* 90 (citing predevelopment abundance estimate for chinook salmon of 4.7 to 9.2 million fish).

[15] *See, e.g.*, B. Harden, *A River Lost* 196.

[16] *See* NMFS, "Factors for Decline: A Supplement to the Notice of Determination for Snake RIver Spring/Summer Chinook Salmon under the Endangered Species Act", June 1991, at 7 (citing Northwest Power Planning Council estimate); NMFS, Biological Opinion, "Reinitiation of Consultation on 1994-98 Operation of the Federal Columbia River Power System and Juvenile Transportation Program in 1995 and

Future Years", Mar. 2, 1995, at 4 (misciting the "Factors for Decline" paper as reciting an estimate by NMFS).

[17] *See, e.g., American Rivers v. NMFS*, No. 96-384-MA, slip op. at 12 (D. Or. April 3, 1997) (citing 1995 Biological Opinion); *NRIC v. NWPPC*, 35 F.3d 1371, 1376 (9th Cir. 1994).

[18] "Numerical Estimates of Hydropower-Related Losses", Appendix E of the Columbia River Basin Fish and Wildlife Program, at 7.

[19] *Id.* at 3-4.

[20] *Id.* at 6.

[21] Reviewing the fishery agencies claims of "optimum sustainable runs" in the Snake River, prepared to support the Lower Snake River Compensation Program, Professor Salo found them "difficult to support". E. Salo, "Special Report to the U.S. Army Corps of Engineers on two reports concerning proposed compensation for losses of fish caused by Ice Harbor, Lower Monumental, Little Goose, and Lower Granite Locks and Dam projects, Washington and Idaho", at 26 (USACE Walla Walla Dist. June 26, 1974).

[22] 1987 Columbia River Basin Fish and Wildlife Program § 203(b)(2), at 38.

[23] *Id.*

[24] Appendix D to 1987 Columbia River Basin Fish and Wildlife Program, at 6.

[25] *Id.* at 212.

[26] *See, e.g.,* ISG, *Return to the River* 397.

[27] K. Petersen, *River of Life, Channel of Death* 60.

[28] H. Price, *Report to the Secretary of the Interior, April 14, 1882*, at 24, *quoted in* C. Smith, *Salmon Fishers of the Columbia* 102.

[29] Quoted in *Wasinington v. Washington State Passenger Fishing Vessel Ass'n*, 443 U.S. 658, 667 n.11 ((1979)

[30] *United States v. Washington*, 384 F. Supp. 312 (W.D. Wash. 1974).

[31] *United States v. Washington*, 573 F.2d 1123 (9th Cir. 1978).

[32] J. Brinckman, "Babbitt promises to help salmon recovery", *The Oregonian*, August 13, 1997, at A18.

[33] *Nez Perce Tribe v. Idaho Power Co.*, 847 F. Supp. 791, 810 (D. Idaho 1994). Although the Tribe appealed this case to the Ninth Circuit, settlement efforts are expected to forestall any ruling by the Ninth Circuit.

[34] I believe this figure comes from a Tribal publication; another source suggests that the "Army Corps of Engineers evaluated the fishery, assigned a monetary value to the difference between the destroyed sites and alternative sites where Indians could work their fisheries, and paid $27.5 million." R. White, *The Organic Machine* 100.

[35] *Id.*

[36] J. LaPlante, "Celilo Falls: Flooded 40 Years Ago But Not Forgotten", *Wana Chinook Tymoo*, Issue Two, 1997, at 11.

[37] Confederated Tribes of the Umatilla Indian Reservation, *Comprehensive Plan*, May 15, 1996, at 22.

[38] Quoted in J. LaPlante, "Celilo Falls: Flooded 40 Years Ago But Not Forgotten", *Wana Chinook Tymoo*, Issue Two, 1997, at 11.

[39] B. Harden, *A River Lost* 115.

[40] "Nez Perce own Oregon land after 120 years", *Stateman Journal*, June 13, 1997.

[41] It should be noted that State fish and wildlife agencies have done better than the tribes. Here is the same data for the four Northwest state fishery agencies.

Oregon Department of Fish and Wildlife	$94,769,625
Idaho Department of Fish and Game	54,734,727
Washington Department of Fish and Wildlife	35,868,927
Montana Department of Fish and Wildlife	27,157,558

These higher numbers have prompted Ted Strong, head of the Columbia River InterTribal Fish Commission to tour the Pacific Northwest with bar charts showing spending levels to complain of anti-Tribal discrimination.

[42] The DPEIS "Impacts of Artificial Salmon and Steelhead Production Strategies in the Columbia River Basin" summarizes (and stretches) some of the relevant cases at pp. 8-9. (CBFWA Dec. 10, 1996).

[43] T. Palmer, *The Snake River* 47.

[44] Draft BPA Fish and Wildlife Budget, Jan. 4, 1996, at 1.

[45] W. Rudolph, "Tribes Mum on MOA After White House Discussions", *Clearing Up*, Aug. 12, 1996, at 8.

[46] W. Rudolph, "Tribes Say Extending Fish Cap Will Strangle Salmon Recovery", *Clearing Up*, June 30, 1997, at 10.

[47] "Has $3 billion effort helped salmon?", *Daily Journal of Commerce (Seattle)*, Aug. 6, 1996.

[48] L. Mapes, "River of No Return", *The Spokesman-Review*, July 28, 1996, at H7 (reprint ed.)

[49] Section 4(h)(10)(A) of the Northwest Power Act, 16 U.S.C. § 839b(h)(10)(A).

[50] Memo, R. Swatfigure to All Enforcement Officers, Feb. 19, 1997.

[51] Memo, R. Swatfigure to Enforcement Captains, Feb. 21, 1997 (emphasis in original).

[52] 1995 Annual Report, at 11.

[53] Quoted in "Has $3 billion effort helped salmon?", *Daily Journal of Commerce (Seattle)*, Aug. 6, 1996.

[54] Quoted in *id.*

[55] J. Cone, *A Common Fate* 18.

[56] NRC, *Upstream* at 49 (Prepub. ed.)

[57] NRC, *Upstream* at 201 (Prepub. ed.).

[58] J. Cone, *A Common Fate* 13. Mr. Cone's protagonist, Gordon Reeves, does not blame biologists who make such certifications, however, because they are "well intentioned". *Id.*

[59] L. Mapes, *The Spokeman-Review*, Sunday, July 28, 1996, at H10.

[60] W. Ebel, pers. comm. (May 5, 1997).

[61] NRC, *Upstream* at 185 (Prepub. ed.).

[62] BPA Programs in Perspective, Technical Appendix, Chapter 7, at 39 (May 1992).

[63] *Id.* at 41.

[64] *Id.* at 42-43.

[65] Quoted in L. Mapes, "River of No Return", *The Spokeman-Review*, Sunday, July 28, 1996, at H10.

[66] B. Brown, *Mountain in the Clouds* 67 (quoting a Dec.28, 1912 letter on the subject).

[67] Final Judgment, *IDFG v. NMFS*, No. 93-1603-MA (D. Or. filed April 28, 1994), at 4.

[68] BPA Comments on Draft 1995 Biological Opinion, at 25.

[69] Memo, M. Field & M. Walker to Council Members, Feb. 20, 1997, at 1.

[70] Letter, J. Volkman to B. Lovelin, Dec. 13, 1996.

[71] H. Rep. No. 104-782, 104th Cong., 2d Sess. 23 (Sept. 12, 1996).

[72] M. Landolt, *Fisheries Forum*, Vol. 3(2), at 1, 7 (May 1995).

[73] J. Hutchings, C. Walters & R. Haedrich, "Is scientific inquiry incompatible with government information control?", 54 Can. J. Fish. Aquat. Sci. 1198, 1208 (1997).

[74] Quoted in C. Enman, "36 Scientists: End the suppression", *The Ottawa Citizen*, July 4, 1997 (Mr. Enman also reports that "[t]wo DFO bureaucrats have also threatened Mr. Myers [another critic of the Department] with a lawsuit").

CHAPTER 14: A SENSIBLE APPROACH TO SALMON RECOVERY

> "... folks need houses and stuff to eat, and the folks need metals and the folks need wheat. Folks need water and power dams. Folks need people and folks need the land." Woody Guthrie, *Talking Columbia*

> "The Church eventually made its peace with Galileo because, after all, the earth does go around the sun." Stephen Jay Gould, *Ever Since Darwin: Reflections in Natural History*

Since 1992, we have been committed to a salmon recovery program that is so complex, inconsistent, and uncertain that attempts to describe it take hundreds of pages. Fish bureaucrats outline intricate decision paths that are seldom actually taken. The most recent statements of the National Marine Fisheries Service, and the statements of other salmon advocates, suggest that the goal of salmon recovery may be fifty years away, and we may never succeed.

Growing salmon does takes longer than growing corn, or rabbits, or even cattle, but not longer than growing trees. Recovering salmon will be like any agricultural enterprise. Its success will depend on the vagaries of the weather. It will depend on luck with the salmon stocks we choose to introduce. Some transplants work, like the salmon in New Zealand. Some don't.

If nature cooperates, every major river in the Pacific Northwest could be running with salmon. We have the hatcheries to do it, if we can focus on making them work before we dismantle them. But if the climate gets warmer and warmer, it's just no realistic to expect to maintain large populations of cold-water fish.

It is surely true that what would be best for salmon would be a Pacific Northwest without humanity at all. But with humanity, and with dams to provide safe and clean electric power, conditions can still be good for salmon—if we choose to use technology to improve conditions for salmon and the salmon themselves. So far, the best has been the enemy of the good, with those pursuing the best destroying the good and achieving nothing.

Reintroducing Economic Considerations to Maximize the Benefits of Salmon Recovery Resources

Economics is the science to be employed to achieve the maximal benefits from a given set of resources. Salmon recovery resources are not unlimited. Even if we throw equity out the window and arbitrarily single out electric ratepayers as the sole taxpayers for salmon recovery, there are limits to how much we can collect. Thus we must prioritize all the available options for assisting salmon recovery in some rational manner, and comparing the cost-effectiveness is the only real way to do this.

We are certainly not doing it now. Right now, "[w]e are spending a lot of money trying to touch all the bases", according to Mike Smith, a program manager for the Corps of Engineers. "Setting priorities, deciding which measures provide the biggest benefit for the least cost, that really hasn't been part of the discussion."[1] Doug Marker, a staff member at the Northwest Power Planning Council, confirms this: "We have these cerebral discussions, but nothing really happens. You can't say what you are getting, what was the result for the money spent."[2]

The main problem is that no one with any fiscal accountability is involved in the process at all. Only at the grossest level was there any management at all through the overall Memorandum of Agreement salmon cap, and that "cap" is subject to constant renegotiation. The salmon budgeting process is a disaster. Congress needs to provide some structure here, and it ought to start by requiring a formal cost-benefit analysis of each salmon measure. And Congress must make sure that interested parties can challenge it in court for accuracy.

Decentralizing Management of Salmon Habitat

Recommendations are always based on experience. My experience has been a little unbalanced, particularly in the area of salmon habitat. That seems to be an area where you really have to be right there at the scene to know what we have to do. Some localities need a lot of work. Others don't. Centralized decisionmaking is incapable of making rational habitat management decisions. This is something that belongs with, and ought to be paid for by, the state and tribal governments with sovereignty over the land at issue.

This is the one area where the government is moving very slowly in the right direction, in that state governments and the Northwest Power Planning Council are paying at least lip service to the concept of watershed-based management. Roy Hemmingway, a former member of the Northwest Power Planning Council and salmon and energy advisor to Oregon Governor

Kitzhaber, stumps the State of Oregon proclaiming Oregon's allegience to a program of watershed management councils. He correctly recognizes that only the locals are going to be able to figure out which streams can or should be cleaned up, fenced, or otherwise made more favorable for salmon.

If these leaders intend for the central government to simply serve as a repository of know-how for how to improve salmon habitat, they are on the right track. Right now there are spectacular habitat successes, like Canada's spawning channels for sockeye in the Skeena River that have created problems of *overabundance*.[3] But there is no agency squarely charged to disseminate knowledge of how habitat and hatchery can really be improved for salmon, so that others can build upon the successes.

Most of the state agencies seem to think that the Council or the federal government can or should provide money for habitat improvement, continuing a system that inherently fails to spend the money in a useful way. And most of the harvest agencies also continue to insist on more and more rules and regulations, not tailored to the needs of particular watersheds, that simply gum up the works.

If habitat improvement really brings salmon back, communities should be willing to invest in it with their own money. If the harvest agencies did not insist on sanctioning the taking of nearly all the salmon before they returned, the agencies could probably convince local communities to invest in habitat. But why should anyone invest in habitat improvement now, when the fish all vanish downstream and never come back? When fishery agencies cannot even report whether they are being caught or not? Local county boards are more likely than the Council or the federal government to ask hard questions about whether programs are going to work before they spend money.

Moving Toward River-Based Harvest Management and Sustainable Salmon Harvest

> "The farther that harvest occurs from the spawning grounds, the less likely accurate stock identification becomes, and the lower the likelihood that effective harvest management can be achieved." ISG, *Return to the River* (1996).[4]

There is one obvious way to get more salmon in the rivers of the Pacific Northwest: ban all salmon fishing on the ocean, so that the entire population returns to the rivers. By catching salmon in rivers, harvest levels can be crafted to protect each and every river in the Pacific Northwest.

Every scientific panel to examine salmon production in the Pacific Northwest has recognized that reduced ocean fishing effort is "necessary for increasing production".[5] The Northwest Power Planning Council's Independent Science Group concluded in 1996 that "[a]ll Columbia River stocks, with the possible exception of Hanford fall chinook, are at such low levels that harvest in the ocean will have to be very low or non-existent to allow the habitat restoration proposed herein to have a reasonable chance to succeed".[6]

Perhaps the greatest single success story in fishery management has been the Bristol Bay, Alaska sockeye fishery. Beginning in the late 1800s up until the 1950s, unrestricted fishing on the river led to catches upwards of 20 million fish annually. Then in 1954, harvesters were limited to "'terminal areas' in the marine waters near the mouth of the rivers where returning spawners were thought to have separated".[7] Nevertheless, catches continued to decline as low as 2.3 million fish, largely due to indiscriminate mixed-stock high seas fishing by Japanese vessels (climate changes may also have been a factor). After the Japanese government agreed to close the high seas fishery, sockeye harvests rose steadily, and recently peaked at over 40 million sockeye in 1995. "Bristol Bay is the largest of a substantial number of salmon fisheries which are successfully managed using stock identification information".[8]

Banning ocean harvest would resolve longstanding quarrels between the United States and Canada over the 1985 Pacific Salmon Treaty, which was supposed to assure equal benefits to each nation from Pacific salmon harvests. Right now, the Canadians on the losing end of the Treaty. In 1994, Americans caught almost 9 million Canadian salmon, while Canadians took about 3.5 milllion American fish.[9] Many of the fish caught by Canadians come from the Columbia River system. If ocean harvest were banned, each nation would catch "its own" salmon. Indeed, for the first time, each major river system would receive the economic returns from good watershed management. *It is only by re-establishing such common-sense incentives for salmon protection that any long-term progress can be made.*

Alaska stands as the principal obstacle to ocean harvest reform. Studies suggest that at least 60% of the salmon caught off the coast of Alaska spawn in Canadian rivers, while only 10% of the salmon caught off the coast of Alaska spawn in Alaskan waters.[10] Backed by powerful politicians, including Senator Ted Stevens and Representative Don Young, Alaska has long adopted a "blame the dams" approach to dealing with the salmon problem, even filing a lawsuit in Alaska against dam operations. Environmentalists and fishermen hope to extract more funding for dam-based recovery programs using Alaskan political power, but the quid pro quo is that the Alaskans will be permitted even greater harvests.[11]

Nearly all the tribes would support a ban on ocean harvest, because they have watched for decades as the ocean harvesters have gotten to their fish first. However, the Quinault Indian Nation, the Makah, Hoh and Quileute Indian Tribes have treaty rights to harvest salmon in the ocean off the Washington Coast.[12] Some sort of special arrangements might be made to permit them to continue, or to substitute river harvest, so that their harvests do not threaten the larger conservation objectives.

Enormous numbers of salmon may still be caught as bycatch in other fisheries. Those salmon that are caught as bycatch should not be dumped into the sea, but kept with a corresponding reduction being made in in-river harvest.

Once harvest is returned to the rivers, improvement in fishing methods will still be required if we choose to protect more than one stock in a river. Gradually, more and more observers are coming to perceive the common-sense truth that stock-specific harvest is the only way to protect specific stocks. One possibility, not yet seriously considered by any government agency is: "We'll go back to where we started, to a logical and efficient fish-catching machine that lends itself to rational management, burns no gas and doesn't catch anybody else's fish. . . . [We'll] bring back the traps."[13] Back when traps were legal, trapmen used to argue that their method of harvest had the least impact on salmon. They didn't throw excess (dead) catch overboard; they could simply close the intakes to the traps when limits were reached. And their product was fresher.[14] Fishwheels have had a long history of success on the Columbia River as well. At their peak in 1899, some 76 wheels were in operation, and caught mostly sockeye salmon.[15]

BPA is also funding a program to develop up to 20 hatchery, rearing, imprinting and return programs on the lower Columbia River.[16] These would promote terminal harvest, whereby the salmon are turned loose to rear in the ocean, and then harvested upon return, with little impact on wild stocks beyond the competition for food in the ocean. Provided somebody is paying attention to problems of carrying capacity, these programs make sense—if they can compete economically with fish farms where the salmon simply stay in pens for their entire lives.

Proposals are often made to buy out particularly destructive harvesters, or to lease their licenses when necessary to curtail harvests. BPA has always been willing to try this, but attempts since 1993 have foundered for two reasons. First, the gillnetters targeted for the buyouts greedily insisted on recovering their gross income, not their net income. Second, the tribes who stood next in line to catch whatever salmon were freed up refused to allow them safe passage to the spawning grounds, asserting a Treaty right to catch additional fish.[17] So long as in-river management is conducted by consensus under Court supervision, this seems unlikely to change.

As discussed in Chapter 2, the most promising means of improving harvest management is mass marking of fish and selective (live) harvest. That is the only way that salmon fishing can take place in the ocean or mainstem Columbia River without disproportionate impact on weaker stocks. Unfortunately, the four main Columbia River tribes are opposed to such reforms, believing that they would only "address a symptom—depressed fish runs—rather than rectifying the underlying problem—declining production and survival of wild and naturally spawning fish".[18] Wendell Hannigan of the Yakama Tribe even goes so far as to promote the specious argument that "[s]elective fisheries may actually increase the impact of fisheries on naturally-spawning stocks".[19]

Beyond selective harvest, it may also be necessary to control marine mammal populations, unless we wish to hold success hostage until natural predators, including great white sharks and killer whales, become more abundant. The large and healthy populations of marine mammals at numerous rivers up and down the West Coast call for more immediate, practical action.

What is sauce for the salmon should be sauce for the marine mammals as well. There is no reason to treat salmon as a resource to be exploited, while protecting their predators, marine mammals, from any exploitation whatsoever. Controlled hunting for marine mammals would keep populations in check, and reduce widespread and well-deserved derision of fish and wildlife management policy in coastal towns that see large herds of sea lions destroying their livelihoods.

The final problem that remains is setting harvest levels. We need a body like the Columbia River Compact and the gathering of parties in *United States v. Oregon*, but in the form of a single regulatory agency with final authority on the subject. But this time, somebody has got to tell them how to do it. It's time Congress grew up and started giving federal agencies some guidance, rather than just listing a bunch of factors for the agency to consider. That's what Congressional hearings used to be for: to figure out the rules that ought to govern the citizenry. Now the hearings are no more than media food, and most of the policy that matters is set in the backrooms of the agencies.

In the long run, the best hope for wild salmon is that commercial fisheries may gradually become an anachronism. Like land-based hunting and gathering, commercial fisheries will be outmarketed by agriculture, or, in this case, aquaculture. As anthropologist Dr. Courtland Smith warned, foreseeing this trend back in 1979, "[t]his pattern of evolution will not help the gillnetter, trapman, seiner, fishwheeler, dipnetter, troller or any of the other fishers. They will continue to attempt to stem the flow of events . . ."[20] And their agency, the National Marine Fisheries Service, will continue to misuse salmon recovery planning to keep commercial salmon harvest alive.

Redefining a Role for Hatcheries

Among politically-correct biologists, there is now an almost fanatical emphasis on preserving the genetic purity of individual salmon stocks. In dozens of conference rooms in Portland and Seattle, federal, state and tribal fishery managers meet to debate whether and to what extent salmon stocks not indigenous to a particular watershed might be introduced there.

Among animal breeders, however, and evolutionary biologists, the power of crossing different stocks is recognized as one of the prime movers in creating new breeds of animals with desired characteristics.[21] So long as the process is not random, and careful records are kept, there is no reason to believe that salmon cannot be bred as well. Most experiments may well result in mongrel salmon that do not fare well as they migrate downstream, grow in the ocean and return. But some may produce salmon with hybrid vigor, better adapted to survive in the modern Columbia River Basin. Salmon breeders might consider the particularly successful strains, like the Lake Okanogan sockeye, which migrate 900 miles over nine dams. Perhaps this breed could be crossed with other sockeye stocks.

Doing this will require abandoning the "hands-off" attitude toward Nature that seems to motivate environmentalists. Like the dam builders who saw in the Grand Coulee an opportunity to improve Nature's original design, those who would work to create better salmon runs would accelerate a natural hybridization process that is common in all fish.

It makes a lot of sense to establish some rivers or tributaries as reserves where hatcheries will be "off limits", as a hedge against catastrophic mismanagement of hatcheries. We might even let communities elect whether to pursue an all-wild, all-hatchery, or mixed approach on a tributary-by-tributary basis, so long as harvest regulation below the tributaries assures that each community reaps the fruits of its own salmon experiments.

Indeed, some smaller rivers might be designated as salmon refuges where neither hatcheries nor harvest (other than catch-and-release) is allowed. Politically-prominent marine biologists believe that such an approach is the only long-term solution for chronically overfished stocks.[22] But in some tributaries, where substantial hatcheries have been operating for years, it makes a lot more sense to bite the bullet and make hatcheries work, without regard for remnant wild stocks.

While hatcheries should be free to experiment with techniques for improving adult returns, all the hatchery releases in the Columbia River Basin need to be coordinated by a single authority to optimize the total returns. There is only one obvious role for the federal government, and that is making sure that the total number of fish released does not exceed the carrying capacity of the ecosystem.

This may include ensuring that hatchery releases do not interfere with each other. For example, if several hatcheries in the same river release their smolts at the same time, they may compete for food and habitat. Release times can also be optimized based on the abundance of estuarine predators. Hatcheries that wind up spreading strays all over the Basin might also need central regulation if they can't cure the problem in a reasonable time. So long as the single authority did not attempt to meddle with the details of hatchery operations, and just kept the pastures from being overgrazed, so to speak, everything would probably work out well.

State governments seem to have failed at managing the hatcheries. There may not be a long-term enough perspective in state government. Personally, as part of a global and final settlement of Treaty rights, I would give the tribes a chance to manage the salmon resource by running most or all of the Columbia Basin hatcheries. New upriver hatcheries, like the Yakama and Umatilla Hatcheries can bring mitigation more in line with geographic demands.

Right now, the tribes control only a fraction of the hatcheries. The United States Fish and Wildlife Service is actively resisting efforts by the Nez Perce Tribe to assume operational control of Kooskia National Fish Hatchery, which is located within the Reservation boundaries. Reportedly, the Tribe would like to change its mission and produce different stocks.[23] The Nez Perce could probably apply some useful common sense to hatchery management. Hundreds of years ago, they and the Palouse were probably the most advanced horse breeders among Native Americans.[24]

A global salmon settlement turning over control of nearly all the hatcheries to the tribes, letting them sort out what works and what doesn't, would probably represent the best hope for improving salmon hatcheries. It could be the tribes' responsibility to create the salmon, to be shared 50/50 in accordance with the *Boldt* principle. Because there are more than a dozen tribes, they will not all be locked into one approach to the problem. The alternative and current path, greater federal regulation, might produce an improved set of guidelines for hatchery operations, but a single set of guidelines is unlikely to be the best approach for many different tributaries and fish stocks.

What Improvements Remain for Mainstem Passage?

> "Only recently have the advantages of surface bypasses been taken seriously, even though the success of surface spill and surface ice/trash collectors for passing juveniles was established decades ago ... Return to the historical river at dam sites is not necessary for successfully passing juveniles when surface spill, surface collectors, and selective use of ice and trash sluiceways are management options that use natural fish behavior." Independent Science Group (1996).[25]

Before turning to structural improvements at the dams, there is one improvement needed of overriding importance. We need to be able to measure what we are doing, and the best way to do that is to complete the installation of PIT-tag detectors so that we can measure what is going on in the lower half of the river. Such measurements represent the first step toward making any improvements in dam passage, yet fishery agencies advocate dam removal even before accurate measurement of the effects of dams.

Reviewing the upriver PIT-tag studies, the National Research Council concluded that the available data "suggest high priority for mitigation efforts directed at increasing survival at the dam rather than speeding fish through pools"[26]—if that could even be accomplished. Yet most of the resources devoted to salmon recovery are devoted to flow augmentation, with essentially no effect on survival *at* the dam. Until we can measure survival in each reach of the river, all of the changes we make are little more than guesswork.

As the Independent Science Group emphasized, there are clear paths to improve "across-the-concrete" survival of fish at dams. Before he became a leading anti-dam radical, Ed Chaney wrote that "fish and hydroelectric energy are not inherently incompatible". If dams were "properly designed", he said, "fish passage would divert a small fraction, perhaps one percent, of the average annual flow of the Columbia River".[27]

The most promising concept is surface bypass/collection. Juvenile salmon travel in the upper portion of the water column and are attracted to currents at dams. It is just common sense, as the Northwest Power Planning Council's Independent Science Group recently observed, "to design fish

367

guidance that accomodates the normal behavior of fish rather than attempts to subvert it".[28]

Unfortunately, at the dams on the mainstem Columbia and Snake Rivers, the spillway is located some distance along the dam away from the powerhouse. Thus when turbines are operating, the current attracts many fish through them, rather than over spillways (unless the salmon are prevented from going into the turbine with screens).[29]

However, at Wells Dam on the middle Columbia River in Washington, the spillway is located over the top of the turbines, so that when currents attract the fish, they can pass over the spillway rather than diving through turbines. At Wells, "on average 89% of the smolts that arrive at the dam pass via the vertical slot bypass".[30] The U.S. Army Corps of Engineers believes that surface bypass is at least as effective as the screens, if not more so, and may speed up juvenile passage as well. They think it also provides a "less stressful method of collection".[31]

Tests using horizontal slots to limit flows through a sluiceway over the powerhouses at Ice Harbor Dam showed that even using a relatively small amount of flow could attract 53% of the fish through the sluiceway.[32] Two researchers at the Oregon Department of Fish and Wildlife calculated indirect estimates of the sluiceway efficiency by estimating the number of fish passing the dam upstream (John Day) and entering from the Deschutes River; they found bypass efficiencies of 78% in 1978, 85% in 1979, 67% in 1980, 68.5% in 1981 (for yearling chinook).[33] This is a remarkable result, since flows through the sluiceway were only about 2.5 to 4 thousand cubic feet per second, or 1-2% of the total river flow. Similar, although less effective, results were obtained using the sluiceway at Bonneville Dam.[34] The method does not work as well for subyearling chinook salmon, but they are smaller and probably have better turbine survival.

Unfortuately, most of the research has been ignored by the salmon managers. I am told power interests share some of the blame here, because in the early 1980s they opposed giving up the even the relatively small amount of flow required to pass smolts through the sluiceway. Indeed, modifications were made to Bonneville Dam that probably blocked this low-cost way of passing most juveniles away from the turbines through sluiceways.[35] But this method of fish passage can be restored, and restored for a tiny fraction of the costs currently spent for salmon recovery.

The Columbia River Alliance has been pushing a transportation and surface bypass/collection strategy for salmon recovery, which it calls Recover 1", since 1993. The plan is largely ignored, and is never included in

368

media listings of salmon restoration plans. Yet sophisticated computer modeling shows that it would produce the greatest population gains for endangered Snake River salmon among all the competing salmon plans.[36]

With the exception of their efforts to re-engineer the dams to spill massive quantities of water without creating dissolved gas, harvest managers in the states and tribes resist any spending for structural improvements in survival at the dams. They continue to fight tests of surface collectors, and have succeeded so far in preventing any expansion of the Lower Granite test. When a contractor's delays in the spring of 1996 forced installation of a test bypass facility in the middle of salmon migration season, triggering extensive spill and gas supersaturation, the states and tribes got an excuse to bash surface bypass. Calling in their political allies Crapo and Furse, they succeeded in holding one of the few oversight hearings in salmon recovery, for the express purpose of discrediting surface bypass.

We need to settle on the surface collector/bypass option. The only place that question can be settled is Congress. But because the public pays little attention to what is going on, Northwest politicians are tending to appease the environmentalists and fishery agency bureaucracies. They and Congress are drifting thoughtlessly toward the "remove the dams" option, propelled in part by biased media reports that label "construction of devices to help fish pass dams safely" as "repeating the failures".[37]

Ironically, one of the four members of the Columbia River Inter-tribal Fish Commission, the Warm Springs Tribe, is attempting to gain control of the hydropower project on Oregon's Deschutes River currently operated by Portland General Electric Company.[38] If the Tribe's petition before Federal Energy Regulatory Commission succeeds, it will be interesting to see if the Tribe develops a more practical recognition of the compatibility of dams and salmon. Given the decline of critical facilities in media and government, the most likely outcome is that the Tribe would defend its dam and attack the other dams, with no accountability for the inconsistency.

Reforming the Endangered Species Act

> "... passed in a blind surge of piety, the Endangered Species Act represents no considered judgment on the worth of the nation's natural heritage, nor a debate on the means for achieving its protection." C. Mann & M. Plummer (1995).[39]

Tracy Warner, citing figures provided by Ike Sugg of the Competitive Enterprise Institute, recently summarized the accomplishments of the Endangered Species Act:

369

"Since the law was enacted, 1,037 plants and animals have been listed for protection, and many more have been considered. Of those, the U.S. Fish and Wildlife Service has removed only 27 from the list. Seven of those species removed are extinct. Nine were removed because corrected 'data errors' showed that they were so numerous they were not threatened and should not have been listed in the first place.

"Eleven species are healthy enough for the 'recovered category', but at least four came about with the discovery of significant populations unknown at the time of the listing. Another, the American alligator, is a hardy species that many scientists agree was never endangered.

"Three other 'recovered' species are kangaroos, which are numerous and have no habitat in U.S. jurisdiction. Two others, the brown pelican and the peregrine falcon, were endangered primarily because of the effects of the pesticide DDT, which was banned the year before the Species Act was passed. The last 'recovered' species, the California gray whale, was saved by international bans on hunting and the protection of breeding waters by the Mexican government."[40]

In short, there is not one since species that has been brought back from the brink of extinction by the Endangered Species Act in nearly twenty-five years of operation. Even for government, that is an impressive record of failure. Despite lofty intentions, in practice the Act is merely a tool for stopping actions that may affect the species, without regard for the magnitude of any benefits obtained.

There are many studies of how to reform the Endangered Species Act. One of the most thoughtful, by Charles Mann and Mark Plummer, *Noah's Choice: The Future of Endangered Species*, acknowledges that "the time has come to question the goal that underlies the act: Save every species, no matter what the cost".[41] From their perspective, "demanding the perfect can prevent us from obtaining the merely good",[42] which is precisely what is happening in the Columbia River Basin. Because we demand to stop any stock from extinction, we prevent the general promotion of healthy salmon runs.

Mann and Plummer think we need to separate decisions about listing species from decisions about what to do once the species are listed. The list itself would be merely "an information device, signaling the identities of species with special conservation needs".[43] A critical part of reform is scaling back the "taking" of endangered species that is forbidden under all circumstances. A minimal definition could prevent intentional, direct harm of an individual member of a listed species; federal agencies should gain authority to balance actions to protect endangered species with other legislative goals.[44] Mann and Plummer recommend coupling these changes with a national trust fund for direct improvements to endangered species habitat, akin to the restoration trust once promoted for the Columbia River.

We also need to re-think just what it is about salmon that we are protecting with the Endangered Species Act. As noted above, anti-dam tracts warning that hundreds of "salmon species face extinction" are simply wrong,[45] if "species" is given its biological meaning. There is no chance that the world will lose the Snake River salmon "species"—*Oncorhynchus tshawytscha* (chinook) and *Onchorhynchus nerka* (sockeye)—anytime soon. Indeed, most of the fish listings that are now front-page news in the Pacific Northwest involve biological species in no danger of disappearing. For example, there are at least seven large groups of bull trout in the Northwest; the Columbia River Basin group, likely to be listed as endangered, includes some 386 distinct stocks, many of which are in no danger at all.[46]

Right now, the Endangered Species applies with full force to "any distinct population segment of any species of vertebrate fish or wildlife which interbreeds when mature".[47] (For some reason, we only expand the Endangered Species Act's protections for creatures with bones.) What is a "distinct population segment"? Congress did not bother to define the term, so it means whatever a federal official wants it to mean. The choice is inherently arbitrary. Under the Endangered Species Act, the federal government could make it a federal crime to kill mice in your house, because the mice in your house are a "distinct population segment that interbreeds when mature."

One environmental reporter concluded that "listings are based on increasingly lenient criteria and now may be registered even when a creature is numerous".[48] A Canadian biologist offered one reason for this phenomenon: "[e]ndangered species lists have been needlessly inflated with taxonomically described subspecies to increase alarm and therefore program funding".[49] In the Pacific Northwest, this effort has reached its zenith, with the largest program funding in the world directed at the smallest of population groups: "distinct population segments" of Snake River salmon.

If Noah had applied the current federal standards for "species" protection, his Ark would have sunk under the weight of functionally-identical animals. Pacific Northwest salmon recovery efforts are sinking too, as the larger and worthy goal of having more salmon in the rivers is subordinated to enormous efforts to protect the genetic purity of tiny individual salmon stocks.

The absolutist approach of the Endangered Species Act makes no sense in the context of dynamic salmon metapopulations with common genes.

At the least, Congress ought to recognize that we should not list endangered "species" that we are going to harvest directly. This is bad government. Yet such a reform can come only from the people. None of the institutions have a stake in fixing it; their agencies are growing in power and influence and they are gaining media exposure.

Indeed, no one at present is seeking any useful reform of the Endangered Species Act insofar as salmon are concerned. Idaho Senator Dirk Kempthorne is leading efforts to amend the Act, but he seems only interested in protecting Idaho's Southern irrigators and private landowners. His proposed Act would simply give the federal government even broader and more unreviewable powers, blindly expanding the legal obligation to recover endangered species. No one, not even the National Endangered Species Act Reform Coalition, is pressing Congress to reform the § 7 consultation process that fish and wildlife agencies misuse to extort funding from other federal agencies.

Congress may well be institutionally incapable of actual reform. Members of Congress are "free to wax rhetorical about the value of the environment while refusing to back necessary increases in the budget for protection".[50] The history of salmon law is a history of layering more and more inconsistent statutes on top of each other, when what is needed is a thorough housecleaning.

Putting Someone in Charge

Back when the Bonneville Power Administration was little more than a gleam in Franklin D. Roosevelt's eye, J.D. Ross, the Superintendent of Seattle's public power system, told him:

> "Mr. President, a single administrator is better than a board. The sooner you come to a one-man administration, the sooner the government's power program will reach success. Fix responsibility on one man and remove him if he does not keep faith. Help him if he does."[51]

President Roosevelt took the advice, and Bonneville was for many decades an unqualified success. The same cannot be said of salmon management, where splintered authority has prevented any success.

In 1995, the Chair of the Snake River Salmon Recovery Team responded to former Oregon Senator Mark Hatfield's request to review legislation concerning BPA and salmon. He told the Senator that the legislation was silent on a key question: "Who is in charge?" While "[w]e recognize the popularity of returning these problems to the region. In the short-term, we think that to be unwise." Failure to achieve regional consensus, he warned, would stand as an insuperable barrier to making any progress in salmon recovery.[52]

At this point, who is in charge is barely of importance. If any single individual were placed in a position of ultimate regulatory authority over the salmon resource, with a fixed budget less than half what we spend now, that person could make enormous strides in returning salmon the rivers of the Columbia River Basin.

If it were up to me, I would create a Columbia Basin Fish and Wildlife Administration with a Presidentially-appointed administrator, with the power to regulate harvest, hatcheries, and to *purchase* improvements in dam passage with a budget inherited from the ruins of the current Memorandum of Agreement, and revenues from selling salmon licenses. The new body would replace the Columbia River Compact, the Northwest Power Planning Council (power planning being an anachronism with a free market in electricity), and accompany an outright elimination of federal grants to the menagerie of fish and wildlife authorities, foundations, commissions and centers.

With a single sensible authority, one might finally begin to answer the basic questions about salmon survival and dams that remain unanswered after decades of poorly coordinated, repetitive, and disorganized research. As the Northwest Power Planning Council's Independent Science Group has emphasized, we need to "[d]evelop estimates of smolt mortality rates assignable specifically to mortality in turbines, tailraces, reservoirs and forebays, to identify areas of highest mortality and to be able to treat them individually with the most appropriate measures".[53] This is just common sense, but it is common sense that has eluded fishery managers for decades. Right now, fishery managers can only guess at which dams cause problems for salmon, and which are not much of a problem.

Despite the elegant simplicity and obvious effectiveness of putting someone in charge, it seems like a goal that is politically impossible to achieve. In November 1995, Congress, led by Oregon Senator Mark Hatfield, directed the Northwest Power Planning Council to report back to Congress on methods to improve salmon governance. They gave the Council 180 days to do this, prompting yet another expensive round of meetings and process, dubbed the "180 day review". This was the Northwest Power Planning Council's opportunity to show some real leadership, and propose some real forms that would cut the Gordian knot of competing statutes and agencies.

The Council could have come up with proposed federal legislation to really fix salmon governance. Instead, they dropped the ball.

The Council held public hearings throughout the Region. Every interest group but one appeared to acknowledge that management was in disarray. But every interest group but one stated that no legislative changes should be considered. I am proud to report that my clients alone frankly acknowledged that only legislative initiatives would likely make a difference.

The problem seems to be that nobody trusts Congress to pass a law that would make sense. The environmentalists are all afraid the Republicans will decide to sell BPA to the highest bidder or exempt it from all environmental laws. Maybe both. As of 1997, with Republicans afraid to introduce bills that would really reform the Endangered Species Act, this does not look likely.

Exhibiting typical salmon leadership, the Council ducked the "no one is in charge" issue, recommending only minimal changes. Specifically, the Council sought an Executive Order that would give their recommendations more weight at the federal agencies. No institution or leader in the Pacific Northwest has been willing to provide the leadership necessary to rationalize salmon management.

Now that Senator Hatfield has retired, prospects for meaningful reform are even slimmer. The man some regard as Senator Hatfield's heir-apparent, Washington Senator Slade Gorton, seems to recognize that impossible problems arise from interpreting the Endangered Species Act to require protection of every single "distinct population segment" of salmon. He may even recognize that the rivers of the Pacific Northwest could run full of salmon again, if only we embraced a scientific hatchery-based approach to stocking rivers. Oregon Senator Gordon Smith does not seem to be making salmon recovery reform one of his priorities, instead telling constituents to resort to the courts.

Environmentalists pursuing the commercial harvester's version of Ecotopia clearly support a new Basin-wide planning board (efforts promoted by Angus Duncan) that would treat the Basin as an "ecosystem", which seems to mean that more regulations of every type are needed. But their command and control approach to environmental regulation is not likely to gain much support. Natural resource groups, knowing the Council's history, are unlikely to support creating expanded regional authority.

The good news is that if we could just elect a President with some common sense on environmental issues, he could solve the problem administratively by making all the federal agencies work together, and appointing a BPA Administrator with the guts to use the power of the purse to straighten things out. There would be some sniping from the Ninth Circuit, but things would probably work out.

As of late 1997, "reform" efforts seem to be going in the opposite direction, seeking to subordinate single and accountable federal authority in favor of a new "three sovereigns" consensus-based approach. Endless government-to-government negotiations produce impressive treaty-like documents, but diplomatic negotiations cannot put more salmon in the rivers of the Pacific Northwest. Only wrenching reforms of the existing fishery management bureaucracies can.

NOTES TO CHAPTER 14

[1] Quoted in L. Mapes, "River of No Return", *The Spokesman-Review*, Sunday, July 28, 1996, at H2 (reprint ed.)

[2] Quoted in *id.* at H7.

[3] "Alaskans Say They're Not Targeting Canadian Sockeye", *NW Fishletter*, July 22, 1997, § 9.

[4] ISG, *Return to the River* 369.

[5] *See, e.g.*, NRC, *Upstream* at 11; *ISG, Return to the River* 366.

[6] ISG, *Return to the River* 375.

[7] This quote and the material in this paragraph is drawn from ISG, *Return to the River* 374.

[8] *Id.*

[9] P. Koberstein, "Shipwreck! Is the Pacific Salmon Treaty Lost at Sea?", *Big River News* (Fall 1996).

[10] P. Koberstein, "Shipwreck! Is the Pacific Salmon Treaty Lost at Sea?", *Big River News* (Fall 1996).

[11] *See* P. Koberstein, "Shipwreck! Is the Pacific Salmon Treaty Lost at Sea?", *Big River News* (Fall 1996)

[12] *United States v. Washington*, 384 F. Supp. 312, 364, 372-74 (W.D. Wash. 1974), *aff'd*, 520 F.2d 676 (9th Cir. 1976), *aff'd*, 443 U.S. 658 (1979).

[13] R. Anderson, "Settle the salmon wars or go back to square one", *The Seattle Times*, Sept. 29, 1996.

[14] C. Smith, *Salmon Fishers of the Columbia* 30-31.

[15] *Id.* at 35.

[16] BPA, *Lower Columbia River Salmon Business Plan for Terminal Hatcheries*

[17] J. Cone, *A Common Fate* 279.

[18] R. Taylor, "Mass Marking: Sportfisher's Dream, Commercial Fisher's Salvation, or Natural Resource Nightmare?", in *Wana Chinook Tymoo* Issue One, at 12 (CRITFC 1997)

[19] Quoted in *id.* at 13.

[20] Smith, *Salmon Fishers of the Columbia* 107.

[21] J. Weiner, *The Beak of the Finch* 157-58.

[22] *See, e.g.*, "Refuges proposed to save fish", *The Herald*, June 17, 1997.

[23] AP, "Tribe's bid on hatchery is rejected", *The Spokesman-Review*, Dec. 15, 1996.

[24] K. Petersen, *River of Life, Channel of Death* 51.

[25] ISG, *Return to the River* 250.

[26] NRC, *Upstream* at 201 (Prepub. ed.).

[27] Quoted in J. Cone, *A Common Fate* 120.

[28] ISG, *Return to the River* 201.

[29] *See generally* "Fish Research: Filling the Gaps", *Salmon Passage Notes*, at 1 (USACE NPD Feb. 1996).

[30] D. Chapman & A. Giorgi, "Comments on Work of Biological and FCPRS Alternative Work Groups", at 15 (1994).

[31] U.S. Army Corps of Engineers, "Interim Status Report", at ES-15.

[32] *See* "Fish Research: Filling the Gaps", *Salmon Passage Notes*, at 1 (USACE NPD Feb. 1996).

[33] D. Nichols and B. Ransom, "Development of The Dalles Dam Trash Sluiceway as a Downstream Migrant Bypass System, 1981", Annual Progress Report, Fish Research Project, Oregon, USACE Contract No. DACW57-78-C-0058, at 28. Results for subyearlings showed only about 40% bypass efficiency.

[34] C. Willis & B. Uremovich, "Evaluation of the ice and trash sluiceway at Bonneville Dam as a bypass system for juvenile salmonids, 1981", Annual Progress Report, Fish Research Project, Oregon, NMFS Contract No. 81-ABC-00173.

[35] *See* "Fish Research: Filling the Gaps", *Salmon Passage Notes*, at 1 (USACE NPD Feb. 1996).

[36] *See* J. Anderson, "Comparison of Mainstem Recovery Options Recover-1 and DFOP", Dec. 13, 1994.

[37] J. Brinckman, "$3 billion later, Columbia Basin salmon dwindle", July 27, 1997.

[38] *Clearing Up*, Jan. 13, 1997, at 10.

[39] C. Mann & M. Plummer, *Noah's Choice: The Future of Endangered Species* 218 (A. Knopf 1995).

[40] T. Warner, "The Endangered Species Act is simply a failure", *The Wenatchee World*, Dec. 8, 1996.

[41] C. Mann & M. Plummer, *Noah's Choice: The Future of Endangered Species* 215

[42] *Id.*

[43] *Id.* at 225.

[44] *Id.* at 226-27.

[45] K. Peterson, *River of Life, Channel of Death: Fish and Dams on the Lower Snake* 5 (Confluence Press 1995).

[46] J. Brinckman, "Agency says bull trout deserve to be listed", *The Oregonian*, Mar. 14, 1997.

[47] 16 U.S.C. § 1532(16).

[48] G. Easterbrook, *A Moment on the Earth* 568.

[49] R. McFetridge, "Commentary on Taxonomic Uses and Abuses in Wildlife Law", Alberta Game Warden 14 (Winter 1994).

[50] *Id.* at 232-33.

[51] Quoted in R. Neuberger, *The Promised Land* 107.

[52] Letter, D. Bevan to M. Hatfield, Sept. 25, 1995.

[53] ISG, *Return to the River* 445.

CHAPTER 15: ORGANIZING TO DEFEND COMMON SENSE IN RESOURCE MANAGEMENT

"A popular government without popular information, or the means of acquiring it, is but a prologue to a farce or a tragedy, or, perhaps, both." James Madison

"Men occasionally stumble over the truth, but most of them pick themselves up and hurry off as if nothing happened." Winston Churchill

People who depend on natural resources for their livelihood need to wake up. As long as there are no salmon in the rivers, environmentalists will raise public concern. The public wants salmon in the rivers, and politicians will do whatever gives them media attention for "saving salmon".

The fishery agencies on which the politicians rely will never solve the problem without external pressure. There are not going to be any salmon in the rivers if we commercially harvest them in destructive mixed-stock fisheries. Particularly given the shad explosion and other natural factors working against salmon, the Columbia River salmon are not going to be the most abundant stocks in the Pacific Ocean, and cannot withstand current fishery management practices in the ocean.

More generally, our society itself is threatened by the decline of science and law. Unless people understand what science is (or should be), and what law is (or should be), governance on natural resource issues will tend to decay. So will democracy itself. As one philosopher has written, "there are fairly good reasons to link the birth of modern democratic theory and the growth of modern science. Karl Popper, among others, made the connection perspicuous, recalling his argument in *The Open Society and Its Enemies* that one of the best senses of 'reason' and 'reasonableness' [is] openness to criticism,' a mark of both science and democracy".[1]

Right now, both science and democracy are dead in the area of salmon recovery, as a $500 million program has been put into effect over the objections of scientists by unelected administrators, operating beyond the control of any law. Relying on dogma rather than data, they have generated a salmon recovery program that is both a farce and a tragedy.

The Need to Educate the Urban Majority

Urban people have no realistic concept of farming or other natural-resource-based industries. Early romantic images of these occupations

377

(*Charlotte's Web* (farming) or *Snow White* (mining)) are beginning to succumb to the anti-business blight spread by the media. A significant portion of the river of salmon recovery money is diverted into "public education" programs that spread propaganda and misinformation. Now farmers are perceived as agribusinesses spreading poison on the land, and the miners as leaching toxic wastes into the streams.

Most urban dwellers seem to live in blissful ignorance that they, too, have an impact on the environment. Fellow human beings are out there working every day to meet their needs in ways that minimize their impact on the environment.

As more and more of the Northwest's population concentrates in cities, including more and more immigrants from urbanized states like California, the voice of these rural citizens becomes more and more diluted. The disenfranchised include the fishermen as well as the farmers. Irene Martin, an Episcopal priest who ministers to a fishing community in Cathlamet, Washington, warns:

> "The shift in terminology from such words as fishing, farming and logging to 'extractive industries' carries a negative moral weight, which in turn justifies turning over of resources to the morally superior nonextractive users. The latent function of such thinking is, however, colonialist in nature. It is a classic case of urban exploitation of the rural hinterland. In this case, the hinterland is no longer permitted to export its raw materials, its wealth, to urban areas for processing as it could in previous eras. Rather, rural sources of income in the form of trees, fish and land are transformed into a means of recreation for tourists. Is there not a disturbing echo here of how the original frontier was created, by means of a land grab from the aboriginal inhabitants of North America?"[2]

As the power and regulatory reach of government grows larger and larger, the urban majority exercises more and more control over the lives and livelihoods of rural communities. The urban majority is quite happy to destroy these communities merely to create the impression of protecting the environment, and has no concept of the damage caused.

Urban dwellers do not really put themselves in the place of rural folk. When an animal threatens their safety in the city—like a pit bull—they do not hesitate to regulate it out of existence, or put it to death summarily. Yet the attitude towards animals "in the wild" is completely different.

Attitudes toward use of federal land are changing rapidly, even as the government acquires more and more land from sellers in depressed rural economies. Fishery agencies have gotten the Bonneville Power Administration to buy land in Eastern Oregon so as to take over the water rights for flow augmentation, and such land purchases are on the rise.

When urbanites advocate zero harvest of trees on federal land, advocacy of no hunting on federal land is probably not far behind. It brings to mind the game parks of medieval England, where the peasants could only walk through, and might be put to death for poaching. Only now the park is not maintained for the pleasure of the King, but for the pleasure of the urban majority, which would be offended by the rude signs of people making their livelihood from the land.

Urban dwellers seem to live in a fantasy world where, because there are no wild animals around, they can imagine themselves as joint and co-equal participants in the world. If people are not to be given dominion over animals, who is? Are the animals to be given dominion over us? It is not as if the people and the animals can live in any peaceful state of natural harmony. Without control of animal populations, people in remote areas cannot let their children play in the yard without fear of cougar or bear attacks. There is a reason that the settlers killed the wolves. Unless hunting is allowed, domestic agriculture might be plagued by ravenous deer populations.

And while the urban majority is quick to push ranchers and farmers to dedicate irrigation water for fish, one will not find a similar willingness to relinquish urban water supplies. The Bull Run watershed on Mount Hood used to support nearly half of the salmon runs in the Sandy River (a tributary of the Columbia). The City of Portland's dam eliminated all that habitat; the City has recently refused to release water that fishery officials claimed would benefit anadromous fish below the dam.[3] Urban centers do not hesitate to export their garbage and even sewage sludge to the East side of the Cascade Mountains, a rapidly-growing practice which one writer has called a "growth industry in Oregon and Washington".[4]

Perhaps we need to change the name environmentalist. We are all environmentalists now. All of us want to minimize our injury to the environment, and preserve more of it to enrich our lives. Gifford Pinchot, the first Chief of the U.S. Forest Service, declared in 1907 that "conservation is the wise use of resources". But over time, "conservation" has come to mean not using resources at all rather than using them wisely. Many groups are working to promote an ethic that recognizes that human beings must use resources, and virtue lies in avoiding unnecessary harm to the environment.[5]

Yet such proponents of "wise use" are portrayed as radical fringe groups, even as environmentalists privately worry that they express mainstream values. And government public relations machines propagate the myth that those who advocate dam removal offer the "environmental perspective" while those who advocate passage improvements at the dams offer the "industry/power-generation perspective".[6] By labeling those who would improve the dams as anti-environmental, the government continues to propagate the Great Salmon Hoax.

The essential creed of environmentalists is that preservation of the environment must be accomplished as an end in itself, irrespective of the costs to human lives. Those who stand in the way are "timber junkies" or "pigs at the trough". Andy Kerr, an environmental activist, brags that "history [is] being rewritten not by resource-sucking East Side whiners", "but by people like himself and other West Side suburbanites with money and education and subscriptions to *Audubon* magazine".[7] Resource-sucking West Siders cannot seem to see their effects on natural resources through their own, higher levels of consumption.

The Need for Rural Participation and Organization

Every time I speak on the subjects in this book, usually to audiences from Eastern Oregon and Eastern Washington, I tell them that the only way we have any chance of bringing reason and balance into salmon recovery (or any other "endangered species" issue, for that matter), is if they get personally involved. People need to show up at public meetings and ask hard questions. The anointed representatives of government are so wrapped up in their own concepts of should be done that it will literally take angry mobs to get through to them.

It is not as if the problem is going to go away. On August 11, 1997, the National Marine Fisheries Service announced that five "distinct population segments" of steelhead would be listed as endangered and threatened. The pages of the *Federal Register* are littered with additional proposed listings of fish up and down the West Coast that are neither "species" nor "endangered" in the sense Congress intended when it passed the Endangered Species Act. Oregon politicians have temporarily avoided a listing of Oregon coastal coho, but the courts and environmentalists may undo that effort. Bull trout throughout the Columbia River and Klamath River basins are likely to be listed as well, in part because of environmentalist lawsuits.

Another significant trend on the horizon is the growth of the "public trust doctrine". Under this doctrine, courts can destroy vested water rights held by farmers and others if they are convinced that "the public interest" requires water to be left in the river. Environmentalists have written that water rights should be "questioned in light of modern times". After all, they say, "society has reconsidered century-old decisions in other respects. Women would otherwise not be voting and slavery would be legal".[8] The attitude that a farmer irrigating his or her crops stands on the same moral plane as a slaver ought to be offensive, but this is the attitude that appears to prevail at the law schools.

The "public trust" doctrine is growing in state courts, but the attack on water rights is proceeding in federal courts as well. As the Endangered Species Act is interpreted to require moratoria on water withdrawals all over the Columbia River Basin, water rights decisions, traditionally the province of state law, are slowly federalized. So far, the farmers aren't doing much about it.

New amendments to the Magnuson Act, passed with no public debate in the Pacific Northwest or elsewhere, empower fishery management councils to designate essential fish habitat. Federal agencies will soon have to engage in time-consuming consultations if they would affect such habitat, akin to the Endangered Species Act consultations that have crippled federal resource planning.

As layers and layers of expensive, duplicative and needless procedures clog government natural resource decisionmaking, environmentalists pose as fiscal conservatives. Having caused the skyrocketing management costs, the environmentalists now claim it is too expensive to manage natural resources, so they should just be left alone.

Bit by bit, the benefits of federal water projects are gradually being eroded away by urban interests. Sometimes, as in the case of flow augmentation, the value is simply destroyed. Sometimes, as in the case of BPA buy-outs of ranches and water rights, productive land is simply set aside. The rural people of the Pacific Northwest are themselves endangered by an environmentalist perspective that seems to see them as little more than blots upon the natural landscape.

Government grants pay environmentalists and salmon advocates to prepare anti-dam propaganda, even funding the collection of excerpts from historical documents, slanted to make the "back-to-nature" philosophy seem both reasonable and the justified product of a long historical struggle.[9] The once powerful pro-dam public relations arms of the U.S. Army Corps of Engineers and the Bonneville Power Administration have been silenced. There is almost no one left to speak for the dams.

Back in the 1930s, when rural areas wanted to bring electric power to themselves, public meetings were held all over the Pacific Northwest to sell the

381

bonds to build the dams. Organizers played Woody Guthrie's songs about the dams to inspire the people.[10] Now rural interests are disorganized and complacent. They seem prepared to stand idly by while urban interests destroy the concrete benefits of BPA projects for the intangible benefit of "doing good" for salmon recovery—whether it brings back more salmon or not.

The Future of Government Decisionmaking and a Potential Role for BPA

Notwithstanding the enormous power of the media and government, the truth has some influence, even in the world of politics. I hope this book can arm you with many the facts you need to fight back. More are available in libraries. There are also a lot of Internet Websites that contain further information on salmon recovery. Like everything else on the Internet, you have to work to separate the wheat from the chaff, but there is much wheat to be had.

It is especially unfortunate that rural people often lack access to the Internet. We are getting very close to a world of haves and have-nots, with the critical variable being access to high-speed two-way communications. We need to remember that it took a major effort to wire the Pacific Northwest for electricity. That, coupled with the creation of millions of acres of productive farmland, was perhaps the greatest achievement of the dams.

Some at the Bonneville Power Administration think that BPA's existing transmission system towers could form the central nervous system of a Northwest-wide transmission system for information. It would be easy, efficient, and environmentally optimal to add fiber optic trunks to all of BPA's existing lines. This would bring Internet access to the rural Northwest more rapidly, perhaps even faster than to the urban Northwest. The rural folk need it more, since they live farther apart. Unfortunately, none of the leaders at BPA have the vision to pursue the idea. They would rather capitulate to demands to waste BPA money on flow and spill.

The electric power establishment is trying to ensure that restructuring of the Northwest electric industry, including BPA, will allow pursuit of the "normative" river by replacing lost electric power revenues with electric transmission revenues. Their tactic is to turn the transmission system into a system for tax collection (called a "system benefit charge", not a tax). The environmentalists go along because the system benefit charge is earmarked for "conservation" and all sorts of other projects whose benefits are unknown, never quantified, and largely imaginary.

Environmentalist organizations with multi-million dollar, publicly-funded budgets have already been created to disburse the spoils. They will agitate for more government to perfect their vision of the Pacific Northwest ecosystem.

Anybody who cares enough to read this book knows that the government isn't very reliable about fixing problems. Monopolies never are. More and more, citizens have to start paying serious attention to the government just to ensure the most basic governmental functions are not all screwed up. We can't afford to be wasting hundreds of millions of dollars on salmon recovery when roads need building, gunfire on the streets keeps communities cowering in their homes, and the educational system is in rampant decay.

Citizens need to get organized for a fight that will take place in the media, before legislators, before administrators, and in the courts. Now that the Supreme Court has let citizens back into court, they can start regaining some legal ground that have been lost over the last twenty years to environmentalists. They can fight for rational approaches to natural resource management. There are many groups in the Pacific Northwest that need your help to fight back, including my client the Columbia River Alliance.

If you don't get involved, don't be surprised if you don't like what the government does. The government long ago ceased to look out for the broad public interests of citizens. One can attend the endless public meetings on salmon recovery, electric industry restructuring, and many other issues without detecting a whiff of principle in the room. Most of what passes for governance is politicians catering to special interest groups in order to gain favorable media attention. Everyone is a special interest group, and if your special interest group doesn't get organized to put pressure on politicians, you lose.

NOTES TO CHAPTER 15

[1] N. Maull, "Science under Scrutiny", *Harvard Magazine* 25-27 (Mar.-April 1997).

[2] I. Martin, *Legacy and Testament: The Story of the Columbia River Gillnetters* 118.

[3] G. Orcutt, Letter to the Editor, *The Oregonian*, Nov. 16, 1996.

[4] B. Harden, *A River Lost* 194.

[5] *See, e.g.*, R. Arnold, *Ecology Wars: Environmentalism As If People Mattered* (The Free Enterprise Press 1987).

[6] These quotes are from a Northwest Power Planning Council press release, reprinted in "Surface bypass versus breaching", *The Northwest Salmon Recovery Report*, March 7, 1997, at 5.

[7] Reported in B. Harden, *A River Lost* 41.

[8] T. Palmer, *The Snake River* 24.

[9] E.g., J. Cone & S. Ridlington, *The Northwest Salmon Crisis: A Documentary History* (funded by federal monies disbursed through the National Atmospheric and Oceanic Administration, and Oregon state funds).

[10] W. Guthrie, *Roll on Columbia: The Columbia River Songs* 26 (BPA).